CLEP® SOCIAL SCIENCES & HISTORY

Scott Dittloff, Ph.D.
University of the Incarnate Word
San Antonio, Texas

Research & Education Association
Visit our website at: www.rea.com

Research & Education Association
258 Prospect Plains Road
Cranbury, New Jersey 08512
Email: info@rea.com

CLEP® Social Sciences & History with Online Practice Exams, 2nd Edition

Published 2020
Copyright © 2018 by Research & Education Association, Inc.
Prior edition copyright © 2010. All rights reserved. No part of this book may be reproduced in any form without permission of the publisher.

Printed in the United States of America

Library of Congress Control Number 2017944062

ISBN-13: 978-0-7386-1233-1
ISBN-10: 0-7386-1233-2

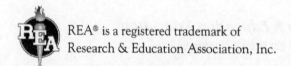

REA® is a registered trademark of
Research & Education Association, Inc.

CONTENTS

ABOUT OUR AUTHOR

Scott Dittloff, Ph.D., is a professor in the Department of Government and International Affairs at the University of the Incarnate Word in San Antonio, Texas. Dr. Dittloff's expertise is in Comparative Democratization, International Relations, and Comparative Politics.

Dr. Dittloff received his Ph.D. from Texas A&M University and his M.A. from Iowa State University. In 2015, he was the recipient of the Incarnate Word Presidential Teaching Award, which is given to a person with extraordinary dedication to teaching that encourages student engagement. Dr. Dittloff serves on the editorial board of the *Journal of Social Sciences* and the *British Journal of Applied Science and Technology*. He is a former member of the College Board's CLEP Social Sciences and History test development committee.

ABOUT REA

Founded in 1959, Research & Education Association (REA) is dedicated to publishing the finest and most effective educational materials—including study guides and test preps—for students of all ages.

Today, REA's wide-ranging catalog is a leading resource for students, teachers, and other professionals. Visit *www.rea.com* to see a complete listing of all our titles.

ACKNOWLEDGMENTS

We would like to thank Pam Weston, Publisher, for setting the quality standards for production integrity and managing the publication to completion; John Cording, Technology Director, for coordinating the design and development of the REA Study Center; Larry B. Kling, Director of Editorial Services, for his assistance in bringing this book to market; Diane Goldschmidt, Managing Editor, for coordinating development of this edition; Transcend Creative Services for typesetting; and Ellen Gong for proofreading.

We also extend our special thanks to Bernard Yanelli for editing our practice exams. Mr. Yanelli teaches history and economics at Saint Stephen's Episcopal School in Bradenton, Florida.

CHAPTER 1

PASSING THE CLEP SOCIAL SCIENCES AND HISTORY EXAM

Congratulations! You're joining the millions of people who have discovered the value and educational advantage offered by the College Board's College-Level Examination Program, or CLEP. This test prep focuses on what you need to know to succeed on the CLEP Social Sciences and History exam, and will help you earn the college credit you deserve while reducing your tuition costs.

GETTING STARTED

There are many different ways to prepare for a CLEP exam. What's best for you depends on how much time you have to study and how comfortable you are with the subject matter. To score your highest, you need a system that can be customized to fit you: your schedule, your learning style, and your current level of knowledge.

This book, and the online tools that come with it, allow you to create a personalized study plan through three simple steps: assessment of your knowledge, targeted review of exam content, and reinforcement in the areas where you need the most help.

Let's get started and see how this system works.

Test Yourself and Get Feedback	Assess your strengths and weaknesses. The score report from your online diagnostic exam gives you a fast way to pinpoint what you already know and where you need to spend more time studying.
Review with the Book	Armed with your diagnostic score report, review the parts of the book where you're weak and study the answer explanations for the test questions you answered incorrectly.
Ensure You're Ready for Test Day	After you've finished reviewing with the book, take our full-length practice tests. Review your score reports and re-study any topics you missed. We give you two full-length practice tests to ensure you're confident and ready for test day.

THE REA STUDY CENTER

The best way to personalize your study plan is to get feedback on what you know and what you don't know. At the online REA Study Center *(www.rea.com/studycenter),* you can access two types of assessment: a diagnostic exam and full-length practice exams. Each of these tools provides true-to-format questions and delivers a detailed score report that follows the topics set by the College Board.

Diagnostic Exam

Before you begin your review with the book, take the online diagnostic exam. Use your score report to help evaluate your overall understanding of the subject, so you can focus your study on the topics where you need the most review.

Full-Length Practice Exams

Our full-length practice tests give you the most complete picture of your strengths and weaknesses. After you've finished reviewing with the book, test what you've learned by taking the first of the two online practice exams. Review your score report, then go back and study any topics you missed. Take the second practice test to ensure you have mastered the material and are ready for test day.

If you're studying and don't have Internet access, you can take the printed tests in the book. These are the same practice tests offered at the REA Study Center, but without the added benefits of timed testing conditions and diagnostic score reports. Because the actual exam is Internet-based, we recommend you take at least one practice test online to simulate test-day conditions.

AN OVERVIEW OF THE EXAM

The CLEP Social Sciences and History exam consists of approximately 120 multiple-choice questions, each with five possible answer choices, to be answered in 90 minutes.

The exam covers the material one would find in college-level introductory classes in the following disciplines: United States history, Western civilization, world history, government/political science, geography, and economics.

The approximate breakdown of topics is as follows:

History	40%
United States History	13-15%
Western Civilization	13-15%
World History	13-15%
Social Sciences	**60%**
Government/Political Science	20%
Geography	20%
Economics	20%

CLEP and technology-enhanced questions

While most of the questions you will find on your CLEP exam will be primarily standard multiple-choice questions, the College Board is now incorporating some technology-enhanced questions. These new question types include: filling in a numeric answer; shading areas of an object; or putting items in the correct order. In addition, several exams now have an optional essay section.

If you're familiar with basic computer skills, you'll have no trouble handling these question types if you encounter them on your exam.

ALL ABOUT THE CLEP PROGRAM

What is CLEP?

More adult learners use CLEP than any other credit-by-examination program in the United States. The CLEP program's 33 exams span five subject areas. The exams assess the material commonly required in an introductory-level college course. Based on recommendations from the American Council on Education, a passing score can earn you at least three credits per exam at more than 2,900 colleges and universities in the U.S. and abroad. Policies vary, so check with your school on the exams it accepts and the scores it requires. For a complete list of the CLEP subject examinations offered, visit the College Board website: *www.collegeboard.org/clep.*

Who takes CLEP exams?

CLEP exams are typically taken by people who have acquired knowledge outside the classroom and wish to bypass certain college courses and earn college credit. The CLEP program is designed to reward examinees for prior learning—no matter where or how that knowledge was acquired.

CLEP appeals to a wide spectrum of candidates, including home-schooled and high school students, adults returning to college, traditional-age college students, military personnel, veterans, and international students. There are no prerequisites, such as age or educational status, for taking CLEP examinations. However, because policies on granting credits vary among colleges, you should contact the particular institution from which you wish to receive CLEP credit.

How is my CLEP score determined?

Your CLEP score is based on two calculations. First, your CLEP raw score is figured; this is just the total number of test items you answer correctly. After the test is administered, your raw score is converted to a scaled score through a process called *equating*. Equating adjusts for minor variations in difficulty across test forms and among test items, and ensures that your score accurately represents your performance on the exam regardless of when or where you take it, or on how well others perform on the same test form.

Your scaled score is the number your college will use to determine if you've performed well enough to earn college credit. Scaled scores for the CLEP exams are delivered on a 20–80 scale. Institutions can set their own scores for granting college credit, but a good passing estimate (based on recommendations from the American Council on Education) is generally a scaled score of 50, which usually requires getting roughly 66% of the questions correct.

For more information on scoring, contact the institution where you wish to be awarded the credit.

Who administers the exam?

CLEP exams are developed by the College Board, administered by Educational Testing Service (ETS), and involve the assistance of educators from throughout the United States. The test development process is designed and implemented to ensure that the content and difficulty level of the test are appropriate.

When and where is the exam given?

CLEP exams are administered year-round at more than 2,000 test centers in the United States and abroad. To find the test center nearest you and to register for the exam, contact the CLEP Program:

CLEP Services

P.O. Box 6600

Princeton, NJ 08541-6600

Phone: (800) 257-9558 (8 a.m. to 6 p.m. ET)

Fax: (610) 628-3726

Website: *www.collegeboard.org/clep*

The CLEP iBT Platform

To improve the testing experience for both institutions and test-takers, the College Board's CLEP Program has transitioned its 33 exams from the eCBT platform to an Internet-based testing (iBT) platform. All CLEP test-takers may now register for exams and manage their personal account information through the "My Account" feature on the CLEP website. This new feature simplifies the registration process and automatically downloads all pertinent information about the test session, making for a more streamlined check-in.

OPTIONS FOR MILITARY PERSONNEL AND VETERANS

CLEP exams are available free of charge to eligible military personnel as well as eligible civilian employees. All the CLEP exams are available at test centers on college campuses and military bases. Contact your Educational Services Officer or Navy College Education Specialist for more information. Visit the DANTES or College Board websites for details about CLEP opportunities for military personnel. Note that only one attempt per exam is funded by the U.S. Department of Defense.

Eligible U.S. veterans may apply for reimbursement of CLEP exam fees pursuant to provisions of the Harry W. Colmery Veterans Educational Assistance Act of 2017, commonly called the "Forever GI Bill." For details on eligibility and how to apply for reimbursement, visit the U.S. Department of Veterans Affairs website at *www.gibill.va.gov*.

CLEP can be used in conjunction with the Post-9/11 GI Bill, which applies to veterans returning from the Iraq and Afghanistan theaters of operation. Because the GI Bill provides tuition for up to 36 months, earning college credits with CLEP exams expedites academic progress and degree completion within the funded timeframe.

SSD ACCOMMODATIONS FOR CANDIDATES WITH DISABILITIES

Many test candidates qualify for extra time to take the CLEP exams, but you must make these arrangements in advance. For information, contact:

College Board SSD Program

P.O. Box 7504

London, KY 40742-7504

Phone: (212) 713-8333 (Monday through Friday, 8 a.m. to 6 p.m. ET)

TTY: (609) 882-4118

Fax: (866) 360-0114

E-mail: *ssd@info.collegeboard.org*

Website: *www.collegeboard.org/students-with-disabilities*

6-WEEK STUDY PLAN

Be sure to set aside enough time—at least two hours each day—to study. The more time you spend studying, the more prepared and relaxed you will feel on the day of the exam.

Week	Activity
1	Take the Diagnostic Exam at the online REA Study Center. The score report will identify topics where you need the most review.
2-4	Study the review focusing on the topics you missed (or were unsure of) on the Diagnostic Exam.
5	Take Practice Test 1 at the REA Study Center. Review your score report and re-study any topics you missed.
6	Take Practice Test 2 at the REA Study Center to see how much your score has improved. If you still got a few questions wrong, go back to the review and study any topics you may have missed.

TEST-TAKING TIPS

Know the format of the test. Familiarize yourself with the CLEP computer screen beforehand by logging on to the College Board website. Waiting until test day to see what it looks like in the pretest tutorial risks injecting needless anxiety into your testing experience. Also, familiarizing yourself with the directions and format of the exam will save you valuable time on the day of the actual test.

Read all the questions—completely. Make sure you understand each question before looking for the right answer. Reread the question if it doesn't make sense.

Read all of the answers to a question. Just because you think you found the correct response right away, do not assume that it's the best answer. The last answer choice might be the correct answer.

Use the process of elimination. Stumped by a question? Don't make a random guess. Eliminate as many of the answer choices as possible. By eliminating just two answer choices, you give yourself a better chance of getting the item correct, since there will only be three choices left from which to make your guess. Remember, your score is based only on the number of questions you answer correctly.

Don't waste time! Don't spend too much time on any one question. Your time is limited, so pacing yourself is very important. Work on the easier questions first. Skip the difficult questions and go back to them if you have the time. Taking our timed practice tests online will help you learn how to budget your time.

Look for clues to answers in other questions. If you skip a question you don't know the answer to, you might find a clue to the answer elsewhere on the test.

Be sure that your answer registers before you go to the next item. Look at the screen to see that your mouse-click causes the pointer to darken the proper oval. If your answer doesn't register, you won't get credit for that question.

THE DAY OF THE EXAM

On test day, you should wake up early (after a good night's rest, of course) and have breakfast. Dress comfortably so you are not distracted by being too hot or too cold while taking the test. (Note that "hoodies" are not allowed.) Arrive at the test center early. This will allow you to collect your thoughts and relax before the test, and it will also spare you the anxiety that comes with being late.

Before you leave for the test center, make sure you have your admission form and another form of identification, which must contain a recent photograph, your name, and signature (i.e., driver's license, student identification card, or current alien registration card). You may not wear a digital watch (wrist or pocket), alarm watch, or wristwatch camera. In addition, no cell phones, dictionaries, textbooks, notebooks, briefcases, or packages will be permitted, and drinking, smoking, and eating are prohibited.

Good luck on the CLEP Social Sciences and History exam!

CHAPTER 2

POLITICAL SCIENCE

INTRODUCTION TO POLITICAL SCIENCE

What is Political Science?

Political Science is the organized study of government and politics. It borrows from the related disciplines of history, philosophy, sociology, economics, and law. **Political scientists** explore such fundamental questions as: What are the philosophical foundations of modern political systems? What makes a government legitimate? What are the duties and responsibilities of those who govern? Who participates in the political process and why? What is the nature of relations among nations?

Overview of Political Philosophy

In the 4th century BCE, the political writings of Plato and Aristotle sought to combine the realms of ethics and politics. Conjoining the two was especially urgent to Plato after he witnessed the tragic death of his great mentor, Socrates, at the hands of the self-serving political leaders of Athens in 399 BCE. Plato is most famous today for writing a series of dialogues in which Socrates played a prominent role. His most famous dialogue on politics is entitled *The Republic*. In it, he includes the timeless story of the "Allegory of the Cave," which inspired the hit movie *The Matrix*.

Aristotle was Plato's most famous student and also a tutor to Alexander the Great. Two of Aristotle's best known works are his *Politics* and *Nicomachean Ethics*, both of which remain important texts in political philosophy classes today. In both books, Aristotle articulates what he calls the "Golden Mean," where "a virtue is the midpoint between two extremes." In politics, Aristotle argues that the best type of government is the one ruled from the middle (class), because at either extreme—either rule by the rich or rule by the poor—negative consequences will occur: either the rich will exploit the poor, or the poor will seek to destroy the rich.

During the early 1500s, Niccolo Machiavelli wrote a famous political treatise entitled *The Prince*. In it, he argued that for a ruler, it is "better to be feared than loved." He also noted that rulers may have to separate politics from morality in order to achieve their ambitions. Today, Machiavelli's name is often used as an adjective. Thus, when someone accuses another person of being "Machiavellian," this typically means that the person in question is acting in an immoral manner, using "the ends" (whatever he or she wants) to "justify the means" (the tactics being used).

During the mid-1600s to the late 1700s, three thinkers emerged who made important contributions to the field of political philosophy—Thomas Hobbes, John Locke, and Jean-Jacques Rousseau. All three became known as "Social Contract" theorists, in that each one postulated a possible "social contract" that people entered into while still living in a hypothetical "state of nature," just prior to moving into an organized society.

The section below highlights some of their thoughts:

I. Thomas Hobbes / Principal Book: *The Leviathan* (1651)

Principal Concepts:

Hobbes had a pessimistic view toward humans. Accordingly, he famously argued that life in the state of nature was "solitary, poor, nasty, brutish, and short."

Hobbes assumed that, by nature, people are violently self-interested and, if necessary, they will kill others to get what they want. Hobbes thus envisioned a "social contract" whereby people gave up *all* their rights to the state (or government) in return for protection against a violent death. He thus promoted a totalitarian-style of government. The graphic novel and movie *V for Vendetta* dramatically depict a Hobbesian type of state.

II. John Locke / Principal Book: *Two Treatises on Government* (1690)

Principal Concepts:

Locke, who had a much more moderate view toward human behavior than Hobbes, believed that while humans are mostly self-interested, extreme self-interest could be held in check by enforcing a rigorous series of laws. Locke thus saw the "social contract" as one in which people gave up only some of their *natural rights* to the state. He further argued (unlike Hobbes) that if the politicians of a state became corrupt, the people had a right and obligation to overthrow them. A fundamental tenet of John Locke is that power forever resides in the people.

It should also be noted that Locke had a greater influence on America's founding fathers than any other political philosopher. For instance, the opening of Jefferson's Declaration of Independence is, in many ways, a paraphrasing of Locke's teachings.

III. Jean-Jacques Rousseau / Principal Book: *Social Contract* (1762)

Principal Concepts:

Rousseau had the most optimistic view toward human nature of the three Social Contract theorists. In that regard, he famously asserted that, "Man is born free, and everywhere he is in chains."

Rousseau argued for a very limited form of government, which was to be held in check by the loosely defined "General Will." Rousseau felt that, in the state of nature, mankind was uncorrupted, but once people entered into society, they were quickly tainted by the abuses of the corrupt church and state, both of which must be stripped of power so that mankind can return to its original, peaceful state of being.

Principal Subfields of Political Science

At the present time, the study of political science in the United States is concerned with the following broad subtopics or subfields:

Political Theory is an historical exploration of the major contributions to political thought from the ancient Greeks to the contemporary theorists. These theorists raise fundamental questions about the individual's existence and his relationship to the political community. **Political theory** also involves the philosophical and speculative consideration of the political world.

American Government and Politics is a survey of the origins and development of the political system in the United States from the colonial days to modern times with an emphasis on the Constitution, various political structures such as the legislative, executive, and judicial branches, the federal system, political parties, voter behavior, and fundamental freedoms.

Comparative Government is a systematic study of the structures of two or more political systems (such as those of Britain and the People's Republic of China) to achieve an understanding of how different societies manage the realities of governing. Also considered are political processes and behavior and the ideological foundations of various systems.

International Relations is a consideration of how nations interact with each other within the frameworks of law, diplomacy, and international organizations such as the United Nations.

▌ The Development of the Discipline of Political Science

Early History

Political science as a systematic study of government developed in the United States and in Western Europe during the nineteenth century as new political institutions evolved. Prior to 1850, during its classical phase, political science relied heavily on philosophy and utilized the deductive method of research.

Post–Civil War Period

The political science curriculum was formalized in the United States by faculty at Columbia and Johns Hopkins, who were deeply influenced by German scholarship on the nation-state and the formation of democratic institutions. Historical and comparative approaches to analysis of institutions were predominant. Emphasis was on constitutional and legal issues, and political institutions were widely regarded as factors in motivating the actions of individuals.

Twentieth-Century Trends

Political scientists worked to strengthen their research base, to integrate quantitative data, and to incorporate comparative studies of governmental structures in developing countries into the discipline.

American Political Science Association (APSA)

The APSA was founded in 1903 to promote the organized study of politics and to distinguish it as a field separate from history.

The Behavioral Period

From the early 1920s to the present, political science has focused on psychological interpretations and the analysis of the behavior of individuals and groups in a political context. Research has been theory-based, values-neutral, and concerned with predicting and explaining political behavior.

Contemporary Developments

Since the 1960s, interest has focused on such subtopics as African-American politics, public policy, urban and ethnic politics, and women in politics. Influenced by the leadership of Harold Lasswell, political scientists showed greater concern for using their discipline to solve social problems.

▎ The Scientific Method of Research in Political Science

The modern method of scientific inquiry in the field aims to compile a body of data based on direct observation (**empirical knowledge**) that can be utilized both to explain what has been observed and to form valid generalizations. The scientific method in political science has resulted in three types of statements: **observational/evidential**, which describe the principal characteristics of what has been studied; **observational laws**, which are hypotheses based on what has been observed; and **theories**, which analyze the data that have been collected and offer plausible general principles that can be drawn from what has been observed.

Examples of Statements Based on the Scientific Method

- **Observational/evidential:** In 1992, 518 out of 535 members of the U.S. Congress were males. In the British Parliament, 550 of the 635 members were males. Eighteen of France's 20 cabinet ministers were males.

- **Observational law (hypothesis):** Legislative and executive bodies in modern democracies tend to be dominated by males.

- **Theory:** Political power in modern democracies is in male hands.

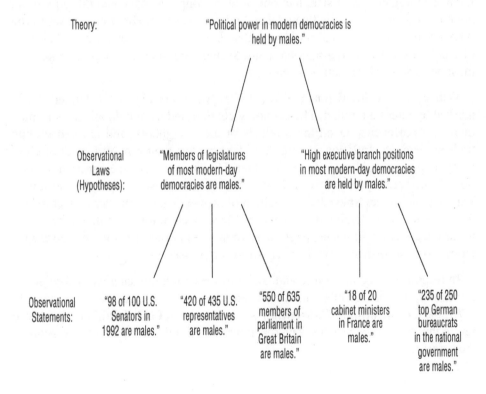

UNITED STATES GOVERNMENT AND POLITICS

█ Constitutional Foundations

The government of the United States rests on a written framework created in an attempt to strengthen a loose confederation that was in crisis in the 1780s. The **Constitution** is a basic plan that outlines the structure and functions of the national government. Clearly rooted in Western political thought, it sets limits on government and protects both property and individual rights.

Historical Background

Following the successful revolt of the British colonies in North America against imperial rule, a plan of government was implemented that was consciously weak and ultimately ineffective: the **Articles of Confederation**. The Articles served as the national government from 1781–1787. The government under the Articles consisted of a **unicameral** (one-house) legislature that was clearly subordinate to the states. Representatives to the Congress were appointed and paid by their respective state legislatures, and their mission was to protect the interests of their home states. Each state, regardless of size, had one vote in Congress, which could request but not require states to provide financial and military support. **Key weaknesses of the Articles** included: their inability to regulate interstate and foreign trade, their lack of a chief executive and a national court system, and their rule that amendments must be approved by unanimous consent.

Dubbed the "**critical period**," the 1780s was a decade in the United States marked by internal conflict. The economy deteriorated as individual states printed their own currencies, taxed the products of their neighbors, and ignored foreign trade agreements. Inflation soared, small farmers lost their property, and states engaged in petty squabbles with one another. The discontent of the agrarian population reached crisis proportions in 1786 in rural Massachusetts when Revolutionary War veteran **Daniel Shays** led a rebellion of farmers against the tax collectors and the banks that were seizing their property. **Shays' Rebellion** symbolized the inability of the government under the Articles to maintain order. Bostonians subscribed money to raise an army, which successfully suppressed the rebels.

In response to the economic and social disorder and the dangers of foreign intervention, a series of meetings to consider reform of the Articles was held. In 1787, the **Constitutional Convention** was convened in **Philadelphia** ostensibly to revise the ineffective Articles. The result was an entirely new plan of government, the Constitution.

Philosophy and Ideology of the Founding Fathers

Among the distinguished men assembled at the Constitutional Convention in 1787 were **James Madison**, who recorded the debate proceedings; **George Washington**, president of the body; **Gouverneur Morris**, who wrote the final version of the document; and **Alexander Hamilton**, one of the authors of the *Federalist Papers* (1787–1788). This collection of essays, to which **Madison** and **John Jay** also contributed, expresses the political philosophy of the Founders and was instrumental in bringing about the ratification of the Constitution.

Clearly the framers of the Constitution were influenced by the ideological heritage of the Enlightenment of the seventeenth and eighteenth centuries in Western Europe. From Hobbes and Locke came the concept of the social contract. The latter had a marked influence upon **Thomas Jefferson**, who incorporated Locke's doctrines with respect to equality; government's responsibility to protect the life, liberty, and property of its constituency; and the right of revolution in his **Declaration of Independence** (1776). The Constitution itself includes Montesquieu's separation of powers and checks and balances. British documents, such as the **Magna Carta** (1215), the **Petition of Right** (1628), and the **Bill of Rights** (1689), all promoting the principle of limited government, were influential in shaping the final form of the Constitution.

Basic Principles of the Constitution

The authors of the Constitution sought to establish a government free from the tyrannies of both monarchs and mobs. Two of the critical principles embedded in the final document, **federalism** and **separation of powers**, address this concern.

The federal system established by the Founders divides the powers of government between the states and the national government. Local matters are handled on a local level, and those issues that affect the general populace are the responsibility of the federal government. Such a system is a natural outgrowth of the colonial relationship between the Americans and the mother country of England. American federalism is defined in the **Tenth Amendment** which declares: "those powers not delegated to the United States by the Constitution, nor prohibited by it to the States, are reserved to the States respectively, or to the people." In practice, the system may be confusing in that powers overlap (i.e., welfare). In cases where they conflict, the federal government is supreme.

The principle of separation of powers is codified in **Articles I, II,** and **III** of the main body of the Constitution. The national government is divided into three branches which have separate functions (**legislative, executive,** and **judicial**). Not entirely independent, each of these branches can check or limit in some way the power of one or both of the others (**checks and balances**). This system of dividing and checking powers is a vehicle for guarding against the extremes the Founders feared. Following are some examples of checks and balances:

- The legislative branch can check the executive by refusing to confirm appointments.

- The executive can check the legislature by vetoing its bills.

- The judiciary can check both the legislature and the executive by declaring laws unconstitutional.

Additional basic principles embodied in the Constitution include:

- The establishment of a representative government (**republic**).

- **Popular sovereignty** or the idea that government derives its power from the people. This concept is expressed in the **Preamble** which opens with the words, "**We the People**."

- The enforcement of government with limits ("**rule of law**").

Structure and Functions of the National Government

The national government consists of the three branches outlined in the Constitution as well as a huge bureaucracy comprised of departments, agencies, and commissions.

The Legislative Branch

Legislative power is vested in a **bicameral** (two-house) Congress which is the subject of Article I of the Constitution. The bicameral structure was the result of a compromise at the Constitutional Convention between the large states, led by Virginia, which presented a plan calling for a strong national government with representation favoring the larger states (**Virginia Plan**) and the smaller states, which countered with the **New Jersey Plan**. The latter would have retained much of the structure of the Articles of Confederation including equal representation of the states in Congress. Connecticut offered a solution in the form of the **Great Compromise**. It called for a two-house legislature with equal representation in the **Senate** and representation in the **House of Representatives** based on population.

The **expressed** or **delegated powers** of Congress are set forth in **Section 8** of Article I. They can be divided into several broad categories including economic, judicial, war, and general peace powers. **Economic powers** include:

- to lay and collect taxes

- to borrow money

- to regulate foreign and interstate commerce

- to coin money and regulate its value

- to establish rules concerning bankruptcy

Judicial powers include:

- to establish courts inferior to the Supreme Court
- to provide punishment for counterfeiting
- to define and punish piracies and felonies committed on the high seas

War powers include:

- to declare war
- to raise and support armies
- to provide and maintain a navy
- to provide for organizing, arming, and calling forth the militia

Peace powers include:

- to establish rules on naturalization
- to establish post offices and post roads
- to promote science and the arts by granting patents and copyrights
- to exercise jurisdiction over the seat of the federal government (**District of Columbia**)

The Constitution includes the so-called "**elastic clause**" which grants Congress **implied powers** to implement the delegated powers.

In addition, Congress maintains the power to discipline federal officials through **impeachment** (formal accusation of wrongdoing) and removal from office.

Article V empowers Congress to propose **amendments** (changes or additions) to the Constitution. A two-thirds majority in both houses is necessary for passage. An alternate method is to have amendments proposed by the legislatures of two-thirds of the states. In order for an amendment to become part of the Constitution, it must be **ratified** (formally approved) by three-fourths of the states (through their legislatures or by way of special conventions as in the case of the repeal of Prohibition).

Article I, Section 9 specifically denies certain powers to the national legislature. Congress is prohibited from suspending the right of **habeas corpus** (writ calling for a party under arrest to be brought before the court where authorities must show cause for detainment) except during war or rebellion. Other prohibitions include: the passage of export taxes, the withdrawal of funds from the treasury without an appropriations law, the passage of **ex post facto** laws (make past actions punishable that were legal when they occurred), and favored treatment of one state over another with respect to commerce.

The work of the Congress is organized around a committee system. The **standing committees** are permanent and deal with such matters as agriculture, the armed services, the budget, energy, finance, and foreign policy. Special or **select committees** are established to deal with specific issues and usually have a limited duration. **Conference committees** iron out differences between the House and the Senate versions of a bill before it is sent on to the President.

One committee unique to the House of Representatives is the powerful **Rules Committee**. Thousands of bills are introduced each term, and the Rules Committee acts as a clearing house to weed out those that are unworthy of consideration before the full House. Constitutionally, all revenue-raising bills must originate in the House of Representatives. They are scrutinized by the powerful House **Ways and Means Committee**.

Committee membership is organized on party lines with **seniority** being a key factor, although in recent years, length of service has diminished in importance in the determination of chairmanships. The composition of each committee is largely based on the ratio of each party in the Congress as a whole. The party that has a **majority** is allotted a greater number of members on each committee. The chairman of the standing committees are selected by the leaders of the majority party.

The legislative process is at once cumbersome and time consuming. A **bill** (proposed law) can be introduced in either house (with the exception of **revenue bills**, which must originate in the House of Representatives). It is referred to the appropriate **committee** and then to a **subcommittee**, which will hold **hearings** if the members agree that it has merit. The bill is reported back to the **full committee**, which must decide whether or not to send it to the **full chamber** to be debated. If the bill passes in the full chamber, it is then sent to the **other chamber** to begin the process all over again. Any differences between the House and Senate versions of the bill must be resolved in a **conference committee** before it is sent to the **President** for consideration. Most of the thousands of bills introduced in Congress die in committee with only a small percentage becoming law.

Debate on major bills is a key step in the legislative process because of the tradition of attaching **amendments** at this stage. In the House, the rules of debate are designed to enforce limits necessitated by the size of the body (435 members). In the smaller Senate (100 members), unlimited debate (**filibuster**) is allowed. Filibustering is a delaying tactic that can postpone action indefinitely. **Cloture** is a parliamentary procedure that can limit debate and bring a filibuster to an end.

Constitutional qualifications for the House of Representatives state that members must be at least **25** years of age, must have been **U.S. citizens for at least seven years,** and must be **residents of the state** that sends them to Congress. According to the **Reapportionment Act of 1929**, the size of the House is fixed at **435** members. They serve terms of **two years** in length. The presiding officer and generally the most powerful member is the **Speaker of the House**, who is the leader of the political party that has a majority in a given term.

Constitutional qualifications for the Senate state that a member must be at least **30** years of age, must have been a **U.S. citizen for at least nine years**, and must be an **inhabitant of the state** that he/she represents. Senators are elected for terms of **six years** in length on a staggered basis so that one-third of the body is up for re-election in each national election. The president of the Senate is the **Vice President**. This role is largely symbolic, with the Vice President casting a vote only in the case of a tie. There is no position in the Senate comparable to that of the Speaker of the House, although the **Majority Leader** is generally recognized as the most powerful member.

The Executive Branch

The **President** is the head of the executive branch of the federal government. **Article II** of the Constitution deals with the powers and duties of the President or chief executive. Following are the President's principal **constitutional responsibilities**:

- serves as **Commander-in-Chief** of the armed forces

- negotiates treaties (with the approval of two-thirds of the Senate)

- appoints ambassadors, judges, and other high officials (with the consent of the Senate)

- grants pardons and reprieves for those convicted of federal crimes (except in impeachment cases)

- seeks counsel of department heads (Cabinet members)

- recommends legislation

- meets with representatives of foreign states

- sees that the laws are faithfully executed

Despite the attempts by the Founders to set clear limits on the power of the chief executive, the importance of the presidency has grown dramatically over the years. Recent trends to reassert the pre-eminence of the Congress notwithstanding, the President remains the most visible and powerful single member of the federal government and the only one (with the exception of the vice president) elected to represent all the people. He shapes foreign policy with his diplomatic and treaty-making powers and largely determines domestic policy. Presidents also possess the power to **veto** legislation. A presidential veto may be overridden by a two-thirds vote in both houses, but such a majority is not easy to build, particularly in the face of the chief executive's opposition. A **pocket veto** occurs when the President neither signs nor rejects a bill, and the Congress adjourns within ten days of his receipt of the legislation. The fact that the President is the head of a vast federal bureaucracy is another indication of the power of the office.

Although the Constitution makes no mention of a formal **Cabinet** as such, since the days of George Washington, chief executives have relied on department heads to aid in the decision-making process. Washington's Cabinet was comprised of the secretaries of **state**, **war**, **treasury**, and an **attorney general**. Today there are 15 Cabinet departments, with **Homeland Security** being the most recently created post. Efforts to trim the federal government in the 1990s have resulted in suggestions to streamline and eliminate some Cabinet posts.

The **Executive Office of the President** is made up of agencies that supervise the daily work of the government. The **White House Staff** manages the President's schedule and is usually headed by a powerful **chief of staff**. Arguably the most critical agency of the Executive Office is the **Office of Management and Budget**, which controls the budget process for the national government. Other key executive agencies include the **Council of Economic Advisors** and the **National Security Council**, which advises the President on matters that threaten the safety of the nation and directs the **Central Intelligence Agency**.

The **Constitutional Requirements** for the office of President and Vice President are as follows: a candidate must be at least **35** years of age, must be a **natural-born** citizen, and must have **resided in the United States for a minimum of 14 years**. Article II provides for an **Electoral College** to elect the President and Vice President. Each state has as many votes in the Electoral College as it has members of Congress plus three additional electors from the District of Columbia—making a grand total of 538 electors. The Founding Fathers established the Electoral College to provide an **indirect** method of choosing the chief executive; as shown in the 2000 and 2016 elections, the Electoral College can still play a decisive role in determining the outcome of presidential elections.

The question of **presidential succession** has been addressed by both legislation and amendment. The Constitution states that if the President dies or cannot perform his duties, the "powers and duties" of the office shall "devolve" on the Vice President. The **Presidential Succession Act** (1947) placed the **speaker of the house** next in line if both the President and the Vice President were unable to serve. Until recently, when the Vice President assumed the office of President, his former position was left vacant. The **Twenty-Fifth Amendment** (1967) gives the President the power to appoint a new Vice President (with the approval of a majority of both houses of Congress). It also provides for the Vice President to serve as **Acting President** if the chief executive is disabled or otherwise unable to carry out the duties of the office. The **Twenty-Second Amendment** (1951) says, "No person shall be elected to the office of the President more than twice...." In addition, anyone who has served more than two years while filling out another person's term may not be elected to the presidency more than once.

The Judicial Branch

Article III of the Constitution establishes the **Supreme Court** but does not define the role of this branch as clearly as it does the legislative and executive branches. Yet our contemporary judicial branch consists of thousands of courts and is in essence a dual system, with each state having its own judiciary functioning simultaneously with a complete set of federal courts. The most significant piece of legislation with respect to establishing a network of federal courts was the **Judiciary Act of 1789**. This law organized the Supreme Court and set up the 13 **federal district courts**. The district courts have **original jurisdiction** (to hear cases in the first instance) for federal cases involving both civil and criminal law. Federal cases on appeal are heard in the **Courts of Appeal**. The decisions of these courts are final, except for those cases that are accepted for review by the Supreme Court.

The **Supreme Court** today is made up of a **Chief Justice** and eight **Associate Justices**. They are appointed for life by the President with the approval of the Senate.

In the early history of the United States, the Supreme Court was largely preoccupied with the relationship between the federal government and the states. In 1803, the process of **judicial review** (power to determine the constitutionality of laws and actions of the legislative and executive branches) was established under **Chief Justice John Marshall** in the case of *Marbury v. Madison*. This power has become the foundation of the American judicial system and underscores the deep significance of the courts in determining the course of United States history.

The Supreme Court chooses cases for review based on whether they address substantial federal issues. If four of the nine justices vote to consider a case, then it will be added to the agenda. In such cases, **writs of certiorari** (orders calling up the records from a lower court) are issued. The justices are given detailed briefs and hear oral arguments. Reaching a decision is a complicated process. The justices scrutinize the case with reference to the Constitution and also consider previous decisions in similar cases (**precedent**). When all of the justices agree, the opinion issued is **unanimous**. In the case of a split decision, a **majority opinion** is written by one of the justices in agreement. Sometimes a justice will agree with the majority but for a different principle, in which case he/she can write a **concurring opinion** explaining the different point of view. Justices who do not vote with the majority may choose to write **dissenting opinions** to air their conflicting arguments.

In addition to the Supreme Court, the federal District Courts, and the Courts of Appeal, several special courts at the federal level have been created by Congress. The **U.S. Tax Court** handles conflicts between citizens and the Internal Revenue Service. The **Court of Claims** was designed to hear cases in which citizens bring suit against the U.S. government. Other special courts include the **Court of International Trade**, the **Court of Customs**, and the **Court of Military Appeals**.

The Federal Bureaucracy

In addition to the President's Cabinet and the Executive Office, a series of independent agencies makes up the federal bureaucracy, the so-called **"fourth branch"** of the national government. Most of these agencies were established to protect consumers and to regulate industries engaged in interstate trade. Others were set up to oversee government programs. From the time of the establishment of the Interstate Commerce Commission in 1887, these departments grew in number and influence. Late in the 1970s, the trend began to reverse, as some agencies were cut back and others eliminated altogether.

Among the most important of these powerful agencies are the **regulatory commissions**. The President appoints their administrators with the approval of the Senate. Unlike Cabinet secretaries and other high appointees, they cannot be dismissed by the chief executive. This system protects the independent status of the agencies. Following are examples of some of the major regulatory agencies and their functions.

Agency	Regulatory Functions
Interstate Commerce Commission	Monitors surface transportation and some pipelines
Federal Reserve Board	Supervises the banking system, sets interest rates, and controls the money supply
Federal Trade Commission	Protects consumers by looking into false advertising and antitrust violations
Federal Communications Commission	Regulates interstate and international communications by radio, television, wire, satellite, and cable.
Securities and Exchange Commission	Protects investors by monitoring the sale of stocks and bonds
National Labor Relations Board	Oversees labor and management practices
Consumer Product Safety Commission	Sets standards of safety for manufactured products
Nuclear Regulatory Commission	Licenses and inspects nuclear power plants

Another category of the "fourth branch" of government is made up of the **independent executive agencies**. These were created by Congress and resemble Cabinet departments, but they do not enjoy Cabinet status. Nonetheless they are powerful entities. Some of the key executive agencies include the Civil Rights Commission, the Environmental Protection Agency, and the National Aeronautics and Space Administration. Their names are indicative of their functions. The top-level

HOW A BILL BECOMES A LAW

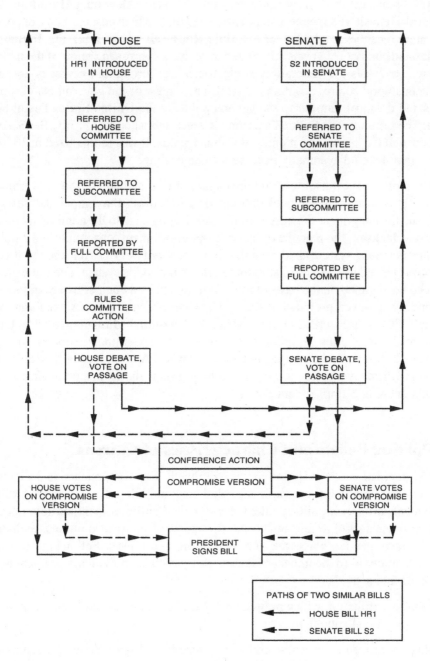

executives of these agencies are appointed by the President with the approval of the Senate.

Some of the independent agencies are actually **government corporations**. These are commercial enterprises created by Congress to perform a variety of necessary services. Their roots can be traced back to the **First Bank of the United States** established in 1791 by Secretary of the Treasury **Alexander Hamilton**. The **Federal Deposit Insurance Corporation** (FDIC), which insures bank deposits, is a more recent example. Under **Franklin Roosevelt's New Deal**, the **Tennessee Valley Authority** (TVA) was authorized to revive a depressed region of the nation. Today it oversees the generation of electric power throughout a vast region and maintains flood control programs as well. The largest of the government corporations and the most familiar to the general public is the **United States Postal Service**. The original Post Office Department was established in 1775 by the Second Continental Congress, and it enjoyed Cabinet status. It was reorganized in 1970 in hopes that it would eventually become self-supporting.

The large and powerful federal bureaucracy shapes and administers government policy. It is inherently political despite sporadic efforts throughout the years to maintain the integrity of the bureaucratic staff. Dating back to the administrations of **Andrew Jackson**, the practice of handing out government jobs in return for political favors (**spoils system**) had been the rule. The **Civil Service Act** (the **Pendleton Act**) was passed in 1883 in an attempt to reform the spoils system. Federal workers were to be recruited on the basis of merit determined by a competitive examination. Veterans were given preferential status. The Civil Service system was reorganized in the 1970s with the creation of the **Office of Personnel Management**. The OPM is charged with recruiting, training, and promoting government workers. Merit is the stated objective when hiring federal employees. A controversial policy of the OPM is affirmative action, a program to help groups discriminated against in the job market to find employment.

Political Beliefs and Characteristics of Citizens

The population of the United States, with its diverse components, is difficult to characterize with respect to political beliefs and attitudes. The process by which individuals form their political allegiances is called **political socialization**. Several factors (**cleavages**) are relevant to the formation of political opinions, including family, race, gender, class, religion, education, and region. Following are some generalizations as to the impact of these cleavages on an individual's political identification and activity.

Family – affiliation with a political party is commonly passed from one generation to another.

Race – African Americans tend to be more liberal than whites on economic, social, and public policy issues.

Gender – women tend to be more liberal than men.

Class – citizens from the middle and upper classes tend to be more politically active than those from the lower socioeconomic brackets. Low income voters tend to identify more with the liberal agenda.

Religion – Protestants tend to be more conservative than Catholics and Jews. Evangelical Protestants seem to be most conservative on ethical and moral issues.

Education – graduate-level education seems to have a liberalizing effect that remains potent after schooling is completed.

Region – Southerners tend to be most conservative, Midwesterners more liberal, and those living on the East and West coasts the most liberal of all.

Despite the categorization of Americans as either **liberals** or **conservatives**, most studies indicate that they do not follow clearly delineated **ideologies** (firm and consistent beliefs with respect to political, economic, and social issues). The terms *liberal* and *conservative* with reference to the political beliefs of Americans are difficult to define in precise terms. Liberals tend to favor change and to view government as a tool for improving the quality of life. Conservatives, on the other hand, are more inclined to view both change and government with suspicion. They emphasize individual initiative and local solutions to problems. A puzzling reversal is seen in the attitudes of liberals and conservatives when confronting moral issues such as abortion and school prayer. Here conservatives see a role for government in ensuring the moral climate of the nation while liberals stress the importance of individual choice.

Political Institutions and Special Interests

Civic culture in the United States is dominated by the two major political parties and is heavily influenced by the activities of interest groups and the mass media. These latter forces, both directly and indirectly, are largely responsible for molding and swaying public opinion.

Political Parties

A **political party** is an organization that seeks to influence government by electing candidates to public office. The party provides a label for candidates, recruits and campaigns, and tries to organize and control the legislative and executive branches of government through a set of leaders.

The Constitution does not mention political parties, and the Founders in general were opposed to them. Yet they developed simultaneously with the organization of the new government in 1789. It was the initial conflict over the interpretation of the powers assigned to the new government by the Constitution that gave rise to the first organized American political parties.

The **Federalist Party** evolved around the policies of Washington's Secretary of the Treasury, **Alexander Hamilton**. He and his supporters favored a "**loose construction**" approach to the interpretation of the Constitution. They advocated a strong federal government with the power to assume any duties and responsibilities not prohibited to it by the text of the document. They generally supported programs designed to benefit banking and commercial interests, and in foreign policy, the Federalists were **pro-British**.

The **Democratic** or **Jeffersonian Republicans** formed in opposition to the Federalists. They rallied around Washington's Secretary of State, **Thomas Jefferson**. The Jeffersonians took a "**strict constructionist**" approach, interpreting the Constitution in a narrow, limited sense. Sympathetic to the needs of the "common man," the Democratic-Republicans were mistrustful of powerful centralized government. They saw the small farmers, shopkeepers, and laborers as the backbone of the nation. In the area of foreign affairs, the Democratic-Republicans were **pro-French**. The present-day Democratic Party traces its roots to the Jeffersonians.

By the 1820s, the Democrats had splintered into factions led by **Andrew Jackson** (the Democrats) and **John Quincy Adams** (National Republicans). The Jacksonians continued with Jefferson's tradition of supporting policies designed to enhance the power of the common man. Their support was largely agrarian. The National Republicans, like their Federalist predecessors, represented the interests of bankers, merchants, and some large planters. Eventually a new party, the **Whigs**, was organized from the remnants of the old Federalists and the National Republicans. The Whigs were prominent during the 1840s, but like their Democratic rivals, they fragmented during the 1850s over the divisive slavery issue. The modern **Republican Party** was born in 1854 as Whigs and anti-slavery Democrats came together to halt the spread of slavery. The Republicans built a constituency around the interests of business, farmers, workers, and the newly emancipated slaves in the post-Civil War era.

Political parties exert a variety of functions essential to the democratic tradition in the United States. Nominating candidates for local, state, and national office is their most visible activity. At the national level, this function has been diluted somewhat by the popularity of **primary elections** allowing voters to express their preference for candidates. Raucous conventions where party bosses chose obscure "**dark horse**" candidates in "smoke-filled rooms" are largely a thing of the past.

Political parties stimulate interest in public issues by highlighting their own strengths and maximizing the flaws of the opposition. They also provide a framework for keeping the machinery of government operating, most notably in their control of Congress and its organization, which is strictly along party lines.

American political parties appear in theory to be highly organized. The geographic size of the country coupled with the federal system of government keep the parties in a state of relative decentralization. At the local level, the fundamental unit of organization is the **precinct**. At this level, there is usually a captain or committee to handle such routine chores as registering voters, distributing party literature, organizing "**grass-roots**" meetings, and getting out the vote on election day.

State central committees are critical to the parties' fund-raising activities. They also organize the state party conventions. There is great variety from state to state regarding the composition and selection of the state committees, which often formulate policies independent from those of the national committee.

In presidential election years, the **national party committees** are most visible. They plan the **national nominating convention**, write the party **platforms** (summaries of positions on major issues), raise money to finance political activities, and carry out the election campaigns. Representatives from each state serve on the national committees, and the **presidential nominee** chooses the individual to serve as the **party chairperson**.

Although the two-party system is firmly established in the United States, over the years, "**third parties**" have left their marks. The national nominating conventions were introduced in the 1830s by the **Anti-Masonic Party** and were soon adopted by the Democrats and the Whigs. The **Prohibition Party** opposed the use of alcohol and worked for the adoption of the **Eighteenth Amendment**. In the 1890s, the **Populist Party** championed the causes of the farmers and workers and impacted the mainstream parties with its reform agenda. Among the Populist innovations were the **initiative petition** (a mechanism allowing voters to put proposed legislation on the ballot) and the **referendum** (allowing voters to approve or reject laws passed by their legislatures). The **Progressive** or **Bull Moose Party** was a **splinter party** (one that breaks away from an established party, in this case the Republican Party) built around the personality of Theodore Roosevelt. Another party formed around the personality of a forceful individual was the 1992 **Reform Party** of **H. Ross Perot**. Perot did not capture any electoral votes but garnered 19 percent of the popular tally.

Elections

In comparison to citizens in other democratic systems, Americans elect a large number of public officials. Elections in the United States are largely regulated by **state** law. The Constitution does assign to Congress the responsibility for determining "the times, places, and manner of holding elections for Senators and Representatives." Article II establishes the Electoral College for presidential elections and specifies that they shall be held on the same day throughout the nation. Several of the Amendments deal with election procedures, voter qualifications, and **suffrage** (the right to vote) for target groups (former slaves, women, and those 18 years of age and older). Nonetheless, the principal responsibility for arranging and supervising elections rests with the states.

The actual election process consists of two phases: nominating the candidates and choosing the final officials. **Primary elections** screen and select the final party candidates. **Closed primaries** allow voters **registered** (legal procedure that must be completed before an individual can vote) in one of the political parties to express their preferences for the final candidate from among the field of hopefuls in that party. **Open primaries** allow voters to select their party affiliations on site. Some states allow "**crossover**" voting which permits voters registered in one party to vote for candidates in the other party. This practice can lead to the tactic of voting for the weakest choice in the opposition party to give an advantage in the final election to the candidate and the party the voter actually supports.

In **national elections** (those held in November of each even-numbered year to choose national officeholders), the **campaign** traditionally begins after Labor Day. **Off-year elections** are those in which only members of Congress are chosen and no presidential contest is held. In both presidential and off-year elections, candidates follow exhausting schedules and spend huge sums on media advertising. Their activities usually dominate the national and local news coverage, and debates are common forums for airing their differences. Funding for political campaigns comes from a variety of sources including the candidates' own resources, private supporters, **Political Action Committees** (PACs), and the federal government. In the election reform drive of the 1970s, the **Federal Election Commission** was created to ensure that laws concerning campaign financing are followed.

The cost of the elections themselves is borne by the state and local governments, which must prepare ballots, designate polling places, and pay workers who participate in administering the elections. **Registrars of voters** oversee the preparation of ballots, the establishment of polling places, and the tallying of the votes. In a close election, the loser may request a **recount**. Some states require them in closely contested races.

Voter Behavior

In recent years, attention has focused on the problem of voter apathy. Despite efforts to extend suffrage to all segments of the adult population, participation in the electoral process has been on the decline. Several theories have been advanced to explain this trend. There is widespread belief that Americans are dissatisfied with their government and mistrust all elected officials. Therefore, they refuse to participate in the electoral process. Some citizens do not vote in a given election, not because they are "turned-off" to the system, but because they are ill, homeless, away on business, or otherwise preoccupied on election day. College students and others away from their legal residences find registration and the use of **absentee ballots** cumbersome and inconvenient. Efforts were made in the 1990s to streamline the registration process with such legislation as the "**motor-voter**" **bill** that makes it possible for citizens to register at their local registries of motor vehicles.

While most attempts to explain voter apathy focus on negatives such as citizen apathy, some analysts disagree. They see disinterest in the ballot as a sign that the majority of Americans are happy with the system and feel no sense of urgency to participate in the political process.

Political participation is not limited to voting in elections. Working for candidates, attending rallies, contacting elected officials and sharing opinions about issues, writing letters to newspapers, marching in protest, and joining in community activities are all forms of political participation. While voter turnout has decreased in recent years, other forms of participation seem to be on the increase.

Interest Groups

American officials and political leaders are continually subjected to pressure from a variety of **interest groups** seeking to influence their actions. Such groups arise from bonds among individuals who share common concerns. Interest groups may be loosely organized (**informal**), with no clear structure or regulations. A good example of such an informal or ad hoc interest group was the "March of the Poor" on Washington, D.C., in 1963 to focus Congress's attention on the needs of the "underclass" in America. A group of neighbors united in opposition to a new shopping mall that threatens a wetland is an example of this type of group. Other interest groups are much more **formal** and permanent in nature. They may have suites of offices and large numbers of employees. Their political objectives are usually clearly defined. Labor unions, professional and public-interest groups, and single-issue organizations fall into this category. The National Rifle Association and the National Right to Life Organization are examples of **single-issue** pressure groups.

Interest groups employ a variety of tactics to accomplish their goals. Most commonly, they **lobby** (influence the passage or defeat of legislation) elected officials, particularly members of Congress. Lobbyists provide legislators with reports and statistics to persuade them of the legitimacy of their respective positions. They may present expert testimony at public hearings and influence the media to portray their causes in a favorable light. Lobbyists are required to register in Washington and to make their positions public. They are barred from presenting false and misleading information and from bribing public officials. Regulatory legislation cannot, however, curb all the abuses inherent to a system of organized persuasion.

One particularly controversial brand of pressure group is the **Political Action Committee** (PAC). PACs were formed in the 1970s in an attempt to circumvent legislation limiting contributions to political campaigns. Critics see these interest groups as another means of diluting the influence individual voters may have on their elected officials. Some politicians refuse to accept PAC money.

Public Opinion

Public opinion refers to the attitudes and preferences expressed by a significant number of individuals about an issue that involves the government or the society at large. It does not necessarily represent the sentiments of all or even most of the citizenry. Nonetheless, it is an important component of a democratic society.

In today's technological society, the influence of the **mass media** on public opinion cannot be over-emphasized. The print and broadcast media can reach large numbers of people cheaply and efficiently, but the electronic media in particular have been criticized for over-simplifying complicated issues and reducing coverage of major events to brief sound bites. Both the print and broadcast media claim to present news in a fair and objective format, but both conservatives and liberals claim that coverage is slanted. In recent years, a number of partisan digital media have taken root on the Internet and in apps. **Paid political advertising** is another vehicle for molding public opinion. In this case, objectivity is neither expected nor attempted, as candidates and interest groups employ "hard-sell" techniques to persuade voters to support their causes.

Measuring the effects of the media on public opinion is difficult, as is gauging where the public stands on a given issue at a particular point in time. **Public opinion polls** have been designed to these ends. Pollsters usually address a **random sample** and try to capture a **cross-section** of the population. Their questions are designed to elicit responses that do not mirror the biases of the interviewer or the polling organization. Results are tabulated and analyzed, and summaries are presented to the media.

Although polls are more accurate today than in the past, they are still subject to criticism for oversimplifying complicated issues and encouraging pat answers to complex problems. Public opinion is constantly in a state of flux, and what may be a valid report today is passé tomorrow. Another criticism is that interviewees may not be entirely candid, particularly with respect to sensitive issues. They may answer as they think they should but not necessarily with full honesty.

A type of election poll that has been the target of sharp criticism is the **exit poll** in which interviewers question subjects about their votes as they leave the polling places. These polls may be accurate, but if the media present the results while voting is still in progress, the outcome may be affected. Predicting the winners before voters throughout the country have had the opportunity to cast their ballots in a national election robs a segment of the electorate of the sense that its participation is of any consequence. In the 2000 election, exit polls led to confusion as Florida results were projected prematurely; the television networks vowed to be more careful.

Civil Rights and Individual Liberties

Civil rights are those legal claims that individuals have to protect themselves from discrimination at the hands of both the government and other citizens. They include the right to vote, equality before the law, and access to public facilities.

Individual or **civil liberties** protect the sanctity of the person from arbitrary governmental interference. In this category belong the fundamental freedoms of speech, religion, press, and rights such as **due process** (government must act fairly and follow established procedures, as in legal proceedings).

The origin of the concept of fundamental rights and freedoms can be traced to the British constitutional heritage and to the theorists of the Enlightenment. Jefferson's **Declaration of Independence** contains several references to the crown's failure to uphold the civil rights that British subjects had come to value and expect. When fashioning the Constitution, the Founding Fathers included passages regarding the protection of civil liberties, such as the provision in Article I for maintaining the right of *habeas corpus*. One of the criticisms of the Constitution lodged by its opponents was that it did not go far enough in safeguarding individual rights. During the first session of Congress in 1789, the first ten amendments (the **Bill of Rights**) were adopted and sent to the states for ratification. These amendments contain many of the protections that define the ideals of American life. The Bill of Rights was meant to limit the power of the federal government to restrict the freedom of individual citizens. The **Fourteenth Amendment** of 1868 prohibits **states** from denying civil rights and individual liberties to their residents. The Supreme Court is charged with interpreting the law, particularly as it applies to civil rights and individual liberties cases. Not until the **Gitlow Case** in 1925 did the Supreme Court begin to exercise this function with respect to state enforcement of the Bill of Rights. States are now expected to conform to the federal standard of civil rights.

The Amendment that is most closely identified with individual liberty in the United States is the **First Amendment**, which protects freedom of religion, speech, press, assembly, and petition. The First Amendment sets forth the principle of **separation of Church and State** with its "**free exercise**" and "**establishment**" clauses. These have led the Supreme Court to rule against such practices as school prayer (***Engel v. Vitale,* 1962**) and Bible reading in public schools (***Abington Township v. Schempp,* 1963**).

The **Fourth Amendment**, which outlawed "**unreasonable searches and seizures,**" mandates that warrants be granted only "**upon probable cause,**" and affirms the "**right of the people to be secure in their persons,**" is fundamental to the Court's interpretation of due process and the rights of the accused. The **Fifth Amendment**, which calls for a grand jury, outlawed **double jeopardy** (trying a person who has been acquitted of a charge for a second time) and states that a person may not be compelled to be a witness against himself, is also the basis for Supreme Court rulings that protect the accused. "**Cruel and unusual punishments**" are banned by the **Eighth Amendment**. This clause has been invoked by opponents of capital punishment to justify their position, but the Supreme Court has ruled that the death penalty can be applied if states are judicious and use equal standards in sentencing to death those convicted of capital crimes.

In the twentieth century, a major concern for litigation and review by the Supreme Court was the area of civil rights for minorities, particularly African Americans. When civil rights organizations such as the NAACP brought a series of cases before the courts under the "**equal protection clause**" of the **Fourteenth Amendment**, they began to enjoy some victories. Earlier when the Supreme Court enforced its "**separate but equal**" doctrine in the 1896 case *Plessy v. Ferguson*, it did not apply the equal protection standard and allowed segregation to be maintained. The Court reversed itself in 1954 in the landmark case *Brown v. Board of Education*, which ruled that separate but equal was unconstitutional. This ruling led to an end to most **de jure** (legally enforced) segregation, but **de facto** (exists in fact) segregation persisted, largely due to housing patterns and racial and ethnic enclaves in urban neighborhoods.

Landmark Supreme Court Cases

In addition to the previously cited Supreme Court rulings in civil rights and individual liberties cases, the following landmark decisions are notable for their relevance to the concepts of civil rights and individual freedoms:

- *Dred Scott v. Sandford* (1857) – ruled that as a slave Scott had no right to sue for his freedom, and further that Congressional prohibitions against slavery in U.S. territories were unlawful.

- *Near v. Minnesota* (1931) – states were barred from using the concept of prior restraint (outlawing something before it has taken place) to discourage the publication of objectionable material except during wartime or in the cases of obscenity or incitement to violence.

- *West Virginia Board of Education v. Barnette* (1943) – overturned an earlier decision and ruled that compulsory saluting of the flag was unconstitutional.

- *Korematsu v. United States* (1944) – upheld the legality of the forced evacuation of persons of Japanese ancestry during World War II as a wartime necessity.

- *Mapp v. Ohio* (1961) – extended the Supreme Court's exclusionary rule, which bars at trial the introduction of evidence that has not been legally obtained. The Court has modified this ruling, particularly with reference to drug cases, so that evidence that might not initially have been obtained legally, but which would eventually have turned up in lawful procedures, can be introduced.

- *Gideon v. Wainwright* (1963) – ruled that courts must provide legal counsel to poor defendants in all felony cases. A later ruling extended this right to all defendants facing possible prison sentences.

- *Escobedo v. Illinois* (1964) – extended the right to counsel to include consultation prior to interrogation by authorities.

- *Miranda v. Arizona* (1966) – mandated that all suspects be informed of their due process rights before questioning by police.

- *Tinker v. Des Moines School District* (1969) – defined the wearing of black armbands in school in protest against the Vietnam War as "symbolic speech" protected by the First Amendment.

- *New York Times v. United States* (1971) – allowed, under the First Amendment's freedom of the press protection, the publication of the controversial Pentagon Papers during the Vietnam War.

- *Roe v. Wade* (1973) – legalized abortion so long as a fetus is not viable (able to survive outside the womb).

- *Bakke v. Regents of the University of California* (1978) – declared the university's quota system to be unconstitutional while upholding the legitimacy of affirmative action policies in which institutions consider race and gender as factors when determining admissions.

- *Hazelwood School District v. Kuhlmeier* (1988) – ruled that freedom of the press does not extend to student publications that might be construed as sponsored by the school.

COMPARATIVE GOVERNMENT AND POLITICS

This subfield of government and politics includes two principal areas of scholarship and information: the theoretical frameworks for the government structures, functions, and political cultures of nations, and a comparative analysis of the political systems of a series of targeted nations or societies.

Theoretical Frameworks for Government Structures, Functions, and Political Culture

Environmental Factors

In order to understand the political institutions and civic life of any nation, several environmental factors need to be considered. Such questions as the **size, location, geographic features, economic strength, level of industrialization**, and **cultural diversity** of a society must be explored. Both the **domestic** and **international** contexts need to be examined as well as the level of **dependence** on or **independence** from the world community. The location of the United States in the Western Hemisphere, separated from both Europe and Asia by vast expanses of ocean, is a critical component in the development of its relatively independent political culture. Conversely, the location of Eastern European countries in the shadow of the post-World War II Soviet Union led to political dependence. The cultural diversity and traditional hostilities of the Balkan peoples are key elements in the political and military volatility of the region. Industrialization and economic stability are conditions that are commonly conducive to a highly developed political system.

The **age** and **historical traditions** of a nation have a great impact on its current political culture. France's contemporary unitary form of government can be viewed as an evolutionary manifestation of earlier traditions that centralized power in divine right monarchs and ambitious emperors. **Legitimacy** (acceptance by citizens) is quite another prospect in such places as Somalia and Haiti with their unstable political histories and economic vulnerability.

Government Structures and Functions

How a government is organized, its mechanisms for carrying out its mission, the scope of that mission, and how its structures and functions compare with other governments are prime considerations in comparative government.

The **geographic distribution of authority and responsibility** is a key variable. **Confederations**, such as the United States under the Articles of Confederation, have weak central governments and delegate principal authority to smaller units such as the states. **Federal systems**, on the other hand, divide sovereignty between a central government and those of their separate states. Brazil, India, and the United States are contemporary examples of federal republics. Highly centralized, **unitary** forms of government concentrate power and authority at the top, as in France and Japan.

Separation of governmental powers is another aspect of structure useful in comparing political systems. **Authoritarian** governments concentrate power in a single or collective executive, with the legislative and judicial bodies having little input. The former Soviet Union is an example. Great Britain typifies the **parliamentary** form of government. Here legislative and executive combine, with a prime minister and cabinet selected from within the legislative body. They maintain power only as long as the legislative assembly supports their major policies. The **democratic presidential** system of the United States clearly separates the legislative, executive, and judicial structures. The branches, particularly the executive and the legislative, must cooperate, however, in order for policy to be consistent and for government operations to be carried out smoothly.

A third aspect of governmental structure and function involves the **limits** placed on the power to govern. This facet of politics closely reflects the theoretical and ideological roots of a system. **Constitutional** systems limit the powers of government through written and/or unwritten sources. Law, custom, and precedent combine to protect individuals from the unchecked power of a central authority. The United States and Great Britain have constitutional governments. **Authoritarian** regimes, such as those found in China and the former Soviet Union, do not limit the power of the central authority over the lives of individuals. Those in control impose their values and their will on the society at large regardless of popular sentiments. Authoritarianism is associated with **fascism**, **Nazism**, and **totalitarianism** in general.

Political Culture, Parties, Participation, and Mechanisms for Change

Understanding a nation's **political culture** is key to analyzing the theoretical foundations, structure, and functions of its government. It can be defined as the aggregate values a society shares about how politics and government should operate. Some societies function from a **consensus** framework, while other political cultures are more **conflicted**. The Soviet Union's political culture after World War II, as contrasted with the post-Soviet situation there in the early 1990s, illustrates the difference between consensual and conflicted societies. The vehicles for transmitting the political culture and the social cleavages that characterize that culture will impact its system of governing and its legitimacy in the minds of its citizenry. Analysis of the extent to which citizens support their political systems is an important component of comparative government.

The methods citizens employ to have an impact upon their political system and the ease of their access to the power structure are the types of questions comparative politics examines. Do elections offer a **choice** between candidates with diverse programs and contrasting agendas, as is often the case in the United States, or do they present citizens the opportunity to show their support for the government in a **one party** system such as in China? The number, nature, and power of political parties are additional factors for analysis with respect to how the demands and concerns of citizens in various nations are represented and met. The presence and proliferation of other interest groups, such as labor unions and environmental activists, provide additional clues as to the values and methods of a political culture.

Beyond voting in elections and joining and supporting political parties and interest groups, **citizen participation** can take other forms. Contacting politicians, lobbying for legislation, and demonstrating in the streets are common vehicles for involvement in the political life of a nation. The degree to which such expressions are encouraged and tolerated by government officials is another facet of political culture that varies from society to society.

Comparative politics and government as a field is concerned with **mechanisms for change** in different nations. Can citizens effect reform through ballots, protest, public opinion polls, or revolts? The underlying factors precipitating the need for change are relevant to an understanding of the overall process.

INTERNATIONAL RELATIONS

The Theoretical Framework

The study of how nations interact with one another can be approached from a variety of perspectives including the following:

- A **traditional analysis** uses the descriptive process and focuses on such topics as global issues, international institutions, and the foreign policies of individual nation-states.

- The **strategists' approach** zeroes in on war and deterrence. Scholars in this camp may employ game theory to analyze negotiations, the effectiveness of weapons systems, and the likelihood of limited versus all-out war in a given crisis situation.

- The **middle range theorists** analyze specific components of international relations, such as the politics of arms races, the escalation of international crises, and the role of prejudice and attitudes toward other cultures in precipitating war and peace.

- A **world politics approach** takes into consideration such factors as economics, ethics, law, and trade agreements and stresses the significance of international organizations and the complexities of interactions among nations.

- The **grand theory** of international relations is presented by **Hans J. Morgenthau** in *Politics Among Nations* (1948). He argues for **realism** in the study of interactions on the international stage. Morgenthau suggests that an analysis of relations among nations reveals such recurring themes as "interest defined as power" and striving for equilibrium/balance of power as a means of maintaining peace.

- The **idealists** assume that human nature is essentially good; hence, people and nations are capable of cooperation and avoiding armed conflict. They highlight global organizations, international law, disarmament, and the reform of institutions that lead to war.

An analysis of international politics can be conducted at various levels by looking at the actions of individual statesmen, the interests of individual nations, and/ or the mechanics of a whole system of international players. In studying the rise of Nazism and its role in precipitating World War II, the **individual** approach would focus on Hitler, the **state** approach would treat the German preoccupation with racial superiority and the need for expansion, and the **systemic** approach would highlight how German military campaigns upset the balance of power and triggered unlikely alliances, such as the linking of the democratic Britain and the United States with the totalitarian Soviet Union in a common effort to restore equilibrium.

Foreign Policy Perspectives

International relations as a discipline is inextricably linked to the field of **foreign policy**. Foreign policy involves the objectives nations seek to gain with reference to other nations and the procedures in which they engage in order to achieve their objectives. The principal foreign policy goals of sovereign states or other political entities may include some or all of the following: independence, national security, economic advancement, encouraging their political values beyond their own borders, gaining respect and prestige, and promoting stability and international peace.

The **foreign policy process** involves the stages a government goes through in formulating policy and arriving at decisions with respect to courses of action. A variety of models have been identified in reference to the process of creating foreign policy. The **primary players** (nations, world organizations, multinational corporations, and non-state ethnic entities such as the Palestine Liberation Organization) are often referred to as **actors**.

The **unitary/rational actor model** assumes that all nations or primary players share similar goals and approach foreign policy issues in like fashion. The actions players take, according to this theory, are influenced by the actions of other players rather than by what may be taking place internally. The rational component in this model is based on the assumption that actors will respond on the world stage by making the best choice after measured consideration of possible alternatives. Maximizing goals and achieving specific objectives motivate the rational actor's course of action.

The **bureaucratic model** assumes that, due to the many large organizations involved in formulating foreign policy, particularly in powerful nation-states, final decisions are the result of struggle among the bureaucratic actors. In the United States, the bureaucratic actors include the Departments of State and Defense, as well as the National Security Council, the Central Intelligence Agency, the Environmental Protection Agency, the Department of Commerce, and/or any other agencies and departments whose agendas might be impacted by a foreign policy decision. While the bureaucratic model is beneficial in that it assumes the consideration of multiple points of view, the downside is that inter-agency competition and compromise often drive the final decision.

A third model assumes that foreign policy results from the intermingling of a variety of political factors including national leaders, bureaucratic organizations, legislative bodies, political parties, interest groups, and public opinion.

The **implementation of foreign policy** depends upon the tools a nation or primary player has at its disposal. The major instruments of foreign policy include **diplomacy**, **military strength/actions**, and **economic initiatives**.

Diplomacy involves communicating with other primary players through official representatives. It might include attending conferences and summit meetings, negotiating treaties and settlements, and exchanging official communications. Diplomacy is an indispensable tool in the successful conduct of an entity's foreign policy.

The extent to which a player may rely on the **military** tool depends upon its technological strength, its readiness, and the support of both its domestic population and the international community. President George H. W. Bush's decision to engage in a military conflict with Iraq's Saddam Hussein in 1991, after Iraq's invasion of Kuwait, largely rested on positive assessments of those factors. Sometimes the buildup of military capabilities is in itself a powerful foreign policy tool and thus a deterrent to armed conflict—as was the case in the Cold War between the United States and the Soviet Union.

Economic development and the ability to employ economic initiatives to achieve foreign policy objectives are effective means by which a principal player can interact on the international scene. The Marshall Plan, through which the United States provided economic aid to a ravaged Europe after World War II, could be viewed as a tool to block Soviet expansion as well as a humanitarian gesture. It was a tool to resurrect the devastated economies of Europe which had been major trading partners and purchasers of U.S. exports before the war. Membership in an economic community such as OPEC (Organization of Petroleum Exporting Countries) or the EC (European Community) can drive the foreign policy of both member nations and those impacted by their decisions.

The Modern Global System

International systems today evidence many of the global forces and foreign policy mechanisms formulated in Western Europe in the eighteenth and nineteenth centuries. Largely due to the influence of Western imperialism and colonialism, the less developed countries of modern times have, to a great extent, embraced ideological and foreign policy values that originated in Europe during the formative centuries. Such concepts as political autonomy, nationalism, economic advancement through technology and industrialization, and gaining respect and prestige in the international community move the foreign policies of major powers and many less developed countries as well.

Historical Context of the Modern Global System

The modern global system or network of relationships among nations owes its origins to the emergence of the nation-state. It is generally recognized that the **Peace of Westphalia** (1648), which concluded the Thirty Years' War in Europe and ended the authority of the Roman Catholic popes to exert their political dominance over secular leaders, gave birth to the concept of the modern nation-state. The old feudal order in Europe that allowed the Holy Roman Emperor to extend his influence over the territories governed by local princes was replaced by a new one in which distinct geographic and political entities interacted under a new set of principles. These allowed the nation-states to conduct business with each other, such as negotiating treaties and settling border disputes, without interference from a higher authority. Hence, the concept of sovereignty evolved.

The eighteenth century in Europe was notable for its relatively even distribution of power among the nation-states. With respect to military strength and international prestige, such nations as England, France, Austria, Prussia, and Russia were on the same scale. Some of the former major powers, such as Spain, the Netherlands, and Portugal, occupied a secondary status. Both the major and secondary players created alliances and competed with each other for control of territories beyond their borders. Alignments, based primarily on economic and colonial considerations, shifted without upsetting the global system. Royal families intermarried and professional soldiers worked for the states that gave them the best benefits without great regard for political allegiances.

Military conflicts in the eighteenth century tended to be conservative with the concept of the **balance of power** at play. Mercenaries and professionals controlled the action mindful of strategic maneuvers to bring about victory. Wiping out the enemy was not the principal goal. Major upheavals were avoided through the formation of alliances and a high regard for the authority of monarchs and the Christian Church. The eighteenth century has been dubbed the **"golden age of diplomacy"** because it was an era of relative stability in which moderation and shared cultural values on the part of the decision-makers were the rule.

Structural changes in the process and implementation of international relations occurred in the nineteenth and twentieth centuries due to major political, technological, and ideological developments.

The nation-state of the eighteenth century was a relatively new phenomenon. Statesmen of the era traded territory with little consideration of ethnic loyalties. This style of diplomacy was irrevocably altered by the French Revolution and the Napoleonic Wars that saw **nationality** emerge as a rallying point for conducting wars and for raising the citizens' armies necessary to succeed in military conflicts. The trend was exacerbated in the mid-nineteenth century by the European drive for unification of distinct ethnic groups and the creation of the Italian and German nation-states. The twentieth century saw a particularly impassioned link between nationalism and war.

The scientific and industrial revolutions of the eighteenth century gave rise to advancements in **military technology** in the nineteenth and twentieth centuries that dramatically altered the concept and the conduct of war. Replacing the eighteenth century conservative, play-by-the-rules approach was a new, fiercely violent brand of warfare that increasingly involved civilian casualties and aimed at utter destruction of the enemy. The World Wars of the twentieth century called for mass mobilization of civilians as well as of the military, prompting leaders to whip up nationalistic sentiments. The development of nuclear weapons in the mid-twentieth century rendered total war largely unfeasible. Nuclear arms buildups, with the goal of **deterrent capabilities** (the means to retaliate so swiftly and effectively that an enemy will avoid conflict) was viewed by the superpowers as the only safety net.

Another factor molding the structural changes in international relations that surfaced in the nineteenth and twentieth centuries was the **ideological component**. Again the French Revolution, anchored in the ideology of "liberty, equality, and fraternity," is viewed as the harbinger of future trends. Those conservative forces valuing legitimacy and monarchy fought the forces of the Revolution and Napoleon to preserve tradition against the rising tide of republican nationalism. In the twentieth century, with its binding "isms"—Communism, democratic republicanism, liberalism, Nazism, socialism—competing for dominance, ideological conflicts became more pronounced.

The Contemporary Global System

The values of the contemporary system are rooted in the currents of eighteenth and nineteenth century Europe, transplanted to the rest of the world through colonialism and imperialism. The forces of nationalism, belief in technological progress, and ideological motivations, as well as the desire for international respect and prestige, are evident worldwide. Principal players in Africa, Asia, Latin America, and the Middle East as often as not dominate the diplomatic arena.

The contemporary scene in international relations is comprised of a number of entities beyond the **nation-state**. These include: **non-state actors** or **principal players, nonterritorial transnational organizations**, and **nonterritorial intergovernmental** or **multinational organizations**.

Contemporary **nation-states** are legal entities occupying well-defined geographic areas and organized under a common set of governmental institutions. They are recognized by other members of the international community as sovereign and independent states.

Non-state actors or **principal players** are movements or parties that function as independent states. They lack sovereignty, but they may actually wield more power than some less developed nation-states. The **Palestine Liberation Organization (PLO)** is an example of a non-state actor that conducts its own foreign policy, purchases armaments, and has committed acts of terror with grave consequences for the contemporary international community. The **Irish Republican Army (IRA)** is another example of a non-state actor that has employed systematic acts of terror to achieve political ends.

Nonterritorial transnational organizations are institutions such as the Catholic Church that conduct activities throughout the world but whose aims are largely nonpolitical. A relatively new nonterritorial transnational organization is the **multinational corporation (MNC)**, such as General Motors, Hitachi, or energy giant BP. These mammoth business entities have bases in a number of countries and exist primarily for economic profit. Despite their apparent nonpolitical agendas, multinational corporations can greatly impact foreign policy, as in the case of the United Fruit Company's suspect complicity in the overthrow of the government of Guatemala in the 1950s. Initially the MNC was largely an American innovation, but in recent years, Asian players, particularly the Chinese, Japanese, and South Koreans, have proliferated, changing the makeup of the scene.

An **intergovernmental organization**, such as the United Nations, NATO, or the European Community (EC), is made up of nation-states and can wield significant power on the international scene. While NATO is primarily a military intergovernmental organization and the EC is mainly economic, the UN is really a multipurpose entity. While its primary mission is to promote world peace, the UN engages in a variety of social, cultural, economic, health, and humanitarian activities.

The contemporary global system tends to classify nation-states based on power, wealth, and prestige in the international community. Such labels as **superpower**, **secondary power**, **middle power**, **small power**, and the like tend to be confusing because they are not based on a single set of criteria or a shared set of standards. Some countries may be strong militarily, as was Iraq prior to the Persian Gulf War, yet lack the wealth and prestige in the international community to classify them as superpowers or secondary powers. Others like Japan may have little in the way of military capabilities, but wide influence due to economic preeminence.

The **structure** of the contemporary global system during the Cold War was distinctly **bipolar**, with the United States and the Soviet Union assuming diplomatic, ideological, and military leadership for the international community. With the breakup of the Soviet Union and the reorganization of the Eastern bloc countries has come the disintegration of the bipolar system. Since the 1970s, when tensions between the United States and the Soviet Union eased, a **multipolar system**, in which new alignments are flexible and more easily drawn, has been emerging. President George H. W. Bush spoke of the **New World Order** at the end of the Cold War. This concept involves alliances that transcend the old bipolar scheme with its emphasis on ideology and military superiority and calls for multinational cooperation as seen in the Persian Gulf War. It also assumes greater non-military, transnational cooperation in scientific research and humanitarian projects. The multipolar system is less cohesive than the bipolar system of the recent past and the orders of the distant past, such as the **hierarchical system** (one unit dominates) of the Holy Roman Empire or the **diffuse system** (power and influence are distributed among a large number of units) of eighteenth-century Europe.

A set of fundamental rules has long governed international relations and, though often ignored, is still held as the standard today. These rules include **territorial integrity**, **sovereignty**, and the **legal equality of nation-states**. However, in an age of covert operations, mass media, multinational corporations, and shifting territorial boundaries, these traditional rules of international conduct are subject to both violation and revision.

International Law

The present system of international law is rooted in the fundamental rules of global relations: territorial integrity, sovereignty, and legal equality of nation-states. It embodies a set of basic principles mandating what countries may or may not do and under what conditions the rules should be applied.

Historical Context

Despite evidence that the legal and ethical norms of modern international law may have guided interactions among political entities in non-Western pre-industrial systems, contemporary international law emanates from the Western legal traditions of Greece, Rome, and modern Europe. The development of the European nation-state gave rise to a system of legal rights and responsibilities in the international sphere that enlarged upon the religious-based code of the feudal era. In medieval Europe, the church's emphasis on hierarchical obligations, duty, and obedience to authority helped shape the notion of the **"just war."** Hugo Grotius (1583–1645), Dutch scholar and statesman, codified the laws of war and peace and has been called the **"father of international law."**

A new era was launched in 1648, with the Peace of Westphalia, that promulgated the idea of the treaty as the basis of international law. Multilateral treaties dominated the eighteenth century, while Britain, with its unparalleled sea power, established and enforced maritime law. By the nineteenth century, advances in military technology rendered the old standard of the "just war" obsolete. Deterrents, rather than legal and ethical principles, provided the means to a relatively stable world order. The concept of **neutrality** evolved during this period, defining the rights and responsibilities of both warring and neutral nations. These restraints helped prevent smaller conflicts from erupting into world wars.

Contemporary International Law

In the twentieth century, international law retreated theoretically from the tradition of using force as a legitimate tool for settling international conflicts. The **Covenant of the League of Nations** (1920), the **Kellogg-Briand Pact** (1929), and the **United Nations Charter** (1945) all emphasize peaceful relations among nations, but the use of force continues to be employed to achieve political ends. The **International Court of Justice**, the judicial arm of the United Nations, and its predecessor, the **Permanent Court of International Justice** represent concerted efforts to replace armed conflict with the rule of law. Unfortunately, the World Court has proven to be an ineffective organ. Nation-states are reluctant to submit vital questions to the Court, and there is a lack of consensus as to the norms to be applied. Members of the United Nations are members of the Court, but they are not compelled to submit their international disputes for consideration.

The UN Charter seeks to humanize the international scene in its admonition that all member nations assist victims of aggression. This approach negates the old idea of neutrality. It further dismisses the tradition of war as a legitimate tool for resolution of disputes between nation-states of equal legal status. Aggressive conflicts can be categorized as crimes against humanity, and individuals may be held personally accountable for launching them.

The concept of international law has been criticized on several fronts. The rise of **multiculturalism**, with its emphasis on multiple perspectives, has called into question the relevance of applying Western legal traditions to the global community. International law has been seen as an instrument of the powerful nations in pursuit of their aims at the expense of weaker nations. Strong nation-states are in a position to both enforce international law and to violate it without fear of reprisal. These observations have led some to conclude that international law is primarily an instrument to maintain the **status quo**.

International law can be effective if parties involved see some **mutual self-advantage** in compliance. **Fear of reprisal** is another factor influencing nations to observe the tenets of international law. **Diplomatic advantage** and **enhanced global prestige** may follow a nation's decisions to abide by international law. It can be argued that international law is valuable in that it seeks to impose **order** on a potentially chaotic system and sets expectations that, while not always met, are positive and affirming.

REVIEW QUESTIONS

1. All of the following are major differences between the Congress of the United States and the parliaments of Western Europe EXCEPT

    (A) campaigns of parliament members are more personalistic.

    (B) members of parliament are more likely to support the party after election.

    (C) Congress functions more separately from the executive than does parliament.

    (D) party discipline is tighter within parliament.

2. During which time period was power in the U.S. House of Representatives most centralized in the leadership?

    (A) 1860s

    (B) Late 1800s and early 1900s

    (C) 1930s

    (D) Today

3. During which period in U.S. history was the House of Representatives more powerful than the Senate?

    (A) The early 1800s   (C) 1920s

    (B) 1870s   (D) 1970s

4. The seniority system of choosing committee chairmen

    (A) is less important today than it was a few years ago.

    (B) has never been particularly important in reality.

    (C) was often opposed openly by powerful Speakers.

    (D) has existed since the early 1800s.

5. The most powerful leader(s) in the Senate is (are) the

    (A) party whips.

    (B) Speaker.

    (C) president *pro tempore*.

    (D) majority and minority leaders.

6. Which of the following powers did the U.S. president lack until 1994?

    (A) Pocket veto

    (B) Executive privilege

    (C) Commander-in-chief of the armed forces

    (D) Line item veto

7. What is the maximum number of terms for which one may be elected president of the U.S.?

    (A) Three terms   (C) Three-and-a-half terms

    (B) Two terms   (D) No limit

8. The number of bureaucrats in the U.S. government

    (A) has grown significantly since the end of World War II.

    (B) has not grown significantly, although the power of the bureaucracy has grown.

    (C) has not grown significantly, and the power of the bureaucracy has declined.

    (D) has grown significantly, as has the power of the bureaucracy.

9. The most important motivation for the limitation of civil liberties and civil rights early in the 20th century was

    (A) national security.

    (B) violence caused by early civil rights leaders.

    (C) the lower percentages of minority groups within the U.S. population.

    (D) the need to control the inequalities caused by an industrialized society.

10. A recently organized country is MOST likely to have problems with

    (A) structures not matching functions.

    (B) survival in the international environment.

    (C) a high GNP.

    (D) establishing legitimacy.

11. The process whereby political culture is transmitted to the citizens is

    (A) political communication.   (C) political socialization.

    (B) domestic environment.   (D) political recruitment.

12. In a consensual political culture,

    (A) citizens always agree with political leaders.

    (B) citizens consent to give all power to a dictator.

    (C) there is usually only one political party.

    (D) citizens are in general agreement about the basics of government.

13. The ways in which a political system encourages individuals to serve in leadership roles is known as

    (A) political socialization.

    (B) political communication.

    (C) a democratic political structure.

    (D) recruitment of elites.

14. The theoretical point of view that focuses on building an understanding of deterrence in the nuclear age is

    (A) traditional analysis.

    (B) the strategists' perspective.

    (C) grand theory.

    (D) middle range theory.

15. A scholar who develops a theory of arms races would MOST likely be studying international relations from which theoretical perspective?

    (A) Traditional analysis

    (B) The strategists' perspective

    (C) Grand theory

    (D) Middle range theory

16. The major purpose of operational definitions in a research design is

    (A) to generate more data.

    (B) to establish criteria for judging reality on a more common basis.

    (C)   to prove a theory to be correct.

    (D)   to define the relationship between hypotheses and theories.

17.   The level of measurement that provides ONLY discreet categories for data is

    (A)   nominal.   (C)   operational.

    (B)   ordinal.   (D)   integral.

18.   Which of the following is an example of ordinal categorization?

    (A)   Republican/Democrat

    (B)   Liberal Democrat/Conservative Democrat; Liberal Republican/Conservative Republican

    (C)   Income levels per year: $10,000-$20,000; $20,000-$30,000; $30,000-$40,000; $40,000-$60,000

    (D)   Democratic regime/totalitarian regime

19.   Procedures that are repeatable and that yield similar readings on repeated applications are said to have

    (A)   validity.   (C)   operationalism.

    (B)   reliability.   (D)   empiricism.

20.   A sample in which a random sample is selected from every sampling unit proportionate to the size of the sampling unit is called

    (A)   cluster sampling.

    (B)   systematic sampling.

    (C)   stratified sampling.

    (D)   multi-stage random sampling.

Answer Key

1.	(A)	6.	(D)	11.	(C)	16.	(B)
2.	(B)	7.	(B)	12.	(D)	17.	(A)
3.	(A)	8.	(B)	13.	(D)	18.	(B)
4.	(A)	9.	(A)	14.	(B)	19.	(B)
5.	(D)	10.	(D)	15.	(D)	20.	(C)

Detailed Explanations

1.   **(A)**   Choice (A) is correct. Candidates can only be elected to parliament through the efforts of a political party, whereas Congressmen may have more personalistic campaigns that are only loosely supported by a party.

2.   **(B)**   Choice (B) is the correct answer. During the late 1800s and early 1900s, power in the House was centralized in the hands of Speakers Thomas B. Reed and Joseph Cannon.

3.   **(A)**   Choice (A) is the correct answer. In the early 1800s, the House of Representatives was more powerful than the Senate, and leadership was strongly centralized under House Speaker Henry Clay.

4.   **(A)**   Choice (A) is the correct answer. In the 1970s, a series of reforms weakened the seniority system, allowing election of chairmen by secret ballot, open committee meetings, and more authority to subcommittees and individual members.

5.   **(D)**   Choice (D) is the correct answer. The real leadership is in the hands of the majority and minority leaders.

6.   **(D)**   Choice (D) is correct. Congress granted the president the line item veto in 1994; however, it came under legal challenge by litigants who claimed it upsets the balance of power between the Executive and Legislative branches.

7.   **(B)**   Choice (B) is the correct answer. The Twenty-Second Amendment, ratified in 1951, says, "No person shall be elected to the office of the President more than twice...."

8.   **(B)**   Choice (B) is the correct answer. Although the number of bureaucrats has not grown significantly, the power of the bureaucracy has grown dramatically since the country's founding.

9.   **(A)**   Choice (A) is correct. Early in the twentieth century, the Supreme Court usually ruled to limit freedoms if national security was at stake.

10.   **(D)**   Choice (D) is the correct answer. A new country with a recently organized government may have trouble with legitimacy (acceptance by the citizens) because no centralization of power has existed before.

11.   **(C)**   Choice (C) is correct. Political socialization is the way in which children and adults learn political values and attitudes. Some governments emphasize political socialization as an important basis for establishing the legitimacy of the government.

12.   **(D)**   Choice (D) is correct. In consensual political culture, citizens are in general agreement about the basics of government. In contrast, in a conflictual

political culture, citizens have conflicting points of view about the way the government should be run.

13. **(D)** Choice (D) is correct. Political recruitment defines the way in which a government encourages citizens to participate in government (citizen recruitment), and the ways in which it encourages individuals to serve in leadership roles (recruitment of elites).

14. **(B)** Choice (B) is the correct answer. The strategists' perspective was particularly strong during the Cold War era. Their main concern has been to understand deterrence in the nuclear age, to analyze the importance of new weapon systems, and to maximize national security and minimize the possibility of nuclear war.

15. **(D)** Choice (D) is correct. Middle range theorists believe that international relations may be best understood by developing more specific explanations, such as a theory of arms races or crisis decision making. A number of middle range theories focus on the study of war and peace. These theories highlight some of the processes leading to escalation of violence, the relationship between prejudice and national hostility, the economic consequences of disarmament, and the sources of public attitudes toward foreign cultures.

16. **(B)** Choice (B) is correct. Operational definitions are required to set agreement on common meanings. Giving a concept an operational definition means providing a set of instructions to indicate how to measure, label, or otherwise designate a given concept.

17. **(A)** Choice (A) is the correct answer. The nominal level of measurement is the simplest measurement, providing only discreet categories for data. There is no metric order in nominal data. There are simply categories.

18. **(B)** Choice (B) is correct. The ordinal level of measurement categorizes *and* orders. For example, an ideological ordering may be attached to the partisan categories of Democratic and Republican by using a liberal/conservative dimension. The ordinal level goes beyond mere categorization and is considered a higher and more meaningful level of measurement than is nominal categorization.

19. **(B)** Choice (B) is the correct answer. One way to assess the adequacy of a research design and its operational definitions and measurement procedures is to determine a measure's reliability. Procedures are deemed to have reliability if they are repeatable and if they yield similar readings on repeated applications.

20. **(C)** Choice (C) is correct. A stratified sample is drawn from different subgroups of a theoretical population to ensure the overall sample's representativeness.

CHAPTER 3

ECONOMICS

INTRODUCTION TO ECONOMICS

What Is Economics?

Economics is "the study of how a society allocates scarce resources amidst unlimited human wants." As such, the concepts of *scarcity* and *human wants* are fundamentally important to the study of economics.

Macroeconomics is the study of the economy as a whole. Some of the topics considered include inflation, unemployment, and economic growth.

Microeconomics is the study of the individual parts that make up the economy. The parts include households, business firms, and government agencies, and particular emphasis is placed on how these units make decisions and the consequences of these decisions.

Economic Analysis

Economic Theory—An economic theory is an explanation of why certain economic phenomena occur. For example, there are theories explaining the rate of inflation, how many hours people choose to work, and the amount of goods and services the U.S. will import. Stripped down to essentials, a theory is a set of statements about cause-and-effect relationships in the economy.

Models—A model is an abstract replica of reality and is the formal statement of a theory. The best models retain the essence of the reality, but do away with extraneous details. Virtually all economic analysis is done by first constructing a model of the situation the economist wants to analyze. The reason for this is because human beings are incapable of fully understanding reality. It is too complex for the human mind. Models, because they avoid many of the messier details of reality, can be comprehended, but good models are always "unrealistic."

It would not be inaccurate to say that economists do not analyze the economy; they analyze models of the economy. Almost every prediction that an economist makes, e.g., the impact of changes in the money supply on interest rates, the effect of the unemployment rate on the rate of inflation, the effect of increased competition in an industry on profits, is based on a model.

Models come in verbal, graphical, or mathematical form.

Empirical Analysis—All models yield predictions about the economy. For example, a widely held model predicts that increases in the rate of growth of the money supply will lead to higher inflation. In empirical analysis, economists compare predictions with the actual performance of the economy as measured by economic data. Good empirical analysis often requires mastery of sophisticated statistical and mathematical tools.

Positive Economics—Positive economics is the analysis of "what is." For example, positive economics tries to answer such questions as these: What will the effect be on the rate of inflation if the rate of growth of the money supply is raised by one percentage point? What will happen to hours of work of welfare recipients if welfare benefits are raised $500? What will the effect be on our trade balance if the exchange rate is devalued five percent? Many economists view positive economics as "objective" or "scientific," and believe their special training gives them the expertise to draw conclusions about these types of issues.

Normative Economics—Normative economics is the analysis of "what should be." For example, normative economics tries to answer such questions as these: What inflation rate should our economy strive for? Should welfare recipients be expected to work? Is reducing our trade deficit a desirable thing? Normative economics is clearly a subjective area. There is nothing in an economist's training that gives his or her opinions on these issues any more validity than anyone else's.

The Economic Way of Thinking

Economics analysis is characterized by an emphasis on certain fundamental concepts.

Scarcity—Human wants and needs (for goods, services, leisure, etc.) exceed the ability of the economy to satisfy those wants and needs. This is true for the economy as a whole as well as each individual in the economy. In other words, there is never enough to go around. Individuals never have enough money to buy all they want. Business firms cannot pay completely satisfactory wages without cutting into profits, and vice versa. Government never has enough money to fund all worthwhile projects.

Opportunity Cost—The reality of scarcity implies that individuals, businesses, and governments must make choices, selecting some opportunities while foregoing others. Buying a car may mean foregoing a vacation; acquiring a new copy machine may mean canceling the company picnic; paying higher welfare benefits may require terminating a weapons system. The opportunity cost of a choice is the value of the best alternative choice sacrificed.

Individualism—Economic analysis emphasizes individual action. Most economic theories attempt to model the behavior of "typical" individuals. All groups, such as "society," business firms, or unions, are analyzed as a collection of individuals each acting in a particular way. In a sense, the preceding sentence represents an ideal. Not all economic theory achieves this goal.

Rational Behavior—Individuals are assumed to act rationally. This is the most misunderstood term in economics. It does not necessarily mean people are cold, calculating, and greedy. Rather, it means that given a person's goals and knowledge, people take actions likely to achieve those goals and avoid actions likely to detract from those goals. A greedy person acts rationally if she spends on herself and does not give to charity. She is irrational if she does the opposite. An altruistic person acts rationally if she gives her money to the needy and does not spend it on herself. Irrational behavior is the opposite.

Marginal Analysis—Economists assume that people make choices by weighing the costs and benefits of particular actions.

Important Economic Concepts and Terms

Specialization and Division of Labor—This is a strategy for producing goods and services. Division of labor means that different members of a team of producers are given responsibility for different aspects of a production plan. Specialization means that producers become quite apt at those aspects of production they concentrate on. Specialization and division of labor is alleged to lead to efficiency which facilitates economic growth and development.

THE ECONOMIC PROBLEM

Universality of the Problem of Scarcity

Goods and Services—Goods and Services refers to anything that satisfies human needs, wants, or desires. Goods are tangible items, such as food, cars, and clothing. Services are intangible items, such as education, health care, and leisure. The consumption of goods and services is a source of happiness, well-being, satisfaction, or utility.

Resources (Factors of Production)—Resources refers to anything that can be used to produce goods and services. A commonly used classification scheme places all resources into one of six categories:

Land—All natural resources, whether on the land, under the land, in the water, or in the air; e.g., fertile agricultural land, iron ore deposits, tuna fish, corn seeds, and quail.

Labor—The work effort of human beings.

Capital—Productive implements made by human beings, e.g., factories, machinery, and tools.

Entrepreneurship—A specialized form of labor. Entrepreneurship is creative labor. It refers to the ability to detect new business opportunities and bring them to fruition. Entrepreneurs also manage the other factors of production.

Technology—The practical application of scientific knowledge. Technology is typically combined with the other factors to make them more productive.

Scarcity—Economists assume that human wants and needs are virtually limitless while acknowledging that the resources to satisfy those needs are limited. Consequently, society is never able to produce enough goods and services to satisfy everybody, or most anyone, completely. Alternatively, resources are scarce relative to human needs and desires.

Scarcity is a problem of all societies, whether rich or poor. As a mental experiment, write down the amount of income you think a typical family needs to be "comfortable" in the United States today. Now compare your figure with the median family income in the United States ($51,939 in 2013). In most instances, what students think is necessary to be comfortable far exceeds median family income, which loosely implies that the typical family in the U.S. is not comfortable, even though the United States is the richest nation in the history of the world. If your figure is less than the median income, think again. Do you think you would really be "comfortable" at that level of income?

Universal Problems Caused by Scarcity

A society without scarcity is a society without problems, and consequently one where there is no need to make decisions. In the real world, all societies must make three crucial decisions:

1. **What goods and services to produce and in what quantities.**

2. **How to produce the goods and services selected**—what resource combinations and production techniques to use.

3. **How to distribute the goods and services produced among people**—who gets how much of each good and service produced.

Universal Economic Goals

Allocative (Economic) Efficiency—A society achieves allocative efficiency if it produces the types and quantities of goods and services that most satisfies its people. Failure to do so wastes resources.

Technical Efficiency—A society achieves technical efficiency when it is producing the greatest quantity of goods and services possible from its resources. Failure to do so is also a waste of resources.

Equity—A society wants the distribution of goods and services to conform with its notions of "fairness."

Standards of Equity—Equity is not necessarily synonymous with equality. There is no objective standard of equity, and all societies have different notions of what constitutes equity. Three widely held standards are:

1. **Contributory standard**—Under a contributory standard, people are entitled to a share of goods and services based on what they contribute to society. Those making larger contributions receive correspondingly larger shares. The measurement of contribution and what to do about those who contribute very little or are unable to contribute (i.e., the disabled) are continuing issues.

2. **Needs standard**—Under a needs standard, a person's contribution to society is irrelevant. Goods and services are distributed based on the needs of different households. Measuring need and inducing people to contribute to society when goods and services are guaranteed are continuing issues.

3. **Equality standard**—Under an equality standard, every person is entitled to an equal share of goods and services, simply because they are a human being. Some of the ongoing issues with this theory are how to allow for needs and how to induce individuals to maximize their productivity when the reward is the same for everyone.

Economists remain divided over whether the goals of equity and efficiency (allocative and technical) are complementary or in conflict.

Production Possibilities Curve

The Production Possibilities Curve is a model of the economy used to illustrate the problems associated with scarcity. It shows the maximum feasible combinations of two goods or services that society can produce, assuming all resources are used in their most productive manner.

Assumptions of the Model

1. Society is only capable of producing two goods (guns and butter).
2. At a given point in time, society has a fixed quantity of resources.
3. All resources are used in their most productive manner.

Table 3-1 shows selected combinations of the two goods that can be produced given the assumptions.

Point	Guns	Butter
A	0	16
B	4	14
C	7	12
D	9	9
E	10	5
F	11	0

Table 3-1–Selected Combinations of Guns and Butter

Figure 3-1 is a graphical depiction of the Production Possibilities Curve (curve FA).

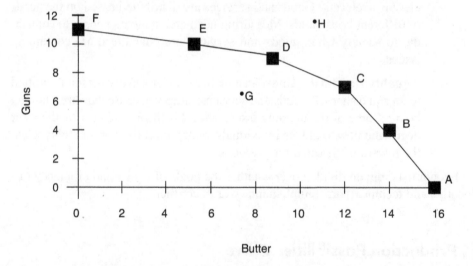

Figure 3-1–Production Possibilities Curve

Technical Efficiency—All points on the curve are points of technical efficiency. By definition, technical efficiency is achieved when more of one good cannot be produced without producing less of the other good. Find point D on the curve. Any move to a point with more guns (i.e., point E) will necessitate a reduction in butter production. Any move to a point with more butter (such as point C) will necessitate a reduction in guns production. Any point inside the curve (such as point

G) represents technical inefficiency. Either inefficient production methods are being used or resources are not fully employed. A movement from G to the curve will allow more of one or both goods to be produced without any reduction in the quantity of the other good. Points outside the curve (such as H) are technically infeasible given society's current stock of resources and technological knowledge.

Opportunity Cost—Consider a move from D to E. Society gets one more unit of guns, but must sacrifice four units of butter. The four units of butter is the opportunity cost of the gun. One gun costs four units of butter.

Law of Increasing Costs—Starting from point A and moving up along the curve, note that the opportunity cost of guns increases. From point A to B, two butter are sacrificed to get four guns (one gun costs one-half butter); from point B to C, two butter are sacrificed to get three guns (one gun costs two-thirds butter); from C to D, three butter are sacrificed for two guns (one gun costs one-and-one-half butter); from D to E, one gun costs four butter; and from E to F, one gun costs five butter.

The law of increasing costs says that as more of a good or service is produced, its opportunity cost will rise. It is a consequence of resources being specialized in particular uses. Some resources are particularly good in gun production and not so good for butter production, and vice versa.

At the commencement of gun production, the resources shifted out of butter will be those least productive in butter (and most productive in guns). Consequently, gun production will rise with little cost in terms of butter. As more resources are diverted, those more productive in butter will be affected, and the opportunity cost will rise. This is what gives the production possibilities curve its characteristic convex shape.

If resources are not specialized in particular uses, opportunity costs will remain constant and the production possibilities curve will be a straight line (see Figure 3-2).

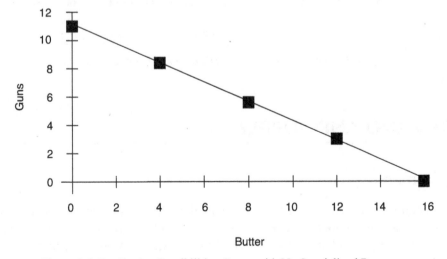

Figure 3-2–Production Possibilities Curve with No Specialized Resources

Allocative Efficiency—Allocative efficiency will be represented by the point on the curve that best satisfies society's needs and wants. It cannot be located without additional knowledge of society's likes and dislikes. A complicating factor is that the allocatively efficient point is not independent of society's distribution of income and wealth.

Economic Growth—Society's production of goods and services is limited by its resources. Economic growth, then, requires that society increases the amount of resources it has or makes those resources more productive through the application of technology. Graphically, economic growth is represented by an outward shift of the curve to IJ (see Figure 3-3). Economic growth will make more combinations of goods and services feasible, but will not end the problem of scarcity.

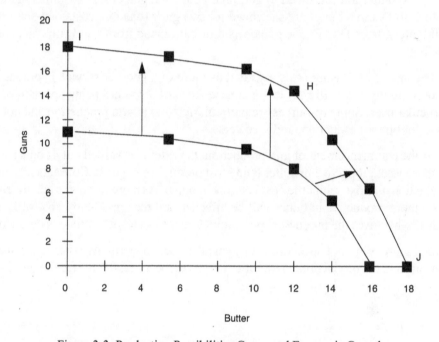

Figure 3-3–Production Possibilities Curve and Economic Growth

DEMAND AND SUPPLY

Demand

Demand is a schedule or a graph showing the relationship between the price of a product and the amount consumers are willing and able to buy, *ceteris paribus*. The schedule or graph does not necessarily show what consumers actually buy at each price. The Law of Demand says there is an inverse relationship between price and quantity demanded; people will be willing and able to buy more if the product gets cheaper.

Ceteris Paribus

All hypothetical relationships between variables in economics include a stated or implied assumption *ceteris paribus*. The term means "all other factors held constant." As we will see, there are many factors affecting the amount of a product people are willing and able to buy. The demand schedule shows the relationship between price and quantity demanded, holding all the other factors constant. This allows us to investigate the independent effect that price changes have on quantity demanded without worrying about the influence the other factors are having.

Demand Schedule—Assume the product is widgets. Let Qd be quantity demanded and P be price.

Qd	P
48.0	1.00
47.5	1.25
47.0	1.50
46.5	1.75
46.0	2.00

Demand Graph

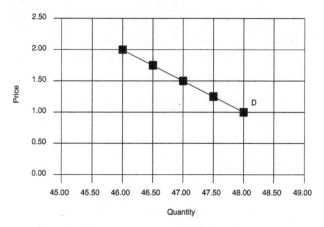

Figure 3-4–Graph of Demand Schedule

Supply

Supply is a schedule or a graph showing the relationship between the price of a product and the amount producers are willing and able to supply, *ceteris paribus*. The schedule or graph does not necessarily show what producers actually sell at each price. There is generally a positive relationship between price and quantity supplied, reflecting higher costs associated with greater production.

Supply Schedule—Assume the product is widgets. Let Qs be quantity supplied.

Qs	P
46.0	1.00
46.5	1.25
47.0	1.50
47.5	1.75
48.0	2.00

Supply Graph

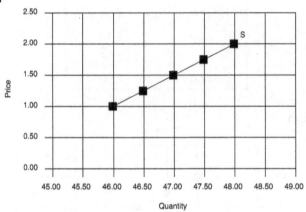

Figure 3-5–Graph of Supply Schedule

Market Equilibrium

The intersection of the demand and supply curves indicates the equilibrium price and quantity in the market (see Figure 3-6). The word *equilibrium* is synonymous with *stable*. The price and quantity in a market will frequently not be equal to the equilibrium, but if that is the case then the market will be adjusting, and, hence, not stable.

If the price of the product is $2.00, then the quantity supplied of the product (48) will be greater than the quantity demanded (46). There will be a surplus in the market of 48 – 46 = 2. The unsold product will force producers to lower their prices. A reduction in price will reduce the quantity supplied while increasing quantity demanded until the surplus disappears. Two dollars is not an equilibrium because the market is forced to adjust.

If the price of the product is $1.00, then the quantity supplied of the product (46) will be less than the quantity demanded (48). There will be a shortage in the market of 48 – 46 = 2. Unsatisfied customers will cause the price of the product to be bid up. The higher price will cause the quantity supplied to increase while decreasing the quantity demanded until the shortage disappears. One dollar is not an equilibrium because the market is forced to adjust.

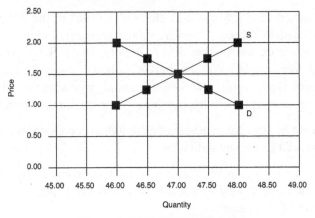

Figure 3-6–Market Equilibrium

If the price of the product is $1.50, then the quantity demanded (47) is just equal to the quantity supplied (47). Producers can sell all they want. Buyers can buy all they want. Since everyone is satisfied, there is no reason for the price to change. Hence, $1.50 is an equilibrium price and 47 is an equilibrium quantity.

ECONOMIC SYSTEMS

Types of Systems

Every society must have some method for making the basic economic decisions.

Tradition—Traditional systems largely rely on custom to determine production and distribution questions. While not static, traditional systems are slow to change and are not well-equipped to propel a society into sustained growth. Traditional systems are found in many of the poorer Third World countries.

Command—Command economies rely on a central authority to make decisions. The central authority may be a dictator or a democratically constituted government.

Market—It is easier to describe what a market system is not than what it is. In a pure market system, there is no central authority and custom plays very little role. Every consumer makes buying decisions based on his or her own needs and desires and income. Individual self-interest rules. Every producer decides for him- or herself what goods or services to produce, what price to charge, what resources to employ, and what production methods to use. Producers are motivated solely by profit considerations. There is vigorous competition in every market.

Mixed—A mixed economy contains elements of each of the three systems defined above. All real-world economies are mixed economies, although the mixture of tradition, command, and market differs greatly. The U.S. economy has traditionally placed great emphasis on the market, although there is a large and active government (command) sector. The Soviet economy placed main reliance on government to direct economic activity, but there was a small market sector.

Capitalism—The key characteristic of a capitalistic economy is that productive resources are owned by private individuals.

Socialism—The key characteristic of a socialist economy is that productive resources are owned collectively by society. Alternatively, productive resources are under the control of government.

Circular Flow

The Circular Flow is a model of economic relationships in a capitalistic market economy. Households, the owners of all productive resources, supply resources to firms through the resource markets, receiving monetary payments in return. Firms use the resources purchased (or rented, as the case may be) to produce goods and services, which are then sold to households and other businesses in the product markets. Household income not spent (consumed) may be saved in the Financial Markets. Firms may borrow from the financial markets to finance capital expansion (investment). Firm saving and household borrowing are not shown.

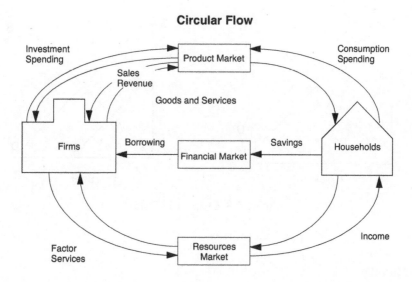

Figure 3-7–The Circular Flow

HOW A MARKET ECONOMY WORKS

Although the description of a market economy may suggest that chaos is the order of the day, economists believe that if certain conditions are met, a market economy is easily capable of achieving the major economic goals.

How a Market Economy Achieves Allocation Efficiency—Market forces will lead firms to produce the mix of goods most desired. Unforeseen events can be responded to in a rational manner.

Change in Tastes

Assume a change in consumer tastes from beef to chicken (see Figure 3-8). An increase in demand in the chicken market will be accompanied by a decrease in demand in the beef market. The higher price of chicken will attract more resources into the market and lead to an increase in the quantity supplied. The lower price of beef will induce a reduction in the quantity supplied and exit of resources to other industries.

Note that the change in the level of output of both goods occurred because it was in the economic self-interest of firms to do so. Greater demand in the chicken market increased the profitability of chicken; lower demand in the beef market decreased the profitability of beef. Chicken and beef producers responded to society's desires not out of a sense of public spiritedness, but out of self-interest.

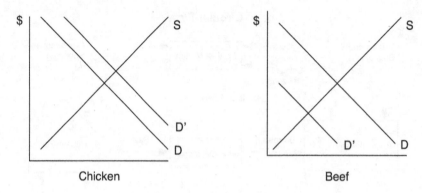

Figure 3-8–Changes in Tastes

Scarcity

An unexpected freeze in Florida will cause a shift in the supply curve of orange juice, driving up its price, and causing consumers to cut back their purchases (see Figure 3-9). The higher price of orange juice will increase the demand for substitute products like apple juice, causing an increase in the quantity supplied of apple juice to take the place of orange juice.

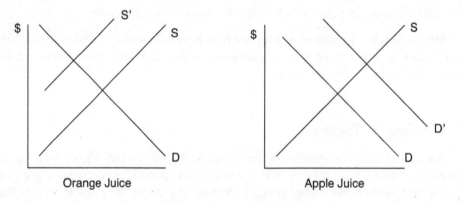

Figure 3-9–Freeze in Florida

As above, the reaction of market participants reflected their evaluation of their own self-interest. Consumers reduced their quantity demanded of orange juice because it was now more expensive. Apple juice producers expanded production because now it was more profitable.

Consumer Sovereignty—"The Consumer is King." Consumer sovereignty means that consumers determine what is produced in the economy. In a market economy, business must cater to the whims of consumer tastes or else go out of business.

How a Market Economy Achieves Technical Efficiency—Market forces will lead firms to produce output in the most efficient manner. The constant struggle for profits will stimulate firms to cut costs. Note that technical efficiency results from attention to self-interest, not the public interest.

The Importance of Competition—A market economy thrives on competition between firms. In their struggle for survival, firms will be forced to cater to consumer demand (leading to allocative efficiency) and force production costs down as far as possible (leading to technical efficiency).

How a Market Economy Achieves Full Employment—Full employment of resources is thought to be the normal state of affairs in a market economy. Resource surpluses will force down the resource's price, leading quickly to re-employment.

How a Market Economy Achieves Growth—Competition between firms for the consumer's dollar will force a constant search for better products and methods of production. The resulting technological change will lead to optimal growth.

The Market Economy and Equity—This is a problematic area for a market economy. Certainly there are financial rewards for those who produce the products that win consumer acceptance. There are losses for those who do not. Yet winners in a market economy are not necessarily the most virtuous of people — they just sell a better product. While consumer demand determines the pattern of production, those consumers with the most income exert the greatest influence on the pattern.

The Role of Prices in a Market Economy—In order for an economy to operate efficiently, there must be information and incentives. There must be information on what goods and services are in demand, which resources are scarce, and so on. There must be an incentive to produce the goods and services desired, conserve on scarce resources, and so on. Both information and incentives are provided by prices. High prices indicate goods and services in demand; low prices indicate goods and services that have lost favor. High prices indicate scarce resources; low prices indicate plentiful. Firms responding "properly" to high prices will earn profits; firms responding "properly" to low prices will avoid losses. Firms exploiting cheap resources will earn profits; firms conserving on expensive resources will avoid losses.

Prices always provide accurate information and appropriate incentives. Since traditional and command economies downplay the role of prices, they have a much more difficult time achieving allocational and technical efficiency.

Conditions that Must Be Met for a Market Economy to Achieve Allocative and Technical Efficiency

A market economy will automatically produce the optimum quantity of every good or service at the lowest possible cost if four conditions are met:

Adequate Information—Consumers must be well-enough informed about prices, quality and availability of products, and other matters so they can make intelligent spending decisions. Workers must be well-enough informed about wages and working conditions so they can choose wisely among job opportunities. Other segments of the economy must be similarly well-informed.

Competition—There must be vigorous competition in every market. Monopolistic elements will reduce output, raise prices, and allow inefficiency in particular markets.

No Externalities—Externalities exist when a transaction between a buyer and seller affects an innocent third party. An example would be if *A* buys a product from *B* that *B* produced under conditions that polluted the air that others breathe. (Not all externalities result in damage to society. Some are beneficial.) Where externalities are present, there is the possibility of over- or under-production of particular goods and services.

No Public Goods—The market is unlikely to produce the appropriate quantity of public goods.

THE PUBLIC SECTOR IN THE AMERICAN ECONOMY

Public Sector

The Public Sector refers to the activities of government.

Government Spending

Government Expenditures on Goods and Services versus Transfer Payments—Government spending can be usefully broken down into two categories. One category is spending on goods and services. When government buys a battleship, a hammer, or the Space Shuttle, it is acquiring goods. When government pays the salary of a soldier, teacher, or bureaucrat, it is getting a service in return. The second category is transfer payments. Transfers are money or in-kind items given to individuals or businesses for which the government receives no equivalent good or service in return. Examples would be social security payments, welfare, or unemployment compensation.

GDP, GNP, AND MEASURING ECONOMIC PERFORMANCE

Gross Domestic Product (GDP) equals the total dollar value of all *final* goods and services produced *within* a country's borders in a given period (usually a quarter or a year). GDP *includes* foreign firms producing in the United States (such as Toyota in Kentucky) and *excludes* U.S. firms producing overseas (such as IBM in Japan).

GDP also excludes "intermediate" goods, such as tires produced by Goodyear but sold to Ford. These types of sales are excluded because Ford, as an automaker, will then install these tires on a car and sell that car to a consumer, which is considered the *final* good for sale.

The formula for GDP is:

Consumer Spending + Business Investment + Government Spending + Net Exports

$$(C + I + G + NX)$$

Consumer spending makes up roughly 70% of GDP.

Note: "Nominal" GDP does *not* take out the effects of inflation, whereas "Real" GDP does.

In contrast to GDP, **Gross National Product (GNP)** equals GDP *plus* all income earned *outside* of the United States by U.S. firms and citizens (such as IBM in Japan) and *less* income earned by foreign firms and citizens *in* the U.S. (such as Toyota in Kentucky).

Note: Given the significant influence that increased globalization has played on the United States' economy since the 1970s, the vast majority of economists today use GDP as the preferred measurement tool rather than GNP.

Technology and Productivity: The four factors of production are (i) land; (ii) labor; (iii) capital; and (iv) entrepreneurial ability. If a country's political and business leaders combine these factors effectively, then that country should have a productive economy.

The United States has the largest economy in the world for several reasons. These include the following elements: (i) ever-growing population; (ii) access to domestic and international capital (or money); (iii) history of technological innovation via a long line of talented entrepreneurs, including Ben Franklin, Thomas Edison, Henry Ford, Steve Jobs, Bill Gates, and Jeff Bezos; (iv) abundant natural resources; and (v) a large national market.

GDP per Capita equals GDP divided by the number of people in the country. For example, in 2016 the U.S. had a GDP of approximately $18.5 trillion and a population of 324 million people. Its GDP per Capita, therefore, was slightly over $57,000.

THE TWO PRIMARY SCHOOLS OF ECONOMIC THOUGHT

I. Classical School

- **Key Person:** Adam Smith / **Principal Book:** *The Wealth of Nations* (1776)

- **Main Period of Influence:** late 1700s to early 1930s

- **Principal Concepts:**

  —**Laissez-faire:** Governments should severely limit their role in markets by taking a *laissez-faire* ("hands-off") approach.

  —**Invisible Hand:** Instead of government involvement, Smith argued that a combination of self-interest, competition, and the laws of supply and demand should direct how markets function. If a firm in a given market is successful in producing the right product at the right price at the right time, it will profit; if not, it will likely fail over time.

  —**Self-Correcting Markets:** In the "long run," markets will correct themselves without government interference.

  —**Labor Specialization:** The concept of labor specialization leads more people to be more efficient and productive, which in turn leads a country to achieving a higher national income (GDP).

  —**Profit Motive/Self Interest:** Smith stated the "unintended consequences of intend actions" tend to benefit a society. He further asserted that, "It is not from the benevolence of the butcher, the brewer, or the baker that we expect our dinner, but from their regard to their own interest."

- **Perceived Strengths:** From the late 1700s through the end of the 1920s, Smith's theories led to long periods of prosperity in the United States. Moreover, a general adherence to Smith's key tenets allowed America to become the most dominant economic and industrial power in the world. If humans are mostly self-interested, then Smith's theories have some obvious merit. The lack of government interference, it should also be noted, led to balanced budgets.

- **Perceived Weaknesses:** Economic busts tend to follow economic booms. For example, there were five panics/depressions in the 1800s—1819, 1837, 1857, 1873, and 1893—and all were preceded by economic booms. The Panic of 1893 was the worst of the five, but its severe consequences were later surpassed by those of the Great Depression, which began with the Stock Market Crash in 1929. Smith's view that governments should not intervene in the business cycle lost favor during the prolonged Great Depression. As a result, by the mid-1930s the theories of John Maynard Keynes gradually took root. Most economists today would agree that Smith's policy of *laissez-faire* led to many excesses during the 1920s, which included both the overproduction of consumer goods and the overextension of credit to both businesses and consumers. Critics of Smith assert that his theories underestimate the human capacity for greed and corruption, which together can take markets to artificial highs before they come crashing back down.

II. Keynesian School

- **Key Person:** John Maynard Keynes / **Principal Book:** *The General Theory of Employment, Interest and Money* (1935)

- **Main Period of Influence:** mid-1930s to 1980

- **Principal Concepts:**

  —A key role of a democratic form of government is to take away the rough edges of capitalism.

  —"In the long run, we're all dead." Keynes agreed with Adam Smith that markets will correct themselves in the long run, but he also noted that, "In the long run, we're all dead." Because Keynes felt there would be too much human suffering during a severe recession, he argued that governments needed to intervene and smooth out the large swings in the business cycle.

  —**Aggregate Demand:** In a severe economic recession, Keynes felt that it was the government's duty to "prime the pump," or increase government spending to lift GDP back up to a healthy level. In making his argument, Keynes provided the basis for fiscal policy (manipulating taxes and government spending) and monetary policy (manipulating interest rates and the money supply) to correct an economy that is surging or flailing.

  — **"Animal Spirits":** Keynes lived through the horrors of World War I and thus concluded that people often act irrationally. To this end, he coined the term "animal spirits," which he defined as "a spontaneous urge to action rather than inaction." Keynes asserted that irrational emotions (such as greed and fear) tend to override our rational instincts at various times, and when they do so in the economic realm, booms and busts may occur.

—**"Paradox of Thrift"**: During a boom time, many people get exuberant and spend all they earn, rather than saving. Conversely, during a recession, people tend to save extensively when governments need them to spend in order to boost national income (GDP).

- **Perceived Strengths:** Keynes' theories did not eliminate the business cycle, but when implemented, especially during the 1950s and 1960s, they did limit the cycle's large swings up and down. Keynes' theories also provided for a greater sense of equality in society, but this benefit was achieved by taking away a certain amount of individual liberty.

- **Perceived Weaknesses:** The implementation of Keynes' theories, critics argue, led to "stagflation"—a combination of high inflation and high unemployment—in the United States during the 1970s. While this is true, the OPEC oil embargo and the resulting surge in oil prices also played a major role in terms of causing stagflation.

- Critics of Keynes have also argued that his theories led to bloated government budgets and massive budget deficits. Moreover, they assert that Keynes was naïve about the role of government. For instance, Keynes argued that when an economy improves, political leaders are supposed to raise taxes and cut government spending to pay off any national debt incurred while propping up the economy. That said, when politicians do in fact raise taxes, they tend to get voted out of office, so there is little incentive for them to do so.

Various Economic Policies Since 1980

After Keynes lost favor around 1980, the "supply-side" economic theories of economist Arthur Laffer gained favor. Adopting a variation of the policies of Andrew Mellon—the U.S. Treasury Secretary during the 1920s—Laffer promoted reducing taxes on businesses and the wealthy in order to induce more production (or supply) of goods and services. In turn, this process would lead to the creation of more jobs. President Ronald Reagan embraced Laffer's theories, and his policies known as Reaganomics did stimulate the economy. These same policies, however, also led to high budget deficits and the tripling of the national debt under Reagan's presidency. A large increase in defense spending also played a major role in the increased budget deficits of the 1980s.

Since the 1980s, political leaders in the United States—in conjunction with the leaders of the Federal Reserve Bank—have used a variation of the theories put forth by both Adam Smith and John Maynard Keynes, including those of their various protégés. As the Great Recession of 2007-2009 recently showed, however, there is no one economic theory today that remains completely dominant in the United States during the various stages of the business cycle. During times of expansion, we tend to lean towards Adam Smith, while during times of economic turbulence, John Maynard Keynes tends to make a comeback.

MACROECONOMIC PROBLEMS OF THE AMERICAN ECONOMY

The Business Cycle

Business Cycles—Business cycles are the alternating periods of prosperity and recession that seem to characterize all market-oriented economies.

Four Phases of the Cycle—Every business cycle consists of four phases. The peak is the high point of business activity. It occurs at a specific point of time. The contraction is a period of declining business activity. It occurs over a period of time. The trough is the low point in business activity. It, too, occurs at a specific point in time. The expansion is a period of growing business activity. It takes place over a period of time.

Although the word "cycle" implies a certain uniformity, that is misleading. Each business cycle differs from every other in terms of duration of contractions and expansions, and height of peak and depth of trough.

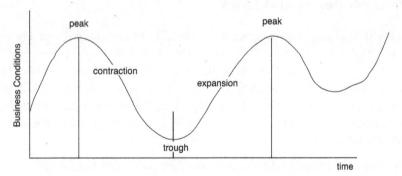

Figure 3-10–Phases of the Business Cycle

Seasonal Fluctuations—Seasonal fluctuations are changes in economic variables that reflect the season of the year. For example, every summer, ice cream sales soar. They decrease during winter. Every December, toy sales increase dramatically. They fall back during January.

Secular Trends—A secular trend is the long run direction of movement of a variable. For example, our economy has become dramatically richer over the past century. We can say that there was a secular upward trend in real GNP. Of course, growth was not steady. There were periods of faster than average followed by slower than average growth, which accounts for business cycles.

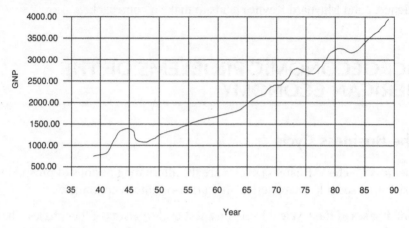

Figure 3-11–Secular Trend and Cycle in Real GNP, 1939–88

MONEY AND BANKING

What Money Is and Does

Money is anything that is generally acceptable in exchange for goods and services and in payment of debts. Suppose you had something you wanted to sell. Few would be willing to part with their product for a commodity like a loaf of bread, a chicken, or an automobile hubcap. All would be willing to exchange their product for coins, currency, or a check. Therefore, these latter items are money because they are generally acceptable. Everybody is willing to accept them in exchange for what they want to sell.

Functions of Money—Money performs four particular functions:

1. **Medium of Exchange**—Money is used to facilitate exchanges of goods and services. Money makes buying and selling easier. Assume we had an economy where nothing was money. Such an economy is known as a **barter economy**. In a barter economy goods and services exchange directly for other goods and services. If you want an axe that someone is selling, you must find an item that person wants to trade for it. Barter requires a **double coincidence of wants**, each party must want what the other party has. If that condition does not hold, then exchange cannot take place, and

valuable resources can be wasted in putting together trades. With money this problem never arises because **everyone always wants money**. Consequently, the resources used to facilitate exchanges can be put to more productive use.

2. **Unit of Value**—We use our monetary unit as the standard measure of value. We say a shirt is worth $25.00, not 14 chickens.

3. **Store of Value**—Money is one of the forms wealth can be stored in. Alternatives include stocks and bonds, real estate, gold, great paintings, and many others. One advantage of storing wealth in money form is that money is the most liquid of all assets. **Liquidity** refers to the ease with which an asset can be transformed into spendable form. Money is already in spendable form. The disadvantage of holding wealth in money form is that money typically pays a lower return than other assets.

4. **Standard of Deferred Payment**—Money is used in transactions involving payments to be made at a future date. An example would be building contracts where full payment is made only when the project is completed. This function of money is implicit in the three already discussed.

What Serves as Money?—Virtually anything can and has served as money. Gold, silver, shells, boulders, cheap metal, paper, and electronic impulses stored in computers are examples of the varied forms money has taken. The only requirement is that the item be generally acceptable. Money does **not** have to have intrinsic value (see below). Typically, the items that have served as money have had the following additional characteristics:

1. durability

2. divisibility

3. homogeneity (uniformity or standardization)

4. portability (high value-to-weight and value-to-volume)

5. relative stability of supply

6. optimal scarcity

What Makes Money Valuable?—Money is valuable if it can be used for or exchanged for something useful. Money's lack of intrinsic value means it cannot be used for anything useful. Why can it be exchanged for something useful? Sellers accept money because they know they can use it anywhere else in the country to buy goods and services and pay off debts. If they could not do that, they would not want it. What this means is that the substance that is used for money need not be valuable, and that money need not be backed by anything valuable. Such is the case. Our money is not backed by gold, silver, or anything else. It is just cheap metal, cheap paper, and electronic impulses stored in computers. Gold can be put to better use filling teeth!

The United States' Money Supply

While there are many different definitions of the money supply available, the two most commonly used are M1 and M2.

M1—M1 consists of currency, demand deposits, other checkable deposits, and traveler's checks.

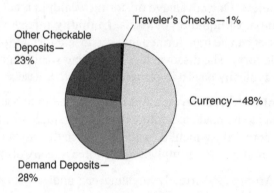

Figure 3-12–Composition of M1

Currency—coins and paper money.

Demand deposits—These are checking accounts held in commercial banks. Funds can be transferred from person to person by means of a check. Demand deposits are considered money because checks are generally acceptable.

Other checkable deposits—This category, includes all other financial institution deposits upon which checks can be written. Among these are NOW accounts, ATS accounts, and credit union share drafts.

Traveler's checks—Most traveler's checks are generally acceptable throughout much of the world.

M2—M2 includes all of M1 plus savings deposits, small-denomination time deposits, money-market mutual funds and deposit accounts, overnight repurchase agreements (known as repos), and Eurodollars.

Savings Deposits—These are the common passbook savings accounts. They do not provide check-writing privileges.

Small-denomination time deposits—Better known as certificates of deposits, or CDs. They typically do not provide check-writing privileges.

Money market mutual funds and deposit accounts—Both mutual funds and deposit accounts are investment funds. Large numbers of people pool their money to allow for diversification and professional investment management. Mutual funds are managed by private financial companies. Deposit accounts are managed by commercial banks. Investors earn a return on their investment and have limited check-writing privileges. Mutual funds are not afforded protection by the government, as is the case with FDIC-insured bank accounts.

Overnight repurchase agreements and Eurodollars—Overnight repos essentially are short-term (literally, overnight) loans. A corporation with excess cash may arrange to purchase a security from a bank with the stipulation that the bank will buy the security back the next day at a slightly higher price. The corporation receives a return on its money, and the bank gets access to funds. Eurodollars are dollar-denominated demand deposits held in banks outside the United States (not just in Europe). From the standpoint of M2, deposits held in Caribbean branches of Federal Reserve member banks are relevant. These deposits are easily accessed by U.S. residents. While both instruments are important in financial affairs, they are negligible in the totality of M2.

A significant proportion of M2 cannot be used as a medium of exchange. Why, then, are the items considered money? First, each of these items is highly liquid. Second, studies indicate that people's economic behavior is not very sensitive to their relative holdings of the various assets in question (see Figure 13).

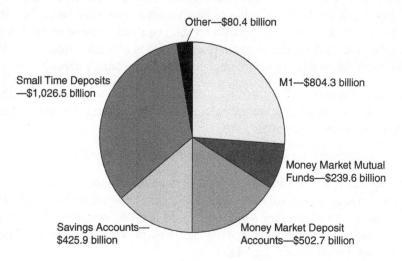

Figure 3-13–Composition of M2.

The Financial System

Financial Intermediaries—Financial intermediaries are organizations such as commercial banks, savings and loan institutions, credit unions, and insurance companies. They play an important role in facilitating the saving and investment process which helps the economy grow. Savers typically look to place their money where the combination of return, liquidity, and safety is best. Through the various types of deposits they offer, financial intermediaries compete for the saved funds. The money so obtained is used to finance borrowing. Through their ability to obtain large pools of money from many depositors, intermediaries are able to service the needs of large borrowers.

Balance Sheet of Typical Bank

Assets	Liabilities
Reserves	Demand Deposits
Loans	Savings Deposits
Securities	Time Deposits
Property	Other Deposits
Other Assets	Net Worth

Reserves—Reserves are a bank's money holdings. Most reserves are held in the form of demand deposits at other banks or the Federal Reserve System. The remainder is cash in the bank's vault. Reserves are held to meet the demand for cash on the part of depositors and to honor checks drawn upon the bank. The amount of reserves a bank must hold is based on the **required reserve ratio**. Set by the Federal Reserve System, the required reserve ratio is a number from 0 to 1.00 and determines the level of reserve holdings relative to the bank's deposits.

Required Reserves—Required reserves are the amount a bank is legally obligated to hold. Required reserves are calculated by multiplying the required reserve ratio by the amount of deposits.

$$\text{Required Reserves} = \text{Required Reserve Ratio} \times \text{Deposits}$$

The required reserve ratio does not make banks safe. In the absence of a requirement, most banks would voluntarily hold adequate reserves to be "safe." In fact, the level of reserves banks are required to hold is probably higher than what they need to be safe. The main purpose of the requirement is to give the Federal Reserve System some control over the banks.

Excess Reserves—Excess reserves are the difference between the amount of reserves a bank holds and what it is required to hold. All banks hold excess reserves at all times for reasons of financial prudence; however, greater excess reserves will be held during periods of financial uncertainty.

$$\text{Excess Reserves} = \text{Reserves} - \text{Required Reserves}$$

Why Can Banks Hold "Fractional" Reserves?—All banks constantly operate with reserve holdings only a fraction of deposit liabilities. This is known as **fractional reserve banking**. If all depositors tried to withdraw their money simultaneously, banks would not be able to honor the demands. Fortunately, this is unlikely to happen because people like to hold deposits because they are safe and convenient. On a normal business day, some withdrawals are made, but these are counterbalanced by new deposits. Reserve holdings need only be a small fraction of deposits for prudent operation.

MONETARY POLICY

The Federal Reserve System

The Federal Reserve System (known as the "Fed") is the central bank of the United States. Its responsibilities are to oversee the stability of the banking system and conduct monetary policy to the end of fighting inflation and unemployment and stimulating economic growth.

Structure—The Fed has an unusual structure. It consists of a Board of Governors, 12 regional banks, money subregional banks, and commercial banks that opt for membership in the system. Although it was created by an Act of Congress (in 1913), nominally the Fed is privately owned by the member banks. Members of the Board of Governors are appointed by the President and confirmed by the Senate for 14 year terms. The Chair of the Board is appointed by the President and confirmed by the Senate for a four year term. The Fed's budget is overseen by a committee of Congress, and it must report to Congress about its operations at least twice a year. To a large extent, the Fed can be considered an independent agency of the government.

The Fed's virtual independence has led to a continuing controversy. Is it wise to give the power to influence the state of the economy to an entity that is not directly accountable to the people? The "pro" side claims the Fed's independence puts it "above" politics and leads to decisions more in the "public interest." The "con" side says that in a democracy, the people should be given a voice in all decisions that affect them.

Functions—The major functions of the Fed are as follows:

1. **Bank Regulation**—The Fed has been given the responsibility of examining member banks to determine if they are financially strong and in conformity with the banking regulations. The Fed also approves mergers.

2. **Clearing Interbank Payments**—The Fed performs a service for member banks in operating the check clearing function. Banks receiving deposit checks drawn on other banks can present them to the Fed. The Fed will

credit the receiving bank's reserve account, reduce the paying bank's reserve account, and send the check back to the paying bank. Banks do not universally avail themselves of this service. Local banks will frequently cooperate and establish their own check clearing process for local checks.

3. **Lender of Last Resort**—One of the original motivations for establishing the Fed was to have a bank that could act as a "lender of last resort."

Bank panics refer to situations where depositors lose faith in their bank and try to withdraw their money. Given the fractional reserve nature of modern banking, under which banks, by law, must set aside a fixed percent of their total deposits as reserves with the Fed, it is impossible for all depositors to withdraw their money simultaneously. The inability of depositors to withdraw their money from any one bank has the potential of scaring other depositors and starting a "run on the banks." By standing ready to loan reserves to banks experiencing difficulties, the Fed helps reduce the danger of panics.

Federal Deposit Insurance was established during the New Deal era. Federal Deposit Insurance provides government guarantees for bank deposits should a bank fail. Both commercial banks and savings and loans are insured. Panics were much more common in the days before the Fed and the Federal Deposit Insurance Corporation, but are not unknown today. Witness the widespread failures of savings and loan institutions in Ohio and Maryland (institutions which *lacked* federal insurance) in the 1980s and '90s.

4. **Monetary Policy**—

Open Market Operations—Open market operations refers to the Fed's buying or selling of U.S. Government bonds in the open market. The purpose is to influence the amount of reserves in the banking system, and, consequently, the banking system's ability to extend credit and create money.

a. **To expand the economy**—The Fed would buy bonds in the open market. If $50 million in bonds was purchased directly from commercial banks, the banks' balance sheet would change as follows:

All Commercial Banks

R + 50 million	
Bonds – 50 million	

Banks are now holding an additional $50 million in excess reserves which they can use to extend additional credit. To induce borrowers, banks are likely to lower interest rates and credit standards. As loans are made, the money supply will expand. The additional credit will stimulate additional spending, primarily for investment goods.

The $50 million in bonds could be purchased directly from private individuals. The private individuals would then deposit the proceeds in their bank accounts. After the money was deposited, the balance sheet of all commercial banks would look as follows:

All Commercial Banks

R	+ 50 million	DD	+ 50 million

As above, the banks are now holding excess reserves which they can use to extend credit. Lower interest rates, a greater money supply, and a higher level of total expenditure will result.

b. **To contract the economy**—The Fed would sell bonds in the open market. If it sold $20 million in bonds directly to the commercial banks, the banks' balance sheet would change as follows:

All Commercial Banks

R	– 20 million	
Bonds	+ 20 million	

Banks are now deficient in reserves. They need to reduce their demand deposit liabilities, and will do so by calling in loans and making new credit more difficult to get. Interest rates will rise, credit requirements will be tightened, and the money supply will fall. Total spending in the economy will be reduced.

If the Fed sells the $20 million in bonds directly to private individuals, payment will be made with checks drawn against the private individuals' bank accounts. The banks' balance sheet will change as follows:

All Commercial Banks

R	– 20 million	DD	– 20 million

Again, banks are deficient in reserves. They are forced to reduce credit availability, which will raise interest rates, reduce the money supply, and lead to a drop in total spending.

Bonds are a financial instrument frequently used by government and business as a way to borrow money. Every bond comes with a par value (often $1,000), a date to maturity (ranging from 90 days to 30 years), a coupon (a promise to pay a certain amount of money each year to the bondholder until maturity), and a promise to repay the par value on the maturity date. The issuing government or business sells the bonds in the bond market for a price determined by supply and demand. The money received from the sale represents the principal of the loan, the annual coupon payment is the interest on the loan, and the principal is repaid at the date of maturity. There is also a secondary market in bonds.

Assume a bond carries a coupon of $100 and is sold for $1,000. Then the annual yield to the purchaser is roughly 10% ($100/$1,000). If the same bond was sold for $950, the yield would be roughly 10.5% ($100/$950). If the same bond was sold for $1,050, the yield would roughly be 9.5% ($100/$1,050). Note the inverse relationship between bond yield and price. Also note that the actual yield formulas are considerably more complicated than those used.

Reserve Ratio—The Fed can set the legal reserve ratio for both member and non-member banks. The purpose is to influence the level of excess reserves in the banking system, and consequently, the banking system's ability to extend credit and create money.

a. **To expand the economy**—The Fed would reduce the reserve requirement. Assume the reserve requirement is 8%, and all banks are "all loaned up."

   If the Fed reduces the reserve requirement to 6%, required reserves fall to $30 million, and there are immediately $10 million in excess reserves. Banks will lower the interest rates they charge and credit requirements in an attempt to make more loans. As the loans are granted, the economy's money supply and total spending will rise.

All Commercial Banks

R	40 million	DD	50 million

b. **To contract the economy**—The Fed would raise the reserve requirement. Assume the reserve requirement is 8%, and all banks are "all loaned up."

All Commercial Banks

R	40 million	DD	50 million

If the Fed raises the reserve requirement to 10%, required reserves rise to $50 million, and banks are immediately $10 million deficient in reserves. Banks will raise the interest rates they charge and credit requirements to reduce the amount of money borrowed. They may also call in loans. As the loans are reduced, the economy's money supply and total spending will fall.

Discount Rate—One of the responsibilities of the Fed is to act as a "lender of last resort." Member banks needing reserves can borrow from the Fed. The interest rate the Fed charges on these loans is called the **discount rate**. By changing the discount rate, the Fed can influence the amount member banks try to borrow, and, consequently, the banking system's ability to extend credit and create money.

a. **To expand the economy**—The Fed would lower the discount rate. A lower discount rate would make it less "painful" for member banks to borrow from the Fed. Consequently, they will be more willing to lend money and hold a low level of excess reserves. A lower discount rate would lead to lower interest rates and credit requirements, a higher money supply, and greater total spending in the economy.

b. **To contract the economy**—The Fed would raise the discount rate. A higher discount rate would make it more "painful" for member banks to borrow from the Fed. Consequently, they will be less willing to lend money and more likely to hold a high level of excess reserves. A higher discount rate would lead to higher interest rates and more stringent credit requirements, a lower money supply, and lower total spending in the economy.

Monetary Policy Summary Table

Tool	Action	Effect on Interest Rates	Effect on Money Supply	Effect on Total Spending	Effect on GNP
Open Market	buy	lower	raise	raise	raise
Operations	sell	raise	lower	lower	lower
Reserve	raise	raise	lower	lower	lower
Ratio	lower	lower	raise	raise	raise
Discount	raise	raise	lower	lower	lower
Rate	lower	lower	raise	raise	raise

REVIEW QUESTIONS

1. In *The Wealth of Nations*, Adam Smith attempted to demonstrate which of the following about international trade?

    (A) Tariffs and quotas should be used to protect domestic industries.

    (B) Countries should produce only those commodities for which they have an absolute advantage.

    (C) When countries specialize and trade, world wealth is enhanced.

    (D) Countries should be self-sufficient and produce all commodities they consume.

2. If the Treasury required the central bank to buy bonds in the amount of $10 million, the effect on the money supply would be the same as the effect of

    (A) the sale of $10 million in bonds by the central bank to commercial banks.

    (B) the purchase of $10 million in U.S. bonds by foreigners.

    (C) the purchase of $10 million in bonds by the central bank from commercial banks.

    (D) the Treasury printing $10 million in new money.

3. Which of the following is NOT a factor that enhances an economy's growth potential?

    (A) Increasing levels of investment

    (B) Relatively high levels of training among the labor force

    (C) A relatively high capital to output ratio

    (D) New technologies

4. Conflicts between the goals of the Treasury and the Federal Reserve Bank exist when

    (A) the GNP is increasing, thus causing tax revenues to increase.

    (B) the Fed restrains money to reduce inflation and the Treasury needs to borrow.

    (C) the Fed follows an easy money policy to reduce unemployment, and the Treasury needs to borrow.

    (D) national debt and interest rates are decreasing due to fiscal restraint.

5. Which of the following represents monetary policy geared to increase the supply of money?

    (A) The purchase of bonds by the Federal Reserve Bank

    (B) The sale of bonds by the central bank

    (C) An increase in reserve requirements

    (D) An increase in the discount rate

6. Prices tend to be inflated during wartime because

    (A) guns cost more than butter.

    (B) there is competition for fully employed resources.

    (C) the Consumer Price Index is calculated differently in wartime.

    (D) the cost of government is not included in the CPI.

7. If people start eating more fish and chicken to reduce their intake of cholesterol, and the importation of Canadian pork is restricted due to a steroid problem, what will happen to meat prices in the U.S.?

    (A) The prices of chicken, pork, and fish will go down.

    (B) The prices of chicken, pork, fish, and beef will go up.

    (C) There will be no substantial effect on prices.

    (D) The price of pork will go down, while the prices of chicken and fish will go up.

8. Both Bank A and Bank B are required to meet a 20% legal reserve requirement. Bank A has excess reserves of $20,000. Bank B has no excess reserves but receives a deposit of $20,000. Which of the following statements is correct?

    (A) Each bank can make a loan of $20,000.

    (B) Bank A can make a loan of $20,000, but Bank B can make a loan of only $16,000.

    (C) Bank B can make a loan of $20,000, but Bank A can make a loan of $16,000.

    (D) The most each bank can loan is $16,000.

9. If the Fed wants to create a situation of "tight" money, which of the following actions would be taken?

    (A) Raise the discount rate, buy government securities, and lower the legal reserve requirement.

    (B) Raise the discount rate, buy government securities, and raise the legal reserve requirement.

    (C) Raise the discount rate, sell government securities, and raise the legal reserve requirement.

    (D) Lower the discount rate, buy government securities, and raise the legal reserve requirement.

10. An economist's definition of investment in human capital would be represented by

    (A) labor costs in producing an intermediate good.

    (B) labor costs in producing a final good.

    (C) federal government's expenses for unemployment compensation.

    (D) the expenditure by an individual on college tuition and other college expenses.

Answer Key

1.	(C)	4.	(B)	7.	(B)	9.	(C)
2.	(D)	5.	(A)	8.	(B)	10.	(D)
3.	(C)	6.	(B)				

Detailed Explanations

1. **(C)** Choice (C) is correct. Adam Smith believed that each country producing what it does best, or relatively better, and trading for those commodities produced to advantage elsewhere, enhanced each nation's wealth and world wealth. Choices (A) and (D) would interfere with the types of specialization and trade described in choice (C). Smith stated that countries should produce those goods that they have an absolute and comparative advantage in, a comparative advantage being the least relative disadvantage.

2. **(D)** Choice (D) is the correct answer. If the central bank buys bonds in the amount of $10 million from the Treasury, it creates $10 million in "new money," the effect of which is identical to the Treasury printing this amount of money.

Conversely, if the central bank buys $10 million in bonds from commercial banks, it creates less money because some must be used as reserves. Choices (A) and (B) reduce the supply of money.

3.   **(C)**   Choice (C) is correct. A growth formula derived from the Harrod-Domar model is:

$$\text{growth rate} = \frac{\text{average propensity to save}}{\text{capital/output ratio}}$$

It should be evident after inspection that as the capital to output ratio decreases, the growth rate increases. Choices (A), (B), and (D) enhance economic growth.

4.   **(B)**   Choice (B) is correct. The Treasury needs to borrow money to finance a debt and wants to do so at the lowest interest rates possible, but monetary restraint and tight money are inconsistent with this goal.

5.   **(A)**   Choice (A) is the correct answer. When the Fed purchases bonds, it pays for them with money which increases money supply. Choices (B), (C), and (D) are contractionary moves by the Fed.

6.   **(B)**   Choice (B) is correct. During wartime, the economy is working to produce more defense than in peacetime, which bids up prices. Choice (C) is false. Choice (D) is true, but if the government were included, it would probably cause more inflation.

7.   **(B)**   Choice (B) is the correct answer. The price of chicken and fish would be bid up by increased demand. The price of pork would go up due to controlled supply, and the price of beef would go up because it is a substitute for pork.

8.   **(B)**   Choice (B) is correct. A single commercial bank can make loans to the extent of its excess reserves. Therefore, Bank A can make loans of $20,000. Bank B, however, must hold 20% of the $20,000 deposit as federal reserve deposit. Therefore, Bank B can only make $16,000 of loans. The loans that banks make depend upon meeting the legal reserve requirements.

9.   **(C)**   Choice (C) is correct. Raising the discount rate raises the cost of commercial banks borrowing from the Fed. Selling government securities to commercial banks or the public takes money or potential money out of circulation. (Money becomes near money.) Raising the legal reserve requirement wipes out excess reserves and lowers the value of the money multiplier. All three of the actions described in (C) are consistent in creating a "tight" money situation.

10.   **(D)**   Choice (D) is the correct answer. When an economist speaks of human capital, the emphasis is on capital theory which includes investment as a large component. Investment is performed to obtain a return. Investment in human capital consists of those expenditures which an individual makes to improve earning power. The concept is very specific and all other answers are not appropriate.

CHAPTER 4

GEOGRAPHY

INTRODUCTION TO GEOGRAPHY

What Is Geography?

Geography is the study of the earth's surface, including such aspects as its climate, topography, vegetation, and population. **Physical geography** is a branch of geography concerned with the natural features of the earth's surface. Physical geography concentrates on such areas as land formation, water, weather, and climate.

Population geography is a form of geography that deals with the relationships between geography and population patterns, including birth and death rates. **Political geography** deals with the effect of geography on politics, especially on national boundaries and relations between states. **Economic geography** is a study of the interaction between the earth's landscape and the economic activity of the human population.

UNITED STATES

San Diego, California	1,394,928
Omaha, Nebraska	443,885
Baltimore, Maryland	621,849
Houston, Texas	2,296,224
Boston, Massachusetts	667,137
New York, New York	8,175,133

Table 4-1 – U.S. City Populations, 2010 (U.S. Census Bureau est.)

Year	Population	Year	Population
1860	31,443,321	1950	151,325,798
1870	38,558,371	1960	179,323,175
1880	50,189,209	1970	203,302,031
1890	62,979,766	1980	226,547,082
1900	76,212,168	1990	248,790,925
1910	92,228,496	2000	282,171,936
1920	106,021,537	2010	308,745,538
1930	123,202,624	2017 (est.)	326,474,013
1940	132,164,569		

Table 4-2 – Population of the United States

There are many sources of energy in the United States that are being developed to lessen the country's dependence on foreign oil. Some of these sources are solar energy, nuclear energy, gasohol, fossil fuels, and others. With the development of these sources of energy, more jobs will be made available and our economy will not be afflicted by adverse situations in oil-rich countries.

The United States is a relatively young country made up of immigrants from all over the world. This country serves as a leader of the free world and has many allies around the world.

It has helped many countries that needed financial help to rebuild their countries and continues to play an important part in world affairs.

The Middle Atlantic states, which include New York, West Virginia, Delaware, Maryland, New Jersey, and Pennsylvania, are a hub of activity. This area is highly industrialized and includes a skilled work force. The financial center of the nation is found in New York and cultural activities of all kinds are found in this area.

The states of North Dakota, South Dakota, Nebraska, Kansas, Minnesota, Iowa, Missouri, Wisconsin, Illinois, Michigan, Indiana, and Ohio make up the Plains states. This area is also referred to as the Midwest Region of the United States. It is known as a great agricultural region. Some of the crops grown are wheat, corn, and oats.

The Plains states are highly industrialized. Their location near waterways and the close proximity to coal and iron deposits have made it relatively easy for industries to develop. Skilled laborers are available and are necessary to work in manufacturing plants.

The South includes the following states: Texas, Oklahoma, Louisiana, Arkansas, Mississippi, Alabama, Florida, Georgia, South Carolina, North Carolina, Tennessee, Kentucky, and Virginia. This area is known for its relatively mild weather and good, rich soil. Agriculture and oil are two of the most important industries in the South. Some of the crops grown are cotton, corn, tobacco, peanuts, and rice. Cattle raising is also very important in some of these states. Five of these states border on the Gulf of Mexico.

Texas is the second-largest state in land area. It is composed of 267,000 square miles and 254 counties. It is broken up into many large physical regions such as piney woods, post oak belt, plains, rolling prairie, high plains, valley, coastal prairie, and West Texas. The estimated population of Texas in 2008 was 24.3 million. Texas is, without a doubt, one of the most geographically varied states in the United States.

The Pacific states include Washington, Oregon, and California, as well as tropical Hawaii. California has the largest population of any state in the United States. It is known for its agriculture and leads all other states in this regard. Oregon and Washington also are known for farming. All three states also have very developed industries.

Some of the major cities located in the Pacific states are Seattle, Spokane, Portland, Olympia, San Francisco, Los Angeles, Salem, and San Diego. Skiing, surfing, and national parks make tourism a major industry in this region.

The Mountain states are Montana, Idaho, Wyoming, Nevada, Utah, Colorado, Arizona, and New Mexico. These states are sparsely populated, even though the combined square mileage is over 800,000. The Rocky Mountains stretch through this area and most people feel they are a beautiful sight to behold.

The New England states include Maine, Massachusetts, New Hampshire, Vermont, Rhode Island, and Connecticut. Territorially, this is a very small region. The total size is about 67,000 square miles. The main industries in this area are fishing, shipping, manufacturing, and dairy farming.

MEXICO

Mexico borders the United States on the south and has about 107 million people. The land area is about 762,000 square miles. The capital is Mexico City. Some of the chief crops are coffee, cotton, corn, sugar cane, and rice.

Mexico has an abundance of natural resources, such as oil, gold, silver, and natural gas. Textiles, steel production, tourism, and petroleum are the major industries in Mexico.

CANADA

Canada is the United States' neighbor to the north. It includes the second-largest territory in the world. The current population is about 32 million people. The capital of Canada is Ottawa.

The United States and Canada are two sprawling countries that make up North America. Each country is an industrial giant and provides a very high standard of living for its population. The population of the United States is about nine or ten times larger than that of Canada.

The United States and Canada have large supplies of natural resources. In the United States, the minerals include coal, copper, gold, nickel, silver, zinc, and others. In Canada, the minerals found are nickel, gold, lead, silver, zinc, and others.

SOUTH AND CENTRAL AMERICA

Country	Population	Square Miles
Argentina	43,132,000	1,065,189
Brazil	204,579,000	3,286,470
Chile	18,006,000	292,257
Venezuela	30,620,000	352,143
Ecuador	16,279,000	109,483

Table 4-3 – Selected South American Countries, 2015 est.

Central America

Central America is the connecting point between North and South America. The countries in Central America have an extremely long coastline. The main industry of this area is agriculture, and most people who live in this area are extremely poor. Bananas, coffee, and corn are some of their chief crops.

The seven nations that make up Central America are Belize, Guatemala, Honduras, El Salvador, Panama, Costa Rica, and Nicaragua.

South America

South America, lying entirely in the Western Hemisphere and mostly south of the Equator, has a Pacific shoreline on the west and an Atlantic shoreline east and north. South America connects with Central America and lies to the south and east of the Caribbean Sea and North America. It is the realm closest to Antarctica.

A few physical characteristics dominate the physiography of South America. The Andes Mountains stretch the length of the west coast while the Amazon Basin covers the north central part of the realm. The remaining parts of the realm consist mainly of plateaus.

Roughly half of the area and half of the population of South America are concentrated in Brazil.

The population of South America resides primarily on the periphery of the continent. The interior is only lightly populated. However, parts of the interior are undergoing extensive development with some population shifts.

Historically, the difficult terrain and the large distances separating the various states have limited the interchange between the different states on the continent. More recently, the states have increased their interconnections, particularly economically. Economic integration has become a significant factor throughout the continent, but primarily so in the southern part of the continent.

South America can be easily divided into four distinct regions: the North, the West, the Southern Cone, and Brazil.

The North consists of Colombia, Venezuela, Guyana, French Guiana, and Suriname. Each of the states has a Caribbean orientation both economically and culturally. All the states followed a plantation development model that involved the importation of slaves and contract laborers. Eventually, those immigrants were absorbed into the culture. While Guyana, French Guiana, and Suriname retained the culture from the colonial period, Colombia and Venezuela expanded into farming, ranching, mining, and oil and became much more diversified.

The West includes the Andean states Ecuador, Peru, Bolivia, and Paraguay. In addition to the influence of Andes, these states also share a strong Amerindian heritage.

The South, or Southern Cone, consists of Argentina, Chile, and Uruguay. These states have a strong European influence and little Amerindian influence.

Brazil distinguishes itself in two respects from the rest of South America. First is the influence of Portugal rather than Spain and second is the importance of Africans as opposed to Amerindians in both culture and demography.

Most states exhibit a marked degree of cultural pluralism. While there are a variety of ethnicities that are remnants of the colonial and slave heritage, these groups exist side by side without mixing. This pluralism is often expressed economically as well. Within the predominant economic activity, agriculture, commercial and subsistence farming exist side by side to a greater extent than any place else in the world. This, too, reflects the history of the continent, as commercial farming is associated with the land distribution of European landholders while subsistence farming is associated with the landholdings of indigenous, African, and Asian peoples.

Urban growth throughout the continent continues its rapid rise. Levels of urbanization overall today are equivalent to those in Europe and the United States.

EUROPE

Europe consists of 39 states and approximately 731 million people, according to the United Nations. On the north, west, and south, it has boundaries facing the Atlantic Ocean and the Mediterranean Sea, as well as a large number of other bodies of water. The eastern boundary is somewhat uncertain, with the line of demarcation lying along the border of Russia or along the Ural Mountains.

The physiography of Europe includes a wide range of topographic, climatic, and soil conditions which have had an impact on the cultural, political, and economic development.

In the south, the coastal areas have hot dry summers that required the development of specially adapted plants. Lacking the richness of natural resources of other regions, the southern region of Europe has nonetheless achieved a continuity of culture that has continuously depended on the exploitation of agriculture. As a result, the region tends to have a lower standard of living than other parts of Europe with the notable exception of Eastern Europe. While not as urbanized as Northern Europe, Southern Europe is actually more populous than Northern Europe.

Eastern Europe encompasses the largest region in Europe as well as the largest range of physiological, cultural, and political characteristics. This is a region of open plains, major rivers, lowlands, highlands, and mountains and valleys that provide key transit corridors. The result is that numerous peoples have converged on the area and kept this rich area in almost continuous conflict. The region is referred to as a shatter belt because of the unrelenting break up of existing orders. The term "balkanization" comes from this region where chronic division and fragmentation occurs.

Northern or Nordic Europe, one of the largest regions in terms of size is also one of the most poorly endowed regions in terms of natural resources. Cold climates with poor soil and limited mineral wealth combined with long distances over mountainous, remote terrain result in an isolated region, yet one that has succeeded economically as is evidenced by Norway's ranking as fourth-richest European country based on per capita income.

The British Isles, off the western coast of Europe consist of two main islands, Ireland and Britain as well as numerous small islands. While its isolation from continental Europe has protected it from attack, that isolation has led the United Kingdom to look outward to fulfill its economic needs. The United Kingdom had one of the largest empires in history and has become a hub of banking and industry.

Western Europe is at the heart of Europe. It provides the hub of economic power, which has led to its leadership in economic and political union.

Europe consists of strong regional distinctions in physical and cultural characteristics. The distinctions extend to functional specializations, thus helping to provide for extensive interchange.

The economy of Europe is well developed and depends in large part on manufacturing for its income. While Europe is considered to be overall highly productive and developed, the further east one goes, the lower the level of development.

Being at the western end of the Eurasian landmass, Europe is located in a prime position to facilitate contact with the rest of the world. Location as well as durable power cores provided necessary elements for the creation of wide ranging colonial empires.

Europe has an aging population that enjoys a high standard of living, is highly urbanized, and has a long life expectancy. The aging population coincides with a drop in fertility rates and thus a population decline in some states. Immigration partially offsets the population decline, but it is changing the cultural make up of the states, with some instability resulting.

Unlike most other parts of the world, Europe has made significant progress toward economic integration through the European Union. Political progress, although also a part of the developing and expanding European Union, has come much more slowly.

NORTH AFRICA

Northern Africa is the northern most part of Africa, separated from Sub-Saharan Africa by the Sahara Desert. Northern Africa is almost completely surrounded by water in all other directions, with only a small connection to Asia at the Sinai Peninsula of Egypt. Northern Africa is bordered by the Atlantic Ocean to the west, the Red Sea to the east, and the Mediterranean Sea to the north. The states of Algeria, Egypt, Libya, Morocco, Sudan, Tunisia, and Western Sahara make up the region. The dominant physical feature of Northern Africa is the Sahara Desert, which covers more than 90% of the region. The other physical feature of note is the Atlas Mountains, which extend across much of Morocco, northern Algeria, and Tunisia. The Atlas Mountains are part of the mountain system, which also runs through much of Southern Europe. The mountains become a steppe landscape as they transition into the Sahara Desert.

Farming has been the traditional economic base of the region, with Atlas Mountain valleys, the Nile valley and delta, and the Mediterranean coast providing good agricultural land. Cereals, rice, cotton, cedar, and cork are important crops. Olives, figs, dates, and citrus fruits are also grown here. The Nile Valley, being fertile and providing its own source of water, is particularly fertile, while elsewhere irrigation is essential to agricultural production. In the 20th century, the economies of Algeria and Libya were transformed by the discovery of oil and natural gas. Morocco depends on phosphates, agriculture, and tourism for its economy. Egypt and Tunisia also depend on tourism. Egypt, also has a varied industrial base, importing technology to develop its electronics and engineering industries.

The population of North Africa can be divided along the main geographic regions of North Africa: the Maghreb (northwest), the Nile Valley (northeast), and the Sahara (south).

SUB-SAHARAN AFRICA

Sub-Saharan Africa is the whole of the African continent south of the Sahara Desert. It is bordered to the north by the Sahara, the largest desert in the world, the Atlantic Ocean to the west, the Indian Ocean to the east, and the Atlantic and Indian Oceans meeting to border Africa to the south. Despite being geographically part of Subsaharan Africa, the Horn of Africa and large parts of Sudan show a strong Middle Eastern influence.

The landforms of Sub-Saharan Africa include rainforests, grasslands, and a few mountain ranges. Equatorial Africa, including the Sahel (a transitional zone just north of the equator between the Sahara and the tropical savanna), is covered by tropical rain forests while farther south there are grassy flat highlands leading to coastal plains. While Northern Africa has the Atlas Mountains, the Ruwenzri on the Uganda-Zaire border is the main mountain range in the Sub-Saharan region. Kilimanjaro, part of the Ruwenzri and Africa's highest mountain, is a dormant volcano. Further to the east is the Great Rift Valley, which contains several lakes. In addition to these landforms, Africa has some of the world's longest rivers, including the Nile, Niger, Zaire, and Zambezi. While there are many great lakes and large river systems, Africa has few natural sea harbors.

Sub-Saharan Africa is culturally rich and diverse with approximately 50 independent states and hundreds of ethnic groups. The large number of states is a legacy of the colonial occupation of Africa by European states. When African states were given their independence, state boundaries were drawn with little thought given to natural geographic boundaries. The result has been great instability that exists to the present day. Governmental fraud, mismanagement, and poor leadership as well as the highest number of refugees and displaced persons in the world compound the instability. In addition to the political instability, health and nutritional conditions in the region are poor. Many diseases remain uncontrolled, malnutrition is rampant, and the AIDS pandemic, which had its genesis in Africa, is a significant health crisis.

Despite the wide variety of cultures, most people in Sub-Saharan Africa depend on farming to earn a living. This is true despite the fact that Sub-Saharan Africa is rich in natural resources. States such as Angola and Nigeria have oil reserves, while South Africa is known for diamonds. The patterns of resource exploitation and transportation still follow those established during the colonial period. Thus, the people of the region have little access to and largely do not benefit from the wealth of raw materials they possess.

RUSSIA

Russia, the largest state in terms of territory, spans most of the northern part of Eurasia. It is almost twice as large as the next biggest state, Canada. It is also the largest and most populous state that lies the farthest north in the world. Russia's climate is largely continental because of its large size and compactness. Most of its land is more than 200 miles from the sea, and the center is approximately 1,600 miles from the sea. Furthermore, Russia's mountain ranges, which are mostly to the south and the east, block moderating temperatures from the Indian and Pacific Oceans.

Despite its large size, comparatively speaking, Russia's population of approximately 143 million people is not very large. Most of that population lives west of the Ural Mountains and that population is very heterogeneous. Russia is a patchwork of many different ethnic groups, which formed the original basis for the 21 internal republics. As such, Russia is multicultural with a multifaceted political geography.

Despite having 80% of its land mass east of the Ural Mountains, most of the development, population, and infrastructure lie west of the Urals. The largest cities with the attendant industrial and transportation structure as well as the most productive farmland exist on the western 20% of Russia. What development does exist east of the Urals follows a narrow corridor near the southern border that reaches the Sea of Japan at Vladivostok. This corridor coincides with the Trans-Siberian Railway, which was built to reach one of the few seaports that is usable all year. Despite the fact that Russia is large, it is almost completely encircled by land within Eurasia.

While having extensive industrial development (at least regionally), Russia also holds the greatest mineral resource reserves in the world. The country is the most abundant in mineral fuels. It may contain up to half of the world's coal reserves and an even larger percentage of petroleum reserves. While Russia is blessed with plentiful resources, they are located in remote areas with extreme climates. For example, deposits of coal are scattered throughout the region, but the largest deposits are located in central and eastern Siberia, making them difficult to reach and expensive to mine.

Despite the wealth of natural resources, Russia has never been an exporter of manufactured goods, with the exception of weapons. Scarcity and low quality have limited the availability of Russian consumer goods outside of Russia (and, in many cases, inside as well).

With the collapse of Soviet Communism in the late 20th century, regions that have been associated with both Russia and the Soviet Union have begun to look outside of the Russian Federation for political, economic, and cultural connections.

SOUTH ASIA

South Asia is a clearly demarcated realm bounded by deserts in the west, the Himalayas to the north, mountains and dense forests to the east, and ocean to the south. Despite containing over 20 percent of the world's population, South Asia consists of only seven states: Bangladesh, Bhutan, India, the Maldives, Nepal, Pakistan, and Sri Lanka. The realm of South Asia is the most populous and densest in the world. The region has been beset by political instability and is the site of frequent military conflicts including wars between India and Pakistan, both of whom possess nuclear weapons.

The bulk of the region's territory is on the Indian subcontinent. Sections of all the states in the realm lie within the subcontinent on the Indian tectonic plate.

The climate varies considerably from area to area being influenced by altitude, proximity to the coast, and seasonal monsoons. The south is hot in summer and subject to vast quantities of rain during monsoon periods. The north is also hot in summer, but cools during winter. As the elevation increases in mountainous areas, the weather is colder and snow falls at higher altitudes in the Himalayas. However, on the plains at the foot of the Himalayas, the temperatures are much more moderate, as the mountains block the bitter winds that make Siberia so cold.

Despite the temperature variations, the climate of the region is called a monsoon climate. The weather is humid during the summer and dry during winter, resulting in two seasons rather than four: wet and dry. In the south, the climate is tropical monsoon while the north has a temperate monsoon climate. The impact of the monsoon climate can be seen on agriculture in the prevalence of jute, tea, rice, and other vegetables being grown in this region.

With more than half its population engaged in subsistence agriculture, it follows that South Asia has a high rate of poverty. Average incomes are low as are levels of education. Moreover, the low income and education levels contribute to poor overall health for the region. All of these factors paint a grim picture of economic prospects.

Sitting on only three percent of the land mass of the world, yet possessing over 22 percent of its population, South Asia has a high population density that will only continue to get worse as it also has one of the highest population growth rates. India, with over 1 billion people, is the world's largest federal republic. Despite having a representative government, economic gains for the majority of the population are limited.

With more than 2,000 ethnic groups, South Asia is one of the most ethnically diverse realms. Ethnic groups range in size from hundreds of millions to small tribal groups. Throughout its history South Asia has been invaded and settled by many ethnic groups. The fusion of the cultures of these different ethnic groups over the centuries has resulted in the creation of a common culture, traditions, and beliefs such as the religions of Hinduism, Jainism, Buddhism, and Sikhism. As a consequence, they share many similar cultural practices, festivals, and traditions.

Religion continues to play a major role in South Asia. Hindus in India, Muslims in Bangladesh and Pakistan, and Buddhists in Sri Lanka display fundamentalist and nationalist tendencies that exacerbate already tendentious religious relationships.

British colonialism created a politically unified South Asia. However, when Britain granted its South Asian colony independence, it split into numerous states along mainly cultural/religious lines. Political friction, particularly between India and Pakistan, remains a constant problem. The cultural and religious differences that contribute to conflict combine with ongoing border disputes between India and Pakistan and India and China to create a potentially disastrous situation, as all three countries possess nuclear weapons.

EAST ASIA

East Asia consists of four states and two other political entities. China, Japan, South Korea, and Mongolia are states, while Taiwan and North Korea cannot be classified as states because they lack general recognition by the states of the world. Taiwan, while considering itself independent, is viewed by the People's Republic of China as a temporarily insubordinate or wayward province. North Korea's political status is uncertain. It is not a full member of the United Nations and there are doubts as to whether the division of Korea into North and South is permanent.

→ REVIEW QUESTIONS

Question 1 is based on Table 1 presented in this chapter.

1.   Which city has the third-largest population?

(A)   Houston   (C)   San Diego

(B)   Boston   (D)   Baltimore

Questions 2 and 3 are based on Table 2 presented in this chapter.

2.   How much did the population increase between 1970 and 1980?

(A)   By approximately 20,000

(B)   By approximately 200,000

(C)   By approximately 2,000,000

(D)   By approximately 20,000,000

3.   The population of the United States has

(A)   steadily declined.   (C)   dropped markedly.

(B)   remained about the same.   (D)   steadily increased.

4.   Two of the main industries of the South are

(A)   oil and agriculture.   (C)   agriculture and fishing.

(B)   oil and mining.   (D)   oil and cattle raising.

5.   The Pacific states have one thing in common. They are

(A)   farming centers.

(B)   extremely cold in the winter.

(C)   located in the Southwest.

(D)   not highly populated.

6.   Mexico has an abundance of

(A)   oil and gold.   (C)   nickel and diamonds.

(B)   natural gas and nickel.   (D)   diamonds and natural gas.

7.   Canada

(A)   is the largest country in the world.

(B)   is located to the south of the United States.

(C)   includes the second-largest territory in the world.

(D)   is a part of the United States.

Question 8 is based on Table 3 presented in this chapter.

8.   Which country in South America is the largest in both population and square miles?

(A)   Ecuador   (C)   Venezuela

(B)   Brazil   (D)   Argentina

9.   One of the chief crops in Central America is

(A)   wheat.   (C)   barley.

(B)   bananas.   (D)   rice.

10.   Which of the following is an example of climate?

(A)   Changes in the temperature from time to time

(B)   Long, extended periods of little or no rainfall in certain areas

(C)   A forecast of sunshine

(D)   An electrical storm

Answer Key

1.	(C)	4.	(A)	7.	(C)	9.	(B)
2.	(D)	5.	(A)	8.	(B)	10.	(B)
3.	(D)	6.	(A)				

Detailed Explanations

1.   **(C)**   Choice (C) is the correct answer. San Diego has the third-largest population, with approximately 1.39 million people. New York City is first with 8.17 million; Houston is second with 2.29 million.

2. **(D)** Choice (D) is the correct answer. Between 1970 and 1980, the population increased by 23,245,051.

3. **(D)** Choice (D) is the correct answer. The population has increased every decade since 1860.

4. **(A)** Choice (A) is the correct answer. Oil and agriculture are two of the main industries in the South. Some of the crops grown in the South are cotton, corn, tobacco, peanuts, and rice.

5. **(A)** Choice (A) is the correct answer. Oregon and Washington are known for farming, and California leads all other states in agriculture.

6. **(A)** Choice (A) is the correct answer. Mexico has an abundance of natural resources, such as oil, gold, silver, and natural gas.

7. **(C)** Choice (C) is the correct answer. Choice (D) is incorrect because Canada is not part of the United States. Choice (B) is wrong because Canada is located north, not south, of the United States.

8. **(B)** Choice (B) is the correct answer. The population of Brazil is 204 million and its area is 3,286,470 square miles.

9. **(B)** Choice (B) is the correct answer. Some of Central America's chief crops are bananas, coffee, and corn.

10. **(B)** Choice (B) is the correct answer. Choices (A), (C), and (D) are incorrect because they refer to day-to-day conditions, not an overall condition over a period of time.

CHAPTER 5

WESTERN CIVILIZATION AND WORLD HISTORY

THE ANCIENT AND MEDIEVAL WORLDS

The Appearance of Civilization

Between 6000 and 3000 BCE, humans invented the plow, utilized the wheel, harnessed the wind, discovered how to smelt copper ores, and began to develop accurate solar calendars. Small villages gradually grew into populous cities. The invention of writing in Mesopotamia around 3500 BCE, in combination with heightened refinement in sculpture, architecture, and metal working from about 3000 BCE, marks the beginning of civilization and divides prehistoric from historic times.

Mesopotamia

Sumer (4000 to 2000 BCE) included the city of Ur. The *Gilgamesh* is an epic Sumerian poem. The Sumerians constructed dikes and reservoirs and established a loose confederation of city-states. They probably invented writing (called "cuneiform" because of its wedge-shaped letters). The Amorites, or Old Babylonians (2000 to 1550 BCE), established a new capital at Babylon, known for its famous Hanging Gardens. King Hammurabi (reigned 1792–1750 BCE) promulgated a legal code that called for retributive punishment ("an eye for an eye") and provided that one's social class determined punishment for a crime.

The Assyrians (1100–612 BCE) conquered Syria, Palestine, and much of Mesopotamia. They controlled a brutal, militaristic empire. The Chaldeans, or New Babylonians (612–538 BCE), conquered the Assyrian territory, including Jerusalem. In

538 BCE, Cyrus, king of the southern Persians, defeated the Chaldeans. The Persians created a huge empire and constructed a road network. Their religion, Zoroastrianism, promoted worship of a supreme being in the context of a cosmic battle with the forces of evil. After 538 BCE, the peoples of Mesopotamia came under the rule of a series of different empires and dynasties.

Egypt

During the end of the Archaic Period (5000–2685 BCE), Menes, or Narmer, unified Upper and Lower Egypt around 3200 BCE. During the Old Kingdom (2685–2180 BCE), the pharaohs came to be considered living gods. The capital moved to Memphis during the Third Dynasty (ca. 2650 BCE). The pyramids at Giza were built during the Fourth Dynasty (ca. 2613–2494 BCE).

After the Hyksos invasion (1785–1560 BCE), the New Kingdom (1560–1085 BCE) expanded into Nubia and invaded Palestine and Syria, enslaving the Jews. King Amenhotep IV or Akhenaton (reigned c. 1372–1362 BCE) promulgated the idea of a single god, Aton, and closed the temples of all other Gods and Goddesses. His successor, Tutankhamen, reestablished pantheism in Egypt.

In the Post-Empire Period (1085–1030 BCE), Egypt came under the successive control of the Assyrians, the Persians, Alexander the Great, and finally, in 30 BCE, the Roman Empire. The Egyptians developed papyrus and made many medical advances. Other peoples would elaborate their ideas of monotheism and the notion of an afterlife.

Palestine and the Hebrews

Phoenicians settled along the present-day coast of Lebanon (Sidon, Tyre, Beirut, Byblos) and established colonies at Carthage and in Spain. They spread Mesopotamian culture through their trade networks.

The Hebrews probably moved to Egypt around 1700 BCE and were enslaved about 1500 BCE. The Hebrews fled Egypt under Moses and around 1200 BCE returned to Palestine. Under King David (reigned ca. 1012–972 BCE), the Philistines were defeated and a capital established at Jerusalem. Ultimately, Palestine divided into Israel (10 tribes) and Judah (two tribes). The 10 tribes of Israel—also known as the Lost Tribes—disappeared after Assyria conquered Israel in 722 BCE.

The poor and less attractive state of Judah continued until 586 BCE, when the Chaldeans transported the Jews to Chaldea as advisors and slaves (Babylonian captivity). When the Persians conquered Babylon in 539 BCE, the Jews were allowed to return to Palestine. Alexander the Great conquered Palestine in 325 BCE. During the Hellenistic period (323–63 BCE), the Jews were allowed to govern themselves.

Under Roman rule, Jewish autonomy was restricted. The Jews revolted in 66–70 CE. The Jews also revolted in 132–135 CE. These uprisings led to the Jews' loss of their Holy Land. The Romans quashed the revolt and ordered the dispersion of the Jews. The Jews contributed the ideas of monotheism and humankind's covenant and responsibility to God to lead ethical lives.

Greece

Homer's *Iliad* and *Odyssey* were poems that dramatized for Ancient Greek civilization ideas like excellence (*arete*), courage, honor, and heroism. Hesiod's *Works and Days* summarized everyday life. His *Theogony* recounted Greek myths. Greek religion was based on their writings.

In the Archaic Period (800–500 BCE), Greek life was organized around the polis (city-state). Oligarchs controlled most of the polis until the end of the sixth century, when individuals holding absolute power (tyrants) replaced them. By the end of the sixth century, democratic governments replaced many tyrants.

Sparta, however, developed into an armed camp. Sparta seized control of neighboring Messenia around 750 BCE. To prevent rebellions, every Spartan entered lifetime military service (as hoplites) beginning at age 7. Around 640 BCE, Lycurgus promulgated a constitution. Around 540 BCE, Sparta organized the Peloponnesian League.

Athens was the principal city of Attica. Draco (ca. 621 BCE) first codified Athenian law. His Draconian Code was known for its harshness. Solon (ca. 630–560 BCE) reformed the laws in 594 BCE. He enfranchised the lower classes and gave the state responsibility for administering justice. Growing indebtedness of small farmers and insufficient land strengthened the nobles. Peisistratus (ca. 605–527 BCE) seized control and governed as a tyrant. In 527 BCE, Cleisthenes led a reform movement that established the basis of Athens's democratic government, including an annual assembly to identify and exile those considered dangerous to the state.

The Fifth Century (Classical Age)

The fifth century marked the high point of Greek civilization. It opened with the Persian Wars (490; 480–479 BCE) after which Athens organized the Delian League. Pericles (ca. 495–429 BCE) used League money to rebuild Athens, including construction of the Parthenon and other Acropolis buildings. Athens's dominance spurred war with Sparta.

The Peloponnesian War between Athens and Sparta (431–404 BCE) ended with Athens's defeat, but weakened Sparta as well. Sparta fell victim to Thebes, and the other city-states warred amongst themselves until Alexander the Great's conquest.

It was his conquest that unified the Greek city-states in the fourth century BCE, the beginning of the Hellenistic Age.

A revolution in philosophy occurred in classical Athens. The Sophists emphasized the individual and his/her attainment of excellence through rhetoric, grammar, music, and mathematics. Socrates (ca. 470–399 BCE) criticized the Sophists' emphasis on rhetoric and emphasized a process of questioning, or dialogues, with his students. Like Socrates, Plato (ca. 428–348 BCE) emphasized ethics. His *Theory of Ideas or Forms* said that what we see is but a dim shadow of the eternal Forms or Ideas. Philosophy should seek to penetrate to the real nature of things. Plato's *Republic* described an ideal state ruled by a philosopher king.

Aristotle (ca. 384–322 BCE) was Plato's pupil. He criticized Plato, arguing that ideas or forms did not exist outside of things. He contended that it was necessary to examine four factors in treating any object: its matter, its form, its cause of origin, and its end or purpose.

Greek art emphasized the individual. In architecture, the Greeks developed the Doric and Ionian forms. Euripides (484–406 BCE) is often considered the most modern tragedian because he was so psychologically minded. In comedy, Aristophanes (ca. 450–388 BCE) was a pioneer who used political themes. The New Comedy, exemplified by Menander (ca. 342–292 BCE), concentrated on domestic and individual themes.

The Greeks were the first to develop the study of history. They were skeptical and critical and banished myth from their works. Herodotus (ca. 484–424 BCE), called the "father of history," wrote *History of the Persian War.* Thucydides (ca. 460–400 BCE) wrote *History of the Peloponnesian War.*

The Hellenistic Age and Macedonia

The Macedonians were a Greek people who were considered semibarbaric by their southern Greek relatives. They never developed a city-state system and had more territory and people than any of the polis.

In 359 BCE, Philip II (382–336 BCE) became king. To finance his state and secure a seaport, he conquered several city-states. In 338 BCE, Athens fell. In 336 BCE, Philip was assassinated.

Philip's son, Alexander the Great (356–323 BCE), killed or exiled rival claimants to his father's throne. He established an empire that included Syria and Persia and extended to the Indus River Valley. At the time of his death, Alexander had established 70 cities and created a vast trading network. With no succession plan, Alexander's realm was divided among three of his generals. By 30 BCE, all of the successor states had fallen to Rome.

Rome

The traditional founding date for Rome is 753 BCE. Between 800 and 500 BCE, Greek tribes colonized southern Italy, bringing their alphabet and religious practices to Roman tribes. In the sixth and seventh centuries, the Etruscans expanded southward and conquered Rome.

Late in the sixth century (the traditional date is 509 BCE), the Romans expelled the Etruscans and established an aristocratically based republic in place of the monarchy. In the early Republic, power was in the hands of the patricians (wealthy landowners). A Senate composed of patricians governed. The Senate elected two consuls to serve one-year terms. Roman executives had great power (the imperium). They were assisted by two quaestors, who managed economic affairs.

Rome's expansion and contact with Greek culture disrupted the traditional agrarian basis of life. Tiberius Gracchus (163–133 BCE) and Gaius Gracchus (153–121 BCE) led the People's party (or *Populares*). They called for land reform and lower grain prices to help small farmers. They were opposed by the *Optimates* (best men). Tiberius was assassinated. Gaius continued his work, assisted by the *Equestrians*. After several years of struggle, Gaius committed suicide.

Power passed into the hands of military leaders for the next 80 years. During the 70s and 60s, Pompey (106–48 BCE) and Julius Caesar (100–44 BCE) emerged as the most powerful men. In 73 BCE, Spartacus led a slave rebellion, which General Crassus suppressed.

In 60 BCE, Caesar convinced Pompey and Crassus (ca. 115–53 BCE) to form the First Triumvirate. When Crassus died, Caesar and Pompey fought for leadership. In 49 BCE, Caesar crossed the Rubicon, the stream separating his province from Italy, and a civil war followed. In 47 BCE, the Senate proclaimed Caesar as dictator, and later named him consul for life. Brutus and Cassius believed that Caesar had destroyed the Republic. They formed a conspiracy, and on March 15, 44 BCE (the Ides of March), Caesar was assassinated in the Roman Forum. His 18-year-old nephew and adopted son, Octavian, succeeded him. Caesar reformed the tax code and eased burdens on debtors. He instituted the Julian calendar, in use until 1582. The Assembly under Caesar had little power.

In literature and philosophy, Plautus (254–184 BCE) wrote Greek-style comedy. Terence, a slave (ca. 186–159 BCE), wrote comedies in the tradition of Menander. Catullus (87–54 BCE) was the most famous lyric poet. Lucretius's (ca. 94–54 BCE) *On the Nature of Things* described Epicurean atomic metaphysics, while arguing against the immortality of the soul. Cicero (106–43 BCE), the great orator and stylist, defended the Stoic concept of natural law. He was an important advocate of the Roman Republic and an opponent of Caesar. His *Orations* described Roman life. Roman religion was family-centered and more civic-minded than Greek religion.

The Roman Empire

After a period of struggle, Octavian (63 BCE–14 CE), named as Caesar's heir, gained absolute control while maintaining the appearance of a republic. When he offered to relinquish his power in 27 BCE, the Senate gave him a vote of confidence and a new title, "Augustus." Augustus ruled for 44 years (31 BCE–14 CE) He introduced many reforms, including new coinage, new tax collection, fire and police protection, and land for settlers in the provinces.

Between 27 BCE and 180 CE, Rome's greatest cultural achievements occurred under the Pax Romana. The period between 27 BCE and 14 CE is called the **Augustan Age**. Virgil (70–19 BCE) wrote the *Aeneid,* an account of Rome's rise. Horace (65–8 BCE) wrote the lyric *Odes.* Ovid (43 BCE–18 CE) published the *Ars Amatoria,* a guide to seduction, and the *Metamorphoses,* about Greek mythology. Livy (57 BCE–17 CE) wrote a narrative history of Rome based on earlier accounts.

The Silver Age lasted from 14–180 CE. Writings in this period were less optimistic. Seneca (5 BCE to 65 CE) espoused Stoicism in his tragedies and satires. Juvenal (50–127 CE) wrote satire, Plutarch's (46–120 CE) *Parallel Lives* portrayed Greek and Roman leaders, and Tacitus (55–120 CE) criticized the follies of his era in his histories.

Stoicism was the dominant philosophy of the era. Epictetus (ca. 60–120 CE), a slave, and Emperor Marcus Aurelius were its chief exponents. In law, Rome made a lasting contribution. It distinguished three orders of law: civil law (*jus civile*), which applied to Rome's citizens, law of the people (*jus gentium*), which merged Roman law with the laws of other peoples of the Empire, and natural law (*jus naturale*), governed by reason.

After the Pax Romana, the third century was a period of great tumult for Rome. Civil war was nearly endemic in the third century. Between 235 and 284 CE, 26 "barracks emperors" governed, taxing the population heavily to pay for the Empire's defense.

Rome's frontiers were attacked constantly by barbarians. Emperors Diocletian (reigned 285–305 CE) and Constantine (reigned 306–337 CE) tried to stem Rome's decline. Diocletian divided the Empire into four parts and moved the capital to Nicomedia in Asia Minor. Constantine moved the capital to Constantinople.

Some historians argue that the rise of Christianity was an important factor in Rome's decline. Jesus was born around 4 BCE, and began preaching and ministering to the poor and sick at the age of 30. The Gospels provide the fullest account of his life and teachings. Saul of Tarsus, or Paul (10–67 CE), transformed Christianity from a small sect of Jews who believed Jesus was the Messiah into a world religion. Paul won followers through his missionary work. He also shifted the focus from the early followers' belief in Jesus' imminent return to concentrate on personal salvation. His *Epistles* (letters to Christian communities) laid the basis for the religion's organization and sacraments.

The Pax Romana allowed Christians to move freely through the Empire. In the Age of Anxiety, many Romans felt confused and alienated, and thus drawn to the new religion. And unlike other mystery religions, Christianity included women. By the first century, the new religion had spread throughout the Empire.

Around 312 CE, Emperor Constantine converted to Christianity and ordered toleration in the Edict of Milan (ca. 313 CE). In 391 CE, Emperor Theodosius I (reigned 371–395 CE) proclaimed Christianity as the Empire's official religion. By the second century, the church hierarchy had developed. Eventually, the Bishop of Rome came to have preeminence, based on the interpretation that Jesus had chosen Peter as his successor.

The Byzantine Empire

Emperor Theodosius II (reigned 408–450 CE) divided his empire between his sons, one ruling the East, the other the West. After the Vandals sacked Rome in 455 CE, Constantinople was the undisputed leading city of the Empire.

In 527 CE, Justinian I (483–565 CE) became emperor in the East and reigned with his controversial wife Theodora until 565 CE The Nika revolt broke out in 532 CE and demolished the city. It was crushed by General Belisarius in 537 CE, after 30,000 had died in the uprising.

The Crusaders further weakened the state. In 1204 CE, Venice contracted to transport the Crusaders to the Near East in return for the Crusaders capturing and looting Constantinople. The Byzantines were defeated in 1204 CE. Though they drove out the Crusaders in 1261 CE, the empire never regained its former power. In 1453 CE, Constantinople fell to the Ottoman Turks.

Islamic Civilization in the Middle Ages

Mohammed was born about 570 CE and received a revelation from the Angel Gabriel around 610 CE. In 630 CE, Mohammed marched into Mecca. The Sharia (code of law and theology) outlines five pillars of faith for Muslims to observe. First is the belief that there is one God and that Mohammed is his prophet. The faithful must pray five times a day, perform charitable acts, fast from sunrise to sunset during the holy month of Ramadan, and make a *haj*, or pilgrimage, to Mecca. The Koran, which consists of 114 *suras* (verses), contains Mohammed's teachings. *Mullahs* (teachers) occupy positions of authority, but Islam did not develop a hierarchical system comparable to that of Christianity.

A leadership struggle developed after Mohammed's death. His father-in-law, Abu Bakr (573–634 CE), succeeded as caliph (successor to the prophet) and governed for two years, until his death in 634 CE Omar succeeded him. Between 634 and 642 CE, Omar established the Islamic Empire.

The Omayyad caliphs, based in Damascus, governed from 661–750 CE. They called themselves Shiites and believed they were Mohammed's true successors. (Most Muslims were Sunnites, from *sunna*, oral traditions about the prophet.) They conquered Spain by 730 CE and advanced into France until they were stopped by Charles Martel (ca. 688–741 CE) in 732 CE at Poitiers and Tours. Muslim armies penetrated India and China. They transformed Damascus into a cultural center and were exposed to Hellenistic culture from the nearby Byzantine Empire.

The Abbasid caliphs ruled from 750–1258 CE. They moved the capital to Baghdad and treated Arab and non-Arab Muslims as equals. Islam assumed a more Persian character under their reign. In the late tenth century, the empire began to disintegrate. In 1055 CE, the Seljuk Turks captured Baghdad, allowing the Abbasids to rule as figureheads. Genghis Khan (ca. 1162–1227 CE) and his army invaded the Abbasids. In 1258 CE, they seized Baghdad and murdered the last caliph.

Feudalism in Japan

Feudalism in Japan began with the arrival of mounted nomadic warriors from throughout Asia during the Kofun Era (300–710). Some members of these nomadic groups formed an elite class and became part of the court aristocracy in the capital city of Kyoto, in Western Japan. During the Heian Era (794–1185), a hereditary military aristocracy arose in the Japanese provinces, and by the late Heian Era, many of these formerly nomadic warriors had established themselves as independent land owners, or as managers of landed estates *(shoen)* owned by Kyoto aristocrats. These aristocrats depended on these warriors to defend their *shoen,* and in response to this need, the warriors organized into small groups called *bushidan*.

As the years passed, these warrior clans grew larger, and alliances formed among them, led by imperial descendants who moved from the capital to the provinces. After victory in the Taira-Minamoto War (1180–1105), Minamoto no Yoritomo forced the emperor to award him the title of *shogun,* which is short for "barbarian subduing generalissimo." He used this power to found the Kamakura Shogunate which survived for 148 years. Under the Kamakura Shogunate, many vassals were appointed to the position of *jitro* or land steward, or the position of provincial governors *(shugo)* to act as liaisons between the Kamakura government and local vassals.

By the fourteenth century, the *shugo* had augmented their power enough to become a threat to the Kamakura, and in 1333 lead a rebellion that overthrew the shogunate. Under the Ashikaga Shogunate, the office of *shogu* was made hereditary, and its powers were greatly extended. These new *shogu* turned their vassals into aggressive local warriors called *kokujin,* or *jizamurai.* Following this move, the Ashikaga shoguns lost a great deal of their power to political fragmentation, which eventually led to the Warring States Era (1467–1568).

By the middle of the sixteenth century, the feudal system had evolved considerably. At the center of this highly evolved system was the *daimyo,* a local feudal lord who ruled over one of the many autonomous domains.

Far-reaching alliances of *daimyo* were forged under the Tokugawa Shogunate, the final and most unified of the three shogunates. Under the Tokugawa, the *daimyo* were considered direct vassals of the shoguns, and were kept under strict control. The warriors were gradually transformed into scholars and bureaucrats under the *bushido,* or code of chivalry, and the principles of Neo-Confucianism. A merchant class, or *chonin* gained wealth as the samurai class began to lose power, and the feudal system effectively ended when power was returned to the emperor under the Meji Restoration of 1868, when all special privileges of the samurai class were abolished.

Chinese and Indian Empires

The Harappan or Indus civilization was confined to the Indus basin. Around 1500 BCE, during the so-called Vedic age, India came to be ruled by the Indo-Aryans, a mainly pastoral people with a speech closely related to the major languages of Europe.

The religion of the Harappan peoples revolved around the god Siva, the belief in reincarnation, in a condition of "liberation" beyond the cycle of birth and death, and in the technique of mental concentration which later came to be called *yoga*. The religion of the Indo-Aryans was based on a pantheon of gods of a rather worldly type, and sacrifices were offered to them. The traditional hymns that accompanied them were the Vedas, which form the basic scriptures for the religion of Hinduism. Indian society also came to be based on a *caste* system.

In the third century BCE, the Indian kingdoms fell under the Mauryan Empire. The grandson of the founder of this empire, named Asoka, opened a new era in the cultural history of India by introducing the Buddhist religion. Buddha had disregarded the Vedic gods and the institutions of caste and had preached a relatively simple ethical religion that had two levels of aspiration—a monastic life of renunciation of the world and a high, but not too difficult morality for the layman. The two religions of Hinduism and Buddhism flourished together for centuries in a tolerant rivalry, and in the end Buddhism virtually disappeared from India by the thirteenth century CE.

Chinese civilization originated in the Yellow River Valley and gradually extended to the southern regions. Three dynasties ruled early China: the Xia or Hsia, the Shang (c. 1500 to 1122 BCE), and the Zhou (c. 1122 to 211 BCE). After the Zhous fell, China welcomed the teachings of Confucius, as warfare between states and philosophical speculation created circumstances ripe for such teachings. Confucius made the good order of society depend on an ethical ruler, who should be advised by scholar-moralists like Confucius himself.

In contrast to the Confucians, the Taoists professed a kind of anarchism; the best kind of government was none at all. The wise man did not concern himself with political affairs, but by means of mystical contemplation identified himself with the forces of nature.

Sub-Saharan Kingdoms and Cultures

The Nok were a people that lived in the area now known as Nigeria. Artifacts indicate that they were peaceful farmers who built small communities consisting of houses of wattle and daub.

The people referred to as the Ghana lived about 500 miles from what we now call Ghana. The Ghana peoples traded with Berber merchants. The Ghana offered these traders gold from deposits found in the south of their territory. In the 1200s the Mali kingdom conquered Ghana and the civilization mysteriously disappeared.

The people known as the Mali lived in a huge kingdom that lay mostly on the savanna bordering the Sahara Desert. The city of Timbuktu, built in the thirteenth century, was a thriving city of culture where traders visited stone houses, shops, libraries, and mosques.

The Songhai lived near the Niger River and gained their independence from the Mali in the early 1400s. The major growth of the empire came after 1464 CE under the leadership of Sunni Ali, who devoted his reign to warfare and expansion of the empire.

The Bantu peoples, numbering about 100,000,000 lived across large sections of Africa. Bantu societies lived in tiny chiefdoms, starting in the third millennium BCE, and each group developed its own version of the original Bantu language.

Civilizations of the Americas

The great civilizations of early America were agricultural, and foremost of these was the Mayan, in Yucatan, Guatemala, and eastern Honduras.

Mayan history is divided into three parts, the Old Empire, Middle Period, and the New Empire. By the time the Spanish conquerors arrived, most of the Mayan religious centers had been abandoned and their civilization had deteriorated seriously, perhaps due to the wide gulf between the majority of the people, who were peasants, and the priests and nobles.

Farther north, in Mexico, there arose a series of advanced cultures that derived much of their substance from the Maya. Such peoples as the Zapotecs, Totonacs, Olmecs, and Toltecs evolved a high level of civilization. By 500 BCE, agricultural peoples had begun to use a ceremonial calendar and had built stone pyramids on which they performed religious observances.

The Aztecs then took over Mexican culture. A major feature of their culture was human sacrifice in repeated propitiation of their chief god. Aztec government was centralized, with an elective king and a large army. Like their predecessors, the Aztecs were skilled builders and engineers, accomplished astronomers and mathematicians.

Andean civilization was characterized by the evolution of beautifully made pottery, intricate fabrics, and flat-topped mounds called *huacas*.

The Incas, a tribe from the interior of South America who termed themselves "Children of the Sun," controlled an area stretching from Ecuador to central Chile. They were Sun worshippers, and believed themselves to be the vice regent on earth of the sun god; the Inca were all powerful; every person's place in society was fixed and immutable; the state and the army were supreme. They were at the apex of their power just before the Spanish conquest.

In the southwestern U.S. and northern Mexico, meanwhile, two ancient cultures are noteworthy. The Anasazi, who lived in the plateau region extending through today's northern Arizona and New Mexico, southern Utah and Colorado, developed adobe architecture, worked the land extensively, had a highly developed system of irrigation, and made cloth and baskets. Their time ran approximately from 100 to 1300 CE. The Hohokam, roughly contemporaneous to the Anasazi, built separate stone and timber houses around central plazas in the desert Southwest.

Europe in Antiquity

Between 486 and 1050 CE, Europe acquired a distinctive identity. In antiquity, much of Europe was occupied by Germanic tribes.

Nomadic tribes from the central Asian steppes invaded Europe and pushed Germanic tribes into conflict with the Roman Empire. Ultimately, in 410 CE, the Visigoths sacked Rome, followed by the Vandals in 455 CE. In 476 CE, the Ostrogoth king forced the boy emperor Romulus Augustulus to abdicate, ending the empire in the West.

The Frankish Kingdom was the most important medieval Germanic state. Under Clovis I (reigned 481–511 CE), the Franks conquered France and the Gauls in 486 CE. Clovis converted to Christianity and founded the Merovingian dynasty.

Pepin's son, known as Charles the Great or Charlemagne (reigned 768–814 CE), founded the Carolingian dynasty. In 800 CE, Pope Leo III named Charlemagne

Emperor of the Holy Roman Empire. In the Treaty of Aix-la-Chapelle (812 CE), the Byzantine emperor recognized Charles's authority in the West.

The Holy Roman Empire was intended to reestablish the Roman Empire in the West. Charles vested authority in 200 counts, who were each in charge of a county. Charles's son, Louis the Pious (reigned 814–840 CE), succeeded him. On Louis's death, his three sons vied for control of the Empire. The three eventually signed the Treaty of Verdun in 843 CE. This gave Charles the Western Kingdom (France), Louis the Eastern Kingdom (Germany), and Lothair the Middle Kingdom, a narrow strip of land running from the North Sea to the Mediterranean.

In the ninth and tenth centuries, Europe was threatened by attacks from the Vikings in the north, the Muslims in the south, and the Magyars in the east. Under the leadership of William the Conqueror (reigned 1066–1087), the Normans conquered England in 1066 CE (Battle of Hastings).

Rome's collapse had ushered in the decline of cities, a reversion to a barter economy from a money economy, and a fall in agricultural productivity with a shift to subsistence agriculture.

Manorialism and feudalism developed in this period. Manorialism refers to the economic system in which large estates, granted by the king to nobles, strove for self-sufficiency. Large manors might incorporate several villages. The lands surrounding the villages were usually divided into long strips, with common land in-between. Ownership was divided among the lord and his serfs (also called villeins).

Feudalism describes the decentralized political system of personal ties and obligations that bound vassals to their lords. The nature of feudalism varied in different areas and changed over time. But at its base were serfs—peasants who were bound to the land. They worked on the demesne, or lord's property, three or four days a week in return for the right to work their own land. In difficult times, the nobles were supposed to provide for the serfs.

The church was the only institution to survive the Germanic invasions intact. The power of the popes grew in this period. Gregory I (reigned 590–604 CE) was the first member of a monastic order to rise to the papacy. He advanced the ideas of penance and purgatory. He centralized church administration and was the first pope to rule as the secular head of Rome. Monasteries preserved the few remnants of antiquity that survived the decline.

The High Middle Ages (1050–1300)

The year 1050 CE marked the beginning of the High Middle Ages. Europe was poised to emerge from five centuries of decline. Between 1000 and 1350 CE, the population grew from 38 million to 75 million. Agricultural productivity grew, aided by new technologies, such as heavy plows, and a slight temperature rise, which produced a longer growing season. Horses were introduced into agriculture in this period, and the three-field system replaced the two-field system.

Enfranchisement, or freeing of serfs, grew in this period, and many other serfs simply fled their manors for the new lands.

The Holy Roman Empire

Charlemagne's grandson, Louis the German, became Holy Roman Emperor under the Treaty of Verdun. Under the weak leadership of his descendants, the dukes in Saxony, Franconia, Swabia, Bavaria, and the Lorraine eroded Carolingian power. The last Carolingian died in 911 CE. The German dukes elected the leader of Franconia to lead the German lands. He was replaced in 919 CE by the Saxon dynasty, which ruled until 1024 CE. Otto became Holy Roman Emperor in 962 CE. His descendants governed the Empire until 1024 CE, when the Franconian dynasty assumed power, reigning until 1125 CE.

When the Franconian line died out in 1125 CE, the Hohenstaufen family (Conrad III, reigned 1138–1152 CE) won power over a contending family. The Hapsburg line gained control of the Empire in 1273 CE.

The Romans abandoned their last outpost in England in the fourth century. Alfred the Great (ca. 849–899 CE) defeated the Danes who had begun invading during the previous century in 878 CE. In 959 CE, Edgar the Peaceable (reigned 959–975 CE) became the first king of all England.

William (reigned 1066–1087 CE) stripped the Anglo-Saxon nobility of its privileges and instituted feudalism. He ordered a survey of all property of the realm, which was recorded in the Domesday Book (1086 CE).

In 1215 CE, the English barons forced John I to sign the Magna Carta Libertatum, acknowledging their "ancient" privileges. The Magna Carta established the principle of a limited English monarchy. Henry III reigned from 1216–1272 CE. In 1272 CE, Edward I became king. His need for revenue led him to convene a parliament of English nobles, which would act as a check upon royal power.

In 710 CE, the Muslims conquered Spain from the Visigoths. Under the Muslims, Spain enjoyed a stable, prosperous government. The caliphate of Córdoba became a center of scientific and intellectual activity. Internal dissent caused the collapse of Córdoba and the division of Spain into more than 20 Muslim states in 1031 CE.

The Reconquista (1085–1340 CE) wrested control from the Muslims. Rodrigo Diaz de Bivar, known as El Cid (ca. 1043–1099 CE) was the most famous of its knights. The fall of Córdoba in 1234 CE completed the Reconquista, except for the small state of Granada.

Most of Russia and Eastern Europe was never under Rome's control, and it was cut off from Western influence by the Germanic invasions. Poland converted to Christianity in the tenth century, and after 1025 CE was dependent on the Holy Roman Empire. In the twelfth and thirteenth centuries, powerful nobles divided control of the country.

In Russia, Vladimir I converted to Orthodox Christianity in 988 CE. He established the basis of Kievian Russia. After 1054 CE, Russia broke into competing principalities. The Mongols (Tatars) invaded in 1221 CE, completing their conquest in 1245 CE, and cutting Russia's contact with the West for almost a century.

The Crusades were an attempt to liberate the Holy Land from infidels. There were seven major crusades between 1096 and 1300 CE Urban II called Christians to the First Crusade (1096–1099 CE) with the promise of a plenary indulgence (exemption from punishment in purgatory). Younger sons who would not inherit their fathers' lands were also attracted. The Crusades helped to renew interest in the ancient world. But thousands of Jews and Muslims were massacred as a result of the Crusades, and relations between Europe and the Byzantine Empire collapsed.

Charlemagne mandated that bishops open schools at each cathedral, and founded a school in his palace for his court. The expansion of trade and the need for clerks and officials who could read and write spurred an 1179 CE requirement that each cathedral set aside enough money to support one teacher.

Scholasticism was an effort to reconcile reason and faith and to instruct Christians on how to make sense of the pagan tradition.

Peter Abelard (ca. 1079–1144 CE) was a controversial proponent of Scholasticism. In *Sic et Non* (Yes and No), Abelard collected statements in the Bible and by church leaders that contradicted each other. Abelard believed that reason could resolve the apparent contradictions between the two authorities, but the church judged his views as heretical.

Thomas Aquinas (ca. 1225–1274 CE) believed that there were two orders of truth. The lower, reason, could demonstrate propositions such as the existence of God, but on a higher level, some of God's mysteries such as the nature of the Trinity must be accepted on faith. Aquinas viewed the universe as a great chain of being, with humans midway on the chain, between the material and the spiritual.

Latin was the language used in universities. But the most vibrant works were in the vernacular. The *chansons de geste* were long epic poems composed between 1050 and 1150 CE. Among the most famous are the *Song of Roland,* the *Song of the Nibelungs,* the Icelandic *Eddas,* and *El Cid.*

The fabliaux were short stories, many of which ridiculed the clergy. Boccaccio (1313–1375 CE) and Chaucer (ca. 1342–1400 CE) belonged to this tradition. The work of Dante (1265–1321 CE), the greatest medieval poet, synthesized the pagan and Christian traditions.

In this period, polyphonic (more than one melody at a time) music was introduced. In architecture, Romanesque architecture (rounded arches, thick stone walls, tiny windows) flourished between 1000 and 1150 CE. After 1150 CE, Gothic architecture, which emphasized the use of light, came into vogue.

THE RENAISSANCE, REFORMATION, AND THE WARS OF RELIGION (1300–1648)

The Late Middle Ages

The Middle Ages fell chronologically between the classical world of Greece and Rome and the modern world. The papacy and monarchs, after exercising much power and influence in the high Middle Ages, were in eclipse after 1300. During the late Middle Ages (1300–1500), all of Europe suffered from the Black Death. While England and France engaged in destructive warfare in northern Europe, in Italy the Renaissance had begun.

Toward the end of the period, monarchs began to assert their power and control. The major struggle, between England and France, was the Hundred Years' War (1337–1453).

The war was fought in France, though the Scots (with French encouragement) invaded northern England. A few major battles occurred—Crécy (1346), Poitiers (1356), Agincourt (1415)—although the fighting consisted largely of sieges and raids. Eventually, the war became one of attrition; the French slowly wore down the English. Technological changes during the war included the use of English longbows and the increasingly expensive plate armor for knights.

Joan of Arc (1412–1431), an illiterate peasant girl who said she heard voices of saints, rallied the French army for several victories. But she was captured by the Burgundians, allies of England, and sold to the English who tried her for heresy (witchcraft). She was burned at the stake at Rouen.

England lost all of its Continental possessions, except Calais. French farmland was devastated, with England and France both expending great sums of money. Population, especially in France, declined. In addition, both countries suffered internal disruption as soldiers plundered and local officials left to fight the war. Trade everywhere was disrupted and England's wool trade with the Low Countries slumped badly. To cover these financial burdens, heavy taxation was inflicted on the peasants.

Because of the war, nationalism grew. Literature also came to express nationalism, as it was written in the language of the people instead of in Latin. Geoffrey Chaucer portrayed a wide spectrum of English life in the *Canterbury Tales*, while

François Villon (1431–1463), in his *Grand Testament*, emphasized the ordinary life of the French with humor and emotion.

The New Monarchs

The defeat of the English in the Hundred Years' War and of the duchy of Burgundy in 1477 removed major military threats. Trade was expanded, fostered by the merchant Jacques Coeur (1395–1456). Louis XI (1461–1483) demonstrated ruthlessness in dealing with his nobility as individuals and collectively in the Estates General.

The marriage of Isabella of Castile (reigned 1474–1504) and Ferdinand of Aragon (reigned 1474–1516) created a united Spain. The Muslims were defeated at Granada in 1492. Navarre was conquered in 1512.

The Black Death and Social Problems

The bubonic plague ("Black Death") is a disease affecting the lymph glands. It causes death quickly. Conditions in Europe encouraged the quick spread of disease. There was no urban sanitation, and streets were filled with refuse, excrement, and dead animals. Living conditions were overcrowded, with families often sleeping in one room or one bed. Poor nutrition was rampant. There was little personal cleanliness.

Carried by fleas on rats, the plague was brought from Asia by merchants, and arrived in Europe in 1347. The plague affected all of Europe by 1350 and killed perhaps 25 to 40 percent of the population, with cities suffering more than the countryside.

The Renaissance (1300–1600)

The Renaissance emphasized new learning, including the rediscovery of much classical material, and new art styles. Italian city-states, such as Venice, Milan, Padua, Pisa, and especially Florence, were the home to many Renaissance developments, which were limited to the rich elite.

Literature, Art, and Scholarship

Humanists, as both orators and poets, were inspired by and imitated works of the classical past. The literature was more secular and wide-ranging than that of the Middle Ages.

Dante (1265–1321) was a Florentine writer whose *Divine Comedy*, describing a journey through hell, purgatory, and heaven, shows that reason can only take people so far and that God's grace and revelation must be used.

Petrarch (1304–1374) encouraged the study of ancient Rome, collected and preserved work of ancient writers, and produced much work in the classical literary style.

Boccaccio (1313–1375) wrote *The Decameron*, a collection of short stories in Italian, which were meant to amuse, not edify, the reader.

Artists also broke with the medieval past, in both technique and content. Renaissance art sometimes used religious topics, but often dealt with secular themes or portraits of individuals. Oil paints, chiaroscuro, and linear perspectives produced works of energy in three dimensions.

Leonardo da Vinci (1452–1519) produced numerous works, including *The Last Supper* and *Mona Lisa*. Raphael (1483–1520), a master of Renaissance grace and style, theory and technique, represented these skills in *The School of Athens*. Michelangelo (1475–1564) produced masterpieces in architecture, sculpture (*David*), and painting (the Sistine Chapel ceiling). His work was a bridge to a new, non-Renaissance style called Mannerism.

Renaissance scholars were more practical and secular than medieval ones. Manuscript collections enabled scholars to study the primary sources and to reject all traditions which had been built up since classical times. Also, scholars participated in the lives of their cities as active politicians.

Leonardo Bruni (1370–1444), a civic humanist, served as chancellor of Florence, where he used his rhetorical skills to rouse the citizens against external enemies.

Machiavelli (1469–1527) wrote *The Prince*, which analyzed politics from the standpoint of expedience. His work, amoral in tone, describes how a political leader could obtain and hold power by acting only in his own self-interest.

The Reformation

The Reformation destroyed Western Europe's religious unity and introduced new ideas about the relationships between God, the individual, and society. Its course was greatly influenced by politics and led, in most areas, to the subjection of the church to the political rulers.

Martin Luther (1483–1546)

Martin Luther, to his personal distress, could not reconcile the problem of the sinfulness of the individual with the justice of God. How could a sinful person attain the righteousness necessary to obtain salvation? he wondered. During his studies of the Bible, especially of Romans 1:17, Luther came to believe that personal efforts—good works such as a Christian life and attention to the sacraments of the church—could not "earn" the sinner salvation, but that belief and faith were the only way to obtain grace. By 1515 Luther believed that "justification by faith alone" was the road to salvation.

On October 31, 1517, Luther nailed 95 theses, or statements, about indulgences, the cancellation of a sin in return for money, to the door of the Wittenberg church and challenged the practice of selling them. At this time he was seeking to reform the church, not divide it.

In 1519, Luther presented various criticisms of the church and was driven to say that only the Bible, not religious traditions or papal statements, could determine correct religious practices and beliefs. In 1521, Pope Leo X excommunicated Luther for his beliefs.

In 1521, Luther appeared in the city of Worms before a meeting (Diet) of the important figures of the Holy Roman Empire, including the Emperor, Charles V. He was again condemned. At the Diet of Worms Luther made his famous statement about his writings and the basis for them: "Here I stand. I can do no other." After this, Luther could not go back; the break with the pope was permanent.

Frederick III of Saxony, the ruler of the territory in which Luther resided, protected Luther in Wartburg Castle for a year. Frederick never accepted Luther's beliefs but protected him because Luther was his subject. The weak political control of the Holy Roman Emperor contributed to Luther's success in avoiding the pope's and the Emperor's penalties.

Other Reformers

Anabaptist (derived from a Greek word meaning to baptize again) is a name applied to people who rejected the validity of child baptism and believed that such children had to be rebaptized when they became adults. A prominent leader was Menno Simons (1496-1561).

Anabaptists sought to return to the practices of the early Christian church, which was a voluntary association of believers with no connection to the state. Anabaptists adopted pacifism and avoided involvement with the state whenever possible.

In 1536, John Calvin (1509–1564), a Frenchman, arrived in Geneva, a Swiss city-state which had adopted an anti-Catholic position. He left after his first efforts at reform failed. Upon his return in 1540, Geneva became the center of the Reformation. Calvin's *Institutes of the Christian Religion* (1536), a strictly logical analysis of Christianity, had a universal appeal.

Calvin emphasized the doctrine of predestination (God knew who would obtain salvation before those people were born) and believed that church and state should be united. Calvinism triumphed as the majority religion in Scotland, under the leadership of John Knox (ca. 1514–1572), and in the United Provinces of the Netherlands. Puritans in England and New England also accepted Calvinism.

Reform in England

England underwent reforms in a pattern different from the rest of Europe. Personal and political decisions by the rulers determined much of the course of the Reformation there, when in 1533 Henry VIII defied the pope and turned to Archbishop Thomas Cranmer to dissolve his marriage to Catherine of Aragon.

Protestant beliefs and practices made little headway during Henry's reign, as he accepted transubstantiation, enforced celibacy among the clergy, and otherwise made the English church conform to most medieval practices.

Under Henry VIII's son, Edward VI (1547–1553), who succeeded to the throne at age 10, the English church adopted Calvinism. Clergy were allowed to marry, communion by the laity expanded, and images were removed from churches. Doctrine included justification by faith, the denial of transubstantiation, and only two sacraments.

Some reformers wanted to purify (hence "Puritans") the church of its remaining Catholic aspects. The resulting church, Protestant in doctrine and practice but retaining most of the physical possessions, such as buildings, and many of the powers, such as church courts, of the medieval church, was called Anglican.

The Counter-Reformation

The Counter-Reformation brought changes to the portion of the Western church that retained its allegiance to the pope.

Ignatius of Loyola (1491–1556), a former soldier, founded the Society of Jesus in 1540 to lead the attack on Protestantism. Jesuits became the leaders of the Counter Reformation.

The Sack of Rome in 1527, when soldiers of the Holy Roman Emperor captured and looted Rome, was seen by many as a judgment of God against the lives of the Renaissance popes. In 1534, Paul III became pope and attacked abuses while reasserting papal leadership.

The Wars of Religion (1560–1648)

The period from approximately 1560 to 1648 witnessed continuing warfare, primarily between Protestants and Catholics. In the latter half of the sixteenth century, the fighting was along the Atlantic seaboard between Calvinists and Catholics; after 1600 the warfare spread to Germany, where Calvinists, Lutherans, and Catholics fought.

The Catholic Crusade

The territories of Charles V, the Holy Roman Emperor, were divided in 1556 between Ferdinand, Charles's brother, and Philip II (1556–1598), Charles's son. Ferdinand received Austria, Hungary, Bohemia, and the title of Holy Roman Emperor. Philip received Spain, Milan, Naples, the Netherlands, and the New World. It was Philip, not the pope, who led the Catholic attack on Protestants.

Spain dominated the Mediterranean following a series of wars led by Philip's half-brother, Don John, against Moslem (largely Turkish) forces. Don John secured the Mediterranean for Christian merchants with a naval victory over the Turks at Lepanto off the coast of Greece in 1571.

Portugal was annexed by Spain in 1580 following the death of the king without a clear successor. This gave Philip the only other large navy of the day as well as Portuguese territories around the globe.

England and Spain

England was ruled by two queens, Mary I (reigned 1553–1558), who married Philip II, and then Elizabeth I (reigned 1558–1603), while three successive kings of France from 1559 to 1589 were influenced by their mother, Catherine de' Medici (1519–1589).

Mary I sought to make England Catholic. She executed many Protestants, earning the name "Bloody Mary" from opponents. Mary married Philip II, king of Spain, and organized her foreign policy around Spanish interests. They had no children.

Elizabeth I, a Protestant, achieved a religious settlement between 1559 and 1563 which left England with a church governed by bishops and practicing Catholic rituals, but maintaining a Calvinist doctrine.

Catholics participated in several rebellions and plots. Mary, Queen of Scots, had fled to England from Scotland in 1568, after alienating the nobles there. In Catholic eyes, she was the legitimate queen of England. Several plots and rebellions to put Mary on the throne led to her execution in 1587. Elizabeth was formally excommunicated by the pope in 1570.

In 1588, as part of his crusade and to stop England from supporting the rebels in the Netherlands, Philip II sent the Armada, a fleet of more than 125 ships, to convey troops from the Netherlands to England as part of a plan to make England Catholic. The Armada was defeated by a combination of superior English naval tactics and a wind which made it impossible for the Spanish to accomplish their goal. A peace treaty between Spain and England was signed in 1604, but England remained an opponent of Spain.

The Thirty Years' War

Calvinism was spreading throughout Germany. The Peace of Augsburg (1555), which settled the disputes between Lutherans and Catholics, had no provision for Calvinists. Lutherans gained more territories through conversions and often took control of previous church-states—a violation of the Peace of Augsburg. A Protestant alliance under the leadership of the Calvinist ruler of the Palatinate opposed a Catholic League led by the ruler of Bavaria. Religious wars were common.

The war brought great destruction to Germany, leading to a decline in population of perhaps one-third, or more, in some areas. Germany remained divided and without a strong government until the nineteenth century.

After 1648, warfare, though often containing religious elements, would not be executed primarily for religious goals.

The Catholic crusade to reunite Europe failed, largely due to the efforts of the Calvinists. The religious distribution of Europe has not changed significantly since 1648.

Nobles, resisting the increasing power of the state, usually dominated the struggle. France, then Germany, fell apart due to the wars. France was reunited in the seventeenth century. Spain began a decline which ended its role as a great power of Europe.

THE GROWTH OF THE STATE AND THE AGE OF EXPLORATION

In the seventeenth century the political systems of the countries of Europe began dividing into two types, absolutist and constitutionalist. England, the United Provinces, and Sweden moved towards constitutionalism, while France was adopting absolutist ideas.

Overseas exploration, begun in the fifteenth century, expanded. Governments supported such activity in order to gain wealth and to preempt other countries.

England

The English church was a compromise of Catholic practices and Protestant beliefs and was criticized by both groups. The monarchs, after 1620, gave leadership of the church to men with Arminian beliefs, a modified Calvinist creed that de-emphasized predestination.

Opponents to this shift in belief were called Puritans, a term that covered a wide range of beliefs and people. To escape the church in England, many Puritans began moving to the New World, especially Massachusetts.

In financial matters, inflation and Elizabeth's wars left the government short of money. Contemporaries blamed the shortage on the extravagance of the courts of James I and Charles I. The monarchs lacked any substantial source of income and had to obtain the consent of a Parliament to levy a tax.

Parliament met only when the monarch summoned it. Though Parliaments had existed since the Middle Ages, there were long periods of time between parliamentary meetings. Parliaments consisted of nobles and gentry, and a few merchants and lawyers. The men in a Parliament usually wanted the government to remedy grievances as part of the agreement to a tax.

Charles I inherited both the English and Scottish thrones at the death of his father, James I. He claimed a "divine right" theory of absolute authority for himself as king and sought to rule without Parliament. That rule also meant control of the Church of England.

Charles stumbled into wars with both Spain and France during the late 1620s. A series of efforts to raise money for the wars led to confrontations with his opponents in Parliament. A "forced loan" was collected from taxpayers with the promise it would be repaid when a tax was voted by a Parliament. Soldiers were billeted in subjects' houses during the wars. In 1628 Parliament passed the Petition of Right, which declared royal actions involving loans and billeting illegal. Charles ruled without calling a Parliament during the 1630s.

In August 1642 Charles abandoned all hope of negotiating with his opponents and instead declared war against them. Charles's supporters were called Royalists or Cavaliers. His opponents were called Parliamentarians or Roundheads, due to many who wore their hair cut short. This struggle is called the Puritan Revolution, the English Civil War, or the Great Rebellion.

Charles was defeated. His opponents had allied with the Scots who still had an army in England. Additionally, the New Model Army, with its general, Oliver Cromwell (1599–1658), was superior to Charles's army, and became a cauldron of radical ideas.

France

The regions of France had long had a large measure of independence, and local parliaments could refuse to enforce royal laws. The centralization of all government proceeded by replacing local authorities with intendants, civil servants who reported to the king.

Henry IV relied on the Duke of Sully (1560–1641), the first of a series of strong ministers in the seventeenth century. Sully and Henry increased the involvement of the state in the economy, acting on a theory known as mercantilism.

Louis XIII reigned from 1610 to 1643, but Cardinal Richelieu became the real power in France. The unique status of the Huguenots was reduced through warfare and the Peace of Alais (1629), when their separate armed cities were eliminated. The nobility was reduced in power through constant attention to the laws and the imprisonment of offenders.

Cardinal Mazarin governed while Louis XIV (reigned 1643–1715) was a minor. During the Fronde, from 1649 to 1652, the nobility controlled Paris, drove Louis XIV and Mazarin from the city, and attempted to run the government. Noble ineffectiveness, the memories of the chaos of the wars of religion, and the overall anarchy convinced most people that a strong king was preferable to a warring nobility.

Louis XIV saw the need to increase royal power and his own glory and dedicated his life to these goals. He steadily pursued a policy of "one king, one law, one faith."

Explorations and Conquests

Portugal. Prince Henry the Navigator (1394–1460) supported exploration of the African coastline, largely in order to seek gold. Bartholomew Dias (1450–1500) rounded the southern tip of Africa in 1487. Vasco da Gama (1460–1524) reached India in 1498 and, after some fighting, soon established trading ports at Goa and Calicut. Albuquerque (1453–1515) helped establish an empire in the Spice Islands after 1510.

Spain. Christopher Columbus (1451–1506), seeking a new route to the (East) Indies, "discovered" the Americas in 1492. Ferdinand Magellan (1480–1521) circumnavigated the globe in 1521–1522. Conquests of the Aztecs by Hernando Cortes (1485–1547), and the Incas by Francisco Pizarro (ca. 1476–1541), enabled the Spanish to send much gold and silver back to Spain.

Other Countries. In the 1490s, the Cabots, John (1450–1498) and Sebastian (ca. 1483–1557), explored North America, and after 1570, various Englishmen, including Francis Drake (ca. 1540–1596), fought the Spanish around the world. Jacques Cartier (1491–1557) explored parts of North America for France in 1534.

Samuel de Champlain (1567–1635) and the French explored the St. Lawrence River, seeking furs to trade. The Dutch established settlements at New Amsterdam and in the Hudson River Valley. The Dutch founded trading centers in the East Indies, the West Indies, and southern Africa. Swedes settled on the Delaware River in 1638.

BOURBON, BAROQUE, AND THE ENLIGHTENMENT

Through the Treaty of Paris (1763), France lost all possessions in North America to Britain. (In 1762, France had ceded to Spain all French claims west of the Mississippi River and New Orleans.)

France entered the French-American Alliance of 1778 in an effort to regain lost prestige in Europe and to weaken her British adversary. In 1779, Spain joined France in the war, hoping to recover Gibraltar and the Floridas.

With the Treaty of Paris (1783) Britain recognized the independence of the United States of America and retroceded the Floridas to Spain. Britain left France no territorial gains by signing a separate and territorially generous treaty with the United States.

Economic Developments

There were several basic assumptions of mercantilism: 1) Wealth is measured in terms of commodities, especially gold and silver, rather than in terms of productivity and income-producing investments; 2) Economic activities should increase the power of the national government in the direction of state controls; 3) Since a favorable balance of trade was important, a nation should purchase as little as possible from nations regarded as enemies. The concept of the mutual advantage of trade was not widely accepted; 4) Colonies existed for the benefit of the mother country, not for any mutual benefit that would be gained by economic development.

Absentee landlords and commercial farms replaced feudal manors, especially in England. Urbanization, increased population, and improvements in trade stimulated the demand for agricultural products.

The steam engine, developed by James Watt between 1765 and 1769, became one of the most significant inventions in human history. It was no longer necessary to locate factories on mountain streams where water wheels were used to supply power. Its portability meant that both steamboats and railroad engines could be built to transport goods across continents. Ocean-going vessels were no longer dependent on winds to power them. At the same time, textile machines revolutionized that industry.

Bourbon France

Louis XIV (reigned 1643–1715) believed in absolute, unquestioned authority. Louis XIV deliberately chose his chief ministers from the middle class in order to keep the aristocracy out of government.

Council orders were transmitted to the provinces by intendants, who supervised all phases of local administration (especially courts, police, and the collection of taxes).

Louis XIV never called the Estates General. His intendants arrested the members of the three provincial estates who criticized royal policy, and the *parlements* were too intimidated by the lack of success of the *Frondes* to offer further resistance.

Control of the peasants, who comprised 95 percent of the French population, was accomplished by numerous means. Some peasants kept as little as 20 percent of their cash crops after paying the landlord, the government, and the Church. Peasants also were subject to the *corvée*, a month's forced labor on the roads. People not at work on the farm were conscripted into the French army or put into workhouses. Finally, rebels were hanged or forced to work as galley slaves.

Under Louis XV (reigned 1715–1774) French people of all classes desired greater popular participation in government and resented the special privileges of the aristocracy. All nobles were exempt from certain taxes. Many were subsidized with regular pensions from the government. The highest offices of government were reserved for aristocrats. Promotions were based on political connections rather than merit.

There was no uniform code of laws and little justice. The king had arbitrary powers of imprisonment. Government bureaucrats were often petty tyrants, many of them merely serving their own interests. The bureaucracy became virtually a closed class. Vestiges of the feudal and manorial systems taxed peasants excessively compared to other segments of society. The *philosophes* gave expression to these grievances and discontent grew.

Louis XVI (reigned 1774–1792) married Marie Antoinette (1770), daughter of the Austrian Empress Maria Theresa. Louis XVI was honest, conscientious, and sought genuine reforms, but he was indecisive and lacking in determination. One of his first acts was to restore judicial powers to the French parlements. When he sought to impose new taxes on the undertaxed aristocracy, the parlements refused to register the royal decrees. In 1787, he granted toleration and civil rights to French Huguenots (Protestants).

In 1787, the king summoned the Assembly of the Notables, a group of 144 representatives of the nobility and higher clergy. Louis XVI asked them to tax all lands, without regard to privilege of family; to establish provincial assemblies; to allow free trade in grain; and to abolish forced labor on the roads. The Notables refused to accept these reforms and demanded the replacement of certain of the king's ministers.

The climax of the crisis came in 1788 when the king was no longer able to achieve either fiscal reform or new loans. He could not even pay the salaries of government officials. By this time one-half of government revenues went to pay interest on the national debt.

For the first time in 175 years, the king called for a meeting of the Estates General (1789). The Estates General formed itself into the National Assembly, and the French Revolution was underway.

England, Scotland, and Ireland

One of the underlying issues in this conflict was the constitutional issue of the relationship between the king and Parliament. In short, the question was whether England was to have a limited constitutional monarchy, or an absolute monarchy as in France and Prussia.

The theological issue focused on the form of church government England was to have. The episcopal form meant that the king, the Archbishop of Canterbury, and the bishops of the church would determine policy, theology, and the form of worship and service in the presbyterian form. Each congregation would have a voice in the life of the church, and a regional group of ministers, or "presbytery," would attempt to ensure "doctrinal purity."

The political implications for representative democracy were present in both issues. That is why most Presbyterians, Puritans, and Congregationalists sided with Parliament and most Anglicans and Catholics sided with the king.

The Parliament in effect bribed the king by granting him a tax grant in exchange for his agreement to the Petition of Right in 1628. It stipulated that no one should pay any tax, gift, loan, or contribution except as provided by an act of Parliament; no one should be imprisoned or detained without due process of law; all were to have the right to the writ of *habeas corpus;* there should be no forced billeting of soldiers in the homes of private citizens; and martial law was not to be declared in England.

In 1629, Charles I dissolved Parliament—for 11 years. Puritan leaders and leaders of the opposition in the House of Commons were imprisoned by the king, some for several years.

The established Church of England was the only legal church under Charles I, a Catholic. Archbishop of Canterbury William Laud (1573–1645) sought to enforce the king's policies vigorously. Arminian clergymen were to be tolerated, but Puritan clergymen silenced. Criticism was brutally suppressed. Several dissenters were executed.

The king, however, had no money, no army, and no popular support. He summoned the Parliament to meet in November 1640. With mobs in the street and rumors of an army enroute to London to dissolve Parliament, a bare majority of an underattended House of Commons passed a bill of attainder to execute the Earl of Strafford, one of the king's principal ministers. Fearing mob violence as well as Parliament itself, the king signed the bill and Strafford was executed in 1641. Archbishop William Laud was also arrested and eventually tried and executed in 1645.

The House of Commons passed a series of laws to strengthen its position and protect civil and religious rights. The Triennial Act (1641) provided that no more than three years should pass between Parliaments. Another act provided that the current Parliament should not be dissolved without its own consent. Various hated laws, taxes, and institutions were abolished: the Star Chamber, the High Commission, and power of the Privy Council to deal with property rights.

Men began identifying themselves as Cavaliers if they supported the king, or Roundheads if they supported Parliament.

The king withdrew to Hampton Court and sent the queen to France for safety. In March 1642 Charles II went to York, and the English Civil War began. Charles put together a sizeable force with a strong cavalry and moved on London, winning several skirmishes.

Oliver Cromwell (1599–1658) led the parliamentary troops to victory, first with his cavalry, which eventually numbered 1,100, and then as lieutenant general in command of the well-disciplined and well-trained New Model Army. He eventually forced the king to flee.

During the Civil War, under the authority of Parliament, the Westminster Assembly convened to write a statement of faith for the Church of England that was Reformed or Presbyterian in content. Ministers and laymen from both England and Scotland participated for six years and wrote the *Westminster Confession of Faith*, still a vital part of Presbyterian theology.

The army tried Charles Stuart, former king of England, and sentenced him to death for treason. After the execution of the king, Parliament abolished the office of king and the House of Lords. The new form of government was to be a Commonwealth, or Free State, governed by the representatives of the people in Parliament. This commonwealth lasted four years, between 1649 and 1653.

Royalists and Presbyterians both opposed Parliament for its lack of broad representation and for regicide. The army was greatly dissatisfied that elections were not held, as one of the promises of the Civil War was popular representation. Surrounded by foreign enemies, the Commonwealth became a military state with a standing army of 44,000. The North American and West Indian colonies were forced to accept the government of the Commonwealth.

When it became clear that Parliament intended to stay in office permanently, Cromwell agreed to serve as Lord Protector from 1653–1659, with a Council of State and a Parliament. The new government permitted religious liberty, except for Catholics and Anglicans.

The new Parliament restored the monarchy from 1660–1688, but the Puritan Revolution clearly showed that the English constitutional system required a limited monarchy. Parliament in 1660 was in a far stronger position in its relationship to the king than it ever had been before.

Two events in 1688 goaded Parliament to action. In May, James reissued the Declaration of Indulgence with the command that it be read on two successive Sundays in every parish church. On June 10, 1688, a son was born to the king and his queen, Mary of Modena. As long as James was childless by his second wife, the throne would go to one of his Protestant daughters, Mary or Anne. The birth of a son, who would be raised Roman Catholic, changed the picture completely.

A group of Whig and Tory leaders, speaking for both houses of Parliament, invited William and Mary to assume the throne of England.

On November 5, 1688, William and his army landed at Torbay in Devon. King James offered many concessions, but it was too late. He finally fled to France. William assumed temporary control of the government and summoned a free Parliament. In February 1689, William and Mary were declared joint sovereigns, with the administration given to William.

The English Declaration of Rights (1689) declared the following:

1) The king could not be a Roman Catholic.

2) A standing army in time of peace was illegal without Parliamentary approval.

3) Taxation was illegal without Parliamentary consent.

4) Excessive bail and cruel and unusual punishments were prohibited.

5) Right to trial by jury was guaranteed.

6) Free elections to Parliament would be held.

The Toleration Act (1689) granted the right of public worship to Protestant Nonconformists, but did not permit them to hold office. The Act did not extend liberty to Catholics or Unitarians, but normally they were left alone. The Trials for Treason Act (1696) stated that a person accused of treason should be shown the accusations against him and should have the advice of counsel. They also could not be convicted except upon the testimony of two independent witnesses. Freedom of the press was permitted, but with very strict libel laws.

Control of finances was to be in the hands of the Commons, including military appropriations. There would no longer be uncontrolled grants to the king. Judges were made independent of the Crown. Thus, England declared itself a limited monarchy and a Protestant nation.

Russia Under the Muscovites and the Romanovs

In 1480, Ivan III (1440–1505), "Ivan the Great," put an end to Mongol domination over Russia. Ivan took the title of Caesar (Czar) as heir of the Eastern Roman Empire (Byzantine Empire). He encouraged the Eastern Orthodox Church and called Moscow the "Third Rome."

Ivan IV (1530–1584), "Ivan the Terrible," grandson of Ivan III, began westernizing Russia. A contemporary of Queen Elizabeth, he welcomed both the English and Dutch and opened new trade routes to Moscow and the Caspian Sea. English merchant adventurers opened Archangel on the White Sea and provided a link with the outer world free from Polish domination.

After a "Time of Troubles" following Ivan's death in 1584, stability returned to Russia in 1613 when the Zemsky Sobor (Estates General representing the Russian Orthodox church, landed gentry, townspeople, and a few peasants) elected Michael Romanov, who ruled as tsar from 1613 to 1645.

Under Michael Romanov, Russia extended its empire to the Pacific. Romanov continued westernization. By the end of the seventeenth century, 20,000 Europeans lived in Russia, developing trade and manufacturing, practicing medicine, and smoking tobacco, while Russians began trimming their beards and wearing Western clothing.

In 1649, three monks were appointed to translate the Bible for the first time into Russian. The Raskolniki (Old Believers) refused to accept any Western innovations or liturgy in the Russian Orthodox church and were severely persecuted as a result.

Peter I (reigned 1682–1725) was one of the most extraordinary people in Russian history. The driving ambitions of Peter the Great's life were to modernize Russia and to compete with the great powers of Europe on equal terms. By the end of Peter's reign, Russia produced more iron than England.

Peter built up the army through conscription and a 25-year term of enlistment. He gave flintlocks and bayonets to his troops instead of the old muskets and pikes. Artillery was improved and discipline enforced. By the end of his reign, Russia had a standing army of 210,000, despite a population of only 13 million. The tsar ruled by decree (*ukase*). Government officials and nobles acted under government authority, but there was no representative body.

All landowners owed lifetime service to the state, either in the army, the civil service, or at court. In return for government service, they received land and serfs to work their fields. Conscription required each village to send recruits for the Russian army. By 1709, Russia manufactured most of its own weapons and had an effective artillery.

After a series of largely ineffective rulers, Catherine II "the Great," (reigned 1762–1796) continued the westernization process begun by Peter the Great. The three partitions of Poland, in 1772, 1793, and 1795 respectively, occurred under Catherine II's rule. Russia also annexed the Crimea and warred with Turkey during her reign.

Italy and the Papacy

Italy in the seventeenth and eighteenth centuries remained merely a geographic expression divided into small kingdoms, most of which were under foreign domination. Unification of Italy into a national state did not occur until the mid-nineteenth century.

THE SCIENTIFIC REVOLUTION AND SCIENTIFIC SOCIETIES

Science and religion were not in conflict in the seventeenth and eighteenth centuries. Scientists universally believed they were studying and analyzing God's creation, not an autonomous phenomenon known as "Nature." There was no attempt, as in the nineteenth and twentieth centuries, to secularize science.

For the first time in human history, the eighteenth century saw the appearance of a secular worldview. This became known as the Age of the Enlightenment. In the past, some kind of a religious perspective had always been central to Western civilization. The philosophical starting point for the Enlightenment was the belief in the autonomy of man's intellect apart from God. The most basic assumption was faith in reason rather than faith in revelation.

The Enlightenment believed in the existence of God as a rational explanation of the universe and its form; "God" was a deistic Creator who made the universe and then was no longer involved in its mechanistic operation. That mechanistic operation was governed by "natural law."

Rationalists stressed deductive reasoning or mathematical logic as the basis for their epistemology (source of knowledge). They started with "self-evident truths," or postulates, from which they constructed a coherent and logical system of thought.

René Descartes (1596–1650) sought a basis for logic and thought he found it in man's ability to think. "I think; therefore, I am" was his most famous statement.

Benedict de Spinoza (1632–1677) developed a rational pantheism in which he equated God and nature. He denied all free will and ended up with an impersonal, mechanical universe.

Gottfried Wilhelm Leibniz (1646–1716) worked on symbolic logic and calculus, and invented a calculating machine. He, too, had a mechanistic world- and life-view and thought of God as a hypothetical abstraction rather than a persona.

Empiricists stressed inductive observation—the "scientific method"—as the basis for their epistemology.

John Locke (1632–1704) pioneered in the empiricist approach to knowledge and stressed the importance of environment in human development. He classified knowledge as 1) according to reason, 2) contrary to reason, or 3) above reason. Locke thought reason and revelation were both complementary and from God.

David Hume (1711–1776) was a Scottish historian and philosopher who began by emphasizing the limitations of human reasoning and later became a dogmatic skeptic.

The Enlightenment believed in a closed system of the universe in which the supernatural was not involved in human life, in contrast to the traditional view of an open system in which God, angels, and devils were very much a part of human life on earth.

The "Counter-Enlightenment" is a comprehensive term encompassing diverse and disparate groups who disagreed with the fundamental assumptions of the Enlightenment and pointed out its weaknesses.

Roman Catholic Jansenism in France argued against the idea of an uninvolved or impersonal God. Hasidism in Eastern European Jewish communities, especially in the 1730s, stressed a joyous religious fervor in direct communion with God.

Culture of the Baroque and Rococo

The Baroque emphasized grandeur, spaciousness, unity, and emotional impact. The splendor of Versailles typifies the baroque in architecture; gigantic frescoes unified around the emotional impact of a single theme is Baroque art; the glory of Bach's *Christmas Oratorio* expresses the baroque in music. Although the Baroque began in Catholic Counter-Reformation countries to teach in a concrete, emotional way, it soon spread to Protestant nations as well, and some of the greatest Baroque artists and composers were Protestant (e.g., Johann Sebastian Bach and George Frideric Handel).

Characteristics of the Rococo can be found in the compositions of both Franz Josef Haydn (1732–1809) and Wolfgang Amadeus Mozart (1756–1791).

REVOLUTION AND THE NEW WORLD ORDER (1789–1848)

The French Revolution I (1789–1799)

Radical ideas about society and government were developed during the eighteenth century in response to the success of the "scientific" and "intellectual" revolutions of the preceding two centuries. Armed with new scientific knowledge of the physical universe, as well as new views of the human capacity to detect "truth," social critics assailed existing modes of thought governing political, social, religious, and economic life. Ten years of upheaval in France (1789–1799) further shaped modern ideas and practices.

Napoleon Bonaparte spread some of the revolutionary ideas about the administration of government as he conquered much of Europe. The modern world that came of age in the eighteenth century was characterized by rapid, revolutionary changes which paved the way for economic modernization and political centralization throughout Europe.

Influence of the Enlightenment (c. 1700–1800)

While they came from virtually every country in Europe, most of the famous social activists were French, and France was the center of this intellectual revolution. Voltaire, Denis Diderot, Baron de Montesquieu, and Jean-Jacques Rousseau were among the more famous philosophers.

The major assumptions of the Enlightenment were as follows:

- Human progress was possible through changes in one's environment; in other words: better people, better societies, better standard of living.

- Humans were free to use reason to reform the evils of society.

- Material improvement would lead to moral improvement.

- Natural science and human reason would discover the meaning of life.

- Laws governing human society would be discovered through application of the scientific method of inquiry.

- Inhuman practices and institutions would be removed from society in a spirit of humanitarianism.

- Human liberty would ensue if individuals became free to choose what reason dictated was good.

The Enlightenment's Effect on Society:

Religion. Deism or "natural religion" rejected traditional Christianity by promoting an impersonal God who did not interfere in the daily lives of the people. The continued discussion of the role of God led to a general skepticism associated with Pierre Bayle (1647–1706), a type of religious skepticism pronounced by David Hume (1711–1776), and a theory of atheism or materialism advocated by Baron d'Holbach (1723–1789).

Political Theory. John Locke (1632–1704) and Jean-Jacques Rousseau (1712–1778) believed that people were capable of governing themselves, either through a political (Locke) or social (Rousseau) contract forming the basis of society. However, most philosophes opposed democracy, preferring a limited monarchy that shared power with the nobility.

Economic Theory. The assault on mercantilist economic theory was begun by the physiocrats in France, who proposed a "laissez-faire" (nongovernmental interference) attitude toward land usage, and culminated in the theory of economic capitalism associated with Adam Smith (1723–1790) and his slogans of free trade, free enterprise, and the law of supply and demand.

Attempting to break away from the strict control of education by the church and state, Jean-Jacques Rousseau advanced the idea of progressive education, where children learn by doing and where self-expression is encouraged. This idea was carried forward by Johann Pestalozzi, Johann Basedow, and Friedrich Fröbel, and influenced a new view of childhood.

Psychological Theory. In the *Essay Concerning Human Understanding* (1690), John Locke offered the theory that all human knowledge was the result of sensory experience, without any preconceived notions.

Causes of the French Revolution

The rising expectations of "enlightened" society were demonstrated by the increased criticism directed toward government inefficiency and corruption, and toward the privileged classes. The clergy (First Estate) and nobility (Second Estate), representing only two percent of the total population of 24 million, were the privileged classes and were essentially tax exempt. The remainder of the population (Third Estate) consisted of the middle class, urban workers, and the mass of peasants, who bore the entire burden of taxation and the imposition of feudal obligations. As economic conditions worsened in the eighteenth century, the French state became poorer, and totally dependent on the poorest and most depressed sections of the economy for support at the very time this tax base had become saturated.

Designed to represent the three estates of France, the Estates General had only met twice, once at its creation in 1302 and again in 1614. When the French parlements insisted that any new taxes must be approved by this body, King Louis XVI reluctantly ordered it to assemble at Versailles by May 1789.

Election fever swept over France for the very first time. The election campaign took place in the midst of the worst subsistence crisis in eighteenth-century France, with widespread grain shortages, poor harvests, and inflated bread prices. Finally, on May 5, 1789, the Estates General met and argued over whether to vote by estate or individual. Each estate was ordered to meet separately and vote as a unit. The Third Estate refused and insisted that the entire assembly stay together.

Phases of Revolution

The National Assembly (1789–1791): After a six-week deadlock over voting methods, representatives of the Third Estate declared themselves the true National Assembly of France (June 17). Defections from the First and Second Estates then caused the king to recognize the National Assembly (June 27) after dissolving the Estates General. At the same time, Louis XVI ordered troops to surround Versailles.

The "Parisian" revolution began at this point. Angry because of food shortages, unemployment, high prices, and fear of military repression, the workers and tradespeople began to arm themselves.

The Legislative Assembly (1791–1792): While the National Assembly had been rather homogeneous in its composition, the new government began to fragment into competing political factions. The most important political clubs were republican groups such as the Jacobins (radical urban) and Girondins (moderate rural), while the *Sans-culottes* (working-class, extremely radical) were a separate faction with an economic agenda.

The National Convention (1792–1795): Meeting for the first time in September 1792, the Convention abolished monarchy and installed republicanism. Louis XVI was charged with treason, found guilty, and executed on January 21, 1793. Later the same year, the queen, Marie Antoinette, met the same fate.

The most notorious event of the French Revolution was the famous "Reign of Terror" (1793–1794), the government's campaign against its internal enemies and counterrevolutionaries.

The Directory (1795–1799): The Constitution of 1795 restricted voting and office holding to property owners. The middle class was in control. It wanted peace in order to gain more wealth and to establish a society in which money and property would become the only requirements for prestige and power. Despite rising inflation and mass public dissatisfaction, the Directory government ignored a growing shift in public opinion. When elections in April 1797 produced a triumph for the royalist right, the results were annulled, and the Directory shed its last pretense of legitimacy.

But the weak and corrupt Directory government managed to hang on for two more years because of great military success. French armies annexed the Austrian Netherlands, the left bank of the Rhine, Nice, and Savoy. The Dutch republic was made a satellite state of France. The greatest military victories were won by Napoleon Bonaparte, who drove the Austrians out of northern Italy and forced them to sign the Treaty of Campo Formio (October 1797), in return for which the Directory government agreed to Bonaparte's scheme to conquer Egypt and threaten English interests in the East.

The French Revolution II: The Era of Napoleon (1799–1815)

Consulate Period, 1799–1804 (Enlightened Reform): The new government was installed on December 25, 1799, with a constitution which concentrated supreme power in the hands of Napoleon. His aim was to govern France by demanding obedience, rewarding ability, and organizing everything in orderly hierarchical fashion. Napoleon's domestic reforms and policies affected every aspect of society.

Empire Period, 1804–1814 (War and Defeat): After being made Consul for Life (1801), Napoleon felt that only through an empire could France retain its strong position in Europe. On December 2, 1804, Napoleon crowned himself emperor of France in Notre Dame Cathedral.

Militarism and Empire Building: Beginning in 1805 Napoleon engaged in constant warfare that placed French troops in enemy capitals from Lisbon and Madrid to Berlin and Moscow, and temporarily gave Napoleon the largest empire since Roman times. Napoleon's Grand Empire consisted of an enlarged France, satellite kingdoms, and coerced allies.

French-ruled peoples viewed Napoleon as a tyrant who repressed and exploited them for France's glory and advantage. Enlightened reformers believed Napoleon had betrayed the ideals of the Revolution. The downfall of Napoleon resulted from his inability to conquer England, economic distress caused by the Continental System (boycott of British goods), the Peninsular War with Spain, the German War of Liberation, and the invasion of Russia. The actual defeat of Napoleon was the result of the Fourth Coalition and the Battle of Leipzig ("Battle of Nations"). Napoleon was exiled to the island of Elba as a sovereign with an income from France.

After learning of allied disharmony at the Vienna peace talks, Napoleon left Elba and began the Hundred Days by seizing power from the restored French king, Louis XVIII. Napoleon's gamble ended at Waterloo in June 1815. He was exiled as a prisoner of war to the South Atlantic island of St. Helena, where he died in 1821.

The Post-War Settlement: The Congress of Vienna (1814–1815)

The Congress of Vienna met in 1814 and 1815 to redraw the map of Europe after the Napoleonic era, and to provide some way of preserving the future peace of Europe. Europe was spared a general war throughout the remainder of the nineteenth century. But the failure of the statesmen who shaped the future in 1814–1815 to recognize the forces, such as nationalism and liberalism, unleashed by the French Revolution, only postponed the ultimate confrontation between two views of the world—change and accommodation, or maintaining the status quo.

The Vienna settlement was the work of the representatives of the four nations that had done the most to defeat Napoleon: England (Lord Castlereagh), Austria (Prince Klemens Von Metternich), Russia (Czar Alexander I), and Prussia (Karl Von Hardenberg).

Arrangements to guarantee the enforcement of the status quo as defined by the Vienna settlement included two provisions: The "Holy Alliance" of Czar Alexander I of Russia, an idealistic and unpractical plan, existed only on paper. No one except Alexander took it seriously. But the "Quadruple Alliance" of Russia, Prussia, Austria, and England provided for concerted action to arrest any threat to the peace or balance of power.

From 1815 to 1822, European international relations were controlled by the series of meetings held by the great powers to monitor and defend the status quo: the Congress of Aix-la-Chapelle (1818), the Congress of Troppau (1820), the Congress of Laibach (1821), and the Congress of Verona (1822).

The Industrial Revolution

Twentieth-century English historian Arnold Toynbee came to refer to the period since 1750 as "the Industrial Revolution." The term was intended to describe a time of transition when machines began to significantly displace human and animal power in methods of producing and distributing goods, and an agricultural and commercial society converted into an industrial one.

These changes began slowly, almost imperceptibly, gaining momentum with each decade, so that by the middle of the nineteenth century, industrialism had swept across Europe west to east, from England to Eastern Europe. Few countries purposely avoided industrialization, because of its promised material improvement and national wealth. The economic changes that constitute the Industrial Revolution have done more than any other movement in Western civilization to revolutionize Western life.

Roots of the Industrial Revolution could be found in the following: 1) the Commercial Revolution (1500–1700), which spurred the great economic growth of Europe and brought about the Age of Discovery and Exploration, which in turn helped to solidify the economic doctrines of mercantilism; 2) the effect of the Scientific Revolution, which produced the first wave of mechanical inventions and technological advances; 3) the increase in population in Europe from 140 million people in 1750, to 266 million people by the mid-part of the nineteenth century (more producers, more consumers); and 4) the political and social revolutions of the nineteenth century, which began the rise to power of the "middle class," and provided leadership for the economic revolution.

The revolution occurred first in the cotton and metallurgical industries, because those industries lent themselves to mechanization. A series of mechanical inventions (1733–1793) would enable the cotton industry to mass-produce quality goods. The need to replace wood as an energy source led to the use of coal, which increased coal mining, and resulted ultimately in the invention of the steam engine and the locomotive. The development of steam power allowed the cotton industry to expand and transformed the iron industry. The factory system, which had been created in response to the new energy sources and machinery, was perfected to increase manufactured goods.

A transportation revolution ensued in order to distribute the productivity of machinery and deliver raw materials to the eager factories. This led to the growth of canal systems, the construction of hard-surfaced "macadam" roads, the commercial use of the steamboat (demonstrated by Robert Fulton, 1765–1815), and the railway locomotive (made commercially successful by George Stephenson, 1781–1848).

A subsequent revolution in agriculture made it possible for fewer people to feed the population, thus freeing people to work in factories, or in the new fields of communications, distribution of goods, or services like teaching, medicine, and entertainment.

The Industrial Revolution created a unique new category of people who were dependent on their job alone for income, a job from which they might be dismissed without cause. Until 1850 workers as a whole did not share in the general wealth produced by the Industrial Revolution. Conditions would improve as the century wore on, as union action combined with general prosperity and a developing social conscience to improve the working conditions, wages, and hours first of skilled labor, and later of unskilled labor.

The most important sociological result of industrialism was urbanization. The new factories acted as magnets, pulling people away from their rural roots and beginning the most massive population transfer in history. Cities made the working class a powerful force by raising consciousness and enabling people to unite for political action and to remedy economic dissatisfaction.

Impact of Thought Systems ("Isms") on the European World

Romanticism was a reaction against the rigid classicism, rationalism, and deism of the eighteenth century. Strongest between 1800 and 1850, the romantic movement differed from country to country and from romanticist to romanticist. Because it emphasized change, it was considered revolutionary in all aspects of life.

English literary Romantics like Wordsworth and Coleridge epitomized the romantic movement. Other romantics included Goethe of Germany, Hugo of France, and Pushkin of Russia. Romanticism also affected music and the visual arts.

Romantic philosophy stimulated an interest in Idealism, the belief that reality consists of ideas, as opposed to materialism. This school of thought (Philosophical Idealism), founded by Plato, was developed through the writings of Immanuel Kant, Johann Gottlieb Fichte, and Georg Wilhelm Friedrich Hegel, the greatest exponent of this school of thought. Hegel believed that an impersonal God rules the universe and guides humans along a progressive evolutionary course by means of a process called dialecticism; this is a historical process by which one thing is constantly reacting with its opposite (the thesis and antithesis), producing a result (synthesis) that automatically meets another opposite and continues the series of reactions.

Conservatism arose in reaction to liberalism and became a popular alternative for those who were frightened by the violence, terror, and social disorder unleashed by the French Revolution. Early conservatism was allied to the restored monarchical governments of Austria, Russia, France, and England. Support for conservatism came from the traditional ruling classes as well as the peasants who still formed the majority of the population. In essence, conservatives believed in order, society, and the state; faith and tradition.

The theory of liberalism was the first major theory in the history of Western thought to teach that the individual is a self-sufficient being whose freedom and well-being are the sole reasons for the existence of society. Liberalism was more closely connected to the spirit and outlook of the Enlightenment than to any of the other "isms" of the early nineteenth century. Liberalism was reformist and political rather than revolutionary in character.

Liberals also advocated economic individualism (i.e., laissez-faire capitalism), heralded by Adam Smith (1723–1790) in his 1776 economic masterpiece, *Wealth of Nations*.

The regenerative force of liberal thought in early nineteenth-century Europe was dramatically revealed in the explosive force of the power of nationalism. Raising the level of consciousness of people having a common language, soil, traditions, history, culture, and experience to seek political unity around an identity of what or who constitutes the nation, nationalism was aroused and made militant during the turbulent French Revolutionary era.

Nationalistic thinkers and writers examined the language, literature, and folkways of their people, thereby stimulating nationalist feelings. Emphasizing the history and culture of the various European peoples reinforced and glorified national sentiment.

Socialism

The Utopian Socialists (from *Utopia*, Saint Thomas More's (1478–1535) book on a fictional ideal society) were the earliest writers to propose an equitable solution to improve the distribution of society's wealth. While they endorsed the productive capacity of industrialism, they denounced its mismanagement. Human society was to be organized as a community rather than a mixture of competing, selfish individuals. All the goods a person needed could be produced in one community.

The Anarchists rejected industrialism and the dominance of government.

"Scientific" Socialism, or Marxism, was the creation of Karl Marx (1818–1883), a German scholar who, with the help of Friedrich Engels (1820–1895), intended to replace utopian hopes and dreams with a militant blueprint for socialist working-class success. The principal works of this revolutionary school of socialism were *The Communist Manifesto* and *Das Kapital*.

The theory of dialectical materialism enabled Marx to explain the history of the world. By borrowing Hegel's dialectic, substituting materialism and realism in place of Hegel's idealism and inverting the methodological process, Marx was able to justify his theoretical conclusions. Marxism consisted of a number of key propositions: 1) An economic interpretation of history, i.e., all human history has been determined by economic factors (mainly who controls the means of production and distribution); 2) Class struggle, i.e., since the beginning of time there has been a class struggle between the rich and the poor or the exploiters and the exploited; 3) Theory of surplus value, i.e., the true value of a product was labor, and since the worker received a small portion of his just labor price, the difference was surplus value, "stolen" from him by the capitalist; and 4) Socialism was inevitable, i.e., capitalism contained the seeds of its own destruction (overproduction, unemployment, etc.); the rich would grow richer and the poor would grow poorer until the gap between each class (proletariat and bourgeoisie) is so great that the working classes would rise up in revolution and overthrow the elite bourgeoisie to install a "dictatorship of the proletariat." As modern capitalism was dismantled, the creation of a classless society guided by the principle "from each according to his abilities, to each according to his needs" would take place.

The Revolutionary Tradition

The year 1848 is considered the watershed of the nineteenth century. The revolutionary disturbances of the first half of the nineteenth century reached a climax in a new wave of revolutions that extended from Scandinavia to southern Italy, and from France to central Europe. Only England and Russia avoided violent upheaval.

The issues were substantially the same as they had been in 1789. What was new in 1848 was that these demands were far more widespread and irrepressible than ever. Whole classes and nations demanded to be fully included in society. Aggravated by rapid population growth and the social disruption caused by industrialism and urbanization, a massive tide of discontent swept across the Western world.

Generally speaking, the 1848 upheavals shared the strong influences of romanticism, nationalism, and liberalism, as well as a new factor of economic dislocation and instability.

Specifically, a number of similar conditions existed in several countries: 1) Severe food shortages caused by poor harvests of grain and potatoes (e.g., Irish potato famine); 2) Financial crises caused by a downturn in the commercial and industrial economy; 3) Business failures; 4) Widespread unemployment; 5) A sense of frustration and discontent among urban artisan and working classes as wages diminished; 6) A system of poor relief which became overburdened; 7) Living conditions, which deteriorated in the cities; 8) The power of nationalism in the Germanies, Italies and in Eastern Europe to inspire the overthrow of existing governments. Middle-class predominance within the unregulated economy continued to drive liberals to push for more government reform and civil liberty. They enlisted the help of the working classes to put more pressure on the government to change.

In France, working-class discontent and liberals' unhappiness with the corrupt regime of King Louis Philippe (reigned 1830–1848)—especially his minister Guizot (1787–1874)—erupted in street riots in Paris on February 22–23, 1848. With the workers in control of Paris, King Louis Philippe abdicated on February 24, and a provisional government proclaimed the Second French Republic.

The "June Days" revolt was provoked when the government closed the national workshop. This new revolution (June 23–26) was unlike previous uprisings in France. It marked the inauguration of genuine class warfare; it was a revolt against poverty and a cry for the redistribution of property. It foreshadowed the great social revolutions of the twentieth century. The revolt was extinguished after General Cavaignac was given dictatorial powers by the government. The June Days confirmed the political predominance of conservative property holders in French life.

The new Constitution of the Second French Republic provided for a unicameral legislature and executive power vested in a popularly elected president of the Republic. When the election returns were counted, the government's candidate was defeated by a "dark horse" candidate, Prince Louis Napoleon Bonaparte (1808–

1873), a nephew of the great emperor. On December 20, 1848, Louis Napoleon was installed as president of the Republic. In December 1852 Louis Napoleon became Emperor Napoleon III (reigned 1852–1870), and France retreated from republicanism again.

Italian nationalists and liberals wanted to end Hapsburg (Austrian), Bourbon (Naples and Sicily), and papal domination and unite these disparate Italian regions into a unified liberal nation. A revolt by liberals in Sicily in January 1848 was followed by the granting of liberal constitutions in Naples, Tuscany, Piedmont, and the Papal States. Milan and Venice expelled their Austrian rulers. In March 1848 upon hearing the news of the revolution in Vienna, a fresh outburst of revolution against Austrian rule occurred in Lombardy and Venetia, with Sardinia-Piedmont declaring war on Austria. Simultaneously, Italian patriots attacked the Papal States, forcing the pope, Pius IX (1792–1878), to flee to Naples for refuge.

The temporary nature of these initial successes was illustrated by the speed with which the conservative forces regained control. In the north Austrian Field Marshal Radetzky (1766–1858) swept aside all opposition, regaining Lombardy and Venetia and crushing Sardinia-Piedmont. In the Papal States the establishment of the Roman Republic (February 1849) under the leadership of Giuseppe Mazzini and the protection of Giuseppe Garibaldi (1807–1882) would fail when French troops took Rome in July 1849 after a heroic defense by Garibaldi. Pope Pius IX returned to Rome cured of his liberal leanings. In the south and in Sicily the revolts were suppressed by the former rulers.

The immediate effect of the 1848 Revolution in France was a series of liberal and nationalistic demonstrations in the German states (March 1848), with the rulers promising liberal concessions. The liberals' demand for constitutional government was coupled with another demand—some kind of union or federation of the German states.

Great Britain and the Victorian Compromise

The Victorian Age (1837–1901) is associated with the long reign of Queen Victoria, who succeeded her uncle King William IV at the age of 18, and married her cousin, Prince Albert. The early years of her reign coincided with the continuation of liberal reform of the British government, accomplished through an arrangement known as the "Victorian Compromise." The Compromise was a political alliance of the middle class and aristocracy to exclude the working class from political power. The middle class gained control of the House of Commons, the aristocracy controlled the government, the army, and the Church of England. This process of accommodation worked successfully.

Parliamentary reforms continued after passage of the 1832 Reform Bill. Laws were enacted abolishing slavery throughout the Empire (1833). The Factory Act (1831) forbade the employment of children under the age of nine. The New Poor

Law (1834) required the needy who were able and unemployed to live in work-houses. The Municipal Reform Law (1835) gave control of the cities to the middle class. The last remnants of the mercantilistic age fell with the abolition of the Corn Laws (1846) and repeal of the old navigation acts (1849).

The revolutions of 1848 began with much promise, but all ended in defeat for a number of reasons. They were spontaneous movements which lost their popular support as people lost their enthusiasm. Initial successes by the revolutionaries were due less to their strength than to the hesitancy of governments to use their superior force. Once this hesitancy was overcome, the revolutions were smashed. They were essentially urban movements, and the conservative landowners and peasants tended, in time, to nullify the spontaneous actions of the urban classes. The middle class, who led the revolutions, came to fear the radicalism of their working-class allies. Divisions among national groups, and the willingness of one nationality to deny rights to other nationalities, helped to destroy the revolutionary movements in Central Europe.

However, the results of 1848–1849 were not entirely negative. Universal male suf-frage was introduced in France; serfdom remained abolished in Austria and the Ger-man states; parliaments were established in Prussia and other German states, though dominated by princes and aristocrats; and Prussia and Sardinia-Piedmont emerged with new determination to succeed in their respective unification schemes.

A new age followed the revolutions of 1848–1849, as Otto von Bismarck (1815–1898), one of the dominant political figures of the second half of the nineteenth century, was quick to realize. If the mistake of these years was to believe that great decisions could be brought about by speeches and parliamentary majorities, the se-quel showed that in an industrial era new techniques involving ruthless force were all too readily available. The period of *Realpolitik*—of realistic, iron-fisted politics and diplomacy—followed.

REALISM AND MATERIALISM (1848–1914)

Realpolitik and the Triumph of Nationalism

After the collapse of the revolutionary movements of 1848, the leadership of Italian nationalism was transferred to Sardinian leaders Victor Emmanuel II (1820–1878), Camillo de Cavour (1810–1861), and Giuseppe Garibaldi (1807–1882). The new leaders did not entertain romantic illusions about the process of transforming Sardinia into a new Italian kingdom; they were practitioners of the politics of realism, *Realpolitik*.

In 1855, under Cavour's direction, Sardinia joined Britain and France in the Crimean War against Russia. At the Paris Peace Conference (1856), Cavour addressed the delegates on the need to eliminate the foreign (Austrian) presence in the Italian peninsula and attracted the attention and sympathy of the French Emperor, Napoleon III.

After being provoked, the Austrians declared war on Sardinia in 1859. French forces intervened and the Austrians were defeated in the battles of Magenta (June 4) and Solferino (June 24).

Napoleon III, without consulting Cavour, signed a secret peace treaty (The Truce of Villafranca) on July 11, 1859. Sardinia received Lombardy but not Venetia; the other terms indicated that Sardinian influence would be restricted and that Austria would remain a power in Italian politics. The terms of Villafranca were clarified and finalized with the Treaty of Zurich (1859).

In 1860, Cavour arranged the annexation of Parma, Modena, Romagna, and Tuscany into Sardinia. These actions were recognized by the Treaty of Turin between Napoleon III and Victor Emmanuel II; Nice and Savoy were transferred to France.

Giuseppe Garibaldi and his Red Shirts landed in Sicily in May 1860 and extended the nationalist activity to the south. Within three months, Sicily was taken and by September 7, Garibaldi was in Naples and the Kingdom of the Two Sicilies had fallen under Sardinian influence. Cavour distrusted Garibaldi, but Victor Emmanuel II encouraged him.

In February 1861, in Turin, Victor Emmanuel was declared King of Italy and presided over an Italian Parliament which represented the entire Italian peninsula with the exception of Venetia and the Patrimony of St. Peter (Rome). Cavour died in June 1861.

Venetia was incorporated into the Italian Kingdom in 1866 as a result of an alliance between Bismarck's Prussia and the Kingdom of Italy which preceded the Austro-Prussian War between Austria and Prussia. In return for opening a southern front against Austria, Prussia, upon its victory, arranged for Venetia to be transferred to Italy.

Bismarck was again instrumental in the acquisition of Rome into the Italian Kingdom in 1870. In 1870, the Franco-Prussian War broke out and the French garrison, which had been in Rome providing protection for the Pope, was withdrawn to serve on the front against Prussia. Italian troops seized Rome, and in 1871, as a result of a plebiscite, Rome became the capital of the Kingdom of Italy.

Bismarck and the Unification of Germany

In the period after 1815, Prussia emerged as an alternative to a Hapsburg-based Germany.

Otto von Bismarck (1810–1898) entered the diplomatic service of Wilhelm I as the Revolutions of 1848 were being suppressed. By the early 1860s, Bismarck had emerged as the principal adviser and minister to the king. Bismarck was an advocate of a Prussian-based (Hohenzollern) Germany.

In 1863, the Schleswig-Holstein crisis broke. These provinces, which were occupied by Germans, were under the personal rule of Christian IX (1818–1906) of Denmark. The Danish government advanced a new constitution which specified that Schleswig and Holstein would be annexed into Denmark. German reaction was predictable and Bismarck arranged for joint Austro-Prussian military action. Denmark was defeated and agreed (Treaty of Vienna, 1864) to give up the provinces, and Schleswig and Holstein were to be jointly administered by Austria and Prussia.

In 1870, deteriorating relations between France and Germany collapsed over the Ems Dispatch. Wilhelm I was approached by representatives of the French government who requested a Prussian pledge not to interfere on the issue of the vacant Spanish throne. Wilhelm I refused to give such a pledge and informed Bismarck of these developments through a telegram from Ems.

Bismarck exploited the situation by initiating a propaganda campaign against the French. Subsequently, France declared war and the Franco-Prussian War (1870–1871) commenced. Prussian victories at Sedan and Metz proved decisive; Napoleon III and his leading general, Marshal MacMahon, were captured. Paris continued to resist but fell to the Prussians in January 1871. The Treaty of Frankfurt (May 1871) concluded the war and resulted in France ceding Alsace-Lorraine to Germany and a German occupation until an indemnity was paid.

The German Empire was proclaimed on January 18, 1871, with Wilhelm I becoming the Emperor of Germany. Bismarck became the Imperial Chancellor. Bavaria, Baden, Württemberg, and Saxony were incorporated into the new Germany.

The Crimean War

The Crimean War originated in the dispute between two differing groups of Christians and their protectors over privileges in the Holy Land. During the nineteenth century, Palestine was part of the Ottoman Turkish Empire. In 1852, the Turks negotiated an agreement with the French to provide enclaves in the Holy Land to Roman Catholic religious orders; this arrangement appeared to jeopardize already existing agreements which provided access to Greek Orthodox religious orders. Czar Nicholas I (reigned 1825–1855), unaware of the impact of his action, ordered Russian troops to occupy several Danubian principalities; his strategy was to withdraw from these areas once the Turks agreed to clarify and guarantee the rights of the Greek Orthodox orders. In October 1853, the Turks demanded that the Russians withdraw from the occupied principalities. The Russians failed to respond, and the Turks declared war. In February 1854, Nicholas advanced a draft for a settlement of the Russo-Turkish War; it was rejected and Great Britain and France joined the Ottoman Turks and declared war on Russia.

With the exception of some naval encounters in the Gulf of Finland off the Aaland Islands, the war was conducted on the Crimean Peninsula in the Black Sea. In September 1854, more than 50,000 British and French troops landed in the Crimea, determined to take the Russian port city of Sebastopol. In December 1854, Austria reluctantly became a co-signatory of the Four Points of Vienna, a statement of British and French war aims. In 1855, Piedmont joined Britain and France in the war. In March 1855, Czar Nicholas I died and was succeeded by Alexander II (reigned 1855–1881), who was opposed to continuing the war. In December 1855, the Austrians, under excessive pressure from the British, French, and Piedmontese, sent an ultimatum to Russia in which they threatened to renounce their neutrality. In response, Alexander II indicated that he would accept the Four Points.

The resulting Peace of Paris had the following major provisions: Russia had to acknowledge international commissions to regulate maritime traffic on the Danube, recognize Turkish control of the mouth of the Danube, renounce all claims to the Danubian Principalities of Moldavia and Wallachia (which later led to the establishment of Romania), agree not to fortify the Aaland Islands, renounce its previously espoused position of protector of the Greek Orthodox residents of the Ottoman Empire, and return all occupied territories to the Ottoman Empire. The Straits Convention of 1841 was revised by neutralizing the Black Sea. The Declaration of Paris specified rules to regulate commerce during periods of war. Lastly, the independence and integrity of the Ottoman Empire were recognized and guaranteed by the signatories.

The Eastern Question and the Congress of Berlin

In 1876, Turkish forces under the leadership of Osman Pasha soundly defeated Serbian armies. In March 1878, the Russians and the Turks signed the Peace of San Stephano; implementation of its provisions would have resulted in Russian hegemony in the Balkans and dramatically altered the balance of power in the eastern Mediterranean.

Britain, under the leadership of Prime Minister Benjamin Disraeli (1804–1881), denounced the San Stephano Accord, dispatched a naval squadron to Turkish waters, and demanded that the San Stephano agreement be scrapped. The German Chancellor, Otto von Bismarck, intervened and offered his services as mediator.

The delegates of the major powers convened in Berlin in June and July 1878 to negotiate a settlement. Prior to the meeting, Disraeli had concluded a series of secret arrangements with Austria, Russia, and Turkey. The combined impact of these accommodations was to restrict Russian expansion in the region, reaffirm the independence of Turkey, and maintain British control of the Mediterranean.

The Russians, who had won the war against Turkey and had imposed the harsh terms of the San Stephano Treaty, found that they left the conference with very little (Kars, Batum, etc.) for their effort. Although Disraeli was the primary agent of this anti-Russian settlement, the Russians blamed Bismarck for its dismal results. Their hostility toward Germany led Bismarck (1879) to embark upon a new system of alliances which transformed European diplomacy and rendered any additional efforts of the Concert of Europe futile.

Capitalism and the Emergence of the New Left (1848–1914)

During the nineteenth century, Europe experienced the full impact of the Industrial Revolution. The Industrial Revolution resulted in improving aspects of the physical lives of a greater number of Europeans; at the same time, it led to a factory system with undesirable working and living conditions and the abuses of child labor.

As the century progressed, the inequities of the system became increasingly evident. Trade-unionism and socialist political parties emerged which attempted to address these problems and improve the lives of the working class.

During the period from 1815 to 1848, Utopian Socialists such as Robert Owen (1771–1858), Saint Simon, and Charles Fourier advocated the establishment of a political-economic system which was based on romantic concepts of the ideal society. The failure of the Revolutions of 1848 and 1849 discredited the Utopian Socialists, and the new "Scientific Socialism" advanced by Karl Marx (1818–1883) became the primary ideology of protest and revolution. Marx stated that the history of humanity was the history of class struggle and that the process of the struggle (the dialectic) would continue until a classless society was realized. The Marxian dialectic was driven by the dynamics of materialism. The proletariat, or the industrial working class, needed to be educated and led towards a violent revolution which would destroy the institutions which perpetuated the struggle and the suppression of the majority. After the revolution, the people would experience the dictatorship of the proletariat, during which the Communist party would provide leadership. Marx advanced these concepts in a series of tracts and books including *The Communist Manifesto* (1848), *Critique of Political Economy* (1859), and *Capital* (1863–1864).

Britain

In 1865, Lord Palmerston died, and during the next two decades significant domestic developments occurred which expanded democracy in Great Britain. The dominant leaders of this period were William Gladstone (1809–1898) and Benjamin Disraeli (1804–1881). As the leader of the Liberal party (until 1895), Gladstone supported Irish Home Rule, fiscal responsibility, free trade, and the extension of democratic principles. He was opposed to imperialism, the involvement of Britain in European affairs, and the further centralization of the British government. Disraeli argued for an aggressive foreign policy, the expansion of the British Empire, and, after opposing democratic reforms, the extension of the franchise.

The Second French Republic and the Second Empire

Louis Napoleon became the president of the Second French Republic in December 1848. During the three-year life of the Second Republic, Louis Napoleon demonstrated his skills as a gifted politician through the manipulation of the various factions in French politics. His deployment of troops in Italy to rescue and restore Pope Pius IX was condemned by the republicans, but strongly supported by the monarchists and moderates.

Louis Napoleon minimized the importance of the Legislative Assembly, capitalized on the developing Napoleonic Legend, and courted the support of the army, the Catholic church, and a range of conservative political groups. The Falloux Law returned control of education to the church. Further, Louis Napoleon was confronted with Article 45 of the constitution, which stipulated that the president was limited to one four-year term; he had no intention of relinquishing power. With the assistance of a core of dedicated supporters, Louis Napoleon arranged for a coup d'état on the night of December 1–2, 1851. The Second Republic fell and was soon replaced by the Second French Empire.

Louis Napoleon drafted a new constitution which resulted in a highly centralized government. On December 2, 1852, he announced that he was Napoleon III, Emperor of the French.

The Second Empire collapsed after the capture of Napoleon III during the Franco-Prussian War (1870–1871). After a regrettable Parisian experience with a communist type of government, the Third French Republic was established; it would survive until 1940.

Imperial Russia

The autocracy of Nicholas I's (reigned 1825–1855) regime was not threatened by the revolutionary movements of 1848. In 1848 and 1849, Russian troops suppressed disorganized Polish attempts to reassert Polish nationalism.

Russian involvement in the Crimean War met with defeat. Russian ambitions in the eastern Mediterranean had been thwarted by a coalition of Western European states. In 1855 Nicholas I died and was succeeded by Alexander II (reigned 1855–1881).

Fearing the transformation of Russian society from below, Alexander II instituted a series of reforms which altered the nature of the social contract in Russia. In 1861, Alexander II declared that serfdom was abolished. Further, he issued the following reforms: 1) The serf (peasant) would no longer be dependent upon the lord; 2) all people were to have freedom of movement and were free to change their means of livelihood; and 3) the serf could enter into contracts and could own property.

The last years of the reign of Alexander II witnessed increased political opposition, manifested in demands for reforms from an ever more hostile group of intellectuals, the emergence of a Russian populist movement, and attempts to assassinate the czar. As the regime matured, greater importance was placed on traditional values. This attitude developed at the same time that nihilism, which rejected romantic illusions of the past in favor of a rugged realism, was being advanced by such writers as Ivan Turgenev in his *Fathers and Sons*.

The notion of the inevitability and desirability of a social and economic revolution was promoted through the Russian populist movement. Originally, the populists were interested in an agrarian utopian order. The populists had no national support. Government persecution of the populists resulted in the radicalization of the movement. In the late 1870s and early 1880s, leaders such as Andrei Zhelyabov and Sophie Perovskaya became obsessed with the need to assassinate Alexander II. In March 1881, the czar was killed in St. Petersburg when his carriage was bombed. He was succeeded by Alexander III (reigned 1881–1894), who advocated a national policy based on "Orthodoxy, Autocracy, and Nationalism." Alexander III died in 1894 and was succeeded by the last of the Romanovs to hold power, Nicholas II (reigned 1894–1917). Nicholas II displayed lack of intelligence, wit, political acumen, and the absence of a firm will throughout his reign. From his ministers to his wife, Alexandra, to Rasputin (1872–1916), Nicholas was influenced by stronger personalities.

The opposition to the czarist government became more focused, and thus more threatening, with the emergence of the Russian Social Democrats and the Russian Social Revolutionaries. Both groups were Marxist. Vladimir Ilyich Ulyanov, also known as Lenin, became the leader of the Bolsheviks, a splinter group of the Social Democrats. By the winter of 1904–1905, the accumulated consequences of inept management of the economy and the prosecution of the Russo-Japanese War reached a critical stage. A group under the leadership of the radical priest Gapon marched on the Winter Palace in St. Petersburg (January 9, 1905) to submit a list of grievances to the czar. Troops fired on the demonstrators and many casualties resulted on this "Bloody Sunday." In June 1905, naval personnel on the battleship *Potemkin* mutinied while the ship was in Odessa. In October 1905, Nicholas II issued the October Manifesto calling for the convocation of a Duma, or assembly of state, which would serve as an advisory body to the czar, extending civil liberties to include freedom of speech, assembly, and press, and announcing that Nicholas II would reorganize his government.

The leading revolutionary forces differed in their responses to the manifesto. The Octobrists indicated that they were satisfied with the arrangements; the Constitutional Democrats, also known as the Kadets, demanded a more liberal representative system. The Duma convened in 1906 and, from its outset to the outbreak of the First World War, was paralyzed by factionalism which was exploited by the czar's ministers. By 1907, Nicholas II's ministers had recovered the real power of government. Russia experienced a general though fragile economic recovery by 1909, which lasted until the war.

Origins, Motives, and Implications of the New Imperialism (1870–1914)

By the 1870s, the European industrial economies required external markets to distribute products which could not be absorbed within their domestic economies. Further, excess capital was available and foreign investment, while risky, appeared to offer high returns. Finally, the need for additional sources of raw materials served as a rationale and stimulant for imperialism. Politicians were also influenced by the numerous missionary societies which sought government protection, in extending Christianity throughout the world. European statesmen were also interested in asserting their national power overseas through the acquisition of strategic (and many not so strategic) colonies.

The focus of most of the European imperial activities during the late nineteenth century was Africa. Initially, European interest in these activities was romantic. With John Hanning Speke's discovery of Lake Victoria (1858), David Livingstone's surveying of the Zambezi, and Henry Stanley's work on the Congo River, Europeans became enraptured with the greatness and novelty of Africa south of the Sahara.

Disraeli was involved in the intrigue which would result in the British acquisition of the Suez Canal (1875), and during the 1870s and 1880s Britain was involved in a Zulu War and announced the annexation of the Transvaal, which the Boers regained after their great victory of Majuba Hill (1881). At about the same time, Belgium established its interest in the Congo; France, in addition to seizing Tunisia, extended its influence into French Equitorial Africa, and Italy established small colonies in East Africa. During the 1880s Germany acquired several African colonies including German East Africa, the Cameroons, Togoland, and German South West Africa. The Berlin Conference (1884–1885) resulted in an agreement which specified the following: 1) The Congo would be under the control of Belgium through an International Association; 2) More liberal use of the Niger and Congo rivers; and 3) European powers could acquire African territory through, first, occupation and, second, notifying the other European states of their occupation and claim.

British movement north of the Cape of Good Hope involved Europeans fighting one another rather than a native African force. The Boers had lived in South Africa since the beginning of the nineteenth century. With the discovery of gold (1882) in the Transvaal, many English Cape settlers moved into the region. The Boers, under the leadership of Paul Kruger, restricted the political and economic rights of the British settlers and developed alternative railroads through Mozambique which would lessen the Boer dependency on the Cape colony. The crisis mounted and, in 1899, the Boer War began. Until 1902, the British and Boers fought a war which was costly to both sides. Britain prevailed and by 1909, the Transvaal, Orange Free State, Natal, and the Cape of Good Hope were united into the Union of South Africa.

Another area of increased imperialist activity was the Pacific. In 1890, the American naval officer Captain Alfred Thayer Mahan published *The Influence of Sea Power Upon History*; in this book he argued that history demonstrated that nations which controlled the seas prevailed. During the 1880s and 1890s naval ships required coaling stations. While Britain, the Netherlands, and France demonstrated that they were interested in Pacific islands, the most active states in this region during the last 20 years of the nineteenth century were Germany and the United States. The United States acquired the Philippines in 1898. Germany gained part of New Guinea, and the Marshall, Caroline, and Mariana island chains. The European powers were also interested in the Asian mainland. Most powers agreed with the American Open Door Policy which recognized the independence and integrity of China and provided economic access for all the powers. Rivalry over China (Manchuria) was a principal cause of the outbreak of the Russo-Japanese War in 1904.

The Age of Bismarck (1871–1890)

During the period from the establishment of the German Empire in January 1871 to his dismissal as chancellor of Germany in March 1890, Otto von Bismarck dominated European diplomacy and established an integrated political and economic structure for the new German state. Bismarck established a statist system which was reactionary in political philosophy and based upon industrialism, militarism, and innovative social legislation.

During the 1870s and 1880s, Bismarck's domestic policies were directed at the establishment of a strong united German state which would be capable of defending itself from a French war of revenge designed to restore Alsace-Lorraine to France. Laws were enacted which unified the monetary system, established an Imperial Bank and strengthened existing banks, developed universal German civil and criminal codes, and required compulsory military service. All of these measures contributed to the integration of the German state.

In order to develop public support for the government and to minimize the threat from the left, Bismarck instituted a protective tariff, to maintain domestic production, and introduced many social and economic laws to provide social security, regulate child labor, and improve working conditions for all Germans.

Bismarck's foreign policy was centered on maintaining the diplomatic isolation of France. In the crisis stemming from the Russo-Turkish War (1877–1878), Bismarck tried to serve as the "Honest Broker" at the Congress of Berlin. Russia did not succeed at the conference and incorrectly blamed Bismarck for its failure. Early in the next year, a cholera epidemic affected Russian cattle herds, and Germany placed an embargo on the importation of Russian beef. The Russians were outraged by the German action and launched an anti-German propaganda campaign in the Russian press. Bismarck, desiring to maintain the peace and a predictable diplomatic environment, concluded a secret defensive treaty with Austria-Hungary in 1879. The Dual Alliance was very significant because it was the first "hard" diplomatic alliance of the era. A "hard" alliance involved the specific commitment of military support; traditional or "soft" alliances involved pledges of neutrality or to hold military conversations in the event of a war. The Dual Alliance, which had a five-year term and was renewable, directed that one signatory would assist the other in the event that one power was attacked by two or more states.

In 1882, another agreement, the Triple Alliance, was signed between Germany, Austria-Hungary, and Italy. In the 1880s, relations between Austria-Hungary and Russia became estranged over Balkan issues. Bismarck, fearing a war, intervened and by 1887, had negotiated the secret Reinsurance Treaty with Russia. This was a "hard" defensive alliance with a three-year term, which was renewable.

In 1888, Wilhelm I died and was succeeded by his son Friedrich III, who also died within a few months. Friedrich's son, Wilhelm II (reigned 1888–1918), came to power and soon found himself in conflict with Bismarck. Early in 1890, two issues developed which led ultimately to Bismarck's dismissal. First, Bismarck had evolved a scheme for a fabricated attempted coup by the Social Democratic Party (SDP); his intent was to use this situation to create a national hysteria through which he could restrict the SDP through legal action. Second, Bismarck intended to renew the Reinsurance Treaty with Russia to maintain his policy of French diplomatic isolation. Wilhelm II opposed both of these plans; in March 1890, Bismarck, who had used the threat of resignation so skillfully in the past, suggested that he would resign if Wilhelm II would not approve of these actions. Wilhelm II accepted his resignation; in fact, Bismarck was dismissed.

The Movement Toward Democracy in Western Europe

Even after the reform measures of 1867 and 1884 to 1885, the movement toward democratic reforms in Great Britain continued unabated.

The most significant political reform of this long-lived Liberal government was the Parliament Act of 1911, which eliminated the powers of the House of Lords and resulted in the House of Commons becoming the unquestioned center of national power.

The most recurring and serious problem which Great Britain experienced during the period from 1890 to 1914 was the "Irish Question." The Irish situation became more complicated when the Protestant counties of the north started to enjoy remarkable economic growth from the mid-1890s; they were adamant in their rejection of all measures of Irish Home Rule. In 1914, an Irish Home Rule Act was passed by both the Commons and the Lords, but the Protestants refused to accept it. Implementation was deferred until after the war.

The Third French Republic

In the fall of 1870, Napoleon III's Second Empire collapsed when it was defeated by the Prussian armies. Napoleon III and his principal aides were captured; later, he abdicated and fled to England. A National Assembly (1871–1875) was created and Adolphe Thiers was recognized as its chief executive. At the same time, a more radical political entity, the Paris Commune (1870–1871), came into existence and exercised extraordinary power during the siege of Paris. After the siege and the peace agreement with Prussia, the Commune refused to recognize the authority of the National Assembly. Led by radical Marxists, anarchists, and republicans, the Paris Commune repudiated the conservative and monarchist leadership of the National Assembly. From March to May 1871, the Commune fought a bloody struggle with the troops of the National Assembly. France began a program of recovery which led to the formulation of the Third French Republic in 1875. The National Assembly sought to 1) put the French political house in order; 2) establish a new constitutional government; 3) pay off an imposed indemnity and, in doing so, remove German troops from French territory; and 4) restore the honor and glory of France. In 1875 a constitution was adopted which provided for a republican government consisting of a president (with little power), a Senate, and a Chamber of Deputies, which was the center of political power. During the early years of the Republic, Leon Gambetta (1838–1882) led the republicans.

The most serious threat to the Republic came through the Dreyfus Affair. In 1894, Captain Alfred Dreyfus (1859–1935) was assigned to the French General Staff. A scandal broke when it was revealed that classified information had been provided to German spies. Dreyfus, a Jew, was charged, tried, and convicted. Later, it was determined that the actual spy was Commandant Marie Charles Esterhazy (1847–1923), who was acquitted in order to save the pride and reputation of the army. In 1906, the case was closed when Dreyfus was declared innocent and returned to the ranks. Rather than lead to the collapse of the Republic, the Dreyfus Affair demonstrated the intensity of anti-Semitism in French society, the level of corruption in the French army, and the willingness of the Catholic church and the monarchists to join in a conspiracy against an innocent man.

From 1905 to 1914 the socialists under Jean Jaurès gained seats in the Chamber of Deputies. The Third French Republic endured the crises which confronted it and, in 1914, enjoyed the support of the vast majority of French citizens.

International Politics and the Coming of the War (1890–1914)

During the late nineteenth century, the economically motivated "New Imperialism" resulted in further aggravating the relations among the European powers. The Fashoda Crisis (1898–1899), the Moroccan Crisis (1905–1906), the Balkan Crisis (1908), and the Agadir Crisis (1911) demonstrated the impact of imperialism in heightening tensions among European states and in creating an environment in which conflict became more acceptable.

In 1908, the decadent Ottoman Empire was experiencing domestic discord which attracted the attention of both the Austrians and the Russians. These two powers agreed that Austria would annex Bosnia and Herzegovina and Russia would be granted access to the Straits and thus the Mediterranean. Great Britain intervened and demanded that there be no change in the status quo in the Straits. Russia backed down from a confrontation, but Austria proceeded to annex Bosnia and Herzegovina.

On June 28, 1914, Archduke Franz Ferdinand (1863–1914), heir to the Austro-Hungarian throne, and his wife were assassinated while on a state visit to Sarajevo, the capital of Bosnia. The assassination resulted in a crisis between Austria-Hungary and Serbia. On July 23, Austria's foreign minister, Count Berchtold, sent a 10-point ultimatum to Serbia. Though the ultimatum was purposely drafted to inflame Serbia, the Serbians argued the validity of only one of its precepts.

German Chancellor Bethmann-Hollweg and British Foreign Secretary Sir Edward Grey attempted to mediate the conflict. It was too late. On July 28, Austria declared war on Serbia and by August 4, Britain, France, and Russia (The Allies) were at war with Germany and Austria-Hungary (The Central Powers); later, other nations would join one of the two camps.

The initial military actions did not proceed as planned. The German Schlieffen Plan failed to succeed in the West as a result of German tactical adjustments and the French and British resistance in the First Battle of the Marne (September 1914). In the East, the Germans scored significant victories over the numerically superior Russians at the battles of Tannenberg and Masurian Lakes (August–September 1914).

WORLD WAR I AND EUROPE IN CRISIS (1914–1935)

The Origins of World War I

The long-range roots of the origins of World War I can be traced to numerous factors, beginning with the creation of modern Germany in 1871. Achieved through a series of wars, the emergence of this new German state completely destroyed Europe's traditional balance of power, and forced its diplomatic and military planners back to their drawing boards to rethink their collective strategies.

From 1871 to 1890, balance of power was maintained through the network of alliances created by the German Chancellor, Otto von Bismarck, and centered around his *Dreikaiserbund* (League of the Three Emperors) that isolated France, and the Dual (Germany, Austria) and Triple (Germany, Austria, Italy) Alliances. Bismarck's fall in 1890 resulted in new policies that saw Germany move closer to Austria, while England and France (Entente Cordiale, 1904), and later Russia (Triple Entente, 1907), drew closer.

Germany's dramatic defeat of France in 1870–1871 coupled with Kaiser William II's decision in 1890 to build up a navy comparable to that of Great Britain created a reactive arms race. This, blended with European efforts to carve out colonial empires in Africa and Asia—plus a new spirit of nationalism and the growing romanticization of war—helped create an unstable international environment in the years before the outbreak of World War I.

Immediate Cause of World War I

The Balkans, the area which today comprises the former Yugoslavia, Albania, Greece, Bulgaria, Macedonia, and Romania, were notably unstable. Part of the rapidly decaying Ottoman (Turkish) Empire, it saw two main forces at work:

(1) ethnic nationalism among the various small groups who lived there, and (2) an intense rivalry between Austria-Hungary and Russia over spheres of influence. Existing friction between Austria and Serbia heated up all the more. In 1912, with Russia's blessing, the Balkan League (Serbia, Montenegro, Greece, and Bulgaria) went to war with Turkey. Serbia, which sought a port on the Adriatic, was rebuffed when Austria and Italy backed the creation of an independent Albania. Russia, meanwhile, grew increasingly protective of its southern Slavic cousins, supporting Serbia's and Montenegro's claims to Albanian lands.

The Outbreak of the World War

As noted earlier, the match that would set Europe ablaze was struck on June 28, 1914, when Archduke Franz Ferdinand, heir to the Austrian throne, was assassinated by Gavrilo Princip, a young Serbian nationalist. Austria consulted with the German government on July 6 and received a "blank check" to take any steps necessary to punish Serbia. On July 23, 1914, the Austrian government presented Serbia with a 10-point ultimatum that required Serbia to suppress and punish all forms of anti-Austrian sentiment there with the help of Austrian officials. On July 25, 1914, three hours after mobilizing its army, the Serbians acceded to most of Austria's terms. In fact, they requested only that Austria's demand to participate in Serbian judicial proceedings be adjudicated by the International Tribunal at The Hague.

Austria immediately broke off official relations with Serbia and mobilized its army. On July 28, 1914, Austria went to war against Serbia, and began to bombard Belgrade the following day. At the same time, Russia gradually prepared for war against Austria and Germany, declaring full mobilization on July 30.

German military strategy, based in part on the plan of the Chief of the General Staff Count Alfred von Schlieffen, viewed Russian mobilization as an act of war. The Schlieffen Plan was based on a two-front war with Russia and France. It was predicated on a swift, decisive blow against France while maintaining a defensive position against slowly mobilizing Russia, which would be dealt with after France.

Germany demanded that Russia demobilize in 12 hours and appealed to the Russian ambassador in Berlin. Russia's offer to negotiate the matter was rejected, and Germany declared war on Russia on August 1, 1914. On August 3, Germany declared war on France. Berlin asked Belgium for permission to send its troops through its territory to attack France, which Belgium refused. On August 4, England, which agreed in 1839 to protect Belgian neutrality, declared war on Germany; Belgium followed suit. Between 1914 and 1915, the alliance of the Central Powers (Germany, Austria-Hungary, Bulgaria, and Turkey) faced the Allied Powers of England, France, Russia, Japan, and in 1917, the United States. A number of smaller countries were also part of the Allied coalition.

The War in 1914

The Western Front: After entering Belgium, the Germans attacked France on five fronts in an effort to encircle Paris rapidly. However, the unexpected Russian attack in East Prussia and Galicia from August 17 to 20 forced Germany to transfer important forces eastward to halt the Russian drive.

To halt a further German advance, the French army, aided by Belgian and English forces, counterattacked. In the Battle of the Marne (September 5–9), they stopped the German drive and forced small retreats. Mutual outflanking maneuvers by France and Germany created a battlefront that would determine the demarcation of the Western Front for the next four years. It ran, in uneven fashion, from the North Sea to Belgium and from northern France to Switzerland.

The Eastern Front: The Germans retreated after their assault against Warsaw in late September. Hindenburg's attack on Lodz, 10 days after he was appointed Commander-in-Chief of the Eastern Front (Nov. 1), was a more successful venture; by the end of 1914 this important textile center was in German hands.

The War in 1915

The Western Front: Wooed by both sides, Italy joined the Allies and declared war on the Central Powers on May 23 after signing the secret Treaty of London (April 26). This treaty gave Italy Austrian provinces in the north and some Turkish territory.

The Eastern Front: On January 23, 1915, Austro-German forces began a coordinated offensive in East Russia and in the Carpathians. The two-pronged German assault in the north was stopped on February 27, while Austrian efforts to relieve their besieged defensive network at Przemyśl failed when it fell into Russian hands on March 22.

German forces, strengthened by troops from the Western Front under August von Mackensen, began a move on May 2 to strike at the heart of the Russian Front. By August 1915, much of Russian Poland was in German hands.

In an effort to provide direct access to the Turks defending Gallipoli, Germany and Austria invaded Serbia in the early fall, aided by their new ally, Bulgaria. On October 7, the defeated Serbian army retreated to Corfu.

The Eastern Mediterranean

Turkey entered the war on the Central Power side on October 28, 1914, which prevented the shipment of Anglo-French aid to Russians through the Straits.

The War in 1916

The Western Front: The Battle for Verdun lasted from February 21 to December 18, 1916. From February until June, German forces, aided by closely coordinated heavy artillery barrages, assaulted the forts around Verdun. The Germans suffered 281,000 casualties while the French, under Marshal Henri Pétain (1856–1951), lost 315,000 while successfully defending their position.

To take pressure off the French, an Anglo-French force mounted three attacks on the Germans to the left of Verdun in July, September, and November. After the Battle of the Somme (July 1–November 18), German pressure was reduced, but at great loss. Anglo-French casualties totaled 600,000.

The Eastern Front: Orchestrated by Aleksei Brusilov (1853–1926), The Brusilov Offensive (June 4–September 20) envisioned a series of unexpected attacks along a lengthy front to confuse the enemy. By late August, he had advanced into Galicia and the Carpathians.

Romania entered the war on the Allied side as a result of Russian successes and the secret Treaty of Bucharest (August 17). The ensuing Romanian thrust into Transylvania was pushed back, and on December 6, a German-Bulgarian army occupied Bucharest as well as the bulk of Romania.

The death of Austrian Emperor Franz Joseph (reigned 1848–1916) on November 21 prompted his successor, Charles I (1887–1922), to discuss the prospect of peace terms with his allies. On December 12, the four Central Powers, strengthened by the fall of Bucharest, offered four separate peace proposals based on their recent military achievements. The Allies rejected them on December 30 because they felt them to be insincere.

By the end of 1914, Allied fleets had gained control of the high seas, which caused Germany to lose control of its colonial empire. Germany's failure in 1914 to weaken British naval strength prompted German naval leaders to begin using the submarine as an offensive weapon to weaken the British. On February 4, Germany announced a war zone around the British Isles, and advised neutral powers to sail there at their own risk. On May 7, 1915, a German submarine sank the *Lusitania*, a British passenger vessel, because it was secretly carrying arms.

New Military Technology

Germany, Russia, and Great Britain all had submarines, but the German U-boats were the most effective. Designed principally for coastal protection, they increasingly used them to reduce British naval superiority through tactical and psychological means.

By the spring of 1915, British war planners finally awoke to the fact that the machine gun had become the mistress of defensive trench warfare. In a search for a weapon to counter trench defenses, the British developed tanks as an armored "land ship," and first used them on September 15, 1916, in the battle of the Somme.

Airplanes were initially used for observation purposes in the early months of the war. As their numbers grew, mid-air struggles using pistols and rifles took place, until the Germans devised a synchronized propeller and machine gun on its Fokker aircraft in May 1915. The Allies responded with similar equipment and new squadron tactics during the early days of the Verdun campaign in February 1916, and briefly gained control of the skies. They also began to use their aircraft for bombing raids against Zeppelin bases in Germany. Air supremacy shifted to the Germans in 1917.

During the first year of the war, the Germans began to use Zeppelin airships to bomb civilian targets in England. Though their significance was neutralized with the development of the explosive shell in 1916, Zeppelins played an important role as a psychological weapon in the first two years of the war.

In the constant search for methods to counter trench warfare, the Germans and the Allied forces experimented with various forms of internationally outlawed gas. On October 27, 1914, the Germans tried a nose/eye irritant gas at Neuve-Chapelle, and by the spring of 1915 had developed a poison chlorine gas at the Battle of Ypres. That fall, the British countered with a similar chemical at the battles of Champagne and Loos.

The Russian Revolutions of 1917

The February Revolution

The government's handling of the war prompted a new wave of civilian unrest. Estimates are that 1,140 riots and strikes swept Russia in January and February 1917. Military and police units ordered to move against the mobs either remained at their posts or joined them.

Despite being ordered by the czar not to meet until April, Duma leaders demanded dramatic solutions to the country's problems. Though dissolved on March 11, the Duma met in special session on March 13 and created a Provisional Committee of Elders to deal with the civil war. After two days of discussions, it decided that the czar must give up his throne, and on March 15, 1917, President Mikhail Rodzianko and Aleksandr Ivanovich Guchkov, leader of the Octobrist Party, convinced the czar to abdicate. He agreed, turning over the throne to his brother, the Grand Duke Mikhail, who himself abdicated the next day. Thus ended the three century-old Romanov dynasty.

The Bolshevik October Revolution

On October 23–24, Lenin returned from Finland to meet with the party's Central Committee to plan the coup. Though he met with strong resistance, the Committee agreed to create a Political Bureau (Politburo) to oversee the revolution.

Leon Trotsky (1879–1940), head of the Petrograd Soviet and its Military Revolutionary Committee, convinced troops in Petrograd to support Bolshevik moves. While Trotsky gained control of important strategic points around the city, Alexander Kerensky, Prime Minister of the Russian Provisional Government at the time, and well-informed of Lenin's plans, finally decided on November 6 to move against the plotters. In response, Lenin and Trotsky ordered their supporters to seize the city's transportation and communication centers. The Winter Palace was captured later that evening, along with most of Kerensky's government.

The Second Congress opened at 11 p.m. on November 7, with Lev Kamenev (1883–1936), a member of Lenin's Politburo, as its head. Soon after it opened, many of the moderate socialists walked out in opposition to Lenin's coup, leaving the Bolsheviks and the Left Socialist Revolutionaries in control of the gathering.

At the Congress, it was announced that the government's new Cabinet, officially called the Council of People's Commissars (Sovnarkom), and responsible to a Central Executive Committee, would include Lenin as Chairman or head of government, Trotsky as Foreign Commissar, and Josef Stalin as Commissar of Nationalities. The Second Congress issued two decrees on peace and land. The first called for immediate peace without any consideration of indemnities or annexations, while the second adopted the Socialist Revolutionary land program that abolished private ownership of land and decreed that a peasant could only have as much land as he could farm. Village councils would oversee distribution.

The Constituent Assembly

The Constituent Assembly, long promised by the Provisional Government as the country's first legally elected legislature, presented serious problems for Lenin, since he knew the Bolsheviks could not win a majority of seats in it. Regardless, Lenin allowed elections for it to be held on November 25 under universal suffrage. When the assembly convened on January 18 in the Tauride Palace, it voted down Bolshevik proposals and elected Victor Chernov, a Socialist Revolutionary, as president, and declared the country a democratic federal republic. The Bolsheviks walked out. The next day, troops dissolved the Assembly.

World War I: The Final Phase (1917–1918)

Russia Leaves the War

As order collapsed among Russian units along the Eastern Front, the Soviet government began to explore cease-fire talks with the Central Powers. Leon Trotsky, now Commissar of Foreign Affairs, offered general negotiations to all sides, and signed an initial armistice as a prelude to peace discussions with Germany at Brest-Litovsk on December 5, 1917.

The Soviets accepted terms that were integrated into the Treaty of Brest-Litovsk of March 3, 1918. According to its terms, in return for peace, Soviet Russia lost its Baltic provinces, the Ukraine, Finland, Byelorussia, and part of Transcaucasia. The area lost totaled 1,300,000 square miles and included 62 million people.

The American Presence: Naval and Economic Support

The United States, which had originally hoped that it could simply supply the Allies with naval and economic support, made its naval presence known immediately and helped Great Britain mount an extremely effective blockade of Germany and, through a convoy system, strengthened the shipment of goods across the Atlantic.

An initial token group, the American Expeditionary Force under General John J. Pershing (1860–1948), arrived in France on June 25, 1917, while by the end of April 1918, 300,000 Americans a month were placed as complete divisions alongside British and French units.

Stirred by the successes on the Marne, the Allies began their offensive against the Germans at Amiens on August 8, 1918. By September 3, the Germans retreated to the Hindenburg Line. On September 26, Foch began his final offensive, and took the Hindenburg Line the following day. Two days later, Ludendorff advised his government to seek a peace settlement. Over the next month, the French took St. Quentin (October 1), while the British occupied Cambrai, Le Cateau, and Ostend.

On September 14, Allied forces attacked in the Salonika area of Macedonia and forced Bulgaria to sue for peace on September 29. On September 19, General Allenby began an attack on Turkish forces at Megiddo in Palestine and quickly defeated them. In a rapid collapse of Turkish resistance, the British took Damascus, Aleppo, and finally forced Turkey from the war at the end of October. On October 24, the Italians began an assault against Austria-Hungary at Vitto Veneto and forced Vienna to sign armistice terms on November 3. Kaiser Wilhelm II, pressured to abdicate, fled the country on November 9, and a republic was declared. On November 11, at 11 a.m., the war ended, with Germany accepting a harsh armistice.

The Paris Peace Conference of 1919–1920

Preliminary Discussions

To a very great extent, the direction and thrust of the discussions at the Paris Peace Conference were determined by the destructive nature of the war itself and the political responsibilities, ideals, and personalities of the principal architects of the settlements at Paris. The sudden, unexpected end of the war, combined with the growing threat of communist revolution throughout Europe created an unsettling atmosphere at the conference. The "Big Four" of Wilson (U.S.), Clemenceau (France), Lloyd-George (England), and Orlando (Italy) took over the peace discussions. The delays caused by uncertainty over direction at the beginning of the conference, Wilson's insistence that the League of Nations be included in the settlement, and fear of European-wide revolution resulted in a hastily prepared, dictated peace settlement.

The Treaty of Versailles

The treaty's war guilt statements were the justification for its harsh penalties. The former German king, Wilhelm II, was accused of crimes against "international morality and the sanctity of treaties," while Germany took responsibility for itself and for its allies for all losses suffered by the Allied Powers and their supporters as a result of German and Central Power aggression.

Germany had to return Alsace and Lorraine to France and Eupen-Malmedy to Belgium. France got Germany's Saar coal mines as reparations, while the Saar Basin was to be occupied by the major powers for 15 years, after which a plebiscite would decide its ultimate fate. Poland got a number of German provinces and Danzig, now a free city, as its outlet to the sea. Additionally, Germany lost all of its colonies in Asia and Africa.

The German Army was limited to 100,000 men and officers with 12-year enlistments for the former and 25 for the latter. The General Staff was also abolished. The Navy lost its submarines and most offensive naval forces, and was limited to 15,000 men and officers with the same enlistment periods as the army. Aircraft and blimps were outlawed. A Reparations Commission was created to determine Germany's war debt to the Allies, which it figured in 1921 to be $32.4 billion, to be paid over an extended period of time. In the meantime, Germany was to begin immediate payments in goods and raw materials.

The Allies presented the treaty to the Germans on May 7, 1919, but the Germans stated that its terms were too much for the German people, and that it violated the spirit of Wilson's Fourteen Points. After some minor changes were made, the Germans were told to sign the document or face an Allied advance into Germany. The treaty was signed on June 28, 1919, at Versailles.

Treaties with Germany's Allies

The Allied treaty with Austria legitimized the breakup of the Austrian Empire in the latter days of the war and saw Austrian territory ceded to Italy and the new states of Czechoslovakia, Poland, and Yugoslavia. The agreement included military restrictions and debt payments.

Weimar Germany (1918–1929)

The dramatic collapse of the German war effort in the second half of 1918 ultimately created a political crisis that forced the abdication of the kaiser and the creation of a German Republic on November 9.

From the outset, the Provisional Government, formed by a coalition of Majority and Independent Social Democratic Socialists, was beset by divisions from within and threats of revolution throughout Germany.

Elections for the new National Constituent Assembly, which was to be based on proportional representation, gave no party a clear majority. A coalition of the Majority Socialists, the Catholic Centre party, and the German Democratic party (DDP) dominated the new assembly. On February 11, 1919, the assembly met in the historic town of Weimar and selected Friedrich Ebert President of Germany. Two days later, Philip Scheidemann (1865–1939) formed the first Weimar Cabinet and became its first Chancellor.

On August 11, 1919, a new constitution was promulgated, which provided for a bicameral legislature.

Politics and Problems of the Weimar Republic (1919–1923)

The territorial, manpower, and economic losses suffered during and after the war, coupled with the $32.4 billion reparations debt, had a severe impact on the German economy and society, and severely handicapped the new government's efforts to establish a stable governing environment.

In an effort of good faith based on hopes of future reparation payment reductions, Germany borrowed heavily and made payments in kind to fulfill its early debt obligations. The result was a spiral of inflation. After the Allied Reparations Commission declared Germany in default on its debt, the French and the Belgians occupied the Ruhr on January 11, 1923.

Chancellor Wilhelm Cuno (1876–1933) encouraged the Ruhr's Germans passively to resist the occupation, and printed worthless currency. The occupation ended on September 26, and helped prompt stronger Allied sympathy to Germany's payment difficulties, though the inflationary spiral had severe economic, social, and political consequences.

Weimar Politics (1919–1923): Germany's economic and social difficulties deeply affected its infant democracy. From February 1919 to August 1923, the country had six chancellors.

Growing right-wing discontent with the Weimar Government resulted in the assassination of the gifted head of the Catholic Center Party, Matthias Erzberger (1875–1921), on August 29, 1921, and the murder of Foreign Minister Walter Rathenau (1867–1922) on June 24, 1922. These were two of the most serious of over 350 political murders in Germany since the end of the war.

Following the death of President Ebert on February 28, 1925, two ballots were held for a new president, since none of the candidates won a majority on the first vote. On the second ballot on April 26, the Reichsblock, a coalition of Conservative parties, was able to get its candidate elected. War hero Paul von Hindenburg was narrowly elected.

The elections of May 20, 1928, saw the Social Democrats get almost one-third of the popular vote which, blended with other moderate groups, created a stable, moderate majority in the Reichstag, which chose Hermann Müller (1876–1931) as chancellor.

Italy (1919–1925)

Benito Mussolini, capitalizing on the sympathy of unfulfilled war veterans, disaffected nationalists, and those fearful of communism, formed the Fascio Italiano di Combattimento (Union of Combat) in Milan on March 23, 1919. Initially, Mussolini's movement had few followers, and it did badly in the November 1919 elections. However, Socialist strikes and unrest enabled him to convince Italians that he alone could bring stability and prosperity to their troubled country.

The resignation of the Bonomi Cabinet on February 9, 1922, underlined the government's inability to maintain stability. In the meantime, the Fascists seized control of Bologna in May and Milan in August. In response, Socialist leaders called for a nationwide strike on August 1, 1922; it was stopped by Fascist street violence within 24 hours. On October 24, 1922, Mussolini told followers that if he was not given power, he would "March on Rome." Three days later, Fascists began to seize control of other cities, while 26,000 began to move towards the capital. On October 29, the king, Victor Emmanuel III (1869–1947), asked Mussolini to form a new government as Premier of Italy.

Beginning in 1925, Mussolini arrested opponents, closed newspapers, and eliminated civil liberties in a new reign of terror. On December 24, 1925, the legislature's powers were greatly limited, while those of Mussolini were increased as the new Head of State. Throughout 1926, Mussolini intensified his control over the country with legislation that outlawed strikes and created the syndicalist corporate system. A failed assassination attempt prompted the "Law for the Defense of the State" of November 25, 1926, that created a Special Court to deal with political crimes and introduced the death penalty for threats against the king, his family, or the Head of State.

Italian Foreign Policy

The nation's wish for post-war peace and stability saw Italy participate in all of the international developments in the 1920s aimed at securing normalcy in relations with its neighbors. Because Italy did not receive its desired portions of Dalmatia at the Paris Peace Conference, Italian nationalist Gabriele D'Annunzio seized Fiume on the Adriatic in the fall of 1919. D'Annunzio's daring gesture as well as his deep sense of Italian national pride deeply affected Mussolini. However, in the atmosphere of detente prevalent in Europe at the time, he agreed to settle the dispute with Yugoslavia in a treaty on January 27, 1924, which ceded most of the port to Italy and the surrounding area to Yugoslavia.

In the fall of 1923, Mussolini used the assassination of Italian officials, who were working to resolve a Greek-Albanian border dispute, as a pretext to seize the island of Corfu. Within a month, however, the British and the French convinced him to return the island for an indemnity.

Soviet Russia (1922–1932)

The Civil War and "War Communism" had brought economic disaster and social upheaval throughout the country. On March 1, 1921, as the Soviet leadership met to decide on policies to guide the country in peace, a naval rebellion broke out at the Kronstadt naval base. The Soviet leadership sent Trotsky to put down the rebellion, which he did brutally by March 18.

Vladimir Ilyich Lenin, the founder of the Soviet State, suffered a serious stroke on May 26, 1922 and a second in December of that year. Lenin died on January 21, 1924.

Iosif Vissarionovich Dzhugashvili (Joseph Stalin, 1879–1953) took over numerous, and in some cases, seemingly unimportant party organizations after the Revolution and transformed them into important bases of power. Among them were Politburo (Political Bureau), which ran the country; the Orgburo (Organizational Bureau), which Stalin headed, and which appointed people to positions in groups that implemented Politiburo decisions, the Inspectorate (Rabkrin,

Commissariat of the Workers' and Peasants' Inspectorate) which tried to eliminate party corruption, and the Secretariat, which worked with all party organs and set the Politburo's agenda. Stalin served as the party's General Secretary after 1921.

Lev Davidovich Bronstein (Trotsky, 1879–1940) was Chairman of the Petrograd Soviet, headed the early Brest-Litovsk negotiating team, served as Foreign Commissar, and was father of the Red Army. A brilliant organizer and theorist, Trotsky was also brusque and, some felt, overbearing.

In China the Soviets helped found a young Chinese Communist party (CCP) in 1921. When it became apparent that Sun Yat-sen's (1866–1925) revolutionary Kuomintang (KMT) was more mature than the infant CCP, the Soviets encouraged an alliance between its party and this movement. Sun's successor, Chiang Kai-shek (1887–1975), was deeply suspicious of the Communists and made their destruction part of his effort to militarily unite China.

Founded in 1919, the Soviet-controlled Comintern (Third International or Communist International) sought to coordinate the revolutionary activities of Communist parties abroad, though it often conflicted with Soviet diplomatic interests. It became an effectively organized body by 1924, and was completely Stalinized by 1928.

Europe in Crisis: Depression and Dictatorship (1929–1935)

In Great Britain in 1929, Ramsay MacDonald formed a minority Labour government that would last until 1931. The most serious problem facing the country was the Depression, which caused unemployment to reach 1,700,000 by 1930 and peaked at over 3 million, or 25 percent of the labor force, by 1932. To meet growing budget deficits caused by heavy subsidies to the unemployed, a special government commission recommended budget cuts and tax increases. Cabinet and labor union opposition helped reduce the total for the cuts but this could not help restore confidence in the government, which fell on August 24, 1931.

The "National Government" (1931–1935)

The following day, King George VI (1895–1952) helped convince MacDonald to return to office as head of a National Coalition cabinet made up of four Conservatives, four Labourites, and two Liberals. MacDonald's coalition swept the November 1931 general elections winning 554 of 615 seats.

The British government abandoned the gold standard on September 21, 1931, and adopted a series of high tariffs on imports. By 1934, unemployment had dropped to 2 million.

MacDonald resigned his position in June 1935 because of ill health and was succeeded by Stanley Baldwin, whose conservative coalition won 428 seats in new elections in November.

France: Return of the Cartel des Gauches (1932–1934)

France remained plagued by differences over economic reform between the Radicals and the Socialists. The latter advocated nationalization of major factories, expanded social reforms, and public works programs for the unemployed, while the Radicals sought a reduction in government spending. This instability was also reflected in the fact that there were six Cabinets between June 1932 and February 1934. The government's inability to deal with the country's economic and political problems saw the emergence of a number of radical groups from across the political spectrum.

Germany: The Depression

The Depression had a dramatic effect on the German economy and politics. The country's national income dropped 20 percent between 1928 and 1932, while unemployment rose from 1,320,000 in 1929 to 6 million by January 1932. This meant that a staggering 43 percent of the German work force were without jobs (compared to one-quarter of the work force in the U.S.).

In 1919, Adolf Hitler joined the German Workers party (DAP), which he soon took over and renamed the National Socialist German Workers' party (NAZI). In 1920, the party adopted a 25-point program that included treaty revision, anti-Semitism, economic, and other social changes. They also created a defense cadre of the *Sturm-abteilung* (SA)—"Storm Troopers" or "brown shirts"—which was to help the party seize power.

The Beer Hall Putsch (1923): In the midst of the country's severe economic crisis in 1923, the party, which now had 55,000 members, tried to seize power, first by a march on Berlin, and then, when this seemed impossible, on Munich. The march was stopped by police, and Hitler and his supporters were arrested. Though sentenced to five years imprisonment, he was released after eight months. While incarcerated, he dictated *Mein Kampf* (My Struggle) to Rudolf Hess.

Hitler's failed coup and imprisonment convinced him to seek power through legitimate political channels, which would require transforming the Nazi party. To do this, he reasserted singular control over the movement from 1924 to 1926. Party districts were set up throughout Germany, overseen by *gauleiters* personally appointed by Hitler.

Hindenburg's seven-year presidential term expired in 1932, and he was convinced to run for reelection to stop Hitler from becoming president on the first ballot of March 13. Hitler got only 30 percent of the vote (11.3 million) to Hindenburg's 49.45 percent (18.6 million).

On June 1, Chancellor Bruenig was replaced by Franz von Papen (1879–1969), who formed a government made up of aristocratic conservatives and others that he and Hindenburg hoped would keep Hitler from power.

Later in the year, Papen convinced Hindenburg to appoint Hitler as chancellor and head of a new coalition cabinet with three seats for the Nazis. Hitler dissolved the Reichstag and called for new elections on March 5. Using presidential decree powers, he initiated a violent anti-Communist campaign that included the lifting of certain press and civil freedoms. On February 27, the Reichstag burned, which enabled Hitler to get Hindenburg to issue the "Ordinances for the Protection of the German State and Nation," that removed all civil and press liberties as part of a "revolution" against communism. In the Reichstag elections of March 5, the Nazis only got 43.9 percent of the vote and 288 Reichstag seats but, through an alliance with the Nationalists, got majority control of the legislature.

Once Hitler had full legislative power, he began a policy of *Gleichschaltung* (coordination) to bring all independent organizations and agencies throughout Germany under his control. All political parties were outlawed or forced to dissolve, and on July 14, 1933, the Nazi party became the only legal party in Germany. In addition, non-Aryans and Nazi opponents were removed from the civil service, the court system, and higher education. On May 2, 1933, the government declared strikes illegal, abolished labor unions, and later forced all workers to join the German Labor Front (DAF) under Robert Ley. In 1934 the Reichsrat was abolished and a special People's Court was created to handle cases of treason. Finally, the secret police or Gestapo (*Geheime Staatspolizei*) was created on April 24, 1933, under Hermann Göring to deal with opponents and operate concentration camps. The party had its own security branch, the SD (*Sicherheitsdienst*) under Reinhard Heydrich.

From the inception of the Nazi state in 1933, anti-Semitism was a constant theme and practice in all *Gleichschaltung* and Nazification efforts. Illegal intimidation and harassment of Jews was coupled with rigid enforcement of civil service regulations that forbade employment of non-Aryans. This first wave of anti-Semitic activity culminated with the passage of the Nuremburg Laws on September 15, 1935, that deprived Jews of German citizenship and outlawed sexual or marital relations between Jews and other Germans, thus effectively isolating them from the mainstream of German society.

Hitler's international policies were closely linked to his rebuilding efforts to give him a strong economic and military base for an active, aggressive, independent foreign policy. The Reich simultaneously quit the League of Nations. On January 26, 1934, Germany signed a non-aggression pact with Poland, which ended Germany's traditional anti-Polish foreign policy and broke France's encirclement of

Germany via the Little Entente. This was followed by the Saarland's overwhelming decision to return to Germany. The culmination of Hitler's foreign policy moves, though, came with his March 15, 1935, announcement that Germany would no longer be bound by the military restrictions of the Treaty of Versailles, that it had already created an air force (Luftwaffe), and that the Reich would institute a draft to create an army of 500,000 men.

Italy (1926–1936)

Until Mussolini's accession to power, the pope had considered himself a prisoner in the Vatican. In 1926, Mussolini's government began talks to resolve this issue, which resulted in the Lateran Accords of February 11, 1929. Italy recognized the Vatican as an independent state, with the pope as its head, while the papacy recognized Italian independence. Catholicism was made the official state religion of Italy, and religious teaching was required in all secondary schools.

In an effort to counter the significance of France's Little Entente with Czechoslovakia, Yugoslavia, and Romania, Mussolini concluded the Rome Protocols with Austria and Hungary which created a protective bond of friendship between the three countries.

In response to Hitler's announcement of German rearmament in violation of the Treaty of Versailles on March 16, 1935, France, England, and Italy met at Stresa in northern Italy on April 11–14, and concluded agreements that pledged joint military collaboration if Germany moved against Austria or along the Rhine.

Ethiopia (Abyssinia) became an area of strong Italian interest in the 1880s. The coastal region was slowly brought under Italian control until the Italian defeat at Ethiopian hands at Adowa in 1894. In 1906, the country's autonomy was recognized and in 1923 it joined the League of Nations. Mussolini, who had been preparing for war with Ethiopia since 1932, established a military base at Walwal in Ethiopian territory. Beginning in December 1934, a series of minor conflicts took place between the two countries, which gave Mussolini an excuse to plan for the full takeover of the country in the near future.

On October 2, 1935, Italy invaded Ethiopia, while the League of Nations, which had received four appeals from Ethiopia since January about Italian territorial transgressions, finally voted to adopt economic sanctions against Mussolini. Unfortunately, the League failed to stop shipments of oil to Italy and continued to allow it to use the Suez Canal. On May 9, 1936, Italy formally annexed the country and joined it to Somalia and Eritrea, which now became known as Italian East Africa.

Soviet Russia (1933–1938)

The Second Five Year Plan (1933–1937) was adopted by the Seventeenth Party Congress in early 1934. Its economic and production targets were less severe than the First Plan, and thus, more was achieved. By the end of the Second Plan, Soviet Russia had emerged as a leading world industrial power, though at great cost. It gave up quality for quantity, and created tremendous social and economic discord that ramifies in the nations of the former Soviet Union even today.

In the spring of 1935, the recently renamed and organized secret police, the NKVD, oversaw the beginnings of a new, violent Purge that eradicated 70 percent of the 1934 Central Committee, and a large percentage of the upper military ranks. Stalin sent between 8 and 9 million to camps and prisons, and caused untold deaths before the Purges ended in 1938.

The period from 1929 to 1933 saw the U.S.S.R. retreat inward as the bulk of its energies were put into domestic economic growth. Regardless, Stalin remained sensitive to growing aggression and ideological threats abroad such as the Japanese invasion of Manchuria in 1931 and Hitler's appointment as Chancellor in 1933. As a result, Russia left its cocoon in 1934, joined the League of Nations, and became an advocate of "collective security" while the Comintern adopted Popular Front tactics, allying with other parties against fascism, to strengthen the U.S.S.R.'s international posture. Diplomatically, in addition to League membership, the Soviet Union completed a military pact with France.

International Developments (1918–1935)

Efforts to create an international body to arbitrate international conflicts gained credence with the creation of a Permanent Court of International Justice to handle such matters at the First Hague Conference (1899). But no major efforts towards this goal were initiated until 1915, when pro-League of Nations organizations arose in the United States and Great Britain. Support for such a body grew as the war lengthened, and creation of such an organization became the cornerstone of President Woodrow Wilson's post-war policy, enunciated in his "Fourteen Points" speech before Congress on January 8, 1918.

The Preamble of the League's Covenant defined the League's purposes, which were to work for international friendship, peace, and security. To attain this, its members agreed to avoid war, maintain peaceful relations with other countries, and honor international law and accords.

Headquartered in Geneva, the League came into existence as the result of an Allied resolution on January 25, 1919, and the signing of the Treaty of Versailles on June 28, 1919. The League had the right, according to Article 8 of the League Covenant, to seek ways to reduce arms strength, while Articles 10 through 17 gave it the authority to search for means to stop war. It could recommend ways to stop aggression, and could suggest economic sanctions and other tactics to enforce its decisions, though its military ability to enforce its decisions was vague.

The Locarno Pact (1925)

Signed on October 16, 1925, by England, France, Italy, Germany, and Belgium, the Locarno Pact guaranteed Germany's western boundaries and accepted the Versailles settlement's demilitarized zones. Italy and Great Britain agreed militarily to defend these lines if flagrantly violated.

In the same spirit, Germany signed arbitration dispute accords that mirrored the Geneva Protocol with France, Belgium, Poland, and Czechoslovakia, and required acceptance of League-determined settlements. Since Germany would only agree to arbitration and not finalize its eastern border, France separately signed guarantees with Poland and Czechoslovakia to defend their frontiers.

The Locarno Pact went into force when Germany joined the League on September 10, 1926, acquiring, after some dispute, the U.S.'s permanent seat on the Council. France and Belgium began to withdraw from the Rhineland, though they left a token force there until 1930.

The Pact of Paris (Kellogg-Briand Pact)

The Locarno Pact heralded a new period in European relations known as the "Era of Locarno" that marked the end of post-war conflict and the beginning of a more normal period of diplomatic friendship and cooperation. It reached its peak, with the Franco-American effort in 1928 to seek an international statement to outlaw war. On August 27, 1928, 15 countries, including the U.S., Germany, France, Italy, and Japan, signed this accord with some minor limitations, which renounced war as a means of solving differences and as a tool of national policy. Within five years, 50 other countries signed the agreement.

League and Allied Response to Aggression

On September 19, 1931, the Japanese Kwantung Army, acting independently of the government in Tokyo, began the gradual conquest of Manchuria after fabricating an incident at Mukden to justify their actions. Ultimately, they created a puppet state, Manchukuo, under the last Chinese emperor, Henry P'u-i. China's League protest resulted in the creation of an investigatory commission under the Earl of Lytton that criticized Japan's actions and recommended a negotiated settlement that would have allowed Japan to retain most of its conquest. Japan responded by resigning from the League on January 24, 1933.

Hitler's announcement on March 15, 1935, of Germany's decisions to rearm and to introduce conscription in violation of the Treaty of Versailles prompted the leaders of England, France, and Italy to meet in Stresa, Italy (April 11–14). They condemned Germany's actions, underlined their commitment to the Locarno Pact, and re-affirmed the support they collectively gave for Austria's independence in early 1934. Great Britain's decision, however, to separately protect its naval strength vis-à-vis a German buildup in the Anglo-German Naval Treaty of June 18, 1935, effectively compromised the significance of the Stresa Front.

FROM WORLD WAR II TO THE POST-COMMUNIST ERA (1935–1996)

The Course of Events

Using a Franco-Soviet agreement of the preceding year as an excuse, Hitler, on March 7, 1936, repudiated the Locarno agreements and reoccupied the Rhineland (an area demilitarized by the Versailles Treaty). Neither France (which possessed military superiority at the time) nor Britain was willing to oppose these moves.

The Spanish Civil War (1936–1939) is usually seen as a rehearsal for World War II because of outside intervention. The government of the Spanish Republic (established in 1931) caused resentment among conservatives by its programs, including land reform and anti-clerical legislation aimed at the Catholic church. Following an election victory by a popular front of republican and radical parties, right-wing generals in July began a military insurrection. Francisco Franco, stationed at the time in Spanish Morocco, emerged as the leader of this revolt, which became a devastating civil war lasting nearly three years.

The democracies, including the United States, followed a course of neutrality. Nazi Germany, Italy, and the U.S.S.R. did intervene despite non-intervention agreements negotiated by Britain and France. Spain became a battlefield for fascist and anti-fascist forces with Franco winning by 1939 in what was seen as a serious defeat for anti-fascist forces everywhere.

The Spanish Civil War was a factor in bringing together Mussolini and Hitler in a Rome-Berlin Axis. Already Germany and Japan had signed the Anti-Comintern Pact in 1936. Ostensibly directed against international communism, this was the basis for a diplomatic alliance between those countries, and Italy soon adhered to this agreement, becoming Germany's ally in World War II.

In 1938 Hitler pressured the Austrian chancellor to make concessions and when this did not work, German troops annexed Austria (the *Anschluss*). Again Britain and France took no effective action, and about six million Austrians were added to Germany.

Hitler turned next to Czechoslovakia. Three million persons of German origin lived in the Sudetenland, a borderland between Germany and Czechoslovakia given to Czechoslovakia in order to provide it with a more defensible boundary. In 1938, after a series of demands from Hitler, a four-power conference was held in Munich with Hitler, Mussolini, Chamberlain, and Daladier in attendance, at which Hitler's terms were accepted. Britain and France, despite the French alliance with Czechoslovakia, put pressure on the Czech government to force it to comply with German demands. Hitler signed a treaty agreeing to this settlement as the limit of his ambitions. At the same time the Poles seized control of Teschen, and Hungary (with the support of Italy and Germany and over the protests of the British and French) seized 7,500 square miles of Slovakia. By the concessions forced on her at Munich, Czechoslovakia lost its frontier defenses and was totally unprotected against any further German encroachments.

In March 1939, Hitler annexed most of the Czech state while Hungary conquered Ruthenia. At almost the same time Germany annexed Memel from Lithuania. In April, Mussolini, taking advantage of distractions created by Germany, landed an army in Albania and seized that Balkan state in a campaign lasting about one week.

Disillusioned by these continued aggressions, Britain and France made military preparations. Guarantees were given to Poland, Romania, and Greece. The two democracies also opened negotiations with the U.S.S.R. for an arrangement to obtain that country's aid against further German aggression. Hitler, with Poland next on his timetable, also began a cautious rapprochement with the U.S.S.R. On August 23, 1939, the world was stunned by the announcement of a Nazi-Soviet Treaty of Friendship. A secret protocol provided that in the event of a "territorial rearrangement" in Eastern Europe the two powers would divide Poland. In addition, Russia would have the Baltic states (Latvia, Lithuania, and Estonia) and Bessarabia (lost to Romania in 1918) as part of her sphere. Stalin agreed to remain neutral in any German war with Britain or France. World War II began with the German invasion of Poland on September 1, 1939, followed by British and French declarations of war against Germany on September 3.

World War II

The German attack (known as the "blitzkrieg" or "lightning war") overwhelmed the poorly equipped Polish army, which could not resist German tanks and airplanes.

On September 17 the Russian armies attacked the Poles from the east. They met the Germans two days later. Stalin's share of Poland extended approximately to the Curzon Line. Russia also made demands on Finland. Later, in June 1940, while Germany was attacking France, Stalin occupied the Baltic states of Latvia, Lithuania, and Estonia.

The only military action of any consequence during the winter of 1939–1940 resulted from Russian demands made on Finland, especially for territory adjacent to Leningrad (then only 20 miles from the border). Finnish refusal led to a Russian attack in November 1939. The Finns resisted with considerable vigor, receiving some supplies from Sweden, Britain, and France, but eventually by March they had to give in to the superior Russian forces. Finland was forced to cede the Karelian Isthmus, Viipuri, and a naval base at Hangoe.

On May 10, the main German offensive was launched against France. Belgium and the Netherlands were simultaneously attacked. According to plan, British and French forces advanced to aid the Belgians. At this point the Germans departed from the World War I strategy by launching a surprise armored attack through Luxembourg and the Ardennes Forest (considered by the British and French to be impassable for tanks). The Dutch could offer no real resistance and collapsed in four days after the May 13 German bombing of Rotterdam.

Paris fell to the Germans in mid-June. The Pétain government quickly made peace with Hitler, who added to French humiliation by dictating the terms of the armistice to the French at Compiègne in the same railroad car used by Marshal Foch when he gave terms to the Germans at the end of the First World War. The complete collapse of France quickly came as a tremendous shock to the British and Americans.

Mussolini declared war on both France and Britain on June 10. Hitler's forces remained in occupation of the northern part of France, including Paris. He allowed the French to keep their fleet and overseas territories probably in the hope of making them reliable allies. Pétain and his chief minister Pierre Laval established their capital at Vichy and followed a policy of collaboration with their former enemies. A few Frenchmen, however, joined the Free French movement started in London by the then relatively unknown General Charles de Gaulle (1890–1970).

From the French Defeat to the Invasion of Russia

By mid-summer 1940, Germany, together with its Italian ally, dominated most of Western and Central Europe. Germany began with no real plans for a long war, but continued resistance by the British made necessary the belated mobilization of German resources. Hitler's policy included exploiting areas Germany conquered. Collaborators were used to establish governments subservient to German policy. Germany began the policy of forcibly transporting large numbers of conquered Europeans to work in German war industries. Jews especially were forced into slave labor for the German war effort, and increasingly large numbers were rounded up and sent to concentration camps, where they were systematically murdered as the Nazis carried out Hitler's "final solution" of genocide against European Jewry. Although much was known about this during the war, the full horror of these atrocities was not revealed until Allied troops entered Germany in 1945.

With the fall of France, Britain remained the only power of consequence at war with the Axis. Hitler began preparations for invading Britain (Operation "Sea

Lion"). Air control over the Channel was vital if an invasion force was to be transported safely to the English Coast. The German Air Force (Luftwaffe) under Herman Göring began its air offensive against the British in the summer of 1940. The Germans concentrated first on British air defenses, then on ports and shipping, and finally in early September they began the attack on London. The Battle of Britain was eventually a defeat for the Germans, who were unable to gain decisive superiority over the British, although they inflicted great damage on both British air defenses and major cities such as London. Despite the damage and loss of life, British morale remained high and necessary war production continued. German losses determined that bombing alone could not defeat Britain. "Operation Sea Lion" was postponed October 12 and never seriously taken up again, although the British did not know this and had to continue for some time to give priority to their coastal and air defenses.

During the winter of 1940–1941, having given up "Operation Sea Lion," Hitler began to shift his forces to the east for an invasion of Russia ("Operation Barbarossa"). Russian expansion towards the Balkans dismayed the Germans, who hoped for more influence there themselves.

The German invasion of Russia began June 22, 1941. The invasion force of three million included Finnish, Romanian, Hungarian, and Italian contingents along with the Germans and advanced on a broad front of about 2,000 miles. They surrounded the city of Leningrad (although they never managed to actually capture it) and came within about 25 miles of Moscow. In November the enemy actually entered the suburbs, but then the long supply lines, early winter, and Russian resistance (strong despite heavy losses) brought the invasion to a halt. During the winter a Russian counterattack pushed the Germans back from Moscow and saved the capital.

With the coming of the Great Depression and severe economic difficulties, Japanese militarists gained more and more influence over the civilian government. On September 18, 1931, the Japanese occupied all of Manchuria. On July 7, 1937, a full-scale Sino-Japanese war began with a clash between Japanese and Chinese at the Marco Polo Bridge in Peking (now Beijing). An indication of ultimate Japanese aims came on November 3, 1938, when Prince Fumimaro Konoye's (1891–1946) government issued a statement on "A New Order in East Asia." This statement envisaged the integration of Japan, Manchuria (now the puppet state of Manchukuo), and China into one "Greater East Asia Co-Prosperity Sphere" under Japanese leadership. In July 1940, the Konoye government was re-formed with General Hideki Tojo (1884–1948) (Japan's principal leader in World War I) as minister of war.

All of these events led to worsening relations between Japan and the two states in a position to oppose her expansion—the Soviet Union and the United States. Despite border clashes with the Russians, Japan avoided any conflict with that state, and Stalin wanted no war with Japan after he became fully occupied with the German invasion. In the few weeks after attacking the U.S. at Pearl Harbor, Japanese forces were able to occupy strategically important islands (including the

Philippines and Dutch East Indies) and territory on the Asian mainland (Malaya, with the British naval base at Singapore, and all of Burma to the border of India).

The Japanese attack brought the United States not only into war in the Pacific, but resulted in German and Italian declarations of war which meant the total involvement of the United States in World War II.

American involvement in the war was ultimately decisive, for it meant that the greatest industrial power of that time was now arrayed against the Axis powers. The United States became, as President Roosevelt put it, "the arsenal of democracy." American aid was crucial to the immense effort of the Soviet Union. Lend-Lease aid was extended to Russia. By 1943 supplies and equipment were reaching Russia in considerable quantities.

The German forces launched a second offensive in the summer of 1942. This attack concentrated on the southern part of the front, aiming at the Caucasus and vital oil fields around the Caspian Sea. At Stalingrad on the Volga River the Germans were stopped. With the onset of winter, Hitler refused to allow the strategic retreat urged by his generals. As a result, the Russian forces crossed the river north and south of the city and surrounded 22 German divisions. On January 31, 1943, following the failure of relief efforts, the German commander Friedrich Paulus (1890–1957) surrendered the remnants of his army. From then on the Russians were almost always on the offensive.

After entering the war in 1940, the Italians invaded British-held Egypt. In December 1940, the British General Archibald Wavell (1883–1950) launched a surprise attack. The Italian forces were driven back about 500 miles and 130,000 were captured. Then Hitler intervened, sending General Erwin Rommel with a small German force (the Afrika Korps) to reinforce the Italians. Rommel took command and launched a counter-offensive which put his forces on the border of Egypt. By mid-1942 Rommel had driven to El Alamein, only 70 miles from Alexandria.

A change in the British high command now placed General Harold Alexander (1891–1969) in charge of Middle Eastern forces, with General Bernard Montgomery (1887–1976) in immediate command of the British Eighth Army. Montgomery attacked at El Alamein, breaking Rommel's lines and starting a British advance which was not stopped until the armies reached the border of Tunisia.

Meanwhile, the British and American leaders decided that they could launch a second offensive in North Africa ("Operation Torch") which would clear the enemy from the entire coast and make the Mediterranean once again safe for Allied shipping.

The landings resulted in little conflict with the French, and the French forces soon joined the war against the Axis. It was only a matter of time before German troops were forced into northern Tunisia and surrendered. American forces, unused to combat, suffered some reverses at the Battle of the Kasserine Pass, but gained valuable experience. The final victory came in May 1943, about the same time as the Russian victory at Stalingrad.

Relatively safe shipping routes across the North Atlantic to Britain were essential to the survival of Britain and absolutely necessary if a force was to be assembled to invade France and strike at Germany proper. New types of aircraft, small aircraft carriers, more numerous and better-equipped escort vessels, new radar and sonar (for underwater detection), extremely efficient radio direction finding, decipherment of German signals plus the building of more ships turned the balance against the Germans despite their development of improved submarines by early 1943, and the Atlantic became increasingly dangerous for German submarines.

Success in these three campaigns—Stalingrad, North Africa, and the Battle of the Atlantic—gave new hope to the Allied cause and made certain that victory was attainable. With the beginning of an Allied offensive in late 1942 in the Solomon Islands against the Japanese, 1943 became the turning point of the war.

At their conference at Casablanca in January 1943, Roosevelt and Churchill developed a detailed strategy for the further conduct of the war. Sicily was to be invaded, then Italy proper. Rome was not captured by the Allied forces until June 4, 1944. With a new Italian government now supporting the Allied cause, Italian resistance movements in northern Italy became a major force in helping to liberate that area from the Germans.

At the Teheran Conference, held in November 1943 and attended by all three major Allied leaders, the final decision reached by Roosevelt and Churchill some six months earlier to invade France in May 1944 was communicated to the Russians. Stalin promised to open a simultaneous Russian offensive.

The Normandy invasion (Operation "Overlord") was the largest amphibious operation in history. The landings actually took place beginning June 6, 1944. The first day, 130,000 men were successfully landed. Strong German resistance hemmed in the Allied forces for about a month. Then the Allies, now numbering about 1,000,000, managed a spectacular breakthrough. By the end of 1944, all of France had been seized. A second invasion force landed on the Mediterranean coast in August, freed southern France, and linked up with Eisenhower's forces. By the end of 1944, the Allied armies stood on the borders of Germany ready to invade from both east and west.

Stalin's armies crossed into Poland July 23, 1944, and three days later the Russian dictator officially recognized a group of Polish Communists (the so-called Lublin Committee) as the government of Poland. As the Russian armies drew near the eastern suburbs of Warsaw, the London Poles, a resistance group, launched an attack. Stalin's forces waited outside the city while the Germans brought in reinforcements and slowly wiped out the Polish underground army in several weeks of heavy street fighting. The offensive then resumed and the city was liberated by the Red Army, but the influence of the London Poles was now virtually nil. Needless to say, this incident aroused considerable suspicion concerning Stalin's motives and led both Churchill and Roosevelt to begin to think through the political implications of their alliance with Stalin.

By late summer of 1944, the German position in the Balkans began to collapse. The Red Army crossed the border into Romania, leading King Michael (1921–) to seize the opportunity to take his country out of its alliance with Germany and to open the way to the advancing Russians. German troops were forced to make a hasty retreat. At this point Bulgaria changed sides. The German forces in Greece withdrew in October.

From October 9–18, Winston Churchill visited Moscow to try to work out a political arrangement regarding the Balkans and Eastern Europe. Dealing from a position of weakness, he simply wrote out some figures on a sheet of paper: Russia to have the preponderance of influence in countries like Bulgaria and Romania, Britain to have the major say in Greece, and a fifty-fifty division in Yugoslavia and Hungary. Stalin agreed. The Americans refused to have anything to do with this "spheres of influence" arrangement.

In Greece, Stalin maintained a hands-off policy when the British used military force to suppress the Communist resistance movement and install a regent for the exiled government.

In early spring of 1945 the Allied armies crossed the Rhine. As the Americans and British and other Allied forces advanced into Germany, the Russians attacked from the east. While the Russian armies were fighting their way into Berlin, Hitler committed suicide in the ruins of the bunker where he had spent the last days of the war. Power was handed over to a government headed by Admiral Karl Dönitz (1891–1980). On May 7, General Alfred Jodl (1890–1946), acting for the German government, made the final unconditional surrender at General Eisenhower's headquarters near Reims.

The future treatment of Germany, and Europe in general, was determined by decisions of the "Big Three" (Churchill, Stalin, and Roosevelt).

The first major conference convened at Teheran on November 28, 1943, and lasted until December 1. Here the two Western allies told Stalin of the May 1944 date for the planned invasion of Normandy. In turn, Stalin confirmed a pledge made earlier that Russia would enter the war against Japan after the war with Germany was concluded. The Yalta Conference was the second attended personally by Stalin, Churchill, and Roosevelt. It lasted from the 4th to the 11th of February 1945. A plan to divide Germany into zones of occupation, which had been devised in 1943 by a committee under British Deputy Prime Minister Clement Attlee, was formally accepted with the addition of a fourth zone taken from the British and American zones for the French to occupy. Berlin, which lay within the Russian Zone, was divided into four zones of occupation also.

The third summit meeting of the Big Three took place at Potsdam outside Berlin after the end of the European war but while the Pacific war was still going on. The conference began July 17, 1945, with Stalin, Churchill, and the new American President Harry Truman attending. A Potsdam Declaration, aimed at Japan, called for immediate Japanese surrender and hinted at the consequences that would ensue if it were not forthcoming. While at the conference, American leaders received the news of the successful testing of the first atomic bomb in the New Mexico desert, but the Japanese were given no clear warning that such a destructive weapon might be used against them.

On August 6, 1945, the bomb was dropped by a single plane on Hiroshima and an entire city disappeared, with the instantaneous loss of 70,000 lives. In time many other persons died from radiation poisoning and other effects. Since no surrender was received, a second bomb was dropped on Nagasaki, obliterating that city. Even the most fanatical of the Japanese leaders saw what was happening and surrender came quickly. The only departure from unconditional surrender was to allow the Japanese to retain their emperor (Hirohito, 1901–1989), but only with the proviso that he would be subject in every respect to the orders of the occupation commander. The formal surrender took place September 2, 1945, in Tokyo Bay on the deck of the battleship *Missouri*, and the occupation of Japan began under the immediate control of the American commander, General Douglas MacArthur (1880–1964).

Europe after World War II: 1945 to 1953

Anglo-American ideas about what the post-war world should be like were expressed by Roosevelt and Churchill at their meeting off the coast of Newfoundland in August 1941. The Atlantic Charter was a general statement of goals: restoration of the sovereignty and self-government of nations conquered by Hitler, free access to world trade and resources, cooperation to improve living standards and economic security, and a peace that would ensure freedom from fear and want and stop the use of force and aggression as instruments of national policy.

At the Casablanca Conference, the policy of requiring unconditional surrender by the Axis powers was announced. This ensured that at the end of the war, all responsibility for government of the defeated nations would fall on the victors, and they would have a free hand in rebuilding government in those countries. No real planning was done in detail before the time arrived to meet this responsibility. It was done for the most part as the need arose.

At Teheran, the Big Three did discuss in a general way the occupation and demilitarization of Germany. They also laid the foundation for a post-war organization—the United Nations Organization—which like the earlier League of Nations was supposed to help regulate international relations and keep the peace and ensure friendly cooperation between the nations of the world.

At Potsdam, agreement was reached to sign peace treaties as soon as possible with former German allies. A Council of Foreign Ministers was established to draft the treaties. Several meetings were held in 1946 and 1947 and treaties were signed with Italy, Romania, Hungary, Bulgaria, and Finland. These states paid reparations and agreed to some territorial readjustments as a price for peace. No agreement could be reached on Japan or Germany. In 1951, the Western powers led by the U.S. concluded a treaty with Japan without Russian participation. The latter made their own treaty in 1956. A final meeting of the Council of Foreign Ministers broke up in 1947 over Germany, and no peace treaty was ever signed with that country. The division of Germany for purposes of occupation and military government became permanent, with the three Western zones joining and eventually becoming the Federal Republic of Germany and the Russian zone becoming the German Democratic Republic.

Arrangements for the United Nations were confirmed at the Yalta Conference: the large powers would predominate in a Security Council, where they would have permanent seats together with several other powers elected from time to time from among the other members of the U.N. Consent of all the permanent members was necessary for any action to be taken by the Security Council (thus, giving the large powers a veto). The General Assembly was to include all members.

Eastern Europe: 1945–1953

Much of European Russia had been devastated, and about 25 million people made homeless. In March 1946 a fourth five-year plan was adopted by the Supreme Soviet intended to increase industrial output to a level 50 percent higher than before the war. A bad harvest and food shortage in 1946 had been relieved by a good harvest in 1947, and in December 1947, the government announced the end of food rationing. At the same time a drastic currency devaluation was put through, which brought immediate hardship to many people but strengthened the Soviet economy in the long run. As a result of these and other forceful and energetic measures, the Soviet Union was able within a few years to make good most of the wartime damage and to surpass pre-war levels of production.

The fate of Eastern Europe (including Poland, Hungary, Romania, Bulgaria, Czechoslovakia, and the Russian zone of Germany) from 1945 on was determined by the presence of Russian armies in that area.

Communization of Eastern Europe and the establishment of regimes in the satellite areas of the Soviet Union occurred in stages over a three-year period following the end of the war. The timetable of events varied in each country.

As relations broke down between the four occupying powers, the Soviet authorities gradually created a Communist state in their zone. On October 7, 1948, a German Democratic Republic was established. In June 1950, an agreement with Poland granted formal recognition of the Oder-Neisse Line as the boundary between the two states. Economic progress was unsatisfactory for most of the population, and on June 16–17, 1953, riots occurred in East Berlin which were suppressed by Soviet forces using tanks. In East Germany, a program of economic reform was announced which eventually brought some improvement.

In Yugoslavia, Marshal Tito (1892–1980) and his Communist partisan movement emerged from the war in a strong position because of their effective campaign against the German occupation. Tito was able to establish a Communist government in 1945 despite considerable pressure from Stalin, and pursue a course independent of the Soviet Union unique among the countries of Eastern Europe.

Western Europe: 1945–1953

The monarchy which had governed Italy since the time of unification in the mid-nineteenth century was now discarded in favor of a republic. King Victor Emmanuel III (1869–1947), compromised by his association with Mussolini, resigned in favor of his son, but a referendum in June 1946 established a republic. In simultaneous elections for a constituent assembly, three parties predominated: the Social Democrats, the Communists, and the Christian Democrats.

In the last two years of the war, France recovered sufficiently under the leadership of General Charles de Gaulle to begin playing a significant military and political role once again. In July 1944, the United States recognized de Gaulle's Committee of National Liberation as the de facto government of areas liberated from the German occupation.

In foreign affairs, France occupied Germany. In addition, the Fourth Republic was faced with two major problems abroad when it attempted to assert its authority over Indochina and Algeria. The Indochina situation resulted in a long and costly war against nationalists and Communists under Ho Chi Minh (1890–1969). French involvement ended with the Geneva Accords of 1954 and French withdrawal. The Algerian struggle reached a crisis in 1958 resulting in General de Gaulle's return to power and the creation of a new Fifth Republic.

In May 1945, when Germany surrendered unconditionally, the country lay in ruins. About three-quarters of city houses had been gutted by air raids, industry was in a shambles, and the country was divided into zones of occupation ruled by foreign military governors. Economic chaos was the rule, currency was virtually worthless, food was in short supply, and the black market flourished for those who could afford to buy in it. By the Potsdam agreements, Germany lost about one-quarter of its pre-war territory. In addition, some 12 million people of German origin driven from their homes in countries like Poland and Czechoslovakia had to be fed, housed, and clothed along with the indigenous population.

Demilitarization, denazification, and democratization were the initial goals of the occupation forces in Germany. All four wartime allies agreed on the imperative to try leading Nazis for a variety of war crimes and "crimes against humanity." An International Military Tribunal was established at Nuremburg to try 22 major war criminals, and lesser courts tried many others. Most of the defendants were executed, although a few like Rudolf Hess were given life imprisonment.

As relations between the three Western powers and the Soviets gradually broke down in Germany, East and West became separate states. In the West, the British and American zones were fused into one in 1946, with the French joining in 1948. Political parties were gradually re-established.

In February 1948, a charter granted further powers of government to the Germans in the American and British zones. Later that year, the Russians and East Germans, in an effort to force the Western powers out of their zones in Berlin, began a blockade of the city which was located within the Russian zone. The response was an allied airlift to supply the city, and eventually, after some months, the blockade was called off.

In 1951 a Conservative majority was returned in Great Britain, and Winston Churchill, who had been defeated in 1945, became prime minister again. The new regime immediately reversed the nationalization of iron and steel. Other measures survived, however, especially the universal health care program which proved to be one of the most popular parts of the Labour achievement. In April 1955, Churchill resigned for reasons of age and health and turned over the prime minister's office to Anthony Eden (1897–1977).

The Marshall Plan

European recovery from the effects of the war was slow for the first two or three years after 1945. The European Recovery Program (Marshall Plan, named after the American secretary of state and World War II army chief of staff) began in 1948 and showed substantial results in all the Western European countries that took part. The most remarkable gains were in West Germany. The Plan aimed to strengthen Western Europe's resistance to communism.

NATO

The United States joined eleven other states in the Atlantic region in a mutual defense pact called the North Atlantic Treaty Organization (NATO) in 1949. NATO was created to counterbalance the Soviet presence in Central and Eastern Europe.

British Overseas Withdrawal

Following World War II, there was a considerable migration of Jews who had survived the Nazi Holocaust to Palestine to join Jews who had settled there earlier. Conflicts broke out with the Arabs. The British occupying forces tried to suppress the violence and to negotiate a settlement between the factions. In 1948, after negotiations failed, the British, feeling they could no longer support the cost of occupation, announced their withdrawal. Zionist leaders then proclaimed the independent state of Israel and took up arms to fight the armies of Egypt, Syria, and other Arab states which invaded the Jewish-held area. The new Israeli state quickly proved its technological and military superiority by defeating the invaders.

The Jews of Israel created a modern parliamentary state on the European model with an economy and technology superior to their Arab neighbors. The new state was thought by many Arabs to be simply another manifestation of European imperialism made worse by religious antagonisms.

In 1967, Israel defeated Egypt, Syria, and Jordan in a six-day war, and the Israelis occupied additional territory including the Jordanian sector of the city of Jerusalem. An additional million Arabs came under Israeli rule as a result of this campaign.

Although defeated, the Arabs refused to sign any treaty or to come to terms with Israel. Palestinian refugees living in camps in states bordering Israel created grave problems. A Palestine Liberation Organization (PLO) was formed to fight for the establishment of an Arab Palestinian state on territory taken from Israel on the west bank of the Jordan River. The PLO resorted to terrorist tactics against both Israel and other states in support of their cause.

In October 1973, the Egyptians and Syrians launched an attack on Israel known as the Yom Kippur War. With some difficulty the attacks were repulsed. A settlement was mediated by American Secretary of State Henry Kissinger.

The government under King Farouk I (1920–1965) did little to alleviate the overriding problem of poverty after the war. In 1952, a group of army officers, including Gamal Abdel Nasser (1918–1970) and Anwar Sadat (1918–1981), plotted against the government, and on July 23 the king was overthrown. Colonel Nasser became premier in April 1954. A treaty with Britain later that year resulted in the withdrawal of all British troops from the Canal Zone.

India under Jawaharlal Nehru (1889–1964) and the Congress Party became a parliamentary democracy. The country made economic progress, but gains were largely negated by a population increase to 600 million from 350 million.

The French in Indochina and Algeria

Following World War II, the French returned to Indochina and attempted to restore their rule there. The opposition nationalist movement was led by the veteran Communist Ho Chi Minh. War broke out between the nationalists and the French forces. In 1954 their army was surrounded at Dien Bien Phu and forced to surrender. This military disaster prompted a change of government in France.

This new government under Premier Pierre Mendès-France (1907–1982) negotiated French withdrawal at a conference held at Geneva, Switzerland in 1954. Cambodia and Laos became independent and Vietnam was partitioned at the 17th parallel. The North, with its capital at Hanoi, became a Communist state under Ho Chi Minh. The South remained non-Communist. Under the Geneva Accords, elections were to be held in the South to determine the fate of that area. However, the United States chose to intervene and support the regime of Ngo Dinh Diem (1901–1963), and elections were never held. Eventually a second Vietnamese war resulted, with the United States playing the role earlier played by France.

In a referendum, on January 8, 1961, the French people approved of eventual Algerian self-determination. In July 1962 French rule ended in Algeria. There was a mass exodus of Europeans from Algeria, but most Frenchmen were grateful to de Gaulle for ending the long Algerian conflict.

The Dutch and Indonesia

During World War II, the Japanese conquered the Dutch East Indies. At the end of the war, they recognized the independence of the area as Indonesia. When the Dutch attempted to return, four years of bloody fighting ensued against the nationalist forces of Achmed Sukarno (1901–1970). In 1949, the Dutch recognized Indonesian independence. In 1954, the Indonesians dissolved all ties with the Netherlands.

The Cold War After the Death of Stalin

Following Stalin's death in 1953, Russian leaders appeared more willing than Stalin to be conciliatory and to consider peaceful coexistence.

In the U.S. the atmosphere also changed with the election of President Dwight Eisenhower, and conciliatory gestures were not always automatically considered appeasement of the Communists. In 1955 a summit conference of Eisenhower, the British and French leaders, and Khrushchev (1894–1971) met at Geneva in an atmosphere more cordial than any since World War II. The "spirit of Geneva" did not last long, however.

After his return to power in France in 1958, General de Gaulle endeavored to make France a leader in European affairs with himself as spokesman for a Europe that he hoped would be a counter to the "dual hegemony" of the U.S. and U.S.S.R. His policies at times were anti-British or anti-American. Despite his prestige as the last great wartime leader, he did not have great success.

A New Era Begins

Joseph Stalin died in March 1953. Eventually a little-known party function-ary, Nikita Khrushchev, became Communist Party General Secretary in 1954. Khrushchev's policy of relaxing the regime of terror and oppression of the Stalin years became known as "The Thaw," after the title of a novel by Ilya Ehrenburg (1891–1967).

Change occurred in foreign affairs also. Khrushchev visited Belgrade and re-established relations with Tito, admitting that there was more than one road to social-ism. He also visited the United States, met with President Eisenhower, and toured the country. Later, relations became more tense after the U-2 spy plane incident.

Following the loss of face sustained by Russia as a result of the Cuban Missile Crisis and the failure of Khrushchev's domestic agricultural policies, he was forced out of the party leadership and lived in retirement in Moscow until his death in 1971.

After Khrushchev's ouster, the leadership in the Central Committee divided power, making Leonid Brezhnev (1906–1982) party secretary and Aleksei Kosy-gin chairman of the council of ministers, or premier.

Stalin's successors rehabilitated many of Stalin's victims. They also permitted somewhat greater freedom in literary and artistic matters and even allowed some political criticism. Controls were maintained, however, and sometimes were tight-ened. Anti-Semitism was also still present, and Soviet Jews were long denied per-mission to emigrate to Israel.

Brezhnev occupied the top position of power until his death in 1982. He was briefly succeeded by Yuri Andropov (1914–1984) (a former secret police chief) and Konstantin Chenenko (1911–1985), then by Mikhail Gorbachev, who carried out a further relaxation of the internal regime. Gorbachev pushed disarmament and dé-tente in foreign relations, and attempted a wide range of internal reforms known as *perestroika* ("restructuring"). Gorbachev resigned in 1991. Boris Yeltsin assumed control over the collapsing Soviet Union, which would later become known as the Commonwealth of Independent States, with Yeltsin as president.

Economic difficulties associated with a transition to a free economy, the mishandled repression of the Chechnya independence movement, and Yeltsin's dissolution of Russia's parliament in 1993 gave ammunition to his opponents. In the 1996 elections, Yeltsin retained office as president, but the poor state of his health, despite successful heart bypass surgery in the fall of 1996, eventually made him step down and yield leadership to Vladimir Putin in late 1999.

Change in Eastern Europe

In the 1980s, the trade union movement known as Solidarity and its leader, Lech Walesa, emerged as a political force, organizing mass protests in 1980–1981 and maintaining almost continuous pressure on the government headed by General Wojciech Jaruzelski. Despite government efforts to maintain strong central control and suppress the opposition, the ruling Communists were forced to recognize the opposition and make concessions. In June 1989, after power had passed to the Polish Parliament, a national election gave Solidarity an overwhelming majority, and Walesa assumed the presidency. By 1993–94, economic problems resulted in a Communist majority and a change of administration, but there was no return to the old Communist dictatorship.

Change in Western Europe

In March 1957, inspired chiefly by Belgian Foreign Minister Paul-Henri Spaak, two treaties were signed in Rome creating a European Atomic Energy Commission (Euratom) and a European Economic Community (the Common Market)—which eventually absorbed Euratom. The EEC was to be a customs union creating a free market area with a common external tariff for member nations. Toward the outside world, the EEC acted as a single bargaining agent for its members in commercial transactions, and it reached a number of agreements with other European and Third World states.

In 1973, the original six were joined by three new members: Britain, Ireland, and Denmark. The name was changed to "European Community." In 1979, there were three more applicants: Spain, Portugal, and Greece. These latter states were less well off and created problems of cheap labor, agricultural products, etc., which delayed their acceptance as members until 1986. With the acceptance of the Maastricht treaty in 1993, the group's name became the "European Union."

Relations with Northern Ireland proved a burden to successive British governments. The 1922 settlement had left Northern Ireland as a self-governing part of the United Kingdom. Of 1.5 million inhabitants, one-third were Roman Catholic and two-thirds were Protestant. Catholics claimed they were discriminated against and pressed for annexation by the Republic of Ireland. Activity by the Irish Republican Army brought retaliation by Protestant extremists. From 1969 on, there was considerable violence, causing the British to bring in troops to maintain order.

Under Prime Minister Margaret Thatcher in the 1980s, the British economy improved somewhat. London regained some of its former power as a financial center. In recent years, an influx of people from former colonies in Asia, Africa, and the West Indies has caused some racial tensions.

Prime Minister Thatcher was a partisan of free enterprise. She fought inflation with austerity and let economic problems spur British employers and unions to change for greater efficiency. She received a boost in popularity when Britain won a brief war with Argentina over the Falkland Islands. She stressed close ties with the Republican administration of Ronald Reagan in the U.S. A Conservative victory in the 1987 elections made Thatcher the longest-serving prime minister in modern British history.

In 1990, having lost the support of Conservatives in Parliament, Thatcher resigned and was replaced by Chancellor of the Exchequer John Major. Under Major's leadership, Conservatives had to deal with slow economic growth, unemployment, and racial tensions caused by resentment over the influx of immigrants from other parts of the Commonwealth. And there remains the seemingly intractable religious strife in Northern Ireland, with its Protestant-Catholic animosities. Tony Blair, prime minister from 1997 to 2007, made Northern Ireland peace a priority. In 2007, the hard-line Roman Catholic Sinn Fein and Protestant Democratic Unionist Party reached a historic power-sharing agreement. Blair also succeeded in achieving closer relations with the European Union, but in 2016, Britain reversed course with a vote to leave the EU— a vote that continued to stir turmoil through 2017.

France under de Gaulle saw a new constitution drafted and approved establishing the Fifth Republic with a much strengthened executive in the form of a president with power to dissolve the legislature and call for elections, to submit important questions to popular referendum, and if necessary to assume emergency powers. De Gaulle used all these powers in his 11 years as president.

In domestic politics, de Gaulle strengthened the power of the president by often using the referendum and bypassing the Assembly. De Gaulle was re-elected in 1965, but people became restless with what amounted to a republican monarch. Labor became restive over inflation and housing while students objected to expenditures on nuclear forces rather than education. In May 1968, student grievances over conditions in the universities caused hundreds of thousands to revolt. They were soon joined by some 10 million workers, who paralyzed the economy.

De Gaulle survived by promising educational reform and wage increases. New elections were held in June 1968, and de Gaulle was returned to power. Promised reforms were begun, but in April 1969, he resigned and died about a year later.

De Gaulle's immediate successors were Georges Pompidou (1969–1974) and Valéry Giscard d'Estaing (1974–1981). Both provided France with firm leadership, and continued to follow an independent foreign policy.

In 1981 François Mitterand succeeded Giscard d'Estaing. He inherited a troubled economy. During his first year Mitterand tried to revitalize economic growth, granted wage hikes, reduced the work week, expanded paid vacations, and nationalized 11 large private companies and banks. The aim was to stimulate the economy by expanding worker purchasing power and confiscating the profits of large corporations for public investment. Loans were made abroad to finance this program. When results were poor, these foreign investors were reluctant to grant more credit. Mitterand then reversed his policy and began to cut taxes and social expenditures. By 1984, this had brought down inflation but increased unemployment.

Mitterand lost his Socialist majority in Parliament in 1986, but regained it in 1988. In 1995, an ailing Mitterand indicated he would retire at the end of his term. He died in January 1996. Out of the election of April 1995 emerged a fractured right-of-center bloc that came to coalesce around Jacques Chirac, the mayor of Paris and former two-time prime minister. Following a second-round runoff, Chirac won 52 percent of the vote. Facing a far-right challenger, Jean-Marie Le Pen, in 2002, Chirac won a decisive victory for re-election.

In Germany in November 1966, the Christian Democrats formed a so-called "great coalition" with the Social Democrats under Willy Brandt. Kurt Georg Kiesinger (1904–1988) became chancellor, and Brandt the Socialist took over as foreign minister. Brandt announced his intention to work step by step for better relations with East Germany, but found that in a coalition of two very dissimilar parties he could make no substantial progress.

Problems with the economy and the environment brought an end to Kiesinger's chancellorship and the rule of the Socialists in 1982. An organization called the Greens, which was a loosely organized coalition of environmentalists alienated from society, detracted from Socialist power. In 1982, the German voters turned to the more conservative Christian Democrats again, and Helmut Kohl became chancellor. Kohl served until 1998, when he was replaced by Social Democrat Gerhard Schroeder.

In Italy, the Christian Democrats, who were closely allied with the Roman Catholic Church, dominated the national scene. Their organization, though plagued by corruption, did provide some unity to Italian politics by supplying the prime ministers for numerous coalitions.

Italy advanced economically. Natural gas and some oil was discovered in the north and the Po valley area especially benefited. Unfortunately, business efficiency found no parallel in the government or civil service. Italy suffered from terrorism, kidnappings, and assassinations by extreme radical groups such as the Red Brigades. These agitators hoped to create conditions favorable to the overthrow of the democratic constitution. The most notorious terrorist act was the assassination in 1978 of Aldo Moro (1916–1978), a respected Christian Democratic leader.

In 1983, Bettino Craxi (Socialist) became prime minister at the head of an uneasy coalition that lasted four years—the longest single government in postwar Italian history. By the 1990s Italian industry and its economy had advanced to a point where Italy was a leading center in high-tech industry, fashion, design, and banking, but instability continued to mark Italian politics. Corruption within a system dominated by the Christian Democrats resulted in criminal trials in the 1990s that sent a number of high government officials to prison. In 1993 the electoral system for the Senate was changed from proportional representation to one that gives power to the majority vote-getting party. The 1994 elections for Parliament brought to power the charismatic, conservative Silvio Berlusconi and his *Forzia Italia* ("Let's go, Italy") movement.

In Portugal, Europe's longest right-wing dictatorship came to an end in September 1968, when a stroke incapacitated Antonio Salazar, who died two years later. A former collaborator, Marcelo Caetano (1906–1980), became prime minister, and an era of change began. Censorship was relaxed and some freedom was given to political parties.

In April 1974, the Caetano regime was overthrown and a "junta of national salvation" took over, headed by General Spinola, who later retired and went into exile. Portugal went through a succession of governments. Its African colonies of Mozambique and Angola were finally granted independence in 1975. Portugal joined the Common Market in 1986.

Spain's Francisco Franco, who had been ruler of a fascist regime since the end of the Civil War in 1939, held on until he was close to 70. He then designated the Bourbon prince, Juan Carlos, to be his successor. In 1975, Franco relinquished power and died three weeks later. Juan Carlos proved an able leader and took the country from dictatorship to constitutional monarchy. Basque and Catalan separatist movements, which had caused trouble for so long, were temporarily appeased by the granting of limited local autonomy. Spain also entered the European Community in 1986.

Under the Maastricht Treaties of 1991, all members of the EC began measured steps toward an economic and political union that would ultimately have its own common currency. In 1996, the 12 member nations of the European Union accounted for one-fifth of world trade.

REVIEW QUESTIONS

1. Renaissance Humanism was a threat to the Church because it

   (A) espoused atheism.

   (B) denounced scholasticism.

   (C) denounced neo-Platonism.

   (D) emphasized a return to the original sources of Christianity.

2. *Defense of the Seven Sacraments* was a tract

   (A) written by Thomas More in which the Church is attacked because of its sacramental theology.

   (B) written by Zwingli which argued that the Eucharist was a symbolic reenactment of the Last Supper.

   (C) in which Luther called upon the German nobility to accept responsibility for cleansing Christianity of the abuses which had developed within the Church.

   (D) written by Henry VIII in which the Roman Catholic Church's position on sacramental theology was supported.

3. Erasmus of Rotterdam was the author of

   (A) *The Praise of Folly.*   (C) *Utopia.*

   (B) *The Birth of Venus.*   (D) *The Prince.*

4. The Henrician reaffirmation of Catholic theology was made in the

   (A) Ten Articles of Faith.

   (B) Six Articles of Faith.

   (C) Forty-two Articles of Faith.

   (D) Act of Supremacy.

5. The Peace of Augsburg

    (A) recognized that Lutheranism was the true interpretation of Christianity.

    (B) recognized the principle that the religion of the leader would determine the religion of the people.

    (C) denounced the Papacy and Charles V.

    (D) resulted in the recognition of Lutheranism, Calvinism, and Catholicism.

6. The Catholic Counter-Reformation included all of the following EXCEPT

    (A) the *Index of Prohibited Books*.

    (B) the Council of Trent.

    (C) a more assertive Papacy.

    (D) a willingness to negotiate non-doctrinal issues with reformers.

7. Where did the Saint Bartholomew's Day Massacre occur?

    (A) France   (C) Spain

    (B) England   (D) The Netherlands

8. The Price Revolution of the 16th century was caused by

    (A) the establishment of monopolies.

    (B) the importation of silver and gold into the European economy.

    (C) a shortage of labor.

    (D) the wars of religion caused by the Reformation.

9. The Peace of Westphalia (1648)

    (A) transferred Louisiana from France to Britain.

    (B) recognized the independence of the Netherlands.

    (C) recognized the unity of the German Empire.

    (D) was a triumph of the Hapsburg polity to unity.

10. Sir Isaac Newton's intellectual synthesis was advanced in

    (A) *Principia*.

    (B) *Discourse on Method*.

    (C) *Novum Organum*.

    (D) *Three Laws of Planetary Motion*.

11. Richelieu served as "Prime Minister" to

    (A) Louis XII.

    (B) Henry IV.

    (C) Louis XIV.

    (D) Louis XIII.

12. In the Edict of Fontainebleau, Louis XIV

    (A) abrogated the Edict of Nantes.

    (B) abrogated the Edict of Potsdam.

    (C) announced his divorce from Catherine de Médici.

    (D) denounced Cardinal Mazarin.

13. In order to seize the Russian throne, Peter the Great had to overthrow his sister

    (A) Theodora.

    (B) Natalia.

    (C) Sophia.

    (D) Catherine.

14. Peter the Great's principal foreign policy achievement was

    (A) the acquisition of ports on the Black Sea.

    (B) the acquisition of ports on the Baltic Sea.

    (C) the Russian gains in the three partitions of Poland.

    (D) the defensive alliance with England.

Unemployment
(Numbers in thousands & percentage of appropriate workforce)

	Germany		Great Britain	
1930	3,076	15.3	1,917	14.6
1932	5,575	30.1	2,745	22.5
1934	2,718	14.9	2,159	17.7
1936	2,151	11.6	1,755	14.3
1938	429	2.1	1,191	13.3

15. The chart above indicates

    (A) that Germany and Great Britain recovered from the Depression at about the same level and rate.

    (B) that Hitler's Germany reduced unemployment at a remarkable rate during the period from 1936 and 1938.

(C)   that Britain was complacent about its double-digit unemployment during the 1930s.

(D)   that the German economic system was superior to that of Great Britain.

16.   A moderate proposal which called on France to adopt a political system similar to Great Britain was an element espoused by Montesquieu in

(A)   *The Social Contract.*

(B)   *The Spirit of the Laws.*

(C)   *The Encyclopédie.*

(D)   *The Declaration of the Rights of Man and the Citizen.*

17.   Which of the following chronological sequences on the French Revolution is correct?

(A)   Directory, Consulate, Legislative Assembly

(B)   Legislative Assembly, Convention, Directory

(C)   Convention, Consulate, Directory

(D)   National Assembly, Convention, Directory

18.   Thomas Hobbes' political philosophy can be most clearly identified with the thought of which of the following?

(A)   Rousseau   (C)   Quesnay

(B)   Voltaire   (D)   Montesquieu

19.   Who was the most important enlightened political ruler of the 18th century?

(A)   Catherine the Great   (C)   Maria Theresa

(B)   Louis XV   (D)   Frederick the Great

20.   The reaction to the Peterloo Massacre was characteristic of the conservative policies advanced by the British government under

(A)   George Canning.   (C)   Lord Melbourne.

(B)   Robert Peel.   (D)   Lord Liverpool.

21.   The Factory Act of 1833

(A)   established the five-day work week in Britain.

(B)   eliminated child labor in the mining of coal and iron.

(C)   required employers to provide comprehensive medical coverage for all employees.

(D)   alleviated some of the abuses of child labor in the textile industry.

22.   The Anglo-French Entente (also known as the Entente Cordiale)

(A)   was a defensive treaty directed at containing German expansion in Europe.

(B)   was a defensive treaty directed at containing German expansion overseas.

(C)   resolved Anglo-French colonial disputes in Egypt and Morocco.

(D)   was a 19th century agreement which ended the diplomatic isolation of Britain.

23.   Who was the most prominent British advocate for the abolition of slavery during the early 19th century?

(A)   William Pitt the Younger

(B)   the Duke of Wellington

(C)   William Wilberforce

(D)   William Wordsworth

24.   English Utilitarianism was identified with the phrase

(A)   all power to the people.

(B)   from each according to his labor, to each according to his need.

(C)   universal reason.

(D)   the greatest good for the greatest number.

25.   An economic philosophy identified with "bullionism" and the need to maintain a favorable balance of trade was

(A)   Utopian Socialism.   (C)   Capitalism.

(B)   Marxism.   (D)   Mercantilism.

26.   Which British Prime Minister was closely associated with the Irish Home Rule bill?

(A)   Benjamin Disraeli   (C)   Lord Salisbury

(B)   William Gladstone   (D)   Joseph Chamberlain

27. The Balfour Declaration (1917)

    (A) denounced the use of chemicals by the Germans on the Western Front.

    (B) was a pledge of British support for the future.

    (C) was a mediation effort to resolve the Anglo-Irish crisis.

    (D) was an attempt to persuade the United States to abandon its neutrality.

28. The Boulanger Crisis

    (A) was a left-wing attempt engineered by Leon Gambetta to overthrow the Third French Republic.

    (B) involved a financial scandal associated with raising funds to build the Panama Canal.

    (C) was caused by a right-wing scheme to overthrow the Third French Republic and install General Georges Boulanger as the political leader.

    (D) broke when the Dreyfus affair became known to the French press.

29. All of the following were plots against Elizabeth I EXCEPT

    (A) the Babington Plot.   (C) the Ridolfi Plot.

    (B) the Throckmorton Plot.   (D) the Wisbech Stirs.

30. The map below indicates the partition of Africa in what year?

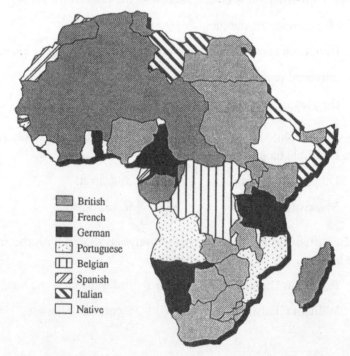

British
French
German
Portuguese
Belgian
Spanish
Italian
Native

(A)   1815   (C)   1870

(B)   1914   (D)   1960

31.   The French essayist Montaigne was representative of which intellectual movement?

(A)   Enlightenment   (C)   Positivism

(B)   Baroque   (D)   Utopian Socialism

32.   The Hundred Days was

(A)   the label given to the reactionary period which followed the Manchester riots in Britain.

(B)   an unsuccessful attempt by Napoleon to restore himself as a credible European leader.

(C)   the worst phase of the Reign of Terror.

(D)   a period which witnessed British defeats in Africa and the Low Countries.

33.   Jeremy Bentham, James Mill, and John Stuart Mill were

(A)   Positivists.   (C)   Utilitarians.

(B)   Romantic Idealists.   (D)   Utopian Socialists.

34.   The Russian blockade of Berlin in 1948–49 was a reaction to

(A)   the unification of the British, French, and American zones into West Germany.

(B)   the Truman Doctrine.

(C)   the Marshall Plan.

(D)   the formation of NATO.

35.   The Heptarchy consisted of the following Anglo-Saxon states:

(A)   Essex, Wessex, Sussex, Kent, East Anglia, Mercia, and Northumbria

(B)   West Cornwall, Essex, Wessex, Sussex, East Anglia, Mercia, and Northumbria

(C)   Wales, West Anglia, Kent, Essex, Wessex, Sussex, and Mercia

(D)   The Danelaw, Cumbria, Essex, Wessex, Sussex, Kent, and East Anglia

36. All of the following were contributors in the Realist-Nominalist Controversy EXCEPT

    (A) Peter Abelard.   (C) Albertus Magnus.

    (B) Peter Lombard.   (D) Hildebrand.

37. The reasons for the formation of the Delian League included

    I.   the Greek victory over Xerxes.

    II.   the Athenian intent to develop a defensive and offensive alliance against Persia.

    III. Athenian strategy to control all of the eastern Mediterranean.

    IV.   an imminent Spartan threat to Athens.

    V.   more than twenty years of crisis caused by Persian aggression.

    (A) I and II only   (C) II and III only

    (B) I, II, and III only   (D) I, II, and V only

38. "Peasant" or "public" uprisings broke out in all of the following places on the dates listed EXCEPT

    (A) France in 1358.   (C) Flanders in 1302.

    (B) Sicily in 1282.   (D) Holy Roman Empire in 1190.

39. During the late 2nd century BCE, Roman political life was dominated by the

    (A) First Triumvirate.

    (B) prevailing political parties; *Populares, Optimates*, and *Equites*.

    (C) Gracchi.

    (D) end of the Punic Wars.

40. After the death of Alexander, which of the following Hellenistic kingdoms emerged?

    I.   Antigonid Macedonia

    II.   Seleucid Asia

    III. Ptolemaic Egypt

    IV.   Bactria

    V.   India

(A)   I and II only   (C)   I, II, III, and IV only

(B)   I, II, and III only   (D)   I, III, and IV only

Answer Key

1.	(D)	11.	(D)	21.	(D)	31.	(B)
2.	(D)	12.	(A)	22.	(C)	32.	(B)
3.	(A)	13.	(C)	23.	(C)	33.	(C)
4.	(B)	14.	(B)	24.	(D)	34.	(A)
5.	(B)	15.	(B)	25.	(D)	35.	(A)
6.	(D)	16.	(B)	26.	(B)	36.	(D)
7.	(A)	17.	(B)	27.	(B)	37.	(D)
8.	(B)	18.	(B)	28.	(C)	38.	(D)
9.	(B)	19.	(D)	29.	(D)	39.	(B)
10.	(A)	20.	(D)	30.	(B)	40.	(B)

Detailed Explanations

1.   **(D)**   Renaissance Humanism was a threat to the Church because it (D) emphasized a return to the original sources of Christianity—the Bible and the writings of the Fathers of Church. In that light, the humanists tended to ignore or denounce the proceedings of Church councils and pontiffs during the Middle Ages. While many Renaissance humanists denounced scholasticism, there was no inherent opposition to it and many retained support of the late Medieval philosophy. Renaissance humanism did not espouse atheism nor did it advance an amoral philosophy; it tended to advance a neo-Platonism through the writings of such individuals as Pico Della Mirandola and Marsiglio.

2.   **(D)**   The *Defense of the Seven Sacraments* was a tract (D) written by Henry VIII in which the Roman Catholic Church's position on sacramental theology was supported. This 1521 publication repudiated Luther's views on the sacraments which he advanced in pamphlets during the preceding year. While some earlier authorities have asserted that the real author of the tract was Thomas More (A), contemporary scholarship has affirmed that, while More no doubt provided assistance, authorship should be attributed to Henry VIII. Zwingli (B) did maintain that the Eucharist was a symbolic reenactment of the Last Supper but he did not write this tract. Obviously, Luther (C), to whom it was directed, was not the author.

3.   **(A)**   Erasmus of Rotterdam was the author of (A) *The Praise of Folly* which was a criticism of the ambitions of the clergy. *The Birth of Venus* (B) was not a literary work. Thomas More was the author of *Utopia* (C); Niccolo Machiavelli wrote (D) *The Prince*.

4.   **(B)**   The Henrican reaffirmation of the Catholic Theology was made in the (B) Six Articles of Faith of 1539. In response to mounting criticism and the vague (A) Ten Articles of Faith (1536) and the dissolution of the monasteries, Henry VIII retreated from the movement toward Protestantism. The (D) Act of Supremacy was passed by the Reformation Parliament to decree and enforce Henry VIII's authority over the Church in England. The Forty-two Articles of Faith (C) was a statement of Protestant doctrines developed by Thomas Cranmer during the early 1550s.

5.   **(B)**   The Peace of Augsburg (1555) (B) recognized the principle that the re-ligion of the leader would determine the religion of the people; it was a major victory for Lutheranism and a defeat of the Hapsburg aspirations to effectively control the Holy Roman Empire. Lutheranism (A) was not recognized as the true interpretation of Christianity. Calvinism (D) was not recognized until the Peace of Westphalia in 1648; (C) Charles V and the Papacy were negotiators in formulating the Peace of Augsburg.

6.   **(D)**   The Catholic Counter-Reformation did not include (D) a willingness to negotiate non-doctrinal issues with reformers; indeed, the Catholic Church con-sidered all confrontational issues to be doctrinal. The Council of Trent (B) was convened in three sessions from 1545 to 1564 and reaffirmed traditional Catholic doctrines; the papacy (C) became more assertive as can be seen in the issuing of the *Index of Prohibited Books* (A) in 1558–59.

7.   **(A)**   The St. Bartholomew's Day Massacre occurred in 1572 in (A) France; it was the work of Queen Catherine De Medici and involved the execution of thou-sands of French Huguenots during the subsequent months. Obviously, this event did not transpire in (B) England, (C) Spain, or (D) the Netherlands.

8.   **(B)**   The Price Revolution of the 16th century was caused by (B) the im-portation of silver and gold into the European economy; the influx of specie from Latin America resulted in eliminating the scarcity of money—the result was a gen-eral fourfold increase in prices. The establishment of monopolies (A) was an im-portant element in 17th century mercantilism. While there were occasional labor shortages (C) and the wars of religion (D) did not disrupt economic activities, these developments did not have any substantive impact on the price revolution.

9.   **(B)**   The Peace of Westphalia (1648) (B) recognized the independence of the Netherlands and Switzerland. Louisiana (A) was not transferred to Britain, and the Hapsburg plan (D) and (C) for a unified central Europe was destroyed.

10.   **(A)**   Sir Isaac Newton's intellectual synthesis was advanced in (A) *Principia* in 1687; he established scientism as a credible alternative to preceding intellectual approaches and methods. *Discourse on Method* (B) was written by René Descartes in 1637; *Novum Organum* (C) was a work by Francis Bacon which addressed the issue of empiricism; Kepler developed the Three Laws of Planetary Motion (D).

11.   **(D)**   Richelieu served as "Prime Minister" to (D) Louis XIII. For over two decades during the turbulence of the Thirty Years' War and the La Rochelle crisis with the Huguenots, Cardinal Richelieu administered France for Louis XIII. Henry

IV (B) was Louis XIII's father; Louis XIV (C) was his son. Louis XII (A) was an earlier French monarch.

12. **(A)** In the Edict of Fontainebleau (1685), Louis XIV (A) abrogated the Edict of Nantes of 1598 in which Henry IV had to extend some religious liberties to French Protestants. Fontainebleau directed that all Frenchmen would conform to Catholicism. The Edict of Potsdam (1686) (B) was issued by Elector Frederick William of Brandenburg-Prussia; it invited French Protestants to migrate to Brandenburg. The Fontainebleau decree was not related to (C) Catherine de Medici or (D) Cardinal Mazarin.

13. **(C)** In order to seize the Russian throne, Peter the Great had to overthrow (1689) his sister (C) Sophia. His mother, Natalia (B), served as regent until 1694 when Peter took over the government. Catherine (D) was a Russian leader in the 18th century. (A) Theodora was not a Romanov ruler.

14. **(B)** Peter the Great's principal foreign policy achievement was (B) the acquisition of ports on the Baltic Sea. His efforts to acquire ports on the Black Sea (A) were not realized; later Catherine the Great would expand in this area at the expense of the Ottoman Turks. The partitions of Poland (C) occurred after Peter's death; Russia did not enter into any alliance with England (D) during this period.

15. **(B)** This chart indicates (B) that Hitler's Germany reduced unemployment at a remarkable rate during the period from 1936 to 1938; the fascist economic controls facilitated this development. (A), (C), and (D) are incorrect; the German economy was not "superior" to Britain's nor was Britain content with excessive unemployment—while there is much to criticize about the manner in which the Labour and Conservative parties handled economic recovery, one must remember that free economies are naturally more difficult to direct than state controlled economic systems.

16. **(B)** A moderate proposal which called on France to adopt a political system similar to that of Great Britain was an element espoused by Montesquieu in (B) *The Spirit of the Laws*. *The Social Contract* (A) was written by Jean-Jacques Rousseau; *The Encyclopédie* (C) was by Denis Diderot; *The Declaration of the Rights of Man and the Citizen* (D) was produced by the National Assembly in August 1789.

17. **(B)** The correct chronological sequence is (B) Legislative Assembly (1791–92), Convention (1792–95), and Directory (1795–99). The National Assembly existed from 1789 to 1791; the Consulate from 1799 to 1804; and the Empire from 1804 to 1814.

18. **(B)** Thomas Hobbes' political philosophy can be most clearly identified with the thought of (B) Voltaire. Voltaire maintained that Enlightened Despotism would be the best form of government for France; this position concurs with the Hobbesian view that people need to be governed, not government by the people; (C) Quesnay's program was similar though not as directly related. (A) Rousseau and (D) Montesquieu entertained political theories which were more revolutionary in the context of sovereign power and the exercise of that power.

19. **(D)**   The most prominent enlightened political ruler of the 18th century was (D) Frederick the Great of Prussia. He had a genuine interest in enlightened government and introduced a wide range of reforms. Catherine the Great (A) of Russia considered herself enlightened but her barbarism did not support that claim. Louis XV (B) and Maria Theresa (C) were opposed to the thought of the enlightenment.

20. **(D)**   The reaction to the Peterloo Massacre was characteristic of the conservative policies advanced by the British government under (D) Lord Liverpool. While George Canning (A) and Robert Peel (B) were involved in the government, they were not very influential at this time. Melbourne (C) became Prime Minister during the 1830s.

21. **(D)**   The Factory Act of 1833 (D) alleviated some of the abuses of child labor in the textile industry. The five-day work week (A) did not become a reality until the 20th century; reforms in the use of children in mining and heavy industry (B) were not implemented until later in the 19th century; employers were never required (C) to provide comprehensive medical coverage for all employees.

22. **(C)**   The Anglo-French Entente (also known as the Entente Cordiale) (C) resolved Anglo-French colonial disputes in Egypt and Morocco; northeast Africa (Egypt and the Sudan) was recognized as a British sphere of influence, northwest Africa (Morocco and Algeria) was recognized as a French sphere of influence. This arrangement was not (A) directed at German expansion in Europe or (B) overseas; it was signed in 1904 and therefore was not (D) a 19th century agreement.

23. **(C)**   The most prominent British advocate for the abolition of slavery during the early 19th century was (C) William Wilberforce. While Wordsworth (D) was sympathetic to abolitionism, he was not in the forefront of opposition to slavery. William Pitt the Younger (A) and the Duke of Wellington (B) were preoccupied with the Napoleonic Wars.

24. **(D)**   English Utilitarianism was identified with the phrase (D) "the greatest good for the greatest number." Jeremy Bentham, James Mill, and John Stuart Mill were prominent Utilitarians. "All power to the people" (A) and "From each according to his labor, to each according to his need" (B) were elements in Lenin's rhetoric. "Universal reason" (C) is identified with Georg Wilhelm Friedrich Hegel.

25. **(D)**   Mercantilism was an economic philosophy identified with "bullionism" and the need to maintain a favorable balance of trade. Utopian Socialism (A) was an early 19th century philosophy which emphasized the need for a more equitable distribution of wealth; (B) Marxism was a leftist approach to economics and politics. (C) Capitalism was the developing condition in which mercantilism operated.

26. **(B)**   The British Prime Minister who was associated closely with Irish Home Rule was (B) William Gladstone. Gladstone maintained through his four ministries that one of his principal tasks was "to pacify Ireland." Benjamin Disraeli

(A), Lord Salisbury (C), and Joseph Chamberlain (D) were not particularly interested or sympathetic to the Irish.

27.   **(B)**   The Balfour Declaration (1917) (B) was a pledge of British support for the future establishment of a Jewish state. It was not related to (A) the German use of chemicals, (C) the Anglo-Irish crisis stemming from the Easter Rebellion, or (D) American neutrality.

28.   **(C)**   The Boulanger Crisis (C) was caused by a right-wing scheme to overthrow the Third French Republic and install General Georges Boulanger as the political leader; it was supported by monarchists and other rightist enemies of the republic. It was not (A) a left-wing scheme, nor was it related to the (B) Panama Canal or (D) the Dreyfus Affair.

29.   **(D)**   While the (A) Babington Plot, (B) the Throckmorton Plot, and (C) the Ridolfi Plot were attempts to overthrow Elizabeth I, the Wisbech Stirs of the late 1590s was a controversy among Catholics over control of the outlawed English Catholic Church.

30.   **(B)**   The map indicates the partition of Africa in (B) 1914 after most of the European powers had participated in establishing colonial empires.

31.   **(B)**   The French essayist Montaigne was representative of an intellectual movement known as (B) Baroque which was an intellectual quest for a new synthesis; it was caused by the chaos of the Reformation/Counter-Reformation era. The Enlightenment (A) developed in the 18th century and constituted an elaboration on the new scientific synthesis which emerged during the 17th century. (C) Positivism and (D) Utopian Socialism were 19th century intellectual movements.

32.   **(B)**   The Hundred Days (1815) was (B) an unsuccessful attempt by Napoleon to restore himself as a credible European leader. The Hundred Days concluded in June 1815 at the Battle of Waterloo when Wellington's army defeated Napoleon. Obviously, the Hundred Days did not relate to (A) the reactionary period in Britain following the Manchester riots, (C) the Reign of Terror, or (D) British defeats in Africa and the Low Countries.

33.   **(C)**   Jeremy Bentham, James Mill, and John Stuart Mill were (C) Utilitarians who argued the case "the greatest good for the greatest number." Auguste Comte established (A) Positivism; Fichte and Hegel were German Romantic Idealists (B); Robert Owen and Charles Fourier were Utopian Socialists (D).

34.   **(A)**   The Russian blockade of Berlin in 1948–49 was a reaction to (A) the unification of the British, French, and American zones into West Germany. While the (B) Truman Doctrine was directed at preventing communist victories in Greece and Turkey, and the Marshall Plan (C) was designed to assist in accelerating the economic recovery of Europe, they were not the direct causes of the blockade. NATO (D) was formed after the blockade began.

35. **(A)** During the 6th century, the Heptarchy of Anglo-Saxon England included Essex, Wessex, Sussex, Kent, East Anglia, Mercia, and Northumbria. By the end of the 6th century, Kent emerged as the primary power in Britain. West Cornwall (B), Wales (C), the Danelaw, and Cumbria (D) were not organized political entities during the 6th century and so were not part of the Heptarchy.

36. **(D)** Hildebrand (D) was a medieval church reformer who became pope. Peter Abelard (A) (*Sic at Non*), Peter Lombard (B) (*Four Books of Sentences*) and Albertus Magnus (C) were all significant contributors to the Realist-Nominalist Controversy. While this controversy was initiated over Plato's Doctrine of Ideas, it was transformed into a discussion of whether truth obtained through reason was reconcilable with truth obtained through revelation.

37. **(D)** The Delian League was established in 477 BCE after more than two decades of war (V) with Persian armies led by Darius and Xerxes (I). Under Athenian leadership, the Delian League was intended to provide a defensive and offensive alliance directed against Persia. Not until later was the Delian League interpreted as an Athenian attempt to dominate the Greek, not Mediterranean, world (III) for its own gain. The Spartan threat to Athens (IV) did not materialize until the early years of the Peloponnesian War in the late 430s.

38. **(D)** In 1190, the Holy Roman Empire (D) was preoccupied with the Third Crusade and did not experience any peasant uprisings. A popular uprising known as the Jacquerie broke out in France in 1358 (A). The "Sicilian Vespers" took place in Sicily in 1282 (B) when the people rebelled against French rule, and the peasants and laborers in Flanders in 1302 (C) followed the Sicilian example and expelled French rulers from Flanders.

39. **(B)** During the late 2nd century BCE, Roman political life was dominated by the prevailing political parties: Populares, the so-called "people's party"; Optimates, the "best men"; and the Equites, rich knights (B). The First Triumvirate (A) did not appear until the next century. The Gracchi (C), Tiberius and Gaius Gracchus, were significant public figures but did not hold substantive power. The Punic Wars (D) concluded in 146 BCE; they did not dominate Roman political life.

40. **(B)** After Alexander the Great's death in 323 BCE, his empire was divided into three major units: Antigonid Macedonia (I), with a monarchy limited by an armed population; Seleucid Asia (II), with a monarchy restricted by autonomous cities; and Ptolemaic Egypt (III), with an unrestricted monarchy. As the Seleucid Empire later disintegrated, Bactria (IV) emerged as a buffer against the barbarians of the East. Most of India (V) was not included in Alexander's empire, although he did penetrate northwest India during his campaigns.

CHAPTER 6

UNITED STATES HISTORY

AMERICAN HISTORY: THE COLONIAL PERIOD (1500–1763)

The Age of Exploration

The Treaty of Tordesillas (1494) drew a line dividing the land in the New World between Spain and Portugal. Lands east of the line were Portuguese. As a result, Brazil eventually became a Portuguese colony, while Spain maintained claims to the rest of the Americas.

To conquer the Americas, the Spanish monarchs used their powerful army, led by independent Spanish adventurers known as conquistadores. The European diseases they unwittingly carried with them devastated the local Native American populations, who had no immunities against such diseases.

Spain administered its new holdings as an autocratic, rigidly controlled empire in which everything was to benefit the parent country. The Spaniards developed a system of large manors or estates (encomiendas), with Indian slaves ruthlessly managed for the benefit of the conquistadores. The encomienda system was later replaced by the similar but somewhat milder hacienda system. As the Indian population died from overwork and European diseases, Spaniards began importing African slaves to supply their labor needs.

English and French Beginnings

In 1497, the Italian John Cabot (Giovanni Caboto, ca. 1450–1499), sailing under the sponsorship of the king of England in search of a Northwest Passage (a water route to the Orient through or around the North American continent), became the first European since the Vikings more than four centuries earlier to reach the main-land of North America, which he claimed for England. Beginning in 1534, Jacques Cartier (1491–1557), authorized by the king of France, mounted three expeditions to the area of the St. Lawrence River, which he believed might be the hoped for Northwest Passage. He explored up the river as far as the site of Montreal.

When the English finally began colonization, commercial capitalism in England had advanced to the point that the English efforts were supported by private rather than government funds, allowing English colonists to enjoy greater freedom from government interference.

The Beginnings of Colonization

Two groups of merchants gained charters from James I, Queen Elizabeth's suc-cessor. One group of merchants was based in London and received a charter to North America between what are now the Hudson and the Cape Fear rivers. The other was based in Plymouth and was granted the right to colonize in North Amer-ica from the Potomac to the northern border of present-day Maine. They were called the Virginia Company of London and the Virginia Company of Plymouth, respectively. They were joint-stock companies that raised their capital by the sale of shares of stock.

The Virginia Company of London settled Jamestown in 1607. It became the first permanent English settlement in North America. During the early years of James-town, the majority of the settlers died of starvation, various diseases, or hostile ac-tions by Native Americans. The colony's survival remained in doubt for a number of years.

Impressed by the potential profits from tobacco growing, King James I was de-termined to have Virginia for himself. In 1624, he revoked the London Company's charter and made Virginia a royal colony. This pattern was followed throughout colonial history; both company colonies and proprietary colonies tended eventu-ally to become royal colonies.

The French opened a lucrative trade in fur with the Native Americans. In 1608, Samuel de Champlain established a trading post in Quebec, from which the rest of what became New France eventually spread. French exploration and settlement spread through the Great Lakes region and the valleys of the Mississippi and Ohio rivers. French settlements in the Midwest were generally forts and trading posts serving the fur trade.

In 1609, Holland sent an Englishman named Henry Hudson (d. 1611) to search for a Northwest Passage. In this endeavor, Hudson discovered the river that bears his name. Arrangements were made to trade with the Iroquois for furs. In 1624,

Dutch trading outposts were established on Manhattan Island (New Amsterdam) and at the site of present-day Albany (Fort Orange).

Many Englishmen came from England for religious reasons. For the most part, these fell into two groups, Puritans and Separatists. Though similar in many respects to the Puritans, the Separatists believed the Church of England was beyond saving and so felt they must separate from it.

Led by William Bradford (1590–1657), a group of Separatists departed in 1620, having obtained from the London Company a charter to settle just south of the Hudson River. Driven by storms, their ship, the *Mayflower*, made landfall at Cape Cod in Massachusetts. This, however, put them outside the jurisdiction of any established government; and so before going ashore they drew up and signed the Mayflower Compact, establishing a foundation for orderly government based on the consent of the governed. After a number of years of hard work, they were able to buy out the investors who had originally financed their voyage, and thus gain greater autonomy.

The Puritans were far more numerous than the Separatists. Charles I determined in 1629 to persecute the Puritans aggressively and to rule without the Puritan-dominated Parliament. In 1629, they chartered a joint-stock company called the Massachusetts Bay Company. The charter neglected to specify where the company's headquarters should be located. Taking advantage of this unusual omission, the Puritans determined to make their headquarters in the colony itself, 3,000 miles from meddlesome royal officials.

Puritans saw their colony not as a place to do whatever might strike one's fancy, but as a place to serve God and build His kingdom. Dissidents would only be tolerated insofar as they did not interfere with the colony's mission.

One such dissident was Roger Williams (ca. 1603–1683). When his activities became disruptive he was asked to leave the colony. He fled to the wilderness around Narragansett Bay, bought land from the Indians, and founded the settlement of Providence (1636).

Another dissident was Anne Hutchinson (1591–1643), who openly taught things contrary to Puritan doctrine. She was banished from the colony. She also migrated to the area around Narragansett Bay and with her followers founded Portsmouth (1638).

In 1663, Charles II, having recently been restored to the throne moved to reward eight of the noblemen who had helped him regain the crown by granting them a charter for all the lands lying south of Virginia and north of Spanish Florida. The new colony was called Carolina, after the king.

In 1664, Charles gave his brother James, Duke of York, title to all the Dutch lands in America, provided James conquered them first. New Amsterdam fell almost without a shot and became New York.

The Colonial World

New England enjoyed a much more stable and well-ordered society than did the Chesapeake colonies. Puritans placed great importance on the family, which in their society was highly patriarchal. Puritans also placed great importance on the ability to read, since they believed everyone should be able to read the Bible. As a result, New England was ahead of the other colonies educationally and enjoyed extremely widespread literacy. Since New England's climate and soil were unsuited to large-scale farming, the region developed a prosperous economy based on small farming, home industry, fishing, and especially trade and a large shipbuilding industry. Boston became a major international port.

On the bottom rung of Southern society were the black slaves. During the first half of the 17th century, blacks in the Chesapeake made up only a small percentage of the population, and were treated more or less as indentured servants. Between 1640 and 1670 this gradually changed, and blacks came to be seen and treated as life-long chattel slaves whose status would be inherited by their children. By 1750, they composed 30 to 40 percent of the Chesapeake population.

While North Carolina tended to follow Virginia in its economic and social development (although with fewer great planters and more small farmers), South Carolina developed a society even more dominated by large plantations and chattel slavery.

Beginning around 1650, British authorities began to take more interest in regulating American trade for the benefit of the mother country. A key idea that underlay this policy was the concept of mercantilism. Each nation's goal was to export more than it imported (i.e., to have a "favorable balance of trade"). To achieve their goals, mercantilists believed economic activity should be regulated by the government. Colonies could fit into England's mercantilist scheme by providing staple crops, such as rice, tobacco, sugar, and indigo, and raw materials, such as timber, that England would otherwise have been forced to import from other countries. Parliament passed a series of Navigation Acts (1651, 1660, 1663, and 1673) to help accomplish these goals.

Pennsylvania was founded as a refuge for Quakers. One of a number of radical religious sects that had sprung up about the time of the English Civil War, the Quakers held many controversial beliefs. They believed all persons had an "inner light" which allowed them to commune directly with God, and therefore they placed little importance on the Bible. They were also pacifists and declined to show customary deference to those who were considered to be their social superiors.

Delaware, though at first part of Pennsylvania, was granted a separate legislature by Penn, but until the American Revolution, Pennsylvania's proprietary governors also functioned as governors of Delaware.

The Eighteenth Century

America's population continued to grow rapidly, both from natural increases due to prosperity and a healthy environment and from large-scale immigration, not only of English but also of other groups such as Scots-Irish and Germans.

It was decided to found a colony as a buffer between South Carolina and Spanish-held Florida. In 1732, a group of British philanthropists, led by General James Oglethorpe (1696–1785), obtained a charter for such a colony, which was named Georgia.

England and France continued on a collision course, as France determined to take complete control of the Ohio Valley and western Pennsylvania. British authorities ordered colonial governors to resist this. George Washington (1732–1799), a young major of the Virginia militia, was sent to western Pennsylvania but was forced by superior numbers to fall back on his hastily built Fort Necessity and then to surrender.

While Washington skirmished with the French, delegates of seven colonies met in Albany, New York, to discuss common plans for defense. Delegate Benjamin Franklin proposed a plan for an intercolonial government. While the other colonies showed no support for the idea, it was an important precedent for the concept of uniting in the face of a common enemy.

Between 1756 and 1763 Britain and France fought the Seven Years' War (also known as the French and Indian War). By the Treaty of Paris of 1763, Britain gained all of Canada and all of what is now the United States east of the Mississippi River. France lost all of its North American holdings.

THE AMERICAN REVOLUTION (1763–1787)

The Coming of the American Revolution

In 1763, George Grenville (1712–1770) became prime minister and set out to solve some of the empire's more pressing problems. Chief among these was the large national debt incurred in the recent war.

In 1764, Grenville pushed through Parliament the Sugar Act (also known as the Revenue Act), which aimed at raising revenue by taxing goods imported by the Americans.

The Stamp Act (1765) imposed a direct tax on Americans for the first time. It required Americans to purchase revenue stamps on everything from newspapers to legal documents, and would have created an impossible drain on hard currency in the colonies. Americans reacted first with restrained and respectful petitions and pamphlets in which they pointed out that "taxation without representation is tyranny." From there, resistance progressed to stronger protests that eventually became violent.

In October 1765, delegates from nine colonies met as the Stamp Act Congress, and passed moderate resolutions against the act, asserting that Americans could not be taxed without the consent of their representatives. The Stamp Act Congress showed that representatives of the colonies could work together, and gave political leaders in the various colonies a chance to become acquainted with each other.

Colonial merchants' boycott of British goods spread throughout the colonies and had a powerful effect on British merchants and manufacturers, who began clamoring for the act's repeal.

Meanwhile, the fickle King George III had dismissed Grenville over an unrelated disagreement and replaced him with a cabinet headed by Charles Lord Rockingham (1730–1782). In March 1766 Parliament repealed the Stamp Act. At the same time, however, it passed the Declaratory Act, which claimed the power to tax or make laws for the Americans "in all cases whatsoever."

The Rockingham ministry was replaced with a cabinet dominated by Chancellor of the Exchequer Charles Townshend (1725–1767). In 1766, Parliament passed his program of taxes on items imported into the colonies. These taxes came to be known as the Townshend duties.

American reaction was at first slow, but the sending of troops, aroused them to resistance. Nonimportation was again instituted, and soon British merchants were calling on Parliament to repeal the acts. In March 1770, Parliament, under the new prime minister, Frederick Lord North (1737–1792), repealed all of the taxes except that on tea, which was retained to prove Parliament had the right to tax the colonies if it so desired.

A relative peace was brought to an end by the Tea Act of 1773. In desperate financial condition—partially because the Americans were buying smuggled Dutch tea rather than the taxed British product—the British East India Company sought and obtained from Parliament concessions that allowed it to ship tea directly to the colonies rather than only by way of Britain. The result would be that East India Company tea, even with the tax, would be cheaper than smuggled Dutch tea. The colonists would thus, it was hoped, buy the tea, tax and all. The East India Company would be saved, and the Americans would be tacitly accepting Parliament's right to tax them.

The Americans, however, proved resistant to this approach; rather than seem to admit Parliament's right to tax, they vigorously resisted the cheaper tea. Various methods, including tar and feathers, were used to prevent the collection of the tax on tea. In most ports, Americans did not allow the tea to be landed.

In Boston, however, pro-British Governor Thomas Hutchinson (1711–1780) forced a confrontation by ordering Royal Navy vessels to prevent the tea ships from leaving the harbor. After 20 days, this would, by law, result in the cargoes being sold at auction and the tax paid. The night before the time was to expire, December 16, 1773, Bostonians thinly disguised as Native Americans boarded the ships and threw the tea into the harbor.

The British responded with four acts collectively titled the Coercive Acts. First, the Boston Port Act closed the port of Boston to all trade until local citizens would agree to pay for the lost tea (they would not). Secondly, the Massachusetts Government Act greatly increased the power of Massachusetts's royal governor at the expense of the legislature. Thirdly, the Administration of Justice Act provided that royal officials accused of crimes in Massachusetts could be tried elsewhere, where chances of acquittal might be greater. Finally, a strengthened Quartering Act allowed the new governor, General Thomas Gage (1721–1787), to quarter his troops anywhere, including unoccupied private homes.

The War for Independence

The British government paid little attention to the First Continental Congress, having decided to teach the Americans a military lesson. More troops were sent to Massachusetts, which was officially declared to be in a state of rebellion. Orders were sent to General Gage to arrest the leaders of the resistance, or failing that, to provoke any sort of confrontation that would allow him to turn British military might loose on the Americans.

Gage decided on a reconnaissance-in-force to find and destroy a reported stockpile of colonial arms and ammunition at Concord. Seven hundred British troops set out on this mission on the night of April 18, 1775, which resulted in skirmishes with the colonists at Lexington and Concord.

Open warfare had begun, and the myth of British invincibility was destroyed. Militia came in large numbers from all the New England colonies to join the force besieging Gage and his army in Boston. The following month the Americans tightened the noose around Boston by fortifying Breed's Hill (a spur of Bunker Hill).

The British determined to remove them by a frontal attack. Twice the British were thrown back, but they finally succeeded when the Americans ran out of ammunition. Over a thousand British soldiers were killed or wounded in what turned out to be the bloodiest battle of the war (June 17, 1775). Yet the British had gained very little and remained bottled up in Boston.

Meanwhile in May 1775, American forces under Ethan Allen (1738–1789) and Benedict Arnold (1741–1801) took Fort Ticonderoga on Lake Champlain.

While these events were taking place in New England and Canada, the Second Continental Congress met in Philadelphia in May 1775. Congress was divided into two main factions. One was composed mostly of New Englanders and leaned toward declaring independence from Britain. The other drew its strength primarily from the Middle Colonies and was not yet ready to go that far.

The Declaration of Independence was primarily the work of Thomas Jefferson (1743–1826) of Virginia. It was a restatement of political ideas by then common-place in America and showed why the former colonists felt justified in separating from Great Britain. It was formally adopted by Congress on July 4, 1776.

The British landed that summer at New York City, where they hoped to find many loyalists. Washington narrowly avoided being trapped there (an escape par-tially due to Howe's slowness). Defeated again at the Battle of Washington Heights (August 29–30, 1776) in Manhattan, Washington was forced to retreat across New Jersey with the aggressive British General Lord Charles Cornwallis (1738–1805) in pursuit.

With his victory almost complete, General Howe decided to wait until spring to finish annihilating Washington's army. Scattering his troops in small detachments so as to hold all of New Jersey, he went into winter quarters.

Washington, with his small army melting away as demoralized soldiers deserted, decided on a bold stroke. On Christmas night 1776, his army crossed the Delaware River and struck the Hessians at Trenton. The Hessians, still groggy from their hard-drinking Christmas party, were easily defeated. A few days later, Washington defeated a British force at Princeton (January 3, 1777). Much of New Jersey was regained, and Washington's army was saved from disintegration.

Hoping to weaken Britain, France began making covert shipments of arms to the Americans early in the war. Shipments from France were vital for the Ameri-cans. The American victory at Saratoga convinced the French to join openly in the war against England. Eventually, the Spanish (1779) and the Dutch (1780) joined as well.

Howe was replaced by General Henry Clinton (1738–1795), who was ordered to abandon Philadelphia and march to New York. Clinton maintained New York as Britain's main base. In November 1778, the British easily conquered Georgia. Late the following year, Clinton moved on South Carolina and in May 1780 Charleston surrendered. Clinton then returned to New York, leaving Cornwallis to continue the Southern campaign.

In the west, George Rogers Clark (1752–1818), led an expedition down the Ohio River and into the area of present-day Illinois and Indiana, defeating a British force at Vincennes, Indiana, and securing the area north of the Ohio River for the United States.

In the south, Cornwallis began to move northward toward North Carolina, but on October 7, 1780, a detachment of his force was defeated by American frontiersmen at the Battle of Kings Mountain in northern South Carolina. Cornwallis unwisely moved north without bothering to secure South Carolina first. The result was that the British would no sooner leave an area than American militia or guerilla bands, such as that under Francis Marion "the Swamp Fox" (ca. 1732–1795), were once again in control.

American commander Nathaniel Greene's (1742–1786) brilliant southern strategy led to a crushing victory at Cowpens, South Carolina (January 17, 1781), by troops under Greene's subordinate, General Daniel Morgan (1736–1802) of Virginia. It also led to a near victory by Greene's own force at Guilford Court House, North Carolina (March 15, 1781).

The frustrated and impetuous Cornwallis now abandoned the southern strategy and moved north into Virginia, taking a defensive position at Yorktown. With the aid of a French fleet which took control of Chesapeake Bay and a French army which joined him in sealing off the land approaches to Yorktown, Washington succeeded in trapping Cornwallis. After three weeks of siege, Cornwallis surrendered (October 17, 1781).

News of the debacle at Yorktown brought the collapse of Lord North's ministry, and the new cabinet opened peace negotiations.

The final agreement became known as the Treaty of Paris of 1783. Its terms stipulated the following: 1) The United States was recognized as an independent nation by the major European powers, including Britain. 2) Its western boundary was set at the Mississippi River. 3) Its southern boundary was set at 31° north latitude (the northern boundary of Florida). 4) Britain retained Canada, but had to surrender Florida to Spain. 5) Private British creditors would be free to collect any debts owed by United States citizens. 6) Congress was to recommend that the states restore confiscated loyalist property.

The Creation of New Governments

After the collapse of British authority in 1775, it became necessary to form new state governments. By the end of 1777, ten new state constitutions had been formed. Most state constitutions included bills of rights—lists of things the government was not supposed to do to the people.

In the summer of 1776, Congress appointed a committee to begin devising a framework for a national government. The end result preserved the sovereignty of the states and created a very weak national government.

The Articles of Confederation provided for a unicameral Congress in which each state would have one vote, as had been the case in the Continental Congress. Executive authority under the articles would be vested in a committee of 13, with one member from each state. In order to amend the articles, the unanimous consent of all the states was required.

The Articles of Confederation government was empowered to make war, make treaties, determine the amount of troops and money each state should contribute to the war effort, settle disputes between states, admit new states to the Union, and borrow money. But it was not empowered to levy taxes, raise troops, or regulate commerce.

Ratification of the Articles of Confederation was delayed by disagreements over the future status of the lands that lay to the west of the original 13 states. Maryland, which had no such claim, withheld ratification until, in 1781, Virginia agreed to surrender its western claims to the new national government.

THE UNITED STATES CONSTITUTION (1787–1789)

Development and Ratification

As time went on, the inadequacy of the Articles of Confederation became increasingly apparent. It was decided in 1787 to call for a convention of all the states to meet in Philadelphia for the purpose of revising the Articles of Confederation.

The men who met in Philadelphia in 1787 were remarkably able, highly educated, and exceptionally accomplished. For the most part they were lawyers, merchants, and planters. Though representing individual states, most thought in national terms.

George Washington was unanimously elected to preside, and the enormous respect that he commanded helped hold the convention together through difficult times.

The delegates shared a basic belief in the innate selfishness of man, which must somehow be kept from abusing the power of government. For this purpose, the document that they finally produced contained many checks and balances, designed to prevent the government, or any one branch of the government, from gaining too much power.

Benjamin Franklin played an important role in reconciling the often heated debates and in making various suggestions that eventually helped the convention arrive at the "Great Compromise," proposed by Roger Sherman (1721–1793) and Oliver Ellsworth (1745–1807). The Great (or Connecticut) Compromise provided for a presidency, a Senate with all states represented equally (by two senators each), and a House of Representatives with representation according to population.

Another crisis involved North-South disagreement over the issue of slavery. Here also a compromise was reached. Slavery was neither endorsed nor condemned by the Constitution. Each slave was to count as three-fifths of a person for purposes of apportioning representation and direct taxation on the states (the Three-Fifths Compromise). The federal government was prohibited from stopping the importation of slaves prior to 1808.

The third major area of compromise was the nature of the presidency. The result was a strong presidency with control of foreign policy and the power to veto Congress's legislation. Should the president commit an actual crime, Congress would have the power to impeach him. Otherwise, the president would serve for a term of four years and be reelectable without limit. As a check to the possible excesses of democracy, the president was to be elected by an electoral college, in which each state would have the same number of electors as it did senators and representatives combined. The person with the second highest total in the electoral college would be vice president. If no one gained a majority in the electoral college, the president would be chosen by the House of Representatives.

The new Constitution was to take effect when nine states, through special state conventions, had ratified it. As the struggle over ratification got under way, those favoring the Constitution astutely named themselves Federalists (i.e., advocates of centralized power) and labeled their opponents Antifederalists.

By June 21, 1788, the required nine states had ratified, but the crucial states of New York and Virginia still held out. Ultimately, the promise of the addition of a bill of rights helped win the final states. In March 1789, George Washington was inaugurated as the nation's first president.

THE NEW NATION (1789–1824)

◾ The Federalist Era

Few Antifederalists were elected to Congress, and many of the new legislators had served as delegates to the Philadelphia Convention two years before.

George Washington received virtually all the votes of the presidential electors, and John Adams received the next highest number, thus becoming the vice-president. After a triumphant journey from Mount Vernon, Washington was inaugurated in New York City, the temporary seat of government (April 30, 1789).

Ten amendments were ratified by the states by the end of 1791 and became the Bill of Rights. The first nine spelled out specific guarantees of personal freedoms, and the Tenth Amendment reserved to the states all those powers not specifically withheld or granted to the federal government.

The Judiciary Act of 1789 provided for a Supreme Court with six justices, and invested it with the power to rule on the constitutional validity of state laws. It was to be the interpreter of the "supreme law of the land." A system of district courts was set up to serve as courts of original jurisdiction, and three courts of appeal were established.

Congress established three departments of the executive branch—state, treasury, and war—as well as the offices of attorney general and postmaster general.

Washington's Administration (1789–1797)

Treasury Secretary Alexander Hamilton, in his "Report on the Public Credit," proposed the funding of the national debt at face value, federal assumption of state debts, and the establishment of a national bank. In his "Report on Manufactures," Hamilton proposed an extensive program for federal stimulation of industrial development through subsidies and tax incentives. The money needed to fund these programs would come from an excise tax on distillers and from tariffs on imports.

Thomas Jefferson, Secretary of State, and others objected to the funding proposal because they believed it would enrich a small elite group at the expense of the more worthy common citizen.

Hamilton interpreted the Constitution as having vested extensive powers in the federal government. This "implied powers" stance claimed that the government was given all powers that were not expressly denied to it. This is the "broad" interpretation.

Jefferson and Madison held the view that any action not specifically permitted in the Constitution was thereby prohibited. This is the "strict" interpretation, and the Republicans opposed the establishment of Hamilton's national bank based on this view of government. The Jeffersonian supporters, primarily under the guidance of James Madison, began to organize political groups in opposition to the Federalist program. They called themselves Republicans.

The Federalists, as Hamilton's supporters were called, received their strongest support from the business and financial groups in the commercial centers of the Northeast and from the port cities of the South. The strength of the Republicans lay primarily in the rural and frontier areas of the South and West.

Foreign and Frontier Affairs

The U.S. proclaimed neutrality when France went to war with Europe in 1792, and American merchants traded with both sides. In retaliation, the British began to seize American merchant ships and force their crews into service with the British navy.

John Jay negotiated a treaty with the British that attempted to settle the conflict at sea, as well as to curtail English agitation of their Native American allies on the western borders in 1794.

In the Pinckney Treaty, ratified by the Senate in 1796, the Spanish opened the Mississippi River to American traffic and recognized the 31st parallel as the northern boundary of Florida.

Internal Problems

In 1794, western farmers refused to pay the excise tax on whiskey which formed the backbone of Hamilton's revenue program. When a group of Pennsylvania farmers terrorized the tax collectors, President Washington sent out a federalized militia force of some 15,000 men and the rebellion evaporated, thus strengthening the credibility of the young government.

John Adams' Administration (1797–1801)

In the election of 1796, John Adams was the Federalist candidate, and Thomas Jefferson the Republican. Jefferson received the second highest number of electoral votes and became vice president.

Repression and Protest

The elections in 1798 increased the Federalists' majorities in both houses of Congress and they used their "mandate" to enact legislation to stifle foreign influences. The Alien Act raised new hurdles in the path of immigrants trying to obtain citizenship, and the Sedition Act widened the powers of the Adams administration to muzzle its newspaper critics.

Republican leaders were convinced that the Alien and Sedition Acts were unconstitutional, but the process of deciding on the constitutionality of federal laws was as yet undefined. Jefferson and James Madison decided that state legislatures should have that power, and they drew up a series of resolutions which were presented to the Kentucky and Virginia legislatures. They proposed that state bodies could "nullify" federal laws within those states. These resolutions were adopted only in these two states, and so the issue died, but the principle of states' rights would have great force in later years.

The Revolution of 1800

Thomas Jefferson and Aaron Burr (1756–1836) ran on the Republican ticket against John Adams and Charles Pinckney (1746–1825) for the Federalists. The Republican candidates won handily, but both received the same number of electoral votes, thus throwing the selection of the president into the House of Representatives. After a lengthy deadlock, Alexander Hamilton threw his support to Jefferson, and Burr had to accept the vice-presidency, the result obviously intended by the electorate. Jefferson appointed James Madison as secretary of state and Albert Gallatin (1761–1849) to the treasury.

The Federalist Congress passed a new Judiciary Act early in 1801, and President Adams filled the newly created vacancies with party supporters, many of them with last-minute commissions. John Marshall (1755–1835) was then appointed chief justice of the United States Supreme Court, thus guaranteeing continuation of Federalist policies from the bench of the high court.

The Jeffersonian Era

Thomas Jefferson and his Republican followers envisioned a nation of independent farmers living under a central government that exercised a minimum of control and served merely to protect the individual liberties guaranteed by the Constitution. This agrarian paradise would be free from the industrial smoke and urban blight of Europe, and would serve as a beacon light of Enlightenment rationalism to a world searching for direction. But Jefferson presided over a nation that was growing more industrialized and urban, and which seemed to need an ever-stronger president.

Domestic Affairs

The Twelfth Amendment was adopted and ratified in 1804, ensuring that a tie vote between candidates of the same party could not again cause the confusion of the Jefferson-Burr affair.

Following the Constitutional mandate, the importation of slaves was stopped by law in 1808.

The Louisiana Purchase: An American delegation purchased the trans-Mississippi territory from Napoleon for $15 million in April 1803, even though they had no authority to buy more than the city of New Orleans.

Exploring the West: Meriwether Lewis (1774–1809) and William Clark's (1770–1838) group left St. Louis in 1804 and returned two years later with a wealth of scientific and anthropological information. At the same time, Zebulon Pike and others had been traversing the middle parts of Louisiana and mapping the land.

Madison's Administration (1809–1817)

The Election of 1808: Republican James Madison won the election over Federalist Charles Pinckney, but the Federalists gained seats in both houses of the Congress.

The Native American tribes of the Northwest and the Mississippi Valley were resentful of the government's policy of pressured removal to the West, and the British authorities in Canada exploited their discontent by encouraging border raids against the American settlements.

At the same time, the British interfered with American transatlantic shipping, including impressing sailors and capturing ships.

The Congress in 1811 contained a strong pro-war group called the War Hawks led by Henry Clay (1777–1852) and John C. Calhoun (1782–1850). They gained control of both houses and began agitating for war with the British. On June 1, 1812, President Madison asked for a declaration of war and Congress complied.

After three years of inconclusive war, in 1815 the Treaty of Ghent provided for the acceptance of the status quo that had existed at the beginning of hostilities, and both sides restored their wartime conquests to the other.

The Federalists had increasingly become a minority party. They vehemently opposed the war, and Daniel Webster (1782–1852) and other New England congressmen consistently blocked the Administration's efforts to prosecute the war effort. On December 15, 1814, delegates from the New England states met in Hartford, Connecticut, and drafted a set of resolutions suggesting nullification—and even secession—if their interests were not protected against the growing influence of the South and the West.

Soon after the convention adjourned, the news of Andrew Jackson's victory over the British on January 8, 1815, at New Orleans was announced and their actions were discredited. The Federalist party ceased to be a political force from this point on.

Postwar Developments

Protective Tariff (1816): The first protective tariff in the nation's history was passed in 1816 to slow the flood of cheap British manufactures into the country.

Rush-Bagot Treaty (1817): An agreement was reached in 1817 between Britain and the United States to stop maintaining armed fleets on the Great Lakes. This first "disarmament" agreement is still in effect.

The Adams-Onis Treaty (1819): Spain had decided to sell the remainder of the Florida territory to the Americans before they took it anyway. Under this agreement, the Spanish surrendered all their claims to Florida. The United States agreed to assume $5 million in debts owed to American merchants.

The Monroe Doctrine

As Latin American nations began declaring independence, British and American leaders feared that European governments would try to restore the former New World colonies to their erstwhile royal owners.

In December 1823, President James Monroe (1758–1831) included in his annual message to Congress a statement that the peoples of the American hemisphere were "henceforth not to be considered as subjects for future colonization by any European powers."

Internal Development (1820–1830)

The years following the War of 1812 were years of rapid economic and social development, followed by a severe depression in 1819. But this slump was temporary, and it became obvious that the country was moving rapidly from its agrarian origins toward an industrial, urban future.

The Monroe Presidency (1817–1823): James Monroe, the last of the "Virginia dynasty," had been handpicked by the retiring Madison and he was elected with only one electoral vote opposed—a symbol of national unity.

The Marshall Court

John Marshall delivered the majority opinions in a number of critical decisions in these formative years, all of which served to strengthen the power of the federal government and restrict the powers of state governments.

Marbury v. Madison (1803): This case established the precedent of the Supreme Court's power to rule on the constitutionality of federal laws.

Gibbons v. Ogden (1824): In a case involving competing steamboat companies, Marshall ruled that commerce included navigation, and that only Congress has the right to regulate commerce among states. Thus, the state-granted monopoly was voided.

National Expansion

The Missouri Compromise (1820): The Missouri Territory, the first to be organized from the Louisiana Purchase, applied for statehood in 1819. Since the Senate membership was evenly divided between slaveholding and free states at that time, the admission of a new state would give the voting advantage either to the North or to the South.

As the debate dragged on, the northern territory of Massachusetts applied for admission as the state of Maine. The two admission bills were combined, with Maine coming in free and Missouri coming in as a slave state. To make the package palatable for the House, a provision was added that prohibited slavery in the remainder of the Louisiana Territory north of the southern boundary of Missouri (latitude 36° 30′).

JACKSONIAN DEMOCRACY AND WESTWARD EXPANSION (1824–1850)

The Election of 1824

Although John Quincy Adams, through the controversial action of the House of Representatives, became president in the 1824 election, Andrew Jackson instigated a campaign for the presidency immediately. He won the election of 1828.

Jackson was popular with the common man. He seemed to be the prototype of the self-made Westerner: rough-hewn, violent, vindictive, with few ideas but strong convictions. He ignored his appointed cabinet officers and relied instead on the counsel of his "Kitchen Cabinet," a group of partisan supporters.

Jackson expressed the conviction that government operations could be performed by untrained, common folk, and he threatened to dismiss large numbers of government employees and replace them with his supporters.

He exercised his veto power more than any other president before him.

The War on the Bank of the United States

The Bank of the United States had operated under the direction of Nicholas Biddle (1786–1844) since 1823. He was a cautious man, and his conservative economic policy enforced conservatism among the state and private banks—which many bankers resented. In 1832, Jackson vetoed the Bank's renewal, and it ceased being a federal institution in 1836.

Jackson had handpicked his Democratic successor, Martin Van Buren (1782–1862) of New York. The opposition Whig party had emerged from the ruins of the National Republicans and other groups who opposed Jackson's policies.

Van Buren inherited all the problems and resentments generated by his mentor. He spent most of his term in office dealing with the financial chaos left by the death of the Second Bank. The best he could do was to eventually persuade Congress to establish an Independent Treasury to handle government funds. It began functioning in 1840.

The Election of 1840

The Whigs nominated William Henry Harrison, "Old Tippecanoe," a western fighter against the Native Americans. Their choice for vice-president was John Tyler (1790–1862), a former Democrat from Virginia. The Democrats put up Van Buren again.

Harrison won but died only a month after the inauguration, having served the shortest term in presidential history.

The Meaning of Jacksonian Politics

The Age of Jackson was the beginning of the modern two-party system. Popular politics, based on emotional appeal, became the accepted style. The practice of meeting in mass conventions to nominate national candidates for office was established during these years.

The Democrats opposed big government and the requirements of modernization: urbanization and industrialization. Their support came from the working classes, small merchants, and small farmers.

The Whigs promoted government participation in commercial and industrial development, the encouragement of banking and corporations, and a cautious approach to westward expansion. Their support came largely from northern business and manufacturing interests and large southern planters. Calhoun, Clay, and Webster dominated the Whig party during the early decades of the nineteenth century.

Remaking Society: Organized Reform

The early antislavery movement advocated only the purchase and colonization of slaves. The American Colonization Society was organized in 1817, and established the colony of Liberia in 1830, but by that time the movement had reached a dead end.

In 1831, William Lloyd Garrison (1805–1879) started his paper, *The Liberator*, and began to advocate total and immediate emancipation. He founded the New England Anti-slavery Society in 1832 and the American Anti-slavery Society in 1833. Theodore Weld (1803–1895) pursued the same goals, but advocated more gradual means.

The movement split into two wings: Garrison's radical followers, and the moderates who favored "moral suasion" and petitions to Congress. In 1840, the Liberty party, the first national anti-slavery party, fielded a presidential candidate on the platform of "free soil" (nonexpansion of slavery into the new western territories).

Diverging Societies—Life in the North

As the nineteenth century progressed, the states seemed to polarize more into the two sections we call the North and the South, with the expanding West becoming ever more identified with the North.

The Role of Minorities

The women's rights movement focused on social and legal discrimination, and women like Lucretia Mott (1793–1880) and Sojourner Truth (ca. 1797–1883) became well-known figures on the speakers' circuit.

By 1850, 200,000 free blacks lived in the North and West. Their lives were restricted everywhere by prejudice, and "Jim Crow" laws separated the races. Black citizens organized separate churches and fraternal orders. The economic security of the free blacks was constantly threatened by the newly arrived immigrants, who were willing to work at the least desirable jobs for lower wages. Racial violence was a daily threat.

The Growth of Industry

By 1850, the value of industrial output had surpassed that of agricultural production. The Northeast produced more than two-thirds of the manufactured goods. Between 1830 and 1850, the number of patents issued for industrial inventions almost doubled.

Diverging Societies—Life in the South

The southern states experienced dramatic growth in the second quarter of the nineteenth century. The economy grew more productive and more prosperous, but still the section called the South was basically agrarian, with few important cities and only scattered industry. The plantation system, with its cash-crop production driven by the use of slave labor, remained the dominant institution.

The most important economic phenomenon of the early decades of the nineteenth century was the shift in population and production from the old "upper South" of Virginia and the Carolinas to the "lower South" of the newly opened Gulf states of Alabama, Mississippi, and Louisiana. In the older Atlantic states, tobacco retained its importance, but shifted westward to the Piedmont. It was replaced in the East by food grains. The southern Atlantic coast continued to produce rice, and southern Louisiana and east Texas retained their emphasis on sugar cane. But the rich black soil of the new Gulf states proved ideal for the production of short-staple cotton, especially after the invention of the "gin." Cotton soon became the center of the southern economy.

Classes in the South

The large plantations growing cotton, sugar, or tobacco used the gang system, in which white overseers directed black drivers who supervised large groups of workers in the fields, all performing the same operation. In the culture of rice, and on the smaller farms, slaves were assigned specific tasks, and when those tasks were finished, the worker had the remainder of the day to himself.

House servants usually were considered the most favored since they were spared the hardest physical labor and enjoyed the most intimate relationship with the owner's family.

Commerce and Industry

The lack of manufacturing and business development has frequently been blamed for the South's losing its bid for independence in 1861–1865. Actually, the South was highly industrialized for its day and compared favorably with most European nations in the development of manufacturing capacity. However, it trailed far behind the North, so much so that when war erupted in 1861, the northern states owned 81 percent of the factory capacity in the United States.

▌Manifest Destiny and Westward Expansion

Although the term "Manifest Destiny" was not actually coined until 1844, the belief that the American nation was destined to eventually expand all the way to the Pacific Ocean, and to possibly embrace Canada and Mexico, had been voiced for years by many who believed that American liberty and ideals should be shared with everyone possible, by force if necessary. The rising sense of nationalism which followed the War of 1812 was fed by the rapidly expanding population, the reform impulse of the 1830s, and the desire to acquire new markets and resources for the burgeoning economy of "Young America."

The Adams-Onis Treaty of 1819 had set the northern boundary of Spanish possessions near the present northern border of California. The territory north of that line and west of the vague boundaries of the Louisiana Territory had been claimed over the years by Spain, England, Russia, France, and the United States. By the 1820s, all these claims had been yielded to Britain and the United States. The United States claimed all the way north to the 54°40′ parallel. Unable to settle the dispute, they had agreed on a joint occupation of the disputed land.

In the 1830s, American missionaries followed the traders and trappers to the Oregon country. They began to publicize the richness and beauty of the land. The result was the "Oregon Fever" of the 1840s, as thousands of settlers trekked across the Great Plains and the Rocky Mountains to settle the new Shangri-la.

Texas had been a state in the Republic of Mexico since 1822, following the Mexican revolution against Spanish control. The new Mexican government invited immigration from the north by offering land grants to Stephen Austin (1793–1836) and other Americans. By 1835, approximately 35,000 "gringos" were homesteading on Texas land.

The Mexican officials saw their power base eroding as the foreigners flooded in, so they moved to tighten control through restrictions on immigration and through tax increases. The Texans responded in 1836 by proclaiming independence and establishing a new republic. The ensuing war was short-lived. The Mexican dictator, Antonio López de Santa Anna (1794–1876), advanced north and annihilated the Texan garrisons at the Alamo and at Goliad. On April 23, 1836, Sam Houston (1793–1863) defeated him at San Jacinto, and the Mexicans were forced to let Texas go its way.

Houston immediately asked the American government for recognition and annexation, but President Andrew Jackson feared the revival of the slavery issue. He also feared war with Mexico and so did nothing. When Van Buren followed suit, the new republic sought foreign recognition and support, which the European nations eagerly provided, hoping thereby to create a counterbalance to rising American power and influence in the Southwest. France and England both quickly concluded trade agreements with the Texans.

The district of New Mexico had, like Texas, encouraged American immigration. Soon that state was more American than Mexican. The Santa Fe Trail, running from Independence, Missouri, to the town of Santa Fe, created a prosperous trade in mules, gold, silver, and furs, which moved north in exchange for manufactured goods. American settlements sprung up all along the route.

Tyler, Polk, and Continued Westward Expansion

A states' rights southerner and a strict constitutionalist who had been placed on the Whig ticket to draw Southern votes, John Tyler, who became president in 1841 upon Harrison's death, rejected the entire Whig program of a national bank, high protective tariffs, and federally funded internal improvements (roads, canals, etc.). In the resulting legislative confrontations, Tyler vetoed a number of Whig-sponsored bills.

The Whigs were furious. In opposition to Tyler over the next few years, the Whigs, under the leadership of Clay, transformed themselves from a loose grouping of diverse factions to a coherent political party with an elaborate organization.

Rejected by the Whigs and without ties to the Democrats, Tyler was a politician without a party. Hoping to gather a political following of his own, he sought an issue with powerful appeal and believed he had found it in the question of Texas annexation. Tyler's new secretary of state, John C. Calhoun, negotiated an annexation treaty with Texas. Calhoun's identification with extreme proslavery forces and his insertion in the treaty of proslavery statements caused the treaty's rejection by the Senate (1844).

The Election of 1844

Democratic front-runner Martin Van Buren and Whig front-runner Henry Clay agreed privately that neither would endorse Texas annexation, and that it would not become a campaign issue, but expansionists at the Democratic convention succeeded in dumping Van Buren in favor of James K. Polk (1795–1849). Polk, called "Young Hickory" by his supporters, was a staunch Jacksonian who opposed protective tariffs and a national bank, but favored territorial expansion, including not only annexation of Texas but also occupation of all the Oregon country (up to latitude 54° 40′) hitherto jointly occupied by the United States and Britain.

The Whigs nominated Clay, who continued to oppose Texas annexation. Later, sensing the mood of the country was against him, he began to equivocate.

The antislavery Liberty party nominated James G. Birney. Apparently because of Clay's wavering on the Texas issue, Birney was able to take enough votes away from Clay in New York to give that state, and thus the election, to Polk.

Tyler, as a lame-duck president, made one more attempt to achieve Texas annexation before leaving office. By means of a joint resolution, which unlike a treaty required only a simple majority rather than a two-thirds vote, he was successful in getting the measure through Congress. Texas was finally admitted to the Union in 1845.

As a good Jacksonian, Polk favored a low, revenue-only tariff rather than a high, protective tariff. This he obtained in the Walker Tariff (1846). He also opposed a national debt and a national bank and reestablished Van Buren's Independent Sub-Treasury system, which remained in effect until 1920.

By the terms of the Oregon Treaty (1846), a compromise with Great Britain was reached. The current United States-Canada boundary east of the Rockies (49°) was extended westward to the Pacific. Some northern Democrats were angered and felt betrayed by Polk's failure to insist on all of Oregon, but the Senate readily accepted the treaty.

Though Mexico broke diplomatic relations with the United States immediately upon Texas's admission to the Union, there was still hope of a peaceful settlement. In the fall of 1845, Polk sent John Slidell (1793–1871) to Mexico City with a proposal for a peaceful settlement.

Nothing came of these attempts at negotiation. Racked by coup and counter-coup, the Mexican government refused even to receive Slidell.

Polk thereupon sent United States troops into the disputed territory in southern Texas. A force under General Zachary Taylor (1784–1850) (who was nicknamed "Old Rough and Ready") took up a position just north of the Rio Grande. Eight days later, April 5, 1846, Mexican troops attacked an American patrol. When news of the clash reached Washington, Polk sought and received from Congress a declaration of war against Mexico on May 13, 1846.

Americans were sharply divided about the war. Some favored it because they felt Mexico had provoked the war, or because they felt it was the destiny of America to spread the blessings of freedom to oppressed peoples. Others, generally northern abolitionists, saw in the war the work of a vast conspiracy of southern slaveholders greedy for more slave territory.

Negotiated peace finally came about when the State Department clerk Nicholas Trist negotiated and signed the Treaty of Guadalupe-Hidalgo (February 2, 1848), ending the Mexican War. Under the terms of the treaty, Mexico ceded to the United States the southwestern territory from Texas to the California coast.

Although the Mexican War increased the nation's territory by one-third, it also brought to the surface serious political issues that threatened to divide the country, particularly the question of slavery in the new territories.

SECTIONAL CONFLICT AND THE CAUSES OF THE CIVIL WAR (1850–1860)

The Crisis of 1850 and America at Mid-Century

The Mexican War had no more than started when, on August 8, 1846, freshman Democratic Congressman David Wilmot (1814–1868) of Pennsylvania introduced his Wilmot Proviso as a proposed amendment to a war appropriations bill. It stipulated that "neither slavery nor involuntary servitude shall ever exist" in any territory to be acquired from Mexico. It was passed by the House, and though rejected by the Senate, it was reintroduced again and again amid increasingly acrimonious debate.

The southern position was expressed by John C. Calhoun, now serving as senator from South Carolina. He argued that the territories were not the property of the United States federal government, but of all the states together, and therefore Congress had no right to prohibit in any territory any type of "property" (by which he meant slaves) that was legal in any of the states.

Antislavery northerners, pointing to the Northwest Ordinance of 1787 and the Missouri Compromise of 1820 as precedents, argued that Congress had the right to make what laws it saw fit for the territories, including, if it so chose, laws prohibiting slavery.

A compromise proposal favored by President Polk and many moderate southerners called for the extension of the 36° 30′ line of the Missouri Compromise westward through the Mexican Cession to the Pacific, with territory north of the line to be closed to slavery.

Another compromise solution, favored by northern Democrats such as Lewis Cass (1782–1866) of Michigan and Stephen A. Douglas (1813–1861) of Illinois, was known as "squatter sovereignty" and later as "popular sovereignty." It held that the residents of each territory should be permitted to decide for themselves whether to allow slavery.

The Election of 1848

The Democrats nominated Lewis Cass, and their platform endorsed his middle-of-the-road popular sovereignty position with regard to slavery in the territories.

The Whigs dodged the issue even more effectively by nominating General Zachary Taylor, whose fame in the Mexican War made him a strong candidate. Taylor knew nothing of politics, had never voted, and liked to think of himself as above politics. He took no position at all with respect to slavery in the territories.

Some antislavery northern Whigs and Democrats, disgusted with their parties' failure to take a clear stand against the spread of slavery, deserted the party ranks to form an antislavery third party. Their party was called the Free Soil party, since it stood for keeping the soil of new western territories free of slavery. Its candidate was Martin Van Buren. The election excited relatively little public interest. Taylor won a narrow victory.

The question of slavery's status in the western territories was made more immediate when, on January 24, 1848, gold was discovered not far from Sacramento, California. The next year, gold seekers from the eastern United States and from many foreign countries swelled California's population from 14,000 to 100,000.

In September 1849, having more than the requisite population and being in need of better government, California petitioned for admission to the Union as a free state.

Southerners were furious. Long outnumbered in the House of Representatives, the South would now find itself, should California be admitted as a free state, also outvoted in the Senate.

At this point, the aged Henry Clay proposed an eight-part package. For the North, California would be admitted as a free state; the land in dispute between Texas and New Mexico would go to New Mexico; the New Mexico and Utah territories (all of the Mexican Cession outside of California) would not be specifically reserved for slavery, the status there would be decided by popular sovereignty; and the slave trade would be abolished in the District of Columbia.

For the South, a tougher Fugitive Slave Law would be enacted; the federal government would pay Texas's $10,000,000 pre-annexation debt; Congress would declare that it did not have jurisdiction over the interstate slave trade and would promise not to abolish slavery itself in the District of Columbia.

President Taylor died (apparently of gastroenteritis) on July 9, 1850, and was succeeded by Vice-President Millard Fillmore (1800–1874). In Congress, the fight for the Compromise was taken up by Senator Stephen A. Douglas of Illinois who broke Clay's proposal into its component parts so that he could use varying coalitions to push each part through Congress. The Compromise was adopted.

The 1852 Democratic convention deadlocked between Cass and Douglas and so settled on dark horse Franklin Pierce (1804–1869) of New Hampshire. The Whigs chose General Winfield Scott, a war hero with no political background.

The result was an easy victory for Pierce, largely because the Whig party, badly divided along North-South lines as a result of the battle over the Compromise of 1850, was beginning to come apart.

President Pierce expressed the nation's hope that a new era of sectional peace was beginning. He sought to distract the nation's attention from the slavery issue to an aggressive program of foreign economic and territorial expansion known as "Young America."

In 1853, Commodore Matthew Perry (1794–1858) led a United States naval force into Tokyo Bay on a peaceful mission to open Japan—previously closed to the outside world—to American diplomacy and commerce.

By means of the Reciprocity Treaty (1854), Pierce succeeded in opening Canada to greater United States trade.

From Mexico he acquired in 1853 the Gadsden Purchase, a strip of land in what is now southern New Mexico and Arizona along the Gila River. The purpose of this purchase was to provide a good route for a transcontinental railroad across the southern part of the country.

The chief factor in the economic transformation of America during the 1840s and 1850s was the dynamic rise of the railroads. They helped link the Midwest to the Northeast rather than just the South, as would have been the case had only water transportation been available.

The 1850s was the heyday of the steamboat on inland rivers, and the clipper ship on the high seas. The period also saw rapid and sustained industrial growth, especially in the textile industry.

In the North, the main centers of agricultural production shifted from the Mid-Atlantic states to the more fertile lands of the Midwest. Mechanical reapers and threshers came into wide use.

America's second two-party system, which had developed during the 1830s, was in the process of breaking down. The Whig party was now in the process of complete disintegration. This was partially the result of the slavery issue, which divided the party along North-South lines, and partially the result of the nativist movement.

The collapse of a viable two-party system made it much more difficult for the nation's political process to contain the explosive issue of slavery.

The Return of Sectional Conflict

The strengthened Fugitive Slave Law enraged northerners. So violent was northern feeling against the law that several riots erupted as a result of attempts to enforce it. Some northern states passed personal liberty laws in an attempt to prevent the enforcement of the Fugitive Slave Law.

One northerner who was outraged by the Fugitive Slave Act was Harriet Beecher Stowe. She wrote *Uncle Tom's Cabin*, a novel depicting what she perceived as the evils of slavery. Furiously denounced in the South, the book became an overnight bestseller in the North, where it turned many toward active opposition to slavery.

All illusion of sectional peace ended abruptly in 1854 when Senator Stephen A. Douglas of Illinois introduced a bill in Congress to organize the area west of Missouri and Iowa as the territories of Kansas and Nebraska on the basis of popular sovereignty.

The Kansas-Nebraska Act aroused a storm of outrage in the North, where its repeal of the Missouri Compromise was seen as the breaking of a solemn agreement. It hastened the disintegration of the Whig party and divided the Democratic party along North-South lines.

In the North, many Democrats left the party and were joined by former Whigs and Know-Nothings in the newly created Republican party. Springing to life almost overnight as a result of northern fury at the Kansas-Nebraska Act, the Republican party included diverse elements whose sole unifying principle was the firm belief that slavery should be banned from all the nation's territories, confined to the states where it already existed, and allowed to spread no further.

For the next several years Kansas was in chaos, including at various times armed conflict, voter fraud, two governments, and a questionable constitution.

In *Dred Scott v. Sandford*, the Supreme Court attempted to finally settle the slavery question. The case involved a Missouri slave, Dred Scott (ca. 1795–1858), who had been encouraged by abolitionists to sue for his freedom on the basis that his owner had taken him for several years to a free state, Illinois, and then to a free territory, Wisconsin.

Under the domination of aging pro-southern Chief Justice Roger B. Taney of Maryland, the Court attempted to read the extreme southern position on slavery into the Constitution, ruling not only that Scott had no standing to sue in federal court, but also that temporary residence in a free state, even for several years, did not make a slave free, and that the Missouri Compromise (already a dead letter by that time) had been unconstitutional all along because Congress did not have the authority to exclude slavery from a territory. Nor did territorial governments have the right to prohibit slavery.

The 1858 Illinois senatorial campaign produced a series of debates that got to the heart of the issues that were threatening to divide the nation. Incumbent Democratic senator and front-runner for the 1860 presidential nomination Stephen A. Douglas was opposed by a Springfield lawyer, little known outside the state, by the name of Abraham Lincoln.

Lincoln, in a series of seven debates that the candidates agreed to hold during the course of the campaign, stressed that Douglas's doctrine of popular sovereignty failed to recognize slavery for the moral wrong it was.

Douglas, for his part, maintained that his guiding principle was democracy, not any moral standard of right or wrong with respect to slavery.

At the debate held in Freeport, Illinois, Lincoln pressed Douglas to reconcile the principle of popular sovereignty to the Supreme Court's decision in the Dred Scott case. How could the people "vote it up or vote it down," if, as the Supreme Court asserted, no territorial government could prohibit slavery? Douglas, in what came to be called his "Freeport Doctrine," replied that the people of any territory could exclude slavery simply by declining to pass any of the special laws that slave jurisdictions usually passed for their protection.

Douglas's answer was good enough to win him reelection to the Senate, although by the narrowest of margins, but hurt him in the coming presidential campaign.

For Lincoln, despite the failure to win the Senate seat, the debates were a major success, propelling him into the national spotlight, and strengthening the resolve of the Republican party to resist compromise on the free-soil issue.

The Coming of the Civil War

On the night of October 16, 1859, John Brown, an abolitionist, led 18 followers in seizing the federal arsenal at Harpers Ferry, Virginia, taking hostages, and endeavoring to incite a slave uprising. Quickly cornered by Virginia militia, he was eventually captured by a force under the command of army Colonel Robert E. Lee (1807–1870).

Brown was quickly tried, convicted, sentenced, and on December 2, 1859, hanged. Many northerners looked upon Brown as a martyr.

Though responsible northerners such as Lincoln denounced Brown's raid as a criminal act which deserved to be punished by death, many southerners became convinced that the entire northern public approved of Brown's action and that the only safety for the South lay in a separate southern confederacy.

As the 1860 presidential election approached, two Democratic conventions failed to reach consensus, and the sundered halves of the party nominated separate candidates. The southern wing of the party nominated Buchanan's vice president, John C. Breckinridge of Kentucky, on a platform calling for a federal slave code in all the territories. What was left of the national Democratic party nominated Douglas on a platform of popular sovereignty.

A third presidential candidate was added by the Constitutional Union party, a collection of aging former Whigs and Know-Nothings from the southern and border states, plus a handful of moderate southern Democrats. It nominated John

Bell of Tennessee on a platform that sidestepped the issues and called simply for the Constitution, the Union, and the enforcement of the laws.

The Republicans met in Chicago, confident of victory and determined to do nothing to jeopardize their favorable position. Accordingly, they rejected as too radical front-running New York Senator William H. Seward in favor of Illinois' favorite son Abraham Lincoln. The platform called for federal support of a transcontinental railroad and for the containment of slavery.

On election day, the voting went along strictly sectional lines. Breckinridge carried the Deep South; Bell, the border states; and Lincoln, the North. Douglas, although second in popular votes, carried only a single state and part of another. Lincoln led in popular votes, and though he was short of a majority in that category, he did have the needed majority in electoral votes and was elected.

The Secession Crisis

On December 20, 1860, South Carolina, by vote of a special convention, declared itself out of the Union. By February 1, 1861, six more states (Alabama, Georgia, Florida, Mississippi, Louisiana, and Texas) had followed suit.

Representatives of the seceded states met in Montgomery, Alabama, in February 1861 and declared themselves to be the Confederate States of America. They elected former Secretary of War and United States senator Jefferson Davis of Mississippi as president and Alexander Stephens (1812–1883) of Georgia as vice president. They also adopted a constitution for the Confederate states which, while similar to the United States Constitution in many ways, contained several important differences:

1) Slavery was specifically recognized, and the right to move slaves from one state to another was guaranteed.

2) Protective tariffs were prohibited.

3) The president was to serve for a single nonrenewable six-year term.

4) The president was given the right to veto individual items within an appropriations bill.

5) State sovereignty was specifically recognized.

THE CIVIL WAR AND RECONSTRUCTION (1860–1877)

Hostilities Begin

In his inaugural address, Lincoln urged southerners to reconsider their actions, but warned that the Union was perpetual, that states could not secede, and that he would therefore hold the federal forts and installations in the South.

Only two remained in federal hands: Fort Pickens, off Pensacola, Florida; and Fort Sumter, in the harbor of Charleston, South Carolina. Lincoln soon received word from Major Robert Anderson, commander of the small garrison at Sumter, that supplies were running low. Desiring to send in the needed supplies, Lincoln informed the governor of South Carolina of his intention, but promised that no attempt would be made to send arms, ammunition, or reinforcements unless southerners initiated hostilities.

Confederate General P.G.T. Beauregard (1818–1893), acting on orders from President Davis, demanded Anderson's surrender. Anderson said he would surrender if not resupplied. Knowing supplies were on the way, the Confederates opened fire at 4:30 a.m. on April 12, 1861. The next day, the fort surrendered.

The day following Sumter's surrender, Lincoln declared an insurrection and called for the states to provide 75,000 volunteers to put it down. In response to this, Virginia, Tennessee, North Carolina, and Arkansas declared their secession.

The remaining slave states, Delaware, Kentucky, Maryland, and Missouri, wavered, but stayed with the Union.

The North enjoyed at least five major advantages over the South. It had overwhelming preponderance in wealth and was vastly superior in industry.

The North also had an advantage of almost three to one in manpower; and over one-third of the South's population was composed of slaves, whom Southerners would not use as soldiers. Unlike the South, the North received large numbers of immigrants during the war. The North retained control of the United States Navy, and thus, would command the sea and be able to blockade the South. Finally, the North enjoyed a much superior system of railroads.

The South did, however, have several advantages. It was vast in size, making it difficult to conquer. Its troops would be fighting on their own ground, a fact that would give them the advantage of familiarity with the terrain, as well as the added motivation of defending their homes and families. Its armies would often have the opportunity of fighting on the defensive, a major advantage in the warfare of that day.

Though Jefferson Davis had extensive military and political experience, Lincoln was much superior to Davis as a war leader, showing firmness, flexibility, mental toughness, great political skill, and, eventually, an excellent grasp of strategy.

At a creek called Bull Run near the town of Manassas Junction, Virginia, just southwest of Washington, D.C., the Union Army met a Confederate force under generals P.G.T. Beauregard and Joseph E. Johnston on July 21, 1861. In the First Battle of Bull Run (called First Manassas in the South), the Union army was forced to retreat in confusion back to Washington.

The Union Is Preserved

To replace the discredited McDowell, Lincoln chose General George B. McClellan (1826–1885). McClellan was a good trainer and organizer and was loved by the troops, but he was unable to effectively use the powerful army (now called the Army of the Potomac) he had built up.

Lee summoned General Thomas J. "Stonewall" Jackson (1824–1863) and his army from the Shenandoah Valley (where Jackson had just finished defeating several superior federal forces), and with the combined forces attacked McClellan.

After two days of bloody but inconclusive fighting, McClellan lost his nerve and began to retreat. In the remainder of what came to be called the Battle of the Seven Days, Lee continued to attack McClellan, forcing him back to his base, though at great cost in lives. McClellan's army was loaded back onto its ships and taken back to Washington.

Before McClellan's army could reach Washington, Lee took the opportunity to thrash Union General John Pope (1822–1892), who was in northern Virginia with another northern army, at the Second Battle of Bull Run.

West of the Appalachian Mountains, matters were proceeding differently. The northern commanders there, Henry W. Halleck (1815–1872) and Don Carlos Buell (1818–1898), were no more enterprising than McClellan, but Halleck's subordinate, Ulysses S. Grant, was.

With permission from Halleck, Grant mounted a combined operation—army troops and navy gunboats—against two vital Confederate strongholds, forts Henry and Donelson, which guarded the Tennessee and Cumberland rivers in northern Tennessee. When Grant captured the forts in February 1862, Johnston was forced to retreat to Corinth in northern Mississippi.

Grant pursued, but ordered by Halleck to wait until all was in readiness before proceeding, halted his troops at Pittsburg Landing on the Tennessee River, 25 miles north of Corinth. On April 6, 1862 General Albert Sidney Johnston, who had received reinforcements and been joined by General P.G.T. Beauregard, surprised

Grant there, but in the two-day battle that followed (Shiloh) failed to defeat him. Johnston was among the many killed in what was, up to this point, the bloodiest battle in American history.

Grant was severely criticized in the North for having been taken by surprise. Yet with other Union victories and Farragut's capture of New Orleans, the North had taken all of the Mississippi River except for a 110-mile stretch between the Confederate fortresses of Vicksburg, Mississippi, and Port Hudson, Louisiana.

Many southerners believed Britain and France would rejoice in seeing a divided and weakened America. They also believed the two countries would likewise be driven by the need of their factories for cotton and thus intervene on the Confederacy's behalf.

This view proved mistaken. Britain already had a large supply of cotton, and had other sources besides the U.S. British leaders may also have weighed their country's need to import wheat from the northern United States against its desire for cotton from the southern states. Finally, British public opinion opposed slavery.

Skillful northern diplomacy had a great impact. In this, Lincoln had the extremely able assistance of Secretary of State William Seward, who took a hard line in warning Europeans not to interfere, and of ambassador to Great Britain Charles Francis Adams (1807–1886). Britain remained neutral, and other European countries, including France followed its lead.

Congress in 1862 passed two highly important acts dealing with domestic affairs in the North. The Homestead Act granted 160 acres of government land free of charge to any person who would farm it for at least five years. Much of the West was eventually settled under the provisions of this act. The Morrill Land Grant Act offered large amounts of the federal government's land to states that would establish "agricultural and mechanical" colleges. Many of the nation's large state universities were later founded under the provisions of this act.

The Emancipation Proclamation

By mid-1862, Lincoln, under pressure from radical elements of his own party and hoping to create a favorable impression on foreign public opinion, determined to issue the Emancipation Proclamation, which declared free all slaves in areas still in rebellion as of January 1, 1863. At Seward's recommendation, Lincoln waited to announce the proclamation until the North won some sort of victory. This was provided by the Battle of Antietam (September 17, 1863).

After his victory at the Second Battle of Bull Run, Lee moved north and crossed into Maryland, where he hoped to win a decisive victory that would force the North to recognize southern independence.

The armies finally met along Antietam Creek, just east of the town of Sharps-burg in western Maryland. In a bloody but inconclusive day-long battle, known as Antietam in the North and Sharpsburg in the South, McClellan's timidity led him to miss another excellent chance to destroy Lee's cornered and badly outnumbered army. After the battle, Lee retreated to Virginia, and Lincoln removed McClellan from command.

To replace him, Lincoln chose General Ambrose E. Burnside (1824–1881), who promptly demonstrated his unfitness by blundering into a lopsided defeat at Fredericksburg, Virginia (December 13, 1862).

Lincoln then replaced Burnside with General Joseph "Fighting Joe" Hooker (1814–1879). He was soundly beaten at the Battle of Chancellorsville (May 5–6, 1863). At this battle, the brilliant Southern general "Stonewall" Jackson was accidentally shot by his own men and died several days later.

Lee received permission from President Davis to invade Pennsylvania. He was pursued by the Army of the Potomac, now under the command of General George G. Meade (1815–1872), who had replaced the discredited Hooker. They met at Gettysburg in a three-day battle (July 1–3, 1863) that was the bloodiest of the war. Lee, who sorely missed the services of Jackson and whose cavalry leader, the normally reliable J.E.B. Stuart (1833–1864), failed to provide him with timely reconnaissance, was defeated. However, he was allowed by the victorious Meade to retreat to Virginia with his army intact if battered, much to Lincoln's disgust.

Meanwhile, Grant moved on Vicksburg, one of the last two Confederate bastions on the Mississippi River. In a brilliant campaign, he bottled up the Confederate forces of General John C. Pemberton (1814–1881) inside the city and placed them under siege. After six weeks, the defenders surrendered on July 4, 1863. Five days later, Port Hudson surrendered, giving the Union complete control of the Mississippi River.

After Union forces under General William Rosecrans (1819–1898) suffered an embarrassing defeat at the Battle of Chickamauga in northwestern Georgia (September 19–20, 1863), Lincoln named Grant overall commander of Union forces in the West.

Grant went to Chattanooga, Tennessee, where Confederate forces under General Braxton Bragg (1817–1876) were virtually besieging Rosecrans, and immediately took control of the situation. Gathering Union forces from other portions of the western theater and combining them with reinforcements from the East, Grant won a resounding victory at the Battle of Chattanooga (November 23–25, 1863), in which federal forces stormed seemingly impregnable Confederate positions on Lookout Mountain and Missionary Ridge. This victory put Union forces in position for a drive into Georgia, which began the following spring.

Early in 1864, Lincoln made Grant commander of all Union armies. Grant devised a coordinated plan for constant pressure on the Confederacy. General William T. Sherman would lead a drive toward Atlanta, Georgia, with the goal of destroying the Confederate army under General Joseph E. Johnston (who had replaced Bragg). Grant would accompany Meade and the Army of the Potomac in advancing toward Richmond with the goal of destroying Lee's Confederate army.

In a series of bloody battles (the Wilderness, Spotsylvania, Cold Harbor) in May and June of 1864, Grant drove Lee to the outskirts of Richmond. Still unable to take the city or get Lee at a disadvantage, Grant circled around, attacking Petersburg, Virginia, an important railroad junction just south of Richmond and the key to that city's—and Lee's—supply lines. Once again turned back by entrenched Confederate troops, Grant settled down to besiege Petersburg and Richmond in a stalemate that lasted some nine months.

Sherman had been advancing simultaneously in Georgia. He maneuvered Johnston back to the outskirts of Atlanta with relatively little fighting. At that point, Confederate President Davis lost patience with Johnston and replaced him with the aggressive General John B. Hood (1831–1879). Hood and Sherman fought three fierce but inconclusive battles around Atlanta in late July, and then settled down to a siege of their own during the month of August.

The Election of 1864 and Northern Victory

Lincoln ran on the ticket of the National Union party, essentially the Republican party with loyal or "War" Democrats. His vice-presidential candidate was Andrew Johnson (1808–1875), a loyal Democrat from Tennessee.

The Democratic party's presidential candidate was General George B. McClellan, who ran on a platform labeling the war a failure, and calling for a negotiated peace settlement even if that meant southern independence.

In September 1864, word came that Sherman had taken Atlanta. The capture of this vital southern rail and manufacturing center brought an enormous boost to northern morale. Along with other northern victories that summer and fall, it ensured a resounding election victory for Lincoln and the continuation of the war to complete victory for the North.

To speed that victory, Sherman marched through Georgia from Atlanta to the sea, arriving at Savannah in December 1864 and turning north into the Carolinas, leaving behind a 60-mile-wide swath of destruction.

Lee abandoned Richmond (April 3, 1865) and attempted to escape with what was left of his army. Pursued by Grant, he was cornered and forced to surrender at Appomattox, Virginia (April 9, 1865). Other Confederate armies still holding out in various parts of the South surrendered over the next few weeks.

Lincoln did not live to receive news of the final surrenders. On April 14, 1865, he was shot in the back of the head while watching a play in Ford's Theatre in Washington.

The Ordeal of Reconstruction

Reconstruction began well before the fighting of the Civil War came to an end. It brought a time of difficult adjustments in the South.

Among those who faced such adjustments were the recently freed slaves. To ease the adjustment for these recently freed slaves, Congress in 1865 created the Freedmen's Bureau to provide food, clothing, and education, and generally look after the interests of former slaves.

To restore legal governments in the seceded states, Lincoln developed a policy that made it relatively easy for southern states to enter the collateral process.

Tennessee, Arkansas, and Louisiana formed loyal governments under Lincoln's plan, but were refused recognition by a Congress dominated by Radical Republicans.

Radical Republicans such as Thaddeus Stevens (1792–1868) of Pennsylvania believed Lincoln's plan did not adequately punish the South, restructure southern society, or boost the political prospects of the Republican party.

Instead, the radicals in Congress drew up the more stringent Wade-Davis Bill which Lincoln killed with a "pocket veto," and the radicals were furious. When Lincoln was assassinated the radicals rejoiced, believing Vice President Andrew Johnson would be less generous to the South, or at least easier to control.

Foreign Policy Under Johnson

In 1866, the Russian minister approached Seward with an offer to sell Alaska to the United States. In 1867, the sale went through and Alaska was purchased for $7,200,000.

Congressional Reconstruction

Determined to reconstruct the South as it saw fit, Congress passed a Civil Rights Act and extended the authority of the Freedmen's Bureau, giving it both quasi-judicial and quasi-executive powers.

Johnson vetoed both bills, claiming they were unconstitutional; but Congress overrode the vetoes. Fearing that the Supreme Court would agree with Johnson and overturn the laws, Congress approved and sent on to the states for ratification (June 1866) the Fourteenth Amendment, making constitutional the laws Congress had just passed. The Fourteenth Amendment defined citizenship and forbade states to deny various rights to citizens, reduced the representation in Congress of states that did not allow blacks to vote, forbade the paying of the Confederate debt, and made former Confederates ineligible to hold public office.

To control the president, Congress passed the Army Act, reducing the president's control over the army. Congress also passed the Tenure of Office Act, forbidding Johnson to dismiss cabinet members without the Senate's permission.

Johnson obeyed the letter but not the spirit of the Reconstruction acts, and Congress, angry at his refusal to cooperate, sought in vain for grounds to impeach him, until in August 1867 Johnson violated the Tenure of Office Act in order to test its constitutionality. The matter was not tested in the courts, however, but in Congress, where Johnson was impeached by the House of Representatives and came within one vote of being removed by the Senate.

The Election of 1868 and the 15th Amendment

In 1868, the Republicans nominated, for president, Ulysses S. Grant, who had no political record and whose views—if any—on national issues were unknown.

The narrow victory of even such a strong candidate as Grant prompted Republican leaders to decide that it would be politically expedient to give the vote to all blacks, North as well as South. For this purpose, the 15th Amendment was drawn up and submitted to the states. Ironically, the idea was so unpopular in the North that it won the necessary three-fourths approval only with its ratification by southern states.

Though personally of unquestioned integrity, Grant naïvely placed his faith in a number of thoroughly dishonest men. His administration was rocked by one scandalous revelation of government corruption after another.

Many of the economic difficulties the country faced during Grant's administration were caused by the necessary readjustments from a wartime economy back to a peacetime economy. The central economic question was deflation versus inflation, or more specifically, whether to retire the unbacked paper money, greenbacks, printed to meet the wartime emergency, or to print more.

Early in Grant's second term, the country was hit by an economic depression known as the Panic of 1873. Brought on by the overexpansive tendencies of railroad builders and businessmen during the immediate postwar boom, the Panic was triggered by economic downturns in Europe, and more immediately, by the failure of Jay Cooke and Company, a major American financial firm.

The Panic led to clamor for the printing of more greenbacks. In 1874, Congress authorized a small new issue of greenbacks, but it was vetoed by Grant. Pro-inflation forces were further enraged when Congress in 1873 demonetized silver, going to a straight gold standard. Silver was becoming more plentiful due to western mining and was seen by some as a potential source of inflation. Pro-inflation forces referred to the demonetization of silver as the "Crime of '73."

In the election of 1876, the Democrats campaigned against corruption and nominated New York Governor Samuel J. Tilden (1814–1886), who had broken the Tweed political machine of New York City.

The Republicans passed over Grant and turned to Governor Rutherford B. Hayes (1822–1893) of Ohio. Like Tilden, Hayes was decent, honest, in favor of hard money and civil service reform, and opposed to government regulation of the economy.

Tilden won the popular vote and led in the electoral vote 184 to 165. However, 185 electoral votes were needed for election, and 20 votes, from the three Southern states still occupied by federal troops and run by Republican governments, were disputed.

A deal was made whereby those 20 votes went to Hayes in return for removal of federal troops from the South. Reconstruction was over.

INDUSTRIALISM, WAR, AND THE PROGRESSIVE ERA (1877–1912)

Politics of the Period (1877–1882)

The presidencies of Abraham Lincoln and Theodore Roosevelt (1858–1919) mark the boundaries of a half century of relatively weak executive leadership and legislative domination by Congress and the Republican party.

"Stalwarts," led by New York senator Roscoe Conkling (1829–1888) favored the old spoils system of political patronage. "Half-Breeds," headed by Maine senator James G. Blaine (1830–1893), pushed for civil service reform and merit appointments to government posts.

The Economy (1877–1882)

Between 1860 and 1894, the United States moved from the fourth-largest manufacturing nation to the world's leader through capital accumulation, natural resources, especially in iron, oil, and coal, an abundance of labor helped by massive immigration, railway transportation, and communications and major technical innovations such as the development of the modern steel industry and electrical energy.

By 1880, northern capital erected the modern textile industry in the New South by bringing factories to the cotton fields.

Social and Cultural Developments (1877–1882)

In time, advocates of the "social gospel" such as Jane Addams (1860–1939) and Washington Gladden (1836–1918) urged the creation of settlement houses and better health and education services to accommodate the new immigrants. In 1881, Booker T. Washington (1856–1915) became president of Tuskegee Institute in Alabama, a school devoted to teaching and vocational education for African Americans.

The Economy (1882–1887)

Captains of industry such as John D. Rockefeller in oil, J. P. Morgan (1837–1919) in banking, Gustavus Swift (1839–1903) in meat processing, Andrew Carnegie in steel, and E. H. Harriman (1848–1909) in railroads put together major industrial empires.

The concentration of wealth and power in the hands of a relatively small number of giant firms led to a monopoly capitalism that minimized competition. This led to a demand by small businessmen, farmers, and laborers for government regulation of the economy in order to promote competition.

The Interstate Commerce Act (1887): Popular resentment of railroad abuses such as price-fixing, kickbacks, and discriminatory freight rates created demands for state regulation of the railway industry. The Interstate Commerce Act was passed, paving the way for a commission to be established to oversee fair and just railway rates, prohibit rebates, end discriminatory practices, and require annual reports and financial statements.

American Federation of Labor (1886): Samuel Gompers (1850–1924) and Adolph Strasser put together a combination of national craft unions to represent labor's concerns with wages, hours, and safety conditions. Although militant in its use of the strike and in its demand for collective bargaining in labor contracts with large corporations, it did not promote violence or radicalism.

Frederick W. Taylor (1856–1915), an engineer credited as the father of scientific management, introduced modern concepts of industrial engineering, plant management, and time and motion studies. This gave rise to a separate class of managers in industrial manufacturing—efficiency experts.

The Emergence of a Regional Empire (1887–1892)

Despite a protective tariff policy, the United States became increasingly international as it sought to export surplus manufactured and agricultural goods. Foreign markets were viewed as a safety valve for labor employment problems and agrarian unrest.

The Economy (1887–1892)

Corporate monopolies (trusts) which controlled whole industries were subject to federal prosecution if they were found to be combinations or conspiracies in restraint of trade. Although supported by smaller businesses, labor unions, and farm associations, the Sherman Antitrust Act of 1890 was in time interpreted by the Supreme Court to apply to labor unions and farmers' cooperatives as much as to large corporate combinations. Monopoly was still dominant over laissez-faire, free-enterprise economics during the 1890s.

Foreign Relations (1887–1892)

As secretary of state, James G. Blaine was concerned with international trade, political stability, and excessive militarism in Latin America. His international Bureau of American Republics was designed to promote a Pan-American customs union and peaceful conflict resolution. To achieve his aims, Blaine opposed U.S. military intervention in the hemisphere.

Economic Depression and Social Crisis (1892–1897)

The economic depression that began in 1893 brought about a collective response from organized labor, militant agriculture, and the business community. Each group called for economic safeguards and a more humane free-enterprise system which would expand economic opportunities in an equitable manner.

Politics of the Period (1892–1897)

The most marked development in American politics was the emergence of a viable third-party movement in the form of the essentially agrarian Populist party.

Democrat Grover Cleveland (New York) regained the White House by defeating Republican president Benjamin Harrison (Indiana). Cleveland's conservative economic stand in favor of the gold standard brought him the support of various business interests. The Democrats won control of both houses of Congress.

The People's party (Populist) nominated James Weaver (Iowa) for president in 1892. The party platform called for the enactment of a program espoused by agrarians, but also for a coalition with urban workers and the middle class. Specific goals were the coinage of silver to gold at a ratio of 16 to 1; federal loans to farmers; a graduated income tax; postal savings banks; public ownership of railroads and telephone and telegraph systems; prohibition of alien land ownership; immigration restriction; a ban on private armies used by corporations to break up strikes; an eight-hour working day; a single six-year term for president and direct election of senators; the right of initiative and referendum; and the use of the secret ballot.

In the election of 1896, the Republicans nominated William McKinley (Ohio) for president on a platform which promised to maintain the gold standard and protective tariffs. The Democratic party repudiated Cleveland's conservative economics and nominated William Jennings Bryan (1860–1925) (Nebraska) for president on a platform similar to the Populists. Bryan delivered one of the most famous speeches in American history when he declared that the people must not be "crucified upon a cross of gold."

The Populist party also nominated Bryan. Having been outmaneuvered by the Silver Democrats, the Populists lost the opportunity to become a permanent political force.

McKinley won a hard-fought election by only about one-half million votes, as Republicans succeeded in creating the fear among business groups and middle-class voters that Bryan represented a revolutionary challenge to the American system. The Republicans retained control over Congress, which they had gained in 1894.

The Economy (1892–1897)

Homestead Strike (1892): Iron and steel workers went on strike in Pennsylvania against the Carnegie Steel Company to protest salary reductions.

The primary causes for the depression of 1893 were dramatic growth of the federal deficit, withdrawal of British investments from the American market and the outward transfer of gold, and loss of business confidence. Twenty percent of the workforce was eventually unemployed. The depression would last four years.

March of Unemployed (1894): The Populist businessman Jacob Coxey (1854–1951) led a march of hundreds of unemployed workers on Washington asking for a government work-relief program.

Pullman Strike (1894): Eugene Debs's (1855–1926) American Railway Union struck the Pullman Palace Car Co. in Chicago over wage cuts and job losses. The strikes were all ended by force.

Wilson-Gorman Tariff (1894): This protective tariff did little to promote overseas trade as a way to ease the depression.

Dingley Tariff (1897): The Dingley Tariff raised protection to new highs for certain commodities.

Social and Cultural Developments (1892–1897)

The Anti-Saloon League was formed in 1893. Women were especially concerned about the increase of drunkenness during the depression.

Immigration declined by almost 400,000 during the depression. Settlement houses helped poor immigrants. Such institutions also lobbied against sweatshop labor conditions, and for bans on child labor.

Foreign Relations (1892–1897)

The Cuban revolt against Spain in 1895 threatened American business interests in Cuba. Sensational "yellow" journalism, and nationalistic statements from officials such as Assistant Secretary of the Navy Theodore Roosevelt (1858–1919), encouraged popular support for direct American military intervention on behalf of Cuban independence. President McKinley, however, proceeded cautiously through 1897.

The Sino-Japanese War (1894–1895)

Japan's easy victory over China signaled to the United States and other nations trading in Asia that China's weakness might result in its colonization by industrial powers, and thus, in the closing of the China market. This concern led the United States to announce the Open Door policy with China, designed to protect equal opportunity of trade and China's political independence (1899 and 1900).

Foreign Policy (1897–1902)

On March 27, President McKinley asked Spain to call an armistice, accept American mediation to end the war, and end the use of concentration camps in Cuba. Spain refused to comply. On April 21, Congress declared war on Spain with the objective of establishing Cuban independence (Teller Amendment). The first U.S. forces landed in Cuba on June 22, 1898 and by July 17 had defeated the Spanish forces.

On May 1, 1898, the Spanish fleet in the Philippines was destroyed, and Manila surrendered on August 13. Spain agreed to a peace conference to be held in Paris in October 1898, where it ceded the Philippines, Puerto Rico, and Guam to the United States, in return for a payment of $20 million to Spain for the Philippines. The Treaty of Paris was ratified by the Senate on February 6, 1900.

Filipino nationalists under Emilio Aguinaldo (1869–1964) rebelled against the United States (February 1899) when they learned the Philippines would not be given independence. The United States used 70,000 men to suppress the revolutionaries by June 1902. A special U.S. commission recommended eventual self-government for the Philippines.

During the war with Spain, the United States annexed Hawaii on July 7, 1898. In 1900, the United States claimed Wake Island, 2,000 miles west of Hawaii.

Although Cuba was granted its independence, the Platt Amendment of 1901 guaranteed that it would become a virtual protectorate of the United States. Cuba could not: 1) make a treaty with a foreign state impairing its independence, or 2) contract an excessive public debt. Cuba was required to: 1) allow the United States to preserve order on the island, and 2) lease a naval base for 99 years to the United States at Guantanamo Bay.

Politics of the Period (1900–1902)

The unexpected death of Vice President Garrett Hobart led the Republican party to choose the war hero and reform governor of New York, Theodore Roosevelt, as President William McKinley's vice-presidential running mate. Riding the crest of victory against Spain, the GOP platform called for upholding the gold standard for full economic recovery, promoting economic expansion and power in the Caribbean and the Pacific, and building a canal in Central America. The Democrats once again nominated William Jennings Bryan on a platform condemning imperialism and the gold standard. McKinley easily won reelection and the Republicans retained control of both houses of Congress.

While attending the Pan American Exposition in Buffalo, New York, the president was shot on September 6 by Leon Czolgosz, an anarchist. The president died on September 14. Theodore Roosevelt became the nation's 25th president, and at age 42, its youngest to date.

Theodore Roosevelt and Progressive Reforms (1902–1907)

President Roosevelt did much to create a bipartisan coalition of liberal reformers whose objective was to restrain corporate monopoly and promote economic competition at home and abroad.

The president pledged strict enforcement of the Sherman Antitrust Act (1890), which was designed to break up illegal monopolies and regulate large corporations for the public good.

Hepburn Act (1906): Membership of the Interstate Commerce Commission was increased from five to seven. The I.C.C. could set its own fair freight rates, had its regulatory power extended over pipelines, bridges, and express companies, and was empowered to require a uniform system of accounting by regulated transportation companies.

Pure Food and Drug Act (1906): This prohibited the manufacture, sale, and transportation of adulterated or fraudulently labeled foods and drugs in accordance with consumer demands.

Meat Inspection Act (1906): This provided for federal and sanitary regulations and inspections in meat packing facilities. Wartime scandals in 1898 involving spoiled canned meats were a powerful force for reform.

The Economy (1902–1907)

Antitrust Policy (1902): Attorney General P. C. Knox (1853–1921) first brought suit against the Northern Securities Company, a railroad holding corporation put together by J. P. Morgan (1837–1913), and then moved against Rockefeller's Standard Oil Company. By the time he left office in 1909, Roosevelt had indictments against 25 monopolies.

Department of Commerce and Labor (1903): A new cabinet position was created to address the concerns of business and labor. Within the department, the Bureau of Corporations was empowered to investigate and report on the illegal activities of corporations.

Coal Strike (1902): Roosevelt interceded with government mediation to bring about negotiations between the United Mine Workers union and the anthracite mine owners after a bitter strike over wages, safety conditions, and union recognition. This was the first time that the government intervened in a labor dispute without automatically siding with management.

A brief economic recession and panic occurred in 1907 as a result, in part, of questionable bank speculations, a lack of flexible monetary and credit policies, and a conservative gold standard. This event called attention to the need for banking reform which would lead to the establishment of the Federal Reserve System in 1913.

Social and Cultural Developments (1902–1907)

There was not one unified progressive movement, but a series of reform causes designed to address specific social, economic, and political problems. Progressive reforms might best be described as evolutionary change from above rather than revolutionary upheaval from below.

Muckrakers (a term coined by Roosevelt) were investigative journalists and authors who were often the publicity agents for reforms.

Foreign Relations (1902–1907)

Panama Canal: Roosevelt engineered the separation of Panama from Colombia and the recognition of Panama as an independent country. The Hay-Bunau-Varilla Treaty of 1903 granted the United States control of the canal zone in Panama for $10 million and an annual fee of $250,000, beginning nine years after ratification of the treaty by both parties. Construction of the canal began in 1904 and was completed in 1914.

Roosevelt Corollary to the Monroe Doctrine: The United States reserved the right to intervene in the internal affairs of Latin American nations to keep European powers from using military force to collect debts in the Western Hemisphere. The United States by 1905 had intervened in the affairs of Venezuela, Haiti, the Dominican Republic, Nicaragua, and Cuba.

Taft-Katsura Memo (1905): The United States and Japan pledged to maintain the Open Door principles in China. Japan recognized American control over the Philippines, and the United States granted a Japanese protectorate over Korea.

Gentleman's Agreement with Japan (1907): After numerous incidents of racial discrimination against Japanese in California, Japan agreed to restrict the emigration of unskilled Japanese workers to the United States.

The Regulatory State and the Ordered Society (1907–1912)

Deciding not to run for reelection, Theodore Roosevelt opened the way for William H. Taft (1857–1930) (Ohio) to run on a Republican platform calling for a continuation of antitrust enforcement, environmental conservation, and a lower tariff policy to promote international trade. The Democrats nominated William Jennings

Bryan for a third time on an antimonopoly and low tariff platform. Taft easily won and the Republicans retained control of both houses of Congress. For the first time, the American Federation of Labor entered national politics officially with an endorsement of Bryan. This decision began a long alliance between organized labor and the Democratic party in the twentieth century.

Antitrust Policy: In pursuing anti-monopoly law enforcement, Taft chose as his attorney general George Wickersham (1858–1936), who brought 44 indictments in antitrust suits.

Taft was less successful in healing the Republican split between conservatives and progressives over such issues as tariff reform, conservation, and the almost dictatorial power held by the reactionary Republican Speaker of the House, Joseph Cannon (Illinois).

The 1912 election was one of the most dramatic in American history. President Taft's inability to maintain party harmony led Theodore Roosevelt to return to national politics. When denied the Republican nomination, Roosevelt and his supporters formed the Progressive (Bull Moose) party and nominated Roosevelt for president on a political platform nicknamed "The New Nationalism." It called for stricter regulation on large corporations, creation of a tariff commission, women's suffrage, minimum wages and benefits, direct election of senators, initiative, referendum and recall, presidential primaries, and prohibition of child labor. Roosevelt also called for a Federal Trade Commission to regulate the economy, a stronger executive, and more government planning. Theodore Roosevelt did not see big business as evil, but as a permanent development that was necessary in a modern economy.

The Republicans: President Taft and Vice President Sherman were nominated on a platform of "Quiet Confidence," which called for a continuation of the progressive programs pursued by Taft.

The Democrats: A compromise gave the nomination to New Jersey Governor Woodrow Wilson. Wilson, who had also served as president of Princeton University, called his campaign the "New Freedom"; it borrowed pieces from the Progressive and Republican platforms. Wilson called for breaking up large corporations rather than just regulating them. He differed from the other two party candidates by favoring independence for the Philippines, and by advocating the exemption from prosecution of labor unions under the Sherman Antitrust Act. Wilson also supported such measures as lower tariffs, a graduated income tax, banking reform, and direct election of senators.

The Republican split set the stage for Wilson's victory. Although a minority president, Wilson garnered the largest electoral majority in American history up to that time. Democrats won control of both houses of Congress.

The Wilson Presidency

Before the outbreak of World War I in 1914, President Wilson, working with cooperative majorities in both houses of Congress, achieved much of the remaining progressive agenda, including lower tariff reform (Underwood-Simmons Act, 1913), the Sixteenth Amendment (graduated income tax, 1913), the Seventeenth Amendment (direct election of senators, 1913), the Federal Reserve banking system (which provided regulation and flexibility to monetary policy, 1913), the Federal Trade Commission (to investigate unfair business practices, 1914), and the Clayton Antitrust Act (improving the old Sherman Act and protecting labor unions and farm cooperatives from prosecution, 1914).

Other goals such as the protection of children in the work force (Keating-Owen Act, 1916), credit reform for agriculture (Federal Farm Loan Act, 1916), and an independent tariff commission (1916) came later. By the end of Wilson's presidency, the New Freedom and the New Nationalism had merged into one government philosophy of regulation, order, and standardization in the interest of an increasingly diverse nation.

Social and Cultural Developments (1907–1912)

In 1905, the African-American intellectual militant W.E.B. DuBois (1868–1963) founded the Niagara Movement which called for federal legislation to protect racial equality and for full rights of citizenship. The National Association for the Advancement of Colored People was organized in 1909.

A radical labor organization called the Industrial Workers of the World (I.W.W., or Wobblies, 1905–1924) was active in promoting violence and revolution. The I.W.W. organized effective strikes in the textile industry in 1912, and among a few western miners groups, but had little appeal to the average American worker. After the Red Scare of 1919, the government worked to smash the I.W.W. and deported many of its immigrant leaders and members.

Foreign Relations (1907–1915)

President Taft sought to avoid military intervention, especially in Latin America, by replacing "big stick" policies with "dollar diplomacy" in the expectation that American financial investments would encourage economic, social, and political stability. This idea proved an illusion.

Wilson urged Huerta to hold democratic elections and adopt a constitutional government. Huerta refused, and Wilson invaded Mexico with troops at Veracruz in 1914. A second U.S. invasion came in northern Mexico in 1916.

The United States kept a military presence in the Dominican Republic and Haiti, and intervened militarily in Nicaragua (1911) to quiet fears of revolution and help manage foreign financial problems.

WILSON AND WORLD WAR I (1912–1920)

The Early Years of the Wilson Administration

Wilson was only the second Democrat (Cleveland was the first) elected president since the Civil War. Key appointments to the cabinet were William Jennings Bryan as secretary of state and William Gibbs McAdoo (1863–1941) as secretary of the treasury.

The Federal Reserve Act of 1913: The law divided the nation into 12 regions, with a Federal Reserve bank in each region. Federal Reserve banks loaned money to member banks at interest less than the public paid to the member banks, and the notes of indebtedness of businesses and farmers to the member banks were held as collateral. This allowed the Federal Reserve to control interest rates by raising or lowering the discount rate.

The money loaned to the member banks was in the form of a new currency — Federal Reserve notes — which was backed 60 percent by commercial paper and 40 percent by gold. This currency was designed to expand and contract with the volume of business activity and borrowing.

The Federal Reserve system serviced the financial needs of the federal government. The system was supervised and policy was set by a national Federal Reserve Board composed of the secretary of the treasury, the comptroller of the currency, and five other members appointed by the president of the United States.

The Clayton Antitrust Act of 1914: This law supplemented and interpreted the Sherman Antitrust Act of 1890. Under its provisions, stock ownership by a corporation in a competing corporation was prohibited, and the same persons were prohibited from managing competing corporations. Price discrimination (charging less in some regions than in others to undercut the competition) and exclusive contracts which reduced competition were prohibited.

The Election of 1916

The Democrats, the minority party nationally in terms of voter registration, nominated Wilson and adopted his platform calling for continued progressive reforms and neutrality in the European war.

The Republican convention bypassed Theodore Roosevelt and chose Charles Evans Hughes (1862–1948), an associate justice of the Supreme Court and formerly a progressive Republican governor of New York.

Wilson won the election.

Social Issues in the First Wilson Administration

In 1913, Treasury Secretary William G. McAdoo and Postmaster General Albert S. Burleson segregated workers in some parts of their departments with no objection from Wilson. Many northern blacks and whites protested, especially black leader W.E.B. DuBois (1868–1963), who had supported Wilson in 1912.

Wilson opposed immigration restrictions and vetoed a literacy test for immigrants in 1915, but in 1917, Congress overrode a similar veto.

Wilson's Foreign Policy and the Road to War

Wilson's Basic Foreign Policy Premise: Wilson promised a more moral foreign policy than that of his predecessors, denouncing imperialism and dollar diplomacy, and advocating the advancement of democratic capitalist governments throughout the world.

Wilson signaled his repudiation of Taft's dollar diplomacy by withdrawing American involvement from the six-power loan consortium of China.

In 1912, American marines had landed in Nicaragua to maintain order, and an American financial expert had taken control of the customs station. The Wilson administration kept the marines in Nicaragua and negotiated the Bryan-Chamorro Treaty of 1914, which gave the United States an option to build a canal through the country.

Claiming that political anarchy existed in Haiti, Wilson sent marines in 1915 and imposed a treaty making the country a protectorate, with American control of its finances and constabulary. The marines remained until 1934.

In 1916, Wilson sent marines to the Dominican Republic to stop a civil war and established a military government under an American naval commander.

Wilson feared in 1915 that Germany might annex Denmark and its Caribbean possession, the Danish West Indies or Virgin Islands. After extended negotiations, the United States purchased the islands from Denmark by treaty on August 4, 1916, for $25 million and took possession of them on March 31, 1917.

In 1913, Wilson refused to recognize the government of Mexican military dictator Victoriano Huerta, and offered unsuccessfully to mediate between Huerta and his Constitutionalist opponent, Venustiano Carranza. When the Huerta government arrested several American seamen in Tampico in April 1914, American forces occupied the port of Veracruz, an action condemned by both Mexican political factions. In July 1914, Huerta abdicated his power to Carranza, who was soon opposed by his former general Francisco "Pancho" Villa (1878–1923). Seeking American intervention as a means of undermining Carranza, Villa shot 16 Americans on a train in northern Mexico in January 1916 and burned the border town of Columbus, New Mexico, in March 1916, killing 19 people. Carranza reluctantly consented to Wilson's request that the United States be allowed to pursue and capture Villa in Mexico, but did not expect the force of about 6,000 army troops under the command of General John J. Pershing which crossed the Rio Grande on March 18. The force advanced more than 300 miles into Mexico, failed to capture Villa, and became, in effect, an army of occupation. The Carranza government demanded an American withdrawal, and several clashes with Mexican troops occurred. War threatened, but in January 1917 Wilson removed the American forces.

▌ The Road to War in Europe

When World War I broke out in Europe, Wilson issued a proclamation of American neutrality on August 4, 1914. The value of American trade with the Central Powers fell from $169 million in 1914 to almost nothing in 1916, but trade with the Allies rose from $825 million to $3.2 billion during the same period. In addition, the British and French had borrowed about $3.25 billion from American sources by 1917. The United States had become a major supplier of Allied munitions, food, and raw materials.

The sinking of the British liner *Lusitania* off the coast of Ireland on May 7, 1915, with the loss of 1,198 lives, including 128 Americans, brought strong protests from Wilson. Secretary of State Bryan, who believed Americans should stay off belligerent ships, resigned rather than insist on questionable neutral rights and was replaced by Robert Lansing.

The House-Grey Memorandum: Early in 1915, Wilson sent his friend and adviser Colonel Edward M. House on an unsuccessful visit to Europe to offer American mediation in the war. Late in the year, House returned to London to propose that Wilson call a peace conference; if Germany refused to attend or was uncooperative at the conference, the United States could enter the war on the Allied side. An agreement to that effect, called the House-Grey memorandum, was signed by the British foreign secretary, Sir Edward Grey, on February 22, 1916.

In an address to Congress on January 22, 1917, Wilson made his last offer to serve as a neutral mediator. He proposed a "peace without victory," based not on a "balance of power" but on a "community of power."

Germany announced on January 31, 1917, that it would sink all ships, belligerent or neutral, without warning in a large war zone off the coasts of the Allied nations in the eastern Atlantic and the Mediterranean. Wilson broke diplomatic relations with Germany on February 3. During February and March several American merchant ships were sunk by submarines.

The British intercepted a secret message from the German foreign secretary, Arthur Zimmermann, to the German minister in Mexico, and turned it over to the United States on February 24, 1917. The Germans proposed that, in the event of a war between the United States and Germany, Mexico attack the United States. After the war, the "lost territories" of Texas, New Mexico, and Arizona would be returned to Mexico. When the telegram was released to the press on March 1, many Americans became convinced that war with Germany was necessary. A declaration of war against Germany was signed by Wilson on April 6.

World War I: The Military Campaign

The American force of about 14,500, which had arrived in France by September 1917, was assigned a quiet section of the line near Verdun. When the Germans mounted a major drive toward Paris in the spring of 1918, the Americans experienced their first important engagements. In June, they prevented the Germans from crossing the Marne at Chateau-Thierry, and cleared the area of Belleau Woods. In July, eight American divisions aided French troops in attacking the German line between Reims and Soissons. The American First Army, with over half a million men under Pershing's immediate command, was assembled in August 1918, and began a major offensive at St. Mihiel on the southern part of the front on September 12. Following the successful operation, Pershing began a drive against the German defenses between Verdun and Sedan, an action called the Meuse-Argonne offensive. He reached Sedan on November 7. During the same period the English in the north and the French along the central front also broke through the German lines. The fighting ended with the armistice on November 11, 1918.

Mobilizing the Home Front

A number of volunteer organizations sprang up around the country to search for draft dodgers, enforce the sale of bonds, and report any opinion or conversation considered suspicious. Such groups publicly humiliated people accused of not buying war bonds, and persecuted, beat, and sometimes killed people of German descent. The anti-German and antisubversive war hysteria in the United States far exceeded similar public moods in Britain and France during the war.

The Espionage Act of 1917 provided for fines and imprisonment for persons who made false statements which aided the enemy, incited rebellion in the military, or obstructed recruitment or the draft. Printed matter advocating treason or insurrection could be excluded from the mails. The Sedition Act of May 1918 forbade any criticism of the government, flag, or uniform, even if there were not detrimental consequences, and expanded the mail exclusion. The laws were applied in ways that trampled on civil liberties. The Espionage Act was upheld by the Supreme Court in the case of *Schenck v. United States* in 1919. The opinion, written by Justice Oliver Wendell Holmes, Jr. (1841–1935), stated that Congress could limit free speech when the words represented a "clear and present danger," and that a person cannot cry "fire" in a crowded theater. The Sedition Act was similarly upheld in *Abrams v. United States* a few months later. Ultimately 2,168 persons were prosecuted under the laws, and 1,055 were convicted, of whom only 10 were charged with actual sabotage.

Wartime Social Trends

Large numbers of women, mostly white, were hired by factories and other enterprises in jobs never before open to them. When the war ended, almost all returned to traditional "women's jobs" or to homemaking. Returning veterans replaced them in the labor market.

The labor shortage opened industrial jobs to Mexican-Americans and to African-Americans. W.E.B. DuBois, the most prominent African-American leader of the time, supported the war effort in the hope that the war would make the world safe for democracy and bring a better life for African-Americans in the United States. About half a million rural southern African-Americans migrated to cities, mainly in the North and Midwest, to obtain employment in war and other industries, especially in steel and meatpacking. In 1917, there were race riots in 26 cities in the North and South, with the worst in East St. Louis, Illinois.

In December 1917, a constitutional amendment to prohibit the manufacture and sale of alcoholic beverages in the United States was passed by Congress and submitted to the states for ratification.

Peacemaking and Domestic Problems (1918–1920)

From the time of the American entry into the war, Wilson had maintained that the war would make the world safe for democracy. He insisted that there should be peace without victory, meaning that the victors would not be vindictive toward the losers, so that a fair and stable international situation in the postwar world would ensure lasting peace. In an address to Congress on January 8, 1918, he presented his specific peace plan in the form of the Fourteen Points. The first five points called for open rather than secret peace treaties, freedom of the seas, free trade, arms reduction, and a fair adjustment of colonial claims. The next eight points were concerned with the national aspirations of various European peoples and the adjustment of boundaries. The fourteenth point, which he considered the most important and had espoused as early as 1916, called for a "general association of nations" to preserve the peace.

Wilson decided that he would lead the American delegation to the peace conference which opened in Paris on January 12, 1919. In doing so he became the first president to leave the country during his term of office. In the negotiations, which continued until May 1919, Wilson found it necessary to make many compromises in forging the text of the treaty.

Following a protest by 39 senators in February 1919, Wilson obtained some changes in the League of Nations structure to exempt the Monroe Doctrine and domestic matters from League jurisdiction. Then, on July 26, 1919, he presented the treaty with the League within it to the Senate for ratification. Almost all of the 47 Democrats supported Wilson and the treaty, but the 49 Republicans were divided. About a dozen were "irreconcilables" who thought that the United States should not be a member of the League under any circumstances. The remainder included 25 "strong" and 12 "mild" reservationists who would accept the treaty with some changes. The main objection centered on Article X of the League Covenant, where the reservationists wanted it understood that the United States would not go to war to defend a League member without the approval of Congress.

On September 3, 1919, Wilson set out on a national speaking tour to appeal to the people to support the treaty and the League and to influence their senators. He collapsed after a speech in Pueblo, Colorado, on September 25, and returned to Washington, where he suffered a severe stroke on October 2 which paralyzed his left side. He was seriously ill for several months, and never fully recovered. The treaty failed to get a two-thirds majority either with or without the reservationists.

Many people, including British and French leaders, urged Wilson to compromise on reservationists, including the issue of Article X. Many historians think that Wilson's ill health impaired his judgment, and that he would have worked out a compromise had he not had the stroke. The Senate took up the treaty again in February 1920, and on March 19 it was again defeated both with and without the reservationists. The United States officially ended the war with Germany by a resolution of Congress signed on July 2, 1921, and a separate peace treaty was ratified on July 25. The United States did not join the League.

Domestic Problems and the End of the Wilson Administration

In January 1919, the Eighteenth Amendment to the Constitution prohibiting the manufacture, sale, transportation, or importation of intoxicating liquors was ratified by the states, and it became effective in January 1920. The Nineteenth Amendment providing for women's suffrage, which had been defeated in the Senate in

1918, was approved by Congress in 1919. It was ratified by the states in time for the election of 1920.

Americans feared the spread of the Russian Communist revolution to the United States, and many interpreted the widespread strikes of 1919 spurred by inflation as Communist-inspired and the beginning of the revolution. Bombs sent through the mail to prominent government and business leaders in April 1919 seemed to confirm their fears, although the origin of the bombs has never been determined. The anti-German hysteria of the war years was transformed into the anti-Communist and antiforeign hysteria of 1919 and 1920, and continued in various forms through the 1920s.

Attorney General A. Mitchell Palmer, who aspired to the 1920 presidential nomination, was one of the targets of the anonymous bombers in the spring of 1919. In August 1919, he named J. Edgar Hoover (1895–1972) to head a new Intelligence Division in the Justice Department to collect information about radicals. After arresting nearly 5,000 people in late 1919 and early 1920, Palmer announced that huge Communist riots were planned for major cities on May Day (May 1, 1920). Police and troops were alerted, but the day passed with no radical activity. Palmer was discredited and the Red Scare subsided.

White hostility based on competition for lower-paying jobs and black encroachment into neighborhoods led to race riots in 25 cities, with hundreds killed or wounded and millions of dollars in property damage. The Chicago riot in July was the worst. Fear of returning African-American veterans in the South led to an increase of lynchings from 34 in 1917 to 60 in 1918 and 70 in 1919. Some of the victims were veterans still in uniform.

THE ROARING TWENTIES AND ECONOMIC COLLAPSE (1920–1929)

The Election of 1920

The Republican Convention: Senator Warren G. Harding (1865–1923) of Ohio was nominated as a dark-horse candidate, and Governor Calvin Coolidge (1872–1933) of Massachusetts was chosen as the vice presidential nominee. The platform opposed the League and promised low taxes, high tariffs, immigration restriction, and aid to farmers.

The Democratic Convention: Governor James Cox was nominated on the 44th ballot, and Franklin D. Roosevelt (1882–1945), an assistant secretary of the Navy and distant cousin of Theodore, was selected as his running mate. The platform endorsed the League, but left the door open for reservations.

The Twenties: Economic Advances and Social Tensions

The principal driving force of the economy of the 1920s was the automobile. Automobile manufacturing stimulated supporting industries such as steel, rubber, and glass, as well as gasoline refining and highway construction. During the 1920s, the United States became a nation of paved roads. The Federal Highway Act of 1916 started the federal highway system and gave matching funds to the states for construction.

Unlike earlier boom periods, which had involved large expenditures for capital investments such as railroads and factories, the prosperity of the 1920s depended heavily on the sale of consumer products. Purchases of "big ticket" items such as automobiles, refrigerators, and furniture were made possible by installment or time payment credit. The idea was not new, but the availability of consumer credit expanded tremendously during the 1920s. Consumer interest and demand was spurred by the great increase in professional advertising, which used newspapers, magazines, radio, billboards, and other media.

There was a trend toward corporate consolidation during the 1920s. In most fields, an oligopoly of two to four firms dominated. This is exemplified by the automobile industry, where Ford, General Motors, and Chrysler produced 83 percent of the vehicles in 1929. Government regulatory agencies such as the Federal Trade Commission and the Interstate Commerce Commission were passive and generally controlled by persons from the business world.

There was also a trend toward bank consolidation. Because corporations were raising much of their money through the sale of stocks and bonds, the demand for business loans declined. Commercial banks then put more of their funds into real estate loans, loans to brokers against stocks and bonds, and the purchase of stocks and bonds themselves.

American Society in the 1920s

By 1920, for the first time, a majority of Americans (51 percent) lived in an urban area with a population of 2,500 or more. A new phenomenon of the 1920s was the tremendous growth of suburbs and satellite cities, which grew more rapidly than the central cities. Streetcars, commuter railroads, and automobiles contributed to the process, as well as the easy availability of financing for home construction. The suburbs had once been the domain of the wealthy, but the technology of the 1920s opened them to working-class families.

Traditional American moral standards regarding premarital sex and marital fidelity were widely questioned for the first time during the 1920s. The automobile, by giving people mobility and privacy, was generally considered to have contributed to sexual license. Birth control, though illegal, was promoted by Margaret Sanger (1883–1966) and others and was widely accepted.

When it became apparent that women did not vote as a block, political leaders gave little additional attention to the special concerns of women. Divorce laws were liberalized in many states at the insistence of women. Domestic service was the largest job category. Most other women workers were in traditional female occupations such as secretarial and clerical work, retail sales, teaching, and nursing. Rates of pay were below those for men. Most women still pursued the traditional role of housewife and mother, and society accepted that as the norm.

The migration of southern rural African-Americans to the cities continued, with about 1.5 million moving during the 1920s. By 1930, about 20 percent of American blacks lived in the North, with the largest concentrations in New York, Chicago, and Philadelphia. While they were generally better off economically in the cities than they had been as tenant farmers, they generally held low-paying jobs and were confined to segregated areas of the cities.

A native of Jamaica, Marcus Garvey (1887–1940) founded the Universal Negro Improvement Association, advocating African-American racial pride and separatism rather than integration, and called for a return of African-Americans to Africa. In 1921, he proclaimed himself the provisional president of an African empire, and sold stock in the Black Star Steamship Line which would take migrants to Africa. The line went bankrupt in 1923, and Garvey was convicted and imprisoned for mail fraud in the sale of the line's stock and then deported. His legacy was an emphasis on African-American pride and self-respect.

Many writers of the 1920s were disgusted with the hypocrisy and materialism of contemporary American society. Often called the "Lost Generation," many of them, such as novelists Ernest Hemingway (1899–1961) and F. Scott Fitzgerald (1896–1940) and poets Ezra Pound (1885–1972) and T. S. Eliot (1888–1965), moved to Europe.

Social Conflicts

Many white Protestant families saw their traditional values gravely threatened. The traditionalists were largely residents of rural areas and small towns, and the clash of farm values with the values of an industrial society of urban workers was evident. The traditionalist backlash against modern urban industrial society expressed itself primarily through intolerance.

On Thanksgiving Day in 1915, the Knights of the Ku Klux Klan, modeled on the organization of the same name in the 1860s and 1870s, was founded near Atlanta by William J. Simmons. Its purpose was to intimidate African-Americans, who were experiencing an apparent rise in status during World War I. By 1923, the Klan had about five million members throughout the nation. The largest concentrations of members were in the South, the Southwest, the Midwest, California, and Oregon.

There had been calls for immigration restriction since the late nineteenth century. Labor leaders believed that immigrants depressed wages and impeded unionization. Some progressives believed that they created social problems. In June 1917, Congress, over Wilson's veto, had imposed a literacy test for immigrants and excluded many Asian nationalists. In 1921, Congress passed the Emergency Quota Act. In practice, the law admitted about as many as wanted to come from such nations as Britain, Ireland, and Germany, while severely restricting Italians, Greeks, Poles, and east European Jews. It became effective in 1922 and reduced the number of immigrants annually to about 40 percent of the 1921 total. Congress then passed the National Origins Act of 1924, which further reduced the number of southern and eastern Europeans, and cut the annual immigration to 20 percent of the 1921 figure. In 1927, the annual maximum was reduced to 150,000.

The Eighteenth Amendment, which prohibited the manufacture, sale, or transportation of intoxicating liquors, took effect in January 1920.

Fundamentalist Protestants, under the leadership of William Jennings Bryan, began a campaign in 1921 to prohibit the teaching of evolution in the schools, and thus protect belief in the literal biblical account of creation. The idea was especially well received in the South.

Sacco and Vanzetti: On April 15, 1920, two unidentified gunmen robbed a shoe factory and killed two men in South Braintree, Massachusetts. Nicola Sacco and Bartolomeo Vanzetti, Italian immigrants and admitted anarchists, were tried for the murders. After they were convicted and sentenced to death in July 1921, there was much protest in the United States and in Europe that they had not received a fair trial. After six years of delays, they were executed on August 23, 1927. Fifty years later, on July 19, 1977, the pair were vindicated by Governor Michael Dukakis.

Government and Politics in the 1920s: The Harding Administration

Harding was a handsome and amiable man of limited intellectual and organizational abilities. He had spent much of his life as the publisher of a newspaper in the small city of Marion, Ohio. He recognized his limitations, but hoped to be a much-loved president.

Harding appointed some outstanding persons to his cabinet, including Secretary of State Charles Evans Hughes, a former Supreme Court justice and presidential candidate; Secretary of the Treasury Andrew Mellon (1855–1937), a Pittsburgh aluminum and banking magnate and reportedly the richest man in America; and Secretary of Commerce Herbert Hoover, a dynamic multimillionaire mine owner famous for his wartime relief efforts. Less impressive was his appointment of his cronies Albert B. Fall as secretary of the interior and Harry M. Daugherty as attorney general.

The Teapot Dome Scandal began when Secretary of the Interior Albert B. Fall in 1921 secured the transfer of several naval oil reserves to his jurisdiction. In 1922, he secretly leased reserves at Teapot Dome in Wyoming to Harry F. Sinclair of Monmouth Oil and at Elk Hills in California to Edward Doheny of Pan-American Petroleum. Sinclair and Doheny were acquitted in 1927 of charges of defrauding the government, but in 1929, Fall was convicted, fined, and imprisoned for bribery.

Vice President Calvin Coolidge became president upon Harding's death in 1923.

The Election of 1924

The Republicans: Calvin Coolidge was nominated. The platform endorsed business development, low taxes, and rigid economy in government. The party stood on its record of economic growth and prosperity since 1922.

The Progressives: Robert M. La Follette, after failing in a bid for the Republican nomination, formed a new Progressive party, with support from Midwest farm groups, socialists, and the American Federation of Labor. The platform attacked monopolies, and called for the nationalization of railroads, the direct election of the president, and other reforms.

The Democrats: John W. Davis was nominated and presented little contrast with the Republicans.

The Election of 1928

The Republicans: Coolidge did not seek another term, and the convention quickly nominated Herbert Hoover, the secretary of commerce, for president. The platform endorsed the policies of the Harding and Coolidge administrations.

The Democrats: Governor Alfred E. Smith (1873–1944) of New York, a Catholic and an anti-prohibitionist, controlled most of the nonsouthern delegations. Southerners supported his nomination with the understanding that the platform would not advocate repeal of prohibition. The platform differed little from the Republican, except in advocating lower tariffs.

The Great Depression: The Crash

Herbert Hoover, an Iowa farm boy and an orphan, graduated from Stanford University with a degree in mining engineering. He became a multimillionaire from mining and other investments around the world. After serving as the director of the Food Administration under Wilson, he became secretary of commerce under Harding and Coolidge. He believed that cooperation between business and government would enable the United States to abolish poverty through continued economic growth.

Stock prices increased throughout the decade. The boom in prices and volume of sales was especially active after 1925, and was intensive during 1928–29.

Careful investors, realizing that stocks were overpriced, began to sell to take their profits. During October 1929, prices declined as more stock was sold. On "Black Thursday," October 24, 1929, almost 13 million shares were traded, a large number for that time, and prices fell precipitously. Investment banks tried to boost the market by buying, but on October 29, "Black Tuesday," the market fell about 40 points, with 16.5 million shares traded.

THE GREAT DEPRESSION AND THE NEW DEAL (1929–1941)

Reasons for the Depression

A stock-market crash does not mean that a depression must follow. In 1929, a complex interaction of many factors caused the decline of the economy.

Many people had bought stock on a margin of 10 percent, meaning that they had borrowed 90 percent of the purchase price through a broker's loan and put up the stock as collateral. When the price of a stock fell more than 10 percent, the lender sold the stock for whatever it would bring and thus further depressed prices. The forced sales brought great losses to the banks and businesses that had financed the broker's loans, as well as to the investors.

There were already signs of recession before the market crash in 1929. The farm economy, which involved almost 25 percent of the population, had been depressed throughout the decade. Coal, railroads, and New England textiles had not been prosperous. After 1927, new construction declined and auto sales began to sag. Many workers had been laid off before the crash of 1929.

During the early months of the depression, most people thought it was just an adjustment in the business cycle which would soon be over. As time went on, the worst depression in American history set in, reaching its bottom point in early 1932.

Hoover's Depression Policies

The Agricultural Marketing Act: Passed in June 1929, before the market crash, this law, proposed by the president, created the Federal Farm Board. It had a revolving fund of $500 million to lend agricultural cooperatives to buy commodities, such as wheat and cotton, and hold them for higher prices.

The Hawley-Smoot Tariff: This law, passed in June 1930, raised duties on both agricultural and manufactured imports.

The Reconstruction Finance Corporation: Chartered by Congress in 1932, the RFC loaned money to railroads, banks, and other financial institutions. It prevented the failure of basic firms, on which many other elements of the economy depended, but was criticized by some as relief for the rich.

The Federal Home Loan Bank Act: This law, passed in July 1932, created home-loan banks to make loans to building and loan associations, savings banks, and insurance companies to help them avoid foreclosures on homes.

Election of 1932

The Republicans renominated Hoover while the Democrats nominated Franklin D. Roosevelt, governor of New York. Although calling for a cut in spending, Roosevelt communicated optimism and easily defeated Hoover.

The First New Deal

In February 1933, before Roosevelt took office, Congress passed the Twenty-First Amendment to repeal prohibition, and sent it to the states. In March, the new Congress legalized light beer. The amendment was ratified by the states and took effect in December 1933.

When Roosevelt was inaugurated on March 4, 1933, the American economic system seemed to be on the verge of collapse. Roosevelt assured the nation that "the only thing we have to fear is fear itself," called for a special session of Congress to convene on March 9, and asked for "broad executive powers to wage war against the emergency." Two days later, he closed all banks and forbade the export of gold or the redemption of currency in gold.

Legislation of the First New Deal

The special session of Congress, from March 9 to June 16, 1933, passed a great body of legislation which has left a lasting mark on the nation. The period has been referred to ever since as the "Hundred Days." Historians have divided Roosevelt's legislation into the First New Deal (1933–1935) and a new wave of programs beginning in 1935 called the Second New Deal.

The Emergency Banking Relief Act was passed on March 9, the first day of the special session. The law provided additional funds for banks from the RFC and the Federal Reserve, allowed the Treasury to open sound banks after 10 days and to merge or liquidate unsound ones, and forbade the hoarding or export of gold. Roosevelt, on March 12, assured the public of the soundness of the banks in the first of many "fireside chats," or radio addresses. People believed him, and most banks were soon open with more deposits than withdrawals.

The Banking Act of 1933, or the Glass-Steagall Act, established the Federal Deposit Insurance Corporation (FDIC) to insure individual deposits in commercial banks, and separated commercial banking from the more speculative activity of investment banking.

The Truth-in-Securities Act required that full information about stocks and bonds be provided by brokers and others to potential purchasers.

The Home Owners Loan Corporation (HOLC) had authority to borrow money to refinance home mortgages and thus prevent foreclosures. Eventually, it lent more than three billion dollars to more than one million home owners.

Gold was taken out of circulation following the president's order of March 6, and the nation went off the gold standard. Eventually, on January 31, 1934, the value of the dollar was set at $35 per ounce of gold, 59 percent of its former value. The object of the devaluation was to raise prices and help American exports.

The Securities and Exchange Commission was created in 1934 to supervise stock exchanges and to punish fraud in securities trading.

The Federal Housing Administration (FHA) was created by Congress in 1934 to insure long-term, low-interest mortgages for home construction and repair.

These programs, intended to provide temporary relief for people in need, were to be disbanded when the economy improved.

The Federal Emergency Relief Act appropriated $500 million for aid to the poor to be distributed by state and local governments. It also established the Federal Emergency Relief Administration under Harry Hopkins (1890–1946).

The Civilian Conservation Corps enrolled 250,000 young men aged 18 to 24 from families on relief to go to camps where they worked on flood control, soil conservation, and forest projects under the direction of the War Department.

The Public Works Administration, under Secretary of the Interior Harold Ickes, had $3.3 billion to distribute to state and local governments for building projects such as schools, highways, and hospitals.

In November 1933, Roosevelt established the Civil Works Administration to hire four million unemployed workers. The temporary and makeshift nature of the jobs, such as sweeping streets, brought much criticism, and the experiment was terminated in April 1934.

The Agricultural Adjustment Act of 1933 created the Agricultural Adjustment Administration (AAA). Farmers agreed to reduce production of principal farm commodities and were paid a subsidy in return. The money came from a tax on the processing of the commodities. Farm prices increased, but tenants and sharecroppers were hurt when owners took land out of cultivation. The law was repealed in January 1936 on the grounds that the processing tax was not constitutional.

The Federal Farm Loan Act consolidated all farm credit programs into the Farm Credit Administration to make low-interest loans for farm mortgages and other agricultural purposes.

The Commodity Credit Corporation was established in October 1933 by the AAA to make loans to corn and cotton farmers against their crops so that they could hold them for higher prices.

The Frazier-Lemke Farm Bankruptcy Act of 1934 allowed farmers to defer foreclosure on their land while they obtained new financing, and helped them to recover property already lost through easy financing.

National Industrial Recovery Act: This law was viewed as the cornerstone of the recovery program. It sought to stabilize the economy by preventing extreme competition, labor-management conflicts, and overproduction. A board composed of industrial and labor leaders in each industry or business drew up a code for that industry which set minimum prices, minimum wages, maximum work hours, production limits, and quotas. The antitrust laws were temporarily suspended.

The TVA, a public corporation under a three-member board, was proposed by Roosevelt as the first major experiment in regional public planning. Starting from the nucleus of the government's Muscle Shoals property on the Tennessee River, the TVA built 20 dams in an area of 40,000 square miles to stop flooding and soil erosion, improve navigation, and generate hydroelectric power. It also manufactured nitrates for fertilizer, conducted demonstration projects for farmers, engaged in reforestation, and attempted to rehabilitate the whole area.

The economy improved but did not recover. The GNP, money supply, salaries, wages, and farm income rose. Unemployment dropped from about 25 percent of nonfarm workers in 1933 to about 20.1 percent, or 10.6 million, in 1935.

The Second New Deal: Opposition

The Share Our Wealth Society was founded in 1934 by Senator Huey "The Kingfish" Long (1893–1935) of Louisiana. Long was a populist demagogue who was elected governor of Louisiana in 1928, established a practical dictatorship over the state, and moved to the United States Senate in 1930. He supported Roosevelt in 1932, but then broke with him, calling him a tool of Wall Street for not doing more to combat the depression. Long called for the confiscation of all fortunes over five million dollars and a tax of one hundred percent on annual incomes over one million. His society had more than five million members when he was assassinated on the steps of the Louisiana Capitol on September 8, 1935.

The Second New Deal Begins

The Works Progress Administration (WPA) was started in May 1935, following the passage of the Emergency Relief Appropriations Act of April 1935. The WPA employed people from the relief rolls for 30 hours of work a week at pay double the relief payment but less than private employment.

The National Youth Administration (NYA) was established as part of the WPA in June 1935, to provide part-time jobs for high school and college students to enable them to stay in school, and to help young adults not in school to find jobs.

The Rural Electrification Administration (REA) was created in May 1935, to provide loans and WPA labor to electric cooperatives so they could build lines into rural areas not served by private companies.

The Social Security Act was passed in August 1935. It established a retirement plan for persons over age 65, which was to be funded by a tax on wages paid equally by employee and employer. The first benefits, ranging from $10 to $85 per month, were paid in 1942. Another provision of the act had the effect of forcing the states to initiate unemployment insurance programs.

The Banking Act of 1935 created a strong central Board of Governors of the Federal Reserve system with broad powers over the operations of the regional banks.

The Election of 1936

Roosevelt had put together a coalition of followers who made the Democratic party the majority party in the nation for the first time since the Civil War. While retaining the Democratic base in the South and among white ethnics in the big cities, Roosevelt also received strong support from Midwestern farmers. Two groups that made a dramatic shift into the Democratic ranks were union workers and African-Americans.

The Last Years of the New Deal

Frustrated by a conservative Supreme Court which had overturned much of his New Deal legislation, Roosevelt, in February 1937, proposed to Congress the Judicial Reorganization Bill, which would allow the president to name a new federal judge for each judge who did not retire by the age of $70^1/_2$. The appointments would be limited to a maximum of 50, with no more than six added to the Supreme Court. The president was astonished by the wave of opposition from Democrats and Republicans alike, but he uncharacteristically refused to compromise. In doing so, he not only lost the bill but control of the Democratic Congress, which he had dominated since 1933. Nonetheless, the Court changed its position, as Chief Justice Charles Evans Hughes and Justice Owen Roberts began to vote with the more liberal members.

Most economic indicators rose sharply between 1935 and 1937. Roosevelt decided that the recovery was sufficient to warrant a reduction in relief programs and a move toward a balanced budget. The budget for fiscal year 1938 was reduced from $8.5 billion to $6.8 billion, with the WPA experiencing the largest cut. During the winter of 1937–1938, the economy slipped rapidly and unemployment rose to 12.5 percent. In April 1938, Roosevelt requested and received from Congress an emergency appropriation of about $3 billion for the WPA, as well as increases for public works and other programs. In July 1938, the economy began to recover, and it regained the 1937 levels in 1939.

Social Dimensions of the New Deal Era

Unemployment for African-Americans was much higher than for the general population, and before 1933 they were often excluded from state and local relief efforts. Roosevelt seems to have given little thought to the special problems of African-Americans, and he was afraid to endorse legislation such as an antilynching bill for fear of alienating the southern wing of the Democratic party. More African-Americans were appointed to government positions by Roosevelt than ever before, but the number was still small. Roosevelt issued an executive order on June 25, 1941, establishing the Fair Employment Practices Committee to ensure consideration for minorities in defense employment.

John Collier, the commissioner of the Bureau of Indian Affairs, persuaded Congress to repeal the Dawes Act of 1887 by passing the Indian Reorganization Act of 1934. The law restored tribal ownership of lands, recognized tribal constitutions and government, and provided loans to tribes for economic development.

Labor Unions

Labor unions lost members and influence during the 1920s and early 1930s. The National Industrial Recovery Act gave them new hope when it guaranteed the right to unionize, and during 1933 about 1.5 million new members joined unions.

The passage of the National Labor Relations or Wagner Act in 1935 resulted in a massive growth of union membership, but at the expense of bitter conflict within the labor movement. The American Federation of Labor was made up primarily of craft unions. Some leaders wanted to unionize the mass-production industries, such as automobiles and rubber, with industrial unions. In November 1935, John L. Lewis and others established the Committee for Industrial Organization to union-ize basic industries, presumably within the AFL. President William Green of the AFL ordered the CIO to disband in January 1936. When the rebels refused, they were expelled by the AFL in March 1937. The insurgents then reorganized the CIO as the independent Congress of Industrial Organizations.

During its organizational period, the CIO sought to initiate several industrial unions, particularly in the steel, auto, rubber, and radio industries. In late 1936 and early 1937, it used a tactic called the sit-down strike, with the strikers occupying the workplace to prevent any production. By the end of 1941, the CIO was larger than the AFL. Union members comprised about 11.5 percent of the work force in 1933 and 28.2 percent in 1941.

New Deal Diplomacy and the Road to War

Roosevelt and Secretary of State Cordell Hull continued the policies of their predecessors by endeavoring to improve relations with Latin American nations, and formalized their position by calling it the Good Neighbor Policy.

At the Montevideo Conference of American Nations in December of 1933, the United States renounced the right of intervention in the internal affairs of Latin American countries. In 1936, in the Buenos Aires Convention, the United States agreed to submit all American disputes to arbitration.

United States Neutrality Legislation

Belief that the United States should stay out of foreign wars and problems began in the 1920s and grew in the 1930s. Examinations of World War I profiteering and revisionist history that asserted Germany had not been responsible for World War I and that the United States had been misled were also influential during the 1930s. A Gallup poll in April 1937 showed that almost two-thirds of those responding thought that American entry into World War I had been a mistake.

The Johnson Act of 1934: This law prohibited any nation in default on World War I payments from selling securities to any American citizen or corporation.

The Neutrality Acts of 1935: On outbreak of war between foreign nations, all exports of American arms and munitions to them would be embargoed for six months. In addition, American ships were prohibited from carrying arms to any belligerent, and the president was to warn American citizens not to travel on belligerent ships.

The Neutrality Acts of 1936: The laws gave the president authority to determine when a state of war existed, and prohibited any loans or credits to belligerents.

The Neutrality Acts of 1937: The laws gave the president authority to determine if a civil war was a threat to world peace and if it was covered by the Neutrality Acts. It also prohibited all arms sales to belligerents, and allowed the cash-and-carry sale of nonmilitary goods to belligerents.

The American Response to the War in Europe

In August 1939, Roosevelt created the War Resources Board to develop a plan for industrial mobilization in the event of war. The next month, he established the Office of Emergency Management in the White House to centralize mobilization activities.

The Neutrality Act of 1939: Roosevelt officially proclaimed the neutrality of the United States on September 5, 1939. The Democratic Congress, in a vote that followed party lines, passed a new Neutrality Act in November. It allowed the cash-and-carry sale of arms and short-term loans to belligerents, but forbade American ships to trade with belligerents or Americans to travel on belligerent ships.

Almost all Americans recognized Germany as a threat. They were divided on whether to aid Britain or to concentrate on the defense of America. The Committee to Defend America by Aiding the Allies was formed in May 1940, and the America First Committee, which opposed involvement, was incorporated in September 1940.

In April 1940, Roosevelt declared that Greenland, a possession of conquered Denmark, was covered by the Monroe Doctrine, and he supplied military assistance to set up a coastal patrol there.

In May 1940, Roosevelt appointed a Council of National Defense, chaired by William S. Knudson (1879–1948), the president of General Motors, to direct defense production and to build 50,000 planes. The Office of Production Management was created to allocate scarce materials, and the Office of Price Administration was established to prevent inflation and protect consumers.

Congress approved the nation's first peacetime draft, the Selective Service and Training Act, in September 1940.

Roosevelt determined that to aid Britain in every way possible was the best way to avoid war with Germany. In September 1940, he signed an agreement to give Britain 50 American destroyers in return for a 99-year lease on air and naval bases in British territories in Newfoundland, Bermuda, and the Caribbean.

The Election of 1940

The Republicans: The Republicans nominated Wendell L. Willkie (1892–1944) of Indiana, a dark-horse candidate. The platform supported a strong defense program, but severely criticized New Deal domestic policies.

The Democrats: Roosevelt was nominated for a third term, breaking a tradition which had existed since George Washington. The platform endorsed the foreign and domestic policies of the administration.

The Election: Roosevelt won by a much narrower margin than in 1936.

American Involvement with the European War

The Lend-Lease Act: This let the United States provide supplies to Britain in exchange for goods and services after the war. It was signed on March 11, 1941.

In April 1941, Roosevelt started the American Neutrality Patrol. The American navy would search out but not attack German submarines in the western half of the Atlantic and warn British vessels of their location. Also in April, U.S. forces occupied Greenland, and in May, the president declared a state of unlimited national emergency.

American marines occupied Iceland, a Danish possession, in July 1941 to protect it from seizure by Germany. The American navy began to convoy American and Icelandic ships between the United States and Iceland.

On August 9, 1941, Roosevelt and Winston Churchill issued the Atlantic Charter.

Germany invaded Russia in June 1941, and in November the United States extended lend-lease assistance to the Russians.

The American destroyer *Greer* was attacked by a German submarine near Iceland on September 4, 1941. Roosevelt ordered the American military forces to shoot on sight any German or Italian vessel in the patrol zone. An undeclared naval war had begun. The American destroyer *Kearny* was attacked by a submarine on October 16, and the destroyer *Reuben James* was sunk on October 30, with 115 lives lost. In November, Congress authorized the arming of merchant ships.

The Road to Pearl Harbor

In late July 1941, the United States placed an embargo on the export of aviation gasoline, lubricants, and scrap iron and steel to Japan, and granted an additional loan to China. In December, the embargo was extended to include iron ore and pig iron, some chemicals, machine tools, and other products.

In October 1941, a new military cabinet headed by General Hideki Tojo took control of Japan. The Japanese secretly decided to make a final effort to negotiate, and to go to war if no solution was found by November 25. A new round of talks followed in Washington, but neither side would make a substantive change in its position, and on November 26, Hull repeated the American demand that the Japanese remove all their forces from China and Indochina immediately. The Japanese gave final approval on December 1 for an attack on the United States.

The Japanese planned a major offensive to take the Dutch East Indies, Malaya, and the Philippines in order to obtain the oil, metals, and other raw materials they needed. At the same time, they would attack Pearl Harbor in Hawaii to destroy the American Pacific fleet to keep it from interfering with their plans.

The United States had broken the Japanese diplomatic codes and knew that trouble was imminent. Between December 1 and December 6, 1941, it became clear to administration leaders that Japanese task forces were being ordered into battle. American commanders in the Pacific were warned of possible aggressive action there, but not forcefully.

At 7:55 a.m. on Sunday, December 7, 1941, the first wave of Japanese carrier-based planes attacked the American fleet in Pearl Harbor. A second wave followed at 8:50 a.m. The United States suffered the loss of two battleships sunk, six damaged and out of action, three cruisers and three destroyers sunk or damaged, and a number of lesser vessels destroyed or damaged. All of the 150 aircraft at Pearl Harbor were destroyed on the ground. Worst of all, 2,323 American servicemen were killed and about 1,100 wounded. The Japanese lost 29 planes, five midget submarines, and one fleet submarine.

WORLD WAR II AND THE POSTWAR ERA (1941–1960)

Declared War Begins

On December 8, 1941, Congress declared war on Japan, with one dissenting vote. On December 11, Germany and Italy declared war on the United States. Great Britain and the United States then established the Combined Chiefs of Staff, headquartered in Washington, to direct Anglo-American military operations.

On January 1, 1942, representatives of 26 nations met in Washington, D.C., and signed the Declaration of the United Nations, pledging themselves to the principles of the Atlantic Charter and promising not to make a separate peace with their common enemies.

The Home Front

War Production Board: The WPD was established in 1942 by President Franklin D. Roosevelt for the purpose of regulating the use of raw materials.

Wage and Price Controls: In April 1942, the General Maximum Price Regulation Act froze prices and extended rationing. In April 1943, prices, wages, and salaries were frozen.

Revenue Act of 1942: The Revenue Act of 1942 extended the income tax to the majority of the population. Payroll deduction for the income tax began in 1944.

Social Changes: Rural areas lost population, while population in coastal areas increased rapidly. Women entered the work force in increasing numbers. African-Americans moved from the rural South to northern and western cities, with racial tensions often resulting, most notably in the June 1943 racial riot in Detroit.

Smith-Connolly Act: Passed in 1943, the Smith-Connolly Antistrike Act authorized government seizure of a plant or mine idled by a strike if the war effort was impeded. It expired in 1947.

Korematsu v. United States: In 1944, the Supreme Court upheld President Roosevelt's 1942 order that Issei (Japanese-Americans who had emigrated from Japan) and Nisei (native born Japanese-Americans) be relocated to concentration camps. The camps were closed in March 1946.

Presidential Election of 1944: President Franklin D. Roosevelt, together with new vice-presidential candidate Harry S. Truman (1884–1972) of Missouri, defeated his Republican opponent, Governor Thomas E. Dewey of New York.

Roosevelt died on April 12, 1945, at Warm Springs, Georgia. Harry S. Truman became president.

The North African and European Theaters

The United States joined in the bombing of the European continent in July 1942. Bombing increased during 1943 and 1944 and lasted to the end of the war.

The Allied army under Dwight D. Eisenhower attacked French North Africa in November 1942. The Vichy French forces surrendered.

In the Battle of Kassarine Pass, North Africa, February 1943, the Allied army met General Erwin Rommel's Afrika Korps. Although the battle is variously interpreted as a standoff or a defeat for the United States, Rommel's forces were soon trapped by the British moving in from Egypt. In May 1943, Rommel's Afrika Korps surrendered.

Allied armies under George S. Patton (1885–1945) invaded Sicily from Africa in July 1943, and gained control by mid-August. Moving from Sicily, the Allied armies invaded the Italian mainland in September. The Germans, however, put up a stiff resistance, with the result that Rome did not fall until June 1944.

In March 1944, the Soviet Union began pushing into Eastern Europe.

On "D-Day," June 6, 1944, Allied armies under Dwight D. Eisenhower, now commander-in-chief of the Allied Expeditionary Forces, began an invasion of Normandy, France.

Allied armies liberated Paris in August. By mid-September, they had arrived at the Rhine, on the edge of Germany.

Beginning December 16, 1944, at the Battle of the Bulge, the Germans counterattacked, driving the Allies back about 50 miles into Belgium. By January, the Allies were once more advancing toward Germany. The Allies crossed the Rhine in March 1945. In the last week of April, Eisenhower's forces met the Soviet army at the Elbe. On May 7, 1945, Germany surrendered.

The Pacific Theater

By the end of December 1941, Guam, Wake Island, the Gilbert Islands, and Hong Kong had fallen to the Japanese. In January 1942, Raboul, New Britain, fell, followed in February by Singapore and Java, and in March by Rangoon, Burma. U.S. forces surrendered at Corregidor, Philippines, on May 6, 1942.

The Battle of the Coral Sea, May 7–8, 1942, stopped the Japanese advance on Australia.

The Battle of Midway, June 4–7, 1942, proved to be the turning point in the Pacific.

A series of land, sea, and air battles took place around Guadalcanal in the Solomon Islands from August 1942 to February 1943, stopping the Japanese.

The Allied strategy of island hopping, begun in 1943, sought to neutralize Japanese strongholds with air and sea power and then move on.

U.S. forces advanced into the Gilberts (November 1943), the Marshalls (January 1944), and the Marianas (June 1944). After the American capture of the Marianas, General Tojo resigned as premier of Japan.

The Battle of Leyte Gulf, October 25, 1944, resulted in Japan's loss of most of its remaining naval power. Forces under General Douglas MacArthur (1880–1964) liberated Manila in March 1945.

Between April and June 1945, in the battle for Okinawa, nearly 50,000 American casualties resulted from the fierce fighting, but the battle virtually destroyed Japan's remaining defenses.

The Atomic Bomb

The Manhattan Engineering District was established by the army engineers in August 1942 for the purpose of developing an atomic bomb (it eventually became known as the Manhattan Project). J. Robert Oppenheimer directed the design and construction of a transportable atomic bomb at Los Alamos, New Mexico.

On December 2, 1942, Enrico Fermi (1901–1954) and his colleagues at the University of Chicago produced the first atomic chain reaction.

On July 16, 1945, the first atomic bomb was exploded at Alamogordo, New Mexico.

The *Enola Gay* dropped an atomic bomb on Hiroshima, Japan, on August 6, 1945, killing about 78,000 persons and injuring 100,000 more. On August 9, a second bomb was dropped on Nagasaki, Japan.

On August 8, 1945, the Soviet Union entered the war against Japan.

Japan surrendered on August 14, 1945. The formal surrender was signed on September 2.

Diplomacy

Casablanca Conference: On January 14–25, 1943, Franklin D. Roosevelt and Winston Churchill, prime minister of Great Britain, declared a policy of unconditional surrender for "all enemies."

Moscow Conference: In October 1943, Secretary of State Cordell Hull obtained Soviet agreement to enter the war against Japan after Germany was defeated, and to participate in a world organization after the war was over.

Declaration of Cairo: Issued on December 1, 1943, after Roosevelt met with General Chiang Kai-shek in Cairo from November 22 to 26, the Declaration of Cairo called for Japan's unconditional surrender and stated that all Chinese territories occupied by Japan would be returned to China and that Korea would be free and independent.

The Emergence of the Cold War and Containment

In 1947, career diplomat and Soviet expert George F. Kennan wrote an anonymous article for *Foreign Affairs* in which he called for a counterforce to Soviet pressures, for the purpose of "containing" communism.

Truman Doctrine: In February 1947, Great Britain notified the United States that it could no longer aid the Greek government in its war against Communist insurgents. The next month President Harry S. Truman asked Congress for $400 million in military and economic aid for Greece and Turkey. In what became known as the "Truman Doctrine," he argued that the United States must support free peoples who were resisting Communist domination.

Marshall Plan: Secretary of State George C. Marshall (1880–1959) proposed in June 1947 that the United States provide economic aid to help rebuild Europe. The following March, Congress passed the European Recovery Program, popularly known as the Marshall Plan, which provided more than $12 billion in aid.

After the United States, France, and Great Britain announced plans to create a West German Republic out of their German zones, the Soviet Union in June 1948 blocked surface access to Berlin. The United States then instituted an airlift to transport supplies to the city until the Soviets lifted their blockade in May 1949.

NATO

In April 1949, the North Atlantic Treaty Organization was signed by the United States, Canada, Great Britain, and nine European nations. The signatories pledged that an attack against one would be considered an attack against all. The Soviets formed the Warsaw Treaty Organization in 1955 to counteract NATO.

International Cooperation

Representatives from Europe and the United States, at a conference held July 1–22, 1944, signed agreements for an international bank and a world monetary fund to stabilize international currencies and rebuild the economies of war-torn nations.

From April to June 1945, representatives from 50 countries met in San Francisco to establish the United Nations. The UN charter created a General Assembly composed of all member nations which would act as the ultimate policy-making body. A Security Council, made up of 11 members, including the United States, Great Britain, France, the Soviet Union, and China as permanent members and six additional nations elected by the General Assembly for two-year terms, would be responsible for settling disputes among UN member nations.

Containment in Asia

General Douglas MacArthur headed a four-power Allied Control Council which governed Japan, allowing it to develop economically and politically.

Between 1945 and 1948, the United States gave more than $2 billion in aid to the Nationalist Chinese under Chiang Kai-shek, and sent George C. Marshall to settle the conflict between Chiang's Nationalists and Mao Tse-tung's Communists. In 1949, however, Mao defeated Chiang and forced the Nationalists to flee to Formosa (Taiwan). Mao established the People's Republic of China on the mainland.

Korean War

On June 25, 1950, North Korea invaded South Korea. President Truman committed U.S. forces commanded by General MacArthur, but under United Nations auspices. By October, the UN forces (mostly American) had driven north of the 38th parallel, which divided North and South Korea. Chinese troops attacked MacArthur's forces on November 26, pushing them south of the 38th parallel, but by spring 1951, the UN forces had recovered their offensive.

In June 1953, an armistice was signed, leaving Korea divided along virtually the same boundary that had existed prior to the war.

Eisenhower-Dulles Foreign Policy

Dwight D. Eisenhower, elected president in 1952, chose John Foster Dulles (1888–1959) as secretary of state. Dulles talked of a more aggressive foreign policy, calling for "massive retaliation" and "liberation" rather than containment. He wished to emphasize nuclear deterrents rather than conventional armed forces.

After several years of nationalist war against French occupation, France, Great Britain, the Soviet Union, and China signed the Geneva Accords in July 1954, dividing Vietnam along the 17th parallel. The North would be under Ho Chi Minh and the South under Emperor Bao Dai. Elections were scheduled for 1956 to unify the country, but Ngo Dinh Diem overthrew Bao Dai and prevented the elections from taking place. The United States supplied economic aid to South Vietnam.

Dulles attempted to establish a Southeast Asia Treaty Organization parallel to NATO, but was able to obtain only the Philippine Republic, Thailand, and Pakistan as signatories in September 1954.

President Eisenhower announced in January 1957 that the United States was prepared to use armed force in the Middle East against Communist aggression. Under this doctrine, U.S. marines entered Beirut, Lebanon, in July 1958 to promote political stability during a change of governments. The marines left in October.

The United States supported the overthrow of President Jacobo Arbenz Guzman of Guatemala in 1954 because he began accepting arms from the Soviet Union.

In January 1959, Fidel Castro overthrew Fulgencio Batista, dictator of Cuba. Castro soon began criticizing the United States and moved closer to the Soviet Union, signing a trade agreement with the Soviets in February 1960. The United States prohibited the importation of Cuban sugar in October 1960, and broke off diplomatic relations in January 1961.

The Politics of Affluence: Demobilization and Domestic Policy

Harry S. Truman, formerly a senator from Missouri and vice president of the United States, became president on April 12, 1945.

Congress created the Atomic Energy Commission in 1946, establishing civilian control over nuclear development and giving the president sole authority over the use of atomic weapons in warfare.

Taft-Hartley Act (1947): The Republicans, who had gained control of Congress in 1946, sought to control the power of the unions through the Taft-Hartley Act. This act made the "closed-shop" illegal; labor unions could no longer force employers to hire only union members. The act slowed down efforts to unionize the South, and by 1954, 15 states had passed "right to work" laws, forbidding the "union-shop."

In 1948, the president banned racial discrimination in federal government hiring practices and ordered desegregation of the armed forces.

The Presidential Succession Act of 1947 placed the Speaker of the House and the president pro tempore of the Senate ahead of the secretary of state and after the vice president in the line of succession. The Twenty-Second Amendment to the Constitution, ratified in 1951, limited the president to election to two terms.

Election of 1948

Truman was the Democratic nominee, but the Democrats were split by the States' Rights Democratic party (Dixiecrats) which nominated Governor Strom Thurmond of South Carolina, and the Progressive party, which nominated former Vice President Henry Wallace. The Republicans nominated Governor Thomas E. Dewey of New York. After traveling widely, and attacking the "do-nothing Congress," Truman won a surprise victory.

Anticommunism

In 1950, Julius and Ethel Rosenberg and Harry Gold were charged with giving atomic secrets to the Soviet Union. The Rosenbergs were convicted and executed in 1953.

On February 9, 1950, Senator Joseph R. McCarthy (1908–1957) of Wisconsin alleged that he had a list of known Communists who were working in the State Department. He later expanded his attacks. After making unproved charges against the army, he was censured by the Senate in 1954.

Eisenhower's Dynamic Conservatism

The Republicans nominated Dwight D. Eisenhower, most recently NATO commander, for the presidency. The Democrats nominated Governor Adlai E. Stevenson (1900–1965) of Illinois for president. Eisenhower won by a landslide; for the first time since Reconstruction, the Republicans won some southern states.

Eisenhower sought to balance the budget and lower taxes but did not attempt to roll back existing social and economic legislation. Eisenhower first described his policy as "dynamic conservatism," and then as "progressive moderation." The administration abolished the Reconstruction Finance Corporation, ended wage and price controls, and reduced farm price supports. It cut the budget and in 1954 lowered tax rates for corporations and individuals with high incomes; an economic slump, however, made balancing the budget difficult.

Social Security was extended in 1954 and 1956 to an additional 10 million people, including professionals, domestic and clerical workers, farm workers, and members of the armed services.

The Rural Electrification Administration announced in 1960 that 97 percent of American farms had electricity.

In 1954, Eisenhower obtained congressional approval for joint Canadian-U.S. construction of the St. Lawrence Seaway, which was to give oceangoing vessels access to the Great Lakes. In 1956, Congress authorized construction of the Interstate Highway System, with the federal government supplying 90 percent of the cost and the states 10 percent.

The launching of the Soviet space satellite *Sputnik* on October 4, 1957, created fear that America was falling behind technologically. Although the United States launched *Explorer I* on January 31, 1958, the concern continued. In 1958, Congress established the National Aeronautics and Space Administration (NASA) to coordinate research and development, and passed the National Defense Education Act to provide grants and loans for education.

On January 3, 1959, Alaska became the 49th state, and on August 21, 1959, Hawaii became the 50th.

Civil Rights

Eisenhower completed the formal integration of the armed forces, desegregated public services in Washington, D.C., naval yards, and veteran's hospitals, and appointed a Civil Rights Commission.

Brown v. Board of Education of Topeka: In this 1954 case, NAACP lawyer Thurgood Marshall challenged the doctrine of "separate but equal" (*Plessy v. Ferguson*, 1896). The Court declared that separate educational facilities were inherently unequal. In 1955, the Court ordered states to integrate "with all deliberate speed."

Although he did not personally support the Supreme Court decision, Eisenhower sent 10,000 National Guardsmen and 1,000 paratroopers to Little Rock, Arkansas, to control mobs and enable African-Americans to enroll at Central High in September 1957.

On December 11, 1955, in Montgomery, Alabama, Rosa Parks, a black woman, refused to give up her seat on a city bus to a white person and was arrested. Under the leadership of Martin Luther King (1929–1968), an African-American pastor, African-Americans of Montgomery organized a bus boycott that lasted for a year, until in December 1956, the Supreme Court refused to review a lower court ruling that stated that separate but equal was no longer legal.

In 1959, state and federal courts nullified Virginia laws that prevented state funds from going to integrated schools. This proved to be the beginning of the end for "massive resistance."

On February 1, 1960, upon being denied service, four African-American students staged a sit-in at a Woolworth lunch counter in Greensboro, North Carolina. This inspired sit-ins by thousands elsewhere in the South and led to the formation of the Student Nonviolent Coordinating Committee.

The Election of 1960

Vice President Richard M. Nixon won the Republican presidential nomination, and the Democrats nominated Senator John F. Kennedy (1917–1963) for the presidency, with Lyndon B. Johnson (1908–1973), majority leader of the Senate, as his running mate.

Kennedy won the election by slightly more than 100,000 popular votes and 94 electoral votes, based on majorities in New England, the Middle Atlantic, and the South.

THE NEW FRONTIER, VIETNAM, AND SOCIAL UPHEAVAL (1960–1972)

Kennedy's "New Frontier" and the Liberal Revival

Kennedy was unable to get much of his program through Congress because of an alliance of Republicans and southern Democrats.

Kennedy did gain congressional approval for raising the minimum wage from $1.00 to $1.25 an hour and extending it to 3 million more workers.

The 1961 Housing Act provided nearly $5 billion over four years for the preservation of open urban spaces, development of mass transit, and the construction of middle-class housing.

Civil Rights

In May 1961, blacks and whites boarded buses in Washington, D.C., and traveled across the South to New Orleans to test federal enforcement of regulations prohibiting discrimination. They met violence in Alabama but continued to New Orleans.

The Justice Department, under Attorney General Robert F. Kennedy (1925–1968), began to push for civil rights, including desegregation of interstate transportation in the South, integration of schools, and supervision of elections.

In the fall of 1962, President Kennedy called the Mississippi National Guard to federal duty to enable an African-American, James Meredith, to enroll at the University of Mississippi.

Kennedy presented a comprehensive civil rights bill to Congress in 1963. With the bill held up in Congress, 200,000 people marched, demonstrating on its behalf on August 28, 1963, in Washington, D.C. Martin Luther King gave his "I Have a Dream" speech.

The Cold War Continues

Under Eisenhower, the Central Intelligence Agency had begun training some 2,000 men for an invasion of Cuba to overthrow Fidel Castro, the left-leaning revolutionary who had taken power in 1959. On April 19, 1961, this force invaded at the Bay of Pigs, but was pinned down and forced to surrender. Some 1,200 men were captured.

In August 1961, Khrushchev closed the border between East and West Berlin and ordered the erection of the Berlin Wall.

The Soviet Union began the testing of nuclear weapons in September 1961. Kennedy then authorized resumption of underground testing by the United States.

On October 14, 1962, a U-2 reconnaissance plane brought photographic evidence that missile sites were being built in Cuba. Kennedy, on October 22, announced a blockade of Cuba and called on Khrushchev to dismantle the missile bases and remove all weapons capable of attacking the United States from Cuba. Six days later, Khrushchev backed down, withdrew the missiles, and Kennedy lifted the blockade.

In July 1963, a treaty banning the atmospheric testing of nuclear weapons was signed by all the major powers except France and China.

In 1961, Kennedy announced the Alliance for Progress, which would provide $20 million in aid to Latin America.

Johnson and the Great Society

On November 22, 1963, Kennedy was assassinated by Lee Harvey Oswald in Dallas, Texas. Jack Ruby, a nightclub owner, killed Oswald two days later.

Succeeding Kennedy, Lyndon B. Johnson had extensive experience in both the House and Senate, and as a Texan, was the first southerner to serve as president since Woodrow Wilson.

A tax cut of more than $10 billion passed Congress in 1964, and an economic boom resulted.

The 1964 Civil Rights Act outlawed racial discrimination by employers and unions, created the Equal Employment Opportunity Commission to enforce the law, and eliminated the remaining restrictions on black voting.

Michael Harrington's *The Other America* (1962) showed that 20 to 25 percent of American families were living below the governmentally defined poverty line. The Economic Opportunity Act of 1964 sought to address the problem by establishing a Job Corps, community action programs, educational programs, work-study programs, job training, loans for small businesses and farmers, and Volunteers in Service to America (VISTA), a "domestic peace corps." The Office of Economic Opportunity administered many of these programs.

Election of 1964

Lyndon Johnson was nominated for president by the Democrats. The Republicans nominated Senator Barry Goldwater, a conservative from Arizona. Johnson won more than 61 percent of the popular vote and could now launch his own "Great Society" program.

The Medicare Act of 1965 combined hospital insurance for retired people with a voluntary plan to cover physician's bills. Medicaid provided grants to states to help the poor below retirement age.

Emergence of Black Power

In 1965, Martin Luther King announced a voter registration drive. With help from the federal courts, he dramatized his effort by leading a march from Selma to Montgomery, Alabama, between March 21 and 25. The Voting Rights Act of 1965 authorized the attorney general to appoint officials to register voters.

Seventy percent of African-Americans lived in city ghettos. In 1966, New York and Chicago experienced riots, and the following year there were riots in Newark and Detroit. The Kerner Commission, appointed to investigate the riots, concluded that they were directed at a social system that prevented African-Americans from getting good jobs and crowded them into ghettos.

Stokely Carmichael, in 1966, called for the civil rights movements to be "black-staffed, black-controlled, and black-financed." Later, he moved on to the Black Panthers, self-styled urban revolutionaries based in Oakland, California. Other leaders such as H. Rap Brown also called for Black Power.

On April 4, 1968, Martin Luther King was assassinated in Memphis by James Earl Ray. Riots in more than 100 cities followed.

The New Left

Students at the University of California at Berkeley staged sit-ins in 1964 to protest the prohibition of political canvassing on campus. In December, police broke up a sit-in; protests spread to other campuses across the country.

Student protests began focusing on the Vietnam War. In the spring of 1967, 500,000 gathered in Central Park in New York City to protest the war, many burning their draft cards. Students for a Democratic Society (SDS) became more militant and willing to use violence.

More than 200 large campus demonstrations took place in the spring, culminating in the occupation of buildings at Columbia University to protest the university's involvement in military research and its poor relations with minority groups. Police wielding billy clubs eventually broke up the demonstration. In August, thousands gathered in Chicago to protest the war during the Democratic convention.

Beginning in 1968, SDS began breaking up into rival factions. By the early 1970s, the New Left had lost political influence, having abandoned its original commitment to democracy and nonviolence.

Women's Liberation

In *The Feminine Mystique* (1963), Betty Friedan argued that middle-class society stifled women and did not allow them to use their individual talents. She attacked the cult of domesticity.

Friedan and other feminists founded the National Organization for Women (NOW) in 1966, calling for equal employment opportunities and equal pay.

Vietnam

After the French defeat in 1954, the United States sent military advisors to South Vietnam to aid the government of Ngo Dinh Diem. The pro-Communist Vietcong forces gradually grew in strength, partly because Diem failed to follow through on promised reforms. They received support from North Vietnam, the Soviet Union, and China.

In August 1964—after claiming that North Vietnamese gunboats had fired on American destroyers in the Gulf of Tonkin—Lyndon Johnson pushed the Gulf of Tonkin resolution through Congress, authorizing him to use military force in Vietnam. After a February 1965 attack by the Vietcong on Pleiku, Johnson ordered operation "Rolling Thunder," the first sustained bombing of North Vietnam. Johnson then sent combat troops to South Vietnam; under the leadership of General William C. Westmoreland, they conducted search and destroy operations. The number of troops increased to 184,000 in 1965, 385,000 in 1966, 485,000 in 1967, and 538,000 in 1968.

"Hawks" defended the president's policy and, drawing on containment theory, said that the nation had the responsibility to resist aggression. If Vietnam should fall, it was said, all Southeast Asia would eventually go. The administration stressed its willingness to negotiate the withdrawal of all "foreign" forces from the war.

Opposition began quickly, with "teach-ins" at the University of Michigan in 1965 and a 1966 congressional investigation led by Senator J. William Fulbright. Antiwar demonstrations were gaining large crowds by 1967. "Doves" argued that the war was a civil war in which the United States should not meddle.

On January 31, 1968, the first day of the Vietnamese new year (Tet), the Vietcong attacked numerous cities and towns, American bases, and even Saigon. Although they suffered large losses, the Vietcong won a psychological victory, as American opinion began turning against the war.

The Election of 1968

In November 1967, Senator Eugene McCarthy of Minnesota announced his candidacy for the 1968 Democratic presidential nomination, running on the issue of opposition to the war.

In February, McCarthy won 42 percent of the Democratic vote in the New Hampshire primary, compared with Johnson's 48 percent. Robert F. Kennedy then announced his candidacy for the Democratic presidential nomination.

Lyndon Johnson withdrew his candidacy on March 31, 1968, and Vice President Hubert H. Humphrey took his place as a candidate for the Democratic nomination.

After winning the California primary over McCarthy, Robert Kennedy was assassinated by Sirhan Sirhan, a young Palestinian. This event assured Humphrey's nomination.

The Republicans nominated Richard M. Nixon. Governor George C. Wallace of Alabama ran for the presidency under the banner of the American Independent party, appealing to fears generated by protestors and big government.

Johnson suspended air attacks on North Vietnam shortly before the election. Nonetheless Nixon, who emphasized stability and order, defeated Humphrey by a margin of 1 percent. Wallace's 13.5 percent was the best showing by a third-party candidate since 1924.

The Nixon Conservative Reaction

The Nixon administration sought to block renewal of the Voting Rights Act and delay implementation of court-ordered school desegregation in Mississippi.

In 1969, Nixon appointed Warren E. Burger, a conservative, as chief justice. Although more conservative than the Warren court, the Burger court did declare the death penalty, as used at the time, unconstitutional in 1972, and struck down state antiabortion legislation in 1973.

Vietnamization

The president turned to "Vietnamization," the effort to build up South Vietnamese forces while withdrawing American troops. In 1969, Nixon reduced American troop strength by 60,000, but at the same time ordered the bombing of Cambodia, a neutral country.

In April 1970, Nixon announced that Vietnamization was succeeding but a few days later, he sent troops into Cambodia to clear out Vietcong sanctuaries and resumed bombing of North Vietnam.

Protests against escalation of the war were especially strong on college campuses. After several students were killed during protests, several hundred colleges were closed down by student strikes, as moderates joined the radicals. Congress repealed the Gulf of Tonkin Resolution.

The publication in 1971 of classified Defense Department documents, called "The Pentagon Papers," revealed that the government had misled the Congress and the American people regarding its intentions in Vietnam during the mid-1960s.

Nixon drew American forces back from Cambodia but increased bombing. In March 1972, after stepped-up aggression from the North, Nixon ordered the mining of Haiphong and other northern ports.

In the summer of 1972, negotiations between the United States and North Vietnam began in Paris. A few days before the 1972 presidential election, Henry Kissinger, the president's national security advisor, announced that "peace was at hand."

Nixon resumed bombing of North Vietnam in December 1972, claiming that the North Vietnamese were not bargaining in good faith. In January 1973, the opponents reached a settlement in which the North Vietnamese retained control over large areas of the South and agreed to release American prisoners of war within 60 days. Nearly 60,000 Americans had been killed and 300,000 more wounded and the war had cost Americans $109 billion. On March 29, 1973, the last American combat troops left South Vietnam.

Foreign Policy

With his national security advisor, Henry Kissinger, Nixon took some bold diplomatic initiatives. In February 1972, Nixon and Kissinger went to China to meet with Mao Tse-tung and his associates. The United States agreed to support China's admission to the United Nations and to pursue economic and cultural exchanges.

Nixon and Kissinger called their policy *détente*, a French term meaning a relaxation in the tensions between two governments.

The Election of 1972

Richard M. Nixon, who had been renominated by the Republicans, won a landslide victory over the Democratic nominee, Senator George McGovern.

WATERGATE, CARTER, AND THE NEW CONSERVATISM, AND POST-COLD WAR CHALLENGES (1972–2008)

Watergate

What became known as the Watergate crisis began during the 1972 presidential campaign. Early on the morning of June 17, James McCord, a security officer for the Committee for the Re-Election of the President, and four other men broke into Democratic headquarters at the Watergate apartment complex in Washington, D.C., and were caught while going through files and installing electronic eavesdropping devices.

In March 1974, a grand jury indicted H.R. Haldeman, John Ehrlichman, former Attorney General John Mitchell, and four other White House aides and named Nixon an unindicted coconspirator.

Meanwhile, the House Judiciary Committee televised its debate over misconduct by the President, adopting three articles of impeachment. It charged the president with obstructing justice, misusing presidential power, and failing to obey the committee's subpoenas.

Before the House began to debate impeachment, Nixon announced his resignation on August 8, 1974, to take effect at noon the following day. Gerald Ford then became president.

The Ford Presidency

Gerald Ford was in many respects the opposite of Nixon. Although a partisan Republican, he was well liked and free from any hint of scandal. Ford almost immediately encountered controversy when in September 1974 he offered to pardon Nixon. Nixon accepted the offer, although he admitted no wrongdoing and had not yet been charged with a crime.

Vietnam

As North Vietnamese forces pushed back the South Vietnamese, Ford asked Congress to provide more arms for the South. Congress rejected the request, and in April 1975 Saigon fell to the North Vietnamese.

Carter's Moderate Liberalism

Ronald Reagan, a former movie actor and governor of California, opposed Ford for the Republican presidential nomination, but Ford won by a slim margin. The Democrats nominated James Earl Carter, formerly governor of Georgia, who ran on the basis of his integrity and lack of Washington connections. Carter narrowly defeated Ford in the election.

Carter offered amnesty to Americans who had fled the draft and gone to other countries during the Vietnam War. He established the Departments of Energy and Education and placed the civil service on a merit basis. He created a "superfund" for cleanup of chemical waste dumps, established controls over strip mining, and protected 100 million acres of Alaskan wilderness from development.

Carter's Foreign Policy

Carter negotiated a controversial treaty with Panama, affirmed by the Senate in 1978, that provided for the transfer of ownership of the canal to Panama in 1999 and guaranteed its neutrality.

Carter ended official recognition of Taiwan and in 1979 recognized the People's Republic of China. Conservatives called the decision a "sell-out."

In 1978, Carter negotiated the Camp David Agreement between Israel and Egypt. Israel promised to return occupied land in the Sinai to Egypt in exchange for Egyptian recognition, a process completed in 1982. An agreement to negotiate the Palestinian refugee problem proved ineffective.

The Iranian Crisis

In 1978, a revolution forced the shah of Iran to flee the country, replacing him with a religious leader, Ayatollah Ruhollah Khomeini. Because the United States had supported the shah with arms and money, the revolutionaries were strongly anti-American, calling the United States the "Great Satan."

After Carter allowed the exiled shah to come to the United States for medical treatment in October 1979, some 400 Iranians broke into the American embassy in Teheran on November 4, taking the occupants captive. They demanded that the shah be returned to Iran for trial and that his wealth be confiscated and given to Iran. Carter rejected these demands; instead, he froze Iranian assets in the United States and established a trade embargo against Iran.

The Election of 1980

Republican Ronald Reagan defeated Carter by a large electoral majority, and the Republicans gained control of the Senate and increased their representation in the House.

After extensive negotiations with Iran, in which Algeria acted as an intermediary, American hostages were freed on January 20, 1981, the day of Reagan's inauguration.

The Reagan Presidency: Attacking Big Government

An ideological though pragmatic conservative, Ronald Reagan acted quickly and forcefully to change the direction of government policy. He placed priority on cutting taxes. His approach was based on "supply-side" economics, the idea that if government left more money in the hands of the people, they would invest rather then spend the excess on consumer goods. The results would be greater production, more jobs, and greater prosperity, and thus more income for the government despite lower tax rates.

Reagan asked for a 30 percent tax cut, and despite fears of inflation on the part of Congress, in August 1983 obtained a 25 percent cut, spread over three years.

Congress passed the Budget Reconciliation Act in 1981, cutting $39 billion from domestic programs, including education, food stamps, public housing, and the National Endowments for the Arts and Humanities. While cutting domestic programs, Reagan increased the defense budget by $12 billion.

From a deficit of $59 billion in 1980, the federal budget was running $195 billion in the red by 1983.

Because of rising deficits, Reagan and Congress increased taxes in various ways. The 1982 Tax Equity and Fiscal Responsibility Act reversed some concessions made to business in 1981. Social Security benefits became taxable income in 1983. In 1984, the Deficit Reduction Act increased taxes by another $50 billion. But the deficit continued to increase.

Reagan ended ongoing antitrust suits against IBM and AT&T, thereby fulfilling his promise to reduce government interference with business.

Asserting American Power

Reagan took a hard line against the Soviet Union, calling it an "evil empire." He placed new cruise missiles in Europe, despite considerable opposition from Europeans.

Reagan also concentrated on obtaining funding for the development of a computer-controlled strategic defense initiative system (SDI), popularly called "Star Wars" after the widely seen movie, that would destroy enemy missiles from outerspace.

In Nicaragua, Reagan encouraged the opposition (*contras*) to the leftist Sand- inista government with arms, tactical support, and intelligence, and supplied aid to the government of El Salvador in its struggles against left-wing rebels. In October 1983, the president also sent American troops into the Caribbean island of Grenada to overthrow a newly established Cuban-backed regime.

The Election of 1984

Walter Mondale, a former senator from Minnesota and vice president under Carter, won the Democratic nomination. Mondale criticized Reagan for his budget deficits, high unemployment and interest rates, and reduction of spending on social services. However, Reagan was elected to a second term in a landslide.

Second-Term Foreign Concerns

After Mikhail S. Gorbachev became the premier of the Soviet Union in March 1985 and took a more flexible approach toward both domestic and foreign affairs, Reagan softened his anti-Soviet stance.

Reagan and Gorbachev had difficulty in reaching an agreement on arms limita- tions at summit talks in 1985 and 1986. Finally, in December 1987, they signed an agreement eliminating medium-range missiles from Europe.

Iran-Contra

In 1985 and 1986, several Reagan officials sold arms to the Iranians in hopes of encouraging them to use their influence in getting American hostages in Lebanon released. The profits from these sales were then diverted to the Nicaraguan *contras* in an attempt to get around congressional restrictions on funding the *contras*. The president was forced to appoint a special prosecutor, and Congress held hearings on the affair in May 1987.

Second-Term Domestic Affairs: The Economy

The Tax Reform Act of 1986 lowered tax rates. At the same time, it removed many tax shelters and tax credits. The law did away with the concept of progressive taxation, the requirement that the percentage of income taxed increased as income increased.

The federal deficit reached $179 billion in 1985. At about the same time, the United States experienced trade deficits of more than $100 billion annually.

Black Monday: On October 19, 1987, the Dow Jones Industrial Average dropped more than 500 points. Between August 25 and October 20, the market lost over a trillion dollars in paper value.

NASA: The explosion of the shuttle *Challenger* soon after take-off on January 28, 1986, damaged NASA's credibility and reinforced doubts about the complex technology required for the SDI program.

Supreme Court: Reagan reshaped the Court in 1986, replacing Chief Justice Warren C. Burger with Associate Justice William H. Rehnquist, probably the most conservative member of the Court. Although failing in his nomination of Robert Bork for associate justice, Reagan did appoint other conservatives to the Court: Sandra Day O'Connor, Antonin Scalia, and Anthony Kennedy.

The Election of 1988

Vice President George H.W. Bush won the Republican nomination. Bush easily defeated Michael Dukakis, the Democratic nominee, but the Republicans were unable to make any inroads in Congress.

The Bush Administration

Soon after Bush took office, the budget deficit for 1990 was estimated at $143 billion. In September, the administration and Congress agreed to increase taxes on gasoline, tobacco, and alcohol, establish an excise tax on luxury items, and raise Medicare taxes. Cuts were also to be made in medicare and other domestic programs. In a straight party vote, Republicans voting against and Democrats voting in favor, Congress in December transferred the power to decide whether new tax and spending proposals violated the deficit cutting agreement from the White House Office of Management and Budget to the Congressional Budget Office.

The Commission on Base Realignment and Closure proposed in December 1989 that 54 military bases be closed. In June 1990, Secretary of Defense Richard Cheney sent Congress a plan to cut military spending by 10 percent and the armed forces by 25 percent over the next five years. The following April, Cheney recommended the closing of 43 domestic military bases, plus many more abroad.

With the savings and loan industry in financial trouble in 1989, largely because of bad real-estate loans, Bush signed a bill which created the Resolution Trust

Corporation to oversee the closure and merging of savings and loans, and which provided $166 billion over 10 years to cover the bad debts. Estimates of the total costs of the debacle were over $300 billion.

Bush's Activist Foreign Policy

Panama: Since coming to office, the Bush administration had been concerned with Panamanian dictator Manuel Noriega because he allegedly served as an important link in the drug traffic between South America and the United States. After economic sanctions, diplomatic efforts, and an October 1989 coup failed to oust Noriega, Bush ordered 12,000 troops into Panama on December 20. The Americans installed a new government headed by Guillermo Endara, who had earlier won a presidential election that was promptly nullified by Noriega. On January 3, 1990, Noriega surrendered to the Americans and was taken to the United States to stand trial on drug trafficking charges; he was convicted and jailed for assisting the Medellín drug cartel. Twenty-three United States soldiers and three American civilians were killed in the operation. The Panamanians lost nearly 300 soldiers and more than 500 civilians.

Nicaragua: After years of civil war, Nicaragua held a presidential election in February 1990. Because of an economy largely destroyed by civil war and large financial debt to the United States, Violeta Barrios de Chamorro of the National Opposition Union defeated Daniel Ortega Saavedra of the Sandinistas, thereby fulfilling a long-standing American objective. The United States lifted its economic sanctions in March and put together an economic aid package for Nicaragua. In September 1991, the Bush administration forgave Nicaragua most of its debt to the United States.

China: After the death in April 1989 of reformer Hu Yaobang, formerly general secretary and chairman of the Chinese Communist party, students began pro-democracy marches in Beijing. By the middle of May, more than one million people were gathering on Beijing's Tiananmen Square, and other protestors elsewhere in China, calling for political reform. Martial law was imposed and in early June the army fired on the demonstrators. Estimates of the death toll in the wake of the nationwide crackdown on demonstrators ranged between 500 and 7,000. In July 1989, United States National Security Advisor Brent Scowcroft and Deputy Secretary of State Lawrence Eagleburger secretly met with Chinese leaders. When they again met the Chinese in December and revealed their earlier meeting, the Bush administration faced a storm of criticism for its policy of "constructive engagement" from opponents arguing that sanctions should be imposed. While establishing sanctions in 1991 on Chinese high-technology satellite-part exports, Bush continued to support renewal of Most Favored Nation trading status.

Africa: To rescue American citizens threatened by civil war, Bush sent 230 marines into Liberia in August 1990, evacuating 125 people. South Africa in 1990 freed Nelson Mandela, the most famous leader of the African National Congress, after 28 years of imprisonment. South Africa then began moving away from apartheid, and in 1991 Bush lifted economic sanctions imposed five years earlier. Mandela and his wife, Winnie, toured the U.S. in June 1990 to a tumultuous welcome, particularly from African-Americans. During their visit, they also addressed Congress.

Collapse of East European Communism

In August 1989 Hungary opened its borders with Austria. The following October, the Communists reorganized their party, calling it the Socialist party. Hungary then proclaimed itself a "Free Republic."

With thousands of East Germans passing through Hungary to Austria, after the opening of the borders in August 1989, Erich Honecker stepped down as head of state in October. On November 1, the government opened the border with Czechoslovakia and eight days later the Berlin Wall fell. On December 6, a non-Communist became head of state, followed on December 11 by large demonstrations demanding German reunification. Reunification took place in October 1990.

After anti-government demonstrations were forcibly broken up in Czechoslovakia in October 1989, changes took place in the Communist leadership the following month. Then, on December 8, the Communists agreed to relinquish power and Parliament elected Václav Havel, a playwright and anti-Communist leader, to the presidency on December 29.

When anti-government demonstrations in Romania were met by force in early December, portions of the military began joining the opposition which captured dictator Nicolae Ceaușescu and his wife, Elena, killing them on December 25, 1989. In May 1990 the National Salvation Front, made up of many former Communists, won the parliamentary elections.

In January 1990 the Bulgarian national assembly repealed the dominant role of the Communist party. A multi-party coalition government was formed the following December.

Albania opened its border with Greece and legalized religious worship in January 1990, and in July ousted hardliners from the government.

Amid the collapse of Communism in Eastern Europe, Bush met with Mikhail Gorbachev in Malta from December 1 through December 3, 1989; the two leaders appeared to agree that the Cold War was over. On May 30 and 31, 1990, Bush and Gorbachev met in Washington to discuss the possible reunification of Germany, and signed a trade treaty between the United States and the Soviet Union. The meeting of the two leaders in Helsinki on September 9 addressed strategies for the developing Persian Gulf crisis. At the meeting of the "Group of 7" nations (Canada, France, Germany, Italy, Japan, United Kingdom, and the United States) in July 1991, Gorbachev requested economic aid from the West. A short time later, on July 30 and 31, Bush met Gorbachev in Moscow where they signed the START treaty, which cut U.S. and Soviet nuclear arsenals by 30 percent, and pushed for Middle Eastern talks.

Persian Gulf Crisis

Saddam Hussein of Iraq charged that Kuwait had conspired with the United States to keep oil prices low and began massing troops at the Iraq-Kuwait border.

On August 2, Iraq invaded Kuwait, an act that Bush denounced as "naked aggression." One day later 100,000 Iraqi soldiers were poised south of Kuwait City near the Saudi Arabian border. The United States quickly banned most trade with Iraq, froze Iraq's and Kuwait's assets in the United States, and sent aircraft carriers to the Persian Gulf. After the United Nations Security Council condemned the invasion, on August 6 Bush ordered the deployment of air, sea, and land forces to Saudi Arabia, dubbing the operation "Desert Shield." At the end of August there were 100,000 American soldiers in Saudi Arabia.

Bush encouraged Egypt to support American policy by forgiving Egypt its debt to the United States and obtaining pledges of financial support from Saudi Arabia, Kuwait, and Japan, among other nations, to help pay for the operation. On October 29, the Security Council warned Saddam Hussein that further actions might be taken if he did not withdraw from Kuwait. In November Bush ordered that U.S. forces be increased to more than 400,000. On November 29, the United Nations set January 15, 1991, as the deadline for Iraqi withdrawal from Kuwait.

On January 9, Iraq's foreign-minister, Tariq Aziz, rejected a letter written by Bush to Hussein. Three days later, after an extensive debate, Congress authorized the use of force in the Gulf. On January 17, an international force including the United States, Great Britain, France, Italy, Saudi Arabia, and Kuwait launched an air and missile attack on Iraq and occupied Kuwait. The U.S. called the effort "Operation Desert Storm." Under the overall command of Army General H. Norman Schwarzkopf, the military effort emphasized high-technology weapons, including F-15 E fighter-bombers, F-117 A stealth fighters, Tomahawk cruise missiles, and Patriot anti-missile missiles. Beginning on January 17, Iraq fired SCUD missiles into Israel in an effort to draw that country into the war and splinter the U.S.-Arabian coalition. On January 22 and 23, Hussein's forces set Kuwaiti oil fields on fire and spilled oil into the Gulf.

On February 23, the allied ground assault began. Four days later Bush announced that Kuwait was liberated and ordered offensive operations to cease. The United Nations established the terms for the cease-fire: Iraqi annexation of Kuwait to be rescinded, Iraq to accept liability for damages and return Kuwaiti property, Iraq to end all military actions and identify mines and booby traps, and Iraq to release captives.

On April 3, the Security Council approved a resolution to establish a permanent cease-fire; Iraq accepted U.N. terms on April 6. The next day the United States began airlifting food to Kurdish refugees on the Iraq-Turkey border who were fleeing the Kurdish rebellion against Hussein, a rebellion that was seemingly encouraged by Bush, who nonetheless refused to become militarily involved. The United States estimated that 100,000 Iraqis had been killed during the war while the Americans had lost about 115 lives.

On February 6, 1991, the United States had set out its postwar goals for the Middle East. These included regional arms control and security arrangements, international aid for reconstruction of Iraq and Kuwait, and resolution of the Israeli-Palestinian conflict. Immediately after cessation of the conflict, Secretary of State James Baker toured the Middle East attempting to promote a conference to address the problems of the region. After several more negotiating sessions, Saudi Arabia, Syria, Jordan, and Lebanon had accepted the U.S. proposal for an Arab-Israeli peace conference by the middle of July; Israel conditionally accepted in early August. Despite continuing conflict with Iraq, including United Nations inspections of its nuclear capabilities, and new Israeli settlements in disputed territory—which kept the conference agreement tenuous—the nations met in Madrid, Spain, at the end of October. Bilateral talks in early November between Israel and the Arabs concentrated on procedural issues.

Breakup of the Soviet Union

Following the collapse of Communism in Eastern Europe, the Baltic republic of Lithuania, which had been taken over by the Soviet Union in 1939 through an agreement with Adolf Hitler, declared its independence from the Soviet Union on March 11, 1990.

Two days later, on March 13, the Soviet Union removed the Communist monopoly of political power, allowing non-Communists to run for office. The process of liberalization went haltingly forward in the Soviet Union. Perhaps the most significant event was the election of Boris Yeltsin, who had left the Communist party, as president of the Russian republic on June 12, 1991.

On August 19, Soviet hard-liners attempted a coup to oust Gorbachev, but a combination of their inability to control communication with the outside world, a failure to quickly establish military control, and the resistance of Yeltsin, members of the military, and people in the streets of cities such as Moscow and Leningrad, ended the coup on August 21, returning Gorbachev to power.

In the aftermath of the coup, much of the Communist structure came crashing down, setting the stage for opposition parties to emerge. The remaining Baltic republics of Latvia and Estonia declared their independence, which was recognized by the United States several days after other nations had done so. Most of the other Soviet republics then followed suit in declaring their independence. The Bush administration wanted some form of central authority to remain in the Soviet Union; hence, it did not seriously consider recognizing the independence of any republics except the Baltics. Bush also resisted offering economic aid to the Soviet Union until it presented a radical economic reform plan to move toward a free market. However, humanitarian aid such as food was pledged in order to preserve stability during the winter.

In September 1991, George Bush announced unilateral removal and destruction of ground-based tactical nuclear weapons in Europe and Asia, removal of nuclear-armed Tomahawk cruise missiles from surface ships and submarines, immediate destruction of intercontinental ballistic missiles covered by START, and an end to the 24-hour alert for strategic bombers that the U.S. had maintained for decades. Gorbachev responded the next month by announcing the immediate deactivation of intercontinental ballistic missiles covered by START, removal of all short-range missiles from Soviet ships, submarines, and aircraft, and destruction of all ground-based tactical nuclear weapons. He also said that the Soviet Union would reduce its forces by 700,000 troops, and he placed all long-range nuclear missiles under a single command. Gorbachev's hold on the presidency progressively weakened in the final months of 1991, with the reforms he had put in place taking on a life of their own. The dissolution of the U.S.S.R. led to his resignation in December, making way for Boris Yeltsin, who had headed popular resistance. The United States was now the world's only superpower.

The Democrats Reclaim the White House

William Jefferson Clinton, governor of Arkansas, overcame several rivals to win the Democratic presidential nomination in 1992 and with his running mate, Senator Albert Gore of Tennessee, went on to win the White House. During the campaign, Clinton and independent candidate H. Ross Perot, a wealthy Texas businessman, emphasized jobs and the economy while attacking the mounting federal debt. The incumbent, Bush, stressed traditional values and his foreign policy accomplishments. In the 1992 election, Clinton won 43 percent of the popular vote and 370 electoral votes, defeating Bush and Perot. Perot took 19 percent of the popular vote, but was unable to garner any electoral votes.

Clinton came to be dogged by a number of controversies, ranging from alleged ill-gotten gains in a complex Arkansas land deal that came to be known as the Whitewater Affair to charges of sexual misconduct, brought by a former Arkansas state employee (with whom he would ultimately reach an out-of-court settlement), that dated to an incident she said had occurred when Clinton was governor. In December 1998 Clinton was impeached by the House on charges that stemmed from an adulterous affair with a White House intern, Monica Lewinsky. The affair had been uncovered by Independent Counsel Kenneth Starr in the course of a long-running investigation into alleged malfeasance by the president and his wife, Hillary, in the Whitewater land deal and other matters. Extraordinary detail about Clinton's encounters with Lewinsky was revealed in a voluminous report from Starr's office. Its release triggered the impeachment proceedings, which ended with Clinton's acquittal by the Senate in February 1999.

On the legislative front, Clinton was strongly rebuffed in an attempt during his first term to reform the nation's healthcare system. In the 1994 mid-term elections, in what Clinton himself considered a repudiation of his administration, the Republicans took both houses of Congress from the Democrats and voted in Newt Gingrich of Georgia as Speaker of the House. Gingrich had helped craft the Republican congressional campaign strategy to dramatically shrink the federal government and give more power to the states.

Clinton, however, was not without his successes, both on the legislative and diplomatic fronts. He signed legislation establishing a five-day waiting period for handgun purchases as well as a crime bill emphasizing community policing. He signed the Family and Medical Leave Act, which requires large companies to provide up to 12 weeks' unpaid leave to workers for family and medical emergencies. He also championed welfare reform (a central theme of his campaign), but made it clear that the legislation he signed into law in August 1996 radically overhauling FDR's welfare system disturbed him on two counts—its exclusion of legal immigrants from getting most federal benefits and its deep cut in federal outlays for food stamps; Clinton said these flaws could be repaired with further legislation. In foreign affairs, Clinton signed the North American Free Trade Agreement (NAFTA), which lifted most trade barriers with Mexico and Canada as of 1994. Clinton sought to ease tensions between Israelis and Palestinians, and he helped bring together Itzhak Rabin, prime minister of Israel, and Yasir Arafat, chairman of the Palestine Liberation Organization, for a summit at the White House. Ultimately, the two Middle East leaders signed an accord in 1994 establishing Palestinian self-rule in the Gaza Strip and Jericho. In October 1994 Israel and Jordan signed a treaty to begin the process of establishing full diplomatic relations. Rabin was assassinated a year later by a radical, right-wing Israeli. The Clinton administration also played a central role in hammering out peace agreements in 1995 in war-torn former Yugoslavia—where armed conflict had broken out four years earlier among Serbs, Croats, Bosnian Muslims, and other factions and groups—and in 1998 in Northern Ireland.

Clinton recaptured the Democratic nomination without a serious challenge, while longtime GOP Senator Robert Dole of Kansas, the Senate majority leader, overcame several opponents but orchestrated a harmonious nominating convention with running mate Jack Kemp, a former New York congressman and Cabinet member. In November 1996, with most voters citing a healthy economy and the lack of an enticing alternative in Dole or the Reform Party's Perot, Clinton received 49 percent of the vote, becoming the first Democrat to be re-elected since FDR, in 1936. The GOP retained control of both houses of Congress.

Clinton, intent on mirroring the diversity of America in his Cabinet appointments, chose Hispanics Henry Cisneros (Housing and Urban Development) and Federico Peña (Transportation and, later, Energy), African Americans Ron Brown (Commerce) and Mike Espy (Agriculture), and women, including the nation's first woman attorney general, Janet Reno, and Madeleine Albright, the first woman secretary of state in U.S. history (Albright succeeded Warren Christopher, who served through Clinton's first term). Brown and 34 others on a trade mission died when his Air Force plane crashed in Croatia in April 1996. Cisneros and Espy both resigned under ethics clouds.

In 2000, Republican George W. Bush defeated Democrat Al Gore in a close and controversial election, with Bush receiving a majority of the electoral votes (after a decision by the Supreme Court to stop a third recount—essentially awarding Florida's electoral votes to him), but Gore receiving a majority of the popular vote. Eight months after being sworn in, the September 11th attacks occurred. In response to the attacks, President Bush declared a War on Terror, which led to the creation of a new cabinet level agency, the Department of Homeland Security, an invasion of Afghanistan, and an invasion of Iraq. On the domestic front, President Bush signed into law tax cuts, the No Child Left Behind Act, and Medicare prescription drug benefits for seniors.

After defeating Democrat John Kerry in the 2004 election, President Bush's second term was beset by scandals and criticism related to the War on Terror, Katrina and the perceived failure of the government's response, and an economy that went into recession. While extremely popular for much of his first term, his public approval ratings went from 90% approval to a low of 25% while finally rising to 34% as he left office. Only Harry Truman and Richard Nixon had lower ratings at the end of their presidencies.

The 2008 presidential election featured two Senators, Democrat Barack Obama from Illinois and Republican John McCain from Arizona. Senator Obama won and became the 44th president of the United States and its first African American president.

Late 20th Century Social and Cultural Developments

AIDS: In 1981 scientists announced the discovery of Acquired Immune Deficiency Syndrome (AIDS), which was especially prevalent among homosexual males and intravenous drug users. Widespread fear resulted, including an upsurge in homophobia. The Centers for Disease Control and Prevention (CDC) and the National Cancer Institute, among others, pursued research on the disease. The Food and Drug Administration responded to calls for fast-tracking evaluation of drugs by approving the drug AZT in February 1991. With the revelation that a Florida dentist had infected three patients, there were calls for mandatory testing of healthcare workers. Supporters of testing argued before a House hearing in September 1991 that testing should be regarded as a public health, rather than a civil rights, issue. In early 1998, the CDC estimated that between 400,000 and 650,000 Americans were HIV-positive, meaning that they had the virus that causes AIDS. Public health officials expressed concern about the difficulties in tracking the spread of AIDS, as the HIV infection was being reported to health agencies only when patients developed symptoms, which could be years after infection. New drug therapies, meanwhile, were preventing AIDS symptoms from ever appearing, creating the specter of growing numbers of people going unseen by public-health agencies as they spread the virus. These developments came against the backdrop of a marked change in the demographic makeup of the epidemic's victims—from mostly white homosexual males to African-Americans, Hispanics, and women, particularly those who were poor, intravenous drug users, or the sex partners of drug users.

Families: More than half the married women in the United States continued to hold jobs outside the home. Nearly one out of every two marriages was ending in divorce, and there was an increase in the number of unmarried couples living together, which contributed to a growing number of illegitimate births. So-called family values became a major theme in presidential politics, powered in part by the publication of leading conservative William J. Bennett's best-selling anthology *The Book of Virtues: A Treasury of Great Moral Stories*. Bennett had served as Bush's secretary of education and, later, as director of the Office of National Drug Control Policy, which the press shortened to "drug czar."

Terrorism Hits Home: While terrorist attacks continued to be a grim reality overseas through the 1980s and early 1990s, with Americans frequently targeted, such incidents had come to be perceived as something the United States wouldn't have to face on its own soil—until February 26, 1993, when a terrorist bomb ripped through the underground parking garage of the World Trade Center in New York City, killing six people and injuring more than 1,000. The blast shattered America's "myth of invulnerability," wrote foreign policy analyst Jeffrey D. Simon in his book *The Terrorist Trap*. Convicted and sentenced to 240 years each were four Islamic militants. On April 19, 1995, the Oklahoma City federal building was bombed: 168 people were killed and 500 injured. Timothy James McVeigh, a gun enthusiast involved in the American militia movement who had often expressed hatred toward the U.S. government and was particularly aggrieved over the government's assault two years earlier on a self-proclaimed prophet's compound in Waco, Texas, was convicted and sentenced to death in June 1997. A second defendant, Terry Nichols, was convicted of conspiracy. These attacks, however, were dwarfed by the September 11, 2001, attacks in which terrorists turned hijacked planes into missiles—two destroying the World Trade Center and one damaging the Pentagon. A fourth plane was brought down in Pennsylvania, apparently by passengers who overtook the hijackers. President Bush immediately cast suspicion upon Saudi exile Osama bin Laden and declared a "war on terrorism" that began with a military strike against Afghanistan, bin Laden's alleged base of operations.

Murder Trial a National Spectacle: In Los Angeles, former pro-football star, broadcaster, and actor O.J. Simpson was tried for the brutal murder in June 1994 of his ex-wife, Nicole Brown Simpson, and her friend Ronald Goldman. The nationally televised trial became a running spectacle for months. Simpson was found not guilty, but later, in a civil trial, would be found responsible for the slaying of Goldman and for committing battery against Nicole.

Crime and Politics: George H.W. Bush had won the presidency in 1988 on a strong anti-crime message, crystallized in a controversial TV spot that demonized Willie Horton, an African-American inmate in the Massachusetts jail system who was released while then-presidential candidate Michael Dukakis was the Democratic governor. Bill Clinton co-opted the traditional Republican crime issue by pushing through legislation for more community policing, an approach that, together with aggressive central management, was credited for the plummeting crime rate in New York City, for example.

U.S. Prisoner Count Grows: Between 1987 and 1997, the period spanning the Bush administration and Clinton's first term, the number of Americans in prison doubled, soaring from 800,000 to 1.6 million.

Drug Abuse Continues: Drug abuse continued to be widespread, with cocaine becoming more readily available, particularly in a cheaper, stronger form called "crack."

Labor: Labor union strength continued to ebb in the 1990s (though some observers pointed to the success of the 1997 Teamsters strike against United Parcel Service as a sign that labor was rebounding), with the U.S. Department of Labor's Bureau of Labor Statistics reporting that union membership dropped to 14.5 percent of wage and salary employment in 1996, down from 14.9 percent in 1995. In 1983, union members made up 20.1 percent of the work force. Unions continued to be responsible for higher wages for their members: organized workers reported median weekly earnings of $615, as against a median of $462 for non-union workers, according to the bureau.

Abortion and the High Court: In a July 1989 decision, *Webster v. Reproductive Health Services*, the U.S. Supreme Court upheld a Missouri law prohibiting public employees from performing abortions, unless the mother's life is threatened. With this decision came a shift in focus on the abortion issue from the courts to the state legislatures. Pro-life (anti-abortion rights) forces moved in several states to restrict the availability of abortions, but their results were mixed. Florida rejected abortion restrictions in October 1989, the governor of Louisiana vetoed similar legislation nine months later, and in early 1991 Maryland adopted a liberal abortion law. In contrast, Utah and Pennsylvania enacted strict curbs on abortion during the same period. At the national level, Bush in October 1989 vetoed funding for Medicaid abortions. The conflict between pro-choice (pro-abortion) and pro-life forces gained national attention through such events as a pro-life demonstration held in Washington in April 1990, and blockage of access to abortion clinics by Operation Rescue, a militant anti-abortion group, in the summer of 1991. Abortion clinics around the country continued to be the targets of protests and violence through the mid-1990s.

Gap Between Rich and Poor Widens: Kevin Phillips's *The Politics of Rich and Poor* (1990) argued that 40 million Americans in the bottom fifth of the population experienced a 1 percent decline in income between 1973 and 1979 and a 10 percent decline between 1979 and 1987. Meanwhile, the top fifth saw a rise of 7 percent and 16 percent during the same periods. The number of single-parent families living below the poverty line (annual income of $11,611 for a family of four) rose by 46 percent between 1979 and 1987. Nearly one-quarter of American children under age six were counted among the poor, said Phillips.

Censorship: The conservative leaning of the electorate in the late 20th century revealed its cultural dimension in a controversy that erupted over the National Endowment for the Arts in September 1989. Criticism of photographer Robert Mapplethorpe's homoerotic and masochistic pictures, among other artworks that had been funded by the Endowment, led Senator Jesse Helms of North Carolina to propose that grants for "obscene or indecent" projects, or those derogatory of religion, be cut off. Although the proposal ultimately failed, it raised questions about the government's role as a sponsor of art in an increasingly pluralistic society. The Mapplethorpe photographs also became an issue the following summer when Cincinnati's Contemporary Art Center was indicted on charges of obscenity when it exhibited the artist's work. A jury later struck down the charges. Meanwhile, in March 1990, the Recording Industry Association of America, in a move advocated by, among others, Tipper Gore, wife of Democratic Senator Al Gore of Tennessee (the man who would be elected vice-president in 1992), agreed to place new uniform warning labels on recordings that contained potentially offensive language.

Crisis in Education: The National Commission on Excellence in Education, appointed in 1981, argued in "A Nation at Risk" that a "rising tide of mediocrity" characterized the nation's schools. In the wake of the report, many states instituted reforms, including higher teacher salaries, competency tests for teachers, and an increase in required subjects for high school graduation. In September 1989 President Bush met with the nation's governors in Charlottesville, Virginia, to work on a plan to improve the schools. The governors issued a call for the establishment of national performance goals to be measured by achievement tests. In February 1990 the National Governors' Association adopted specific performance goals, stating that achievement tests should be administered in grades four, eight, and twelve. As the new millennium approached, however, signs began to emerge that the tide might be turning: a major global comparison found in June 1997 that America's 9- and 10-year-olds were among the world's best in science and also scored well above average in math.

Literary Trends: The 1980s and 1990s saw the emergence of writers who concentrated on marginal or regional aspects of national life. William Kennedy wrote a series of novels about Albany, New York, most notably *Ironweed* (1983). The small-town West attracted attention from Larry McMurtry, whose *Lonesome Dove* (1985) used myth to explore the history of the region. The immigrant experience gave rise to Amy Tan's *The Joy-Luck Club* (1989) and Oscar Hijuelos's *The Mambo Kings Play Songs of Love* (1990). Tom Wolfe satirized greed, and class and racial tensions in New York City in *The Bonfire of the Vanities* (1987). Toni Morrison's *Beloved* (1987) dramatized the African-American slavery experience.

➲ REVIEW QUESTIONS

1. Which of the following statements is true of the Kansas-Nebraska Act?

    (A) It led to the disintegration of the Democratic party.

    (B) It was a measure that the South had been demanding for decades.

    (C) It led directly to the formation of the Republican party.

    (D) By applying "popular sovereignty" to territories formerly closed to slavery by the Missouri Compromise, it succeeded in maintaining the tenuous sectional peace that had been created by the Compromise of 1850.

2. All of the following were steps taken by the United States to aid Great Britain prior to U.S. entry into World War II EXCEPT

    (A) the sale of 50 destroyers to the British in exchange for 99-year leases on certain overseas naval bases.

    (B) gradual assumption by the U.S. Navy of an increasing role in patrolling the Atlantic against German submarines.

    (C) institution of the Lend-Lease Act for providing war supplies to Britain beyond its ability to pay.

    (D) the stationing of U.S. Marines in Scotland to protect it against possible German invasion.

3. Thomas Nast achieved fame and influence as a

    (A) radio commentator.   (C) photographer.

    (B) newspaper publisher.   (D) political cartoonist.

4. Which of the following is true of the Stamp Act Congress?

    (A) It was the first unified government for all the American colonies.

    (B) It provided an important opportunity for colonial stamp agents to discuss methods of enforcing the act.

    (C) It was attended only by Georgia, Virginia, and the Carolinas.

    (D) It provided an important opportunity for colonial leaders to meet and establish ties with one another.

5.   The map below depicts the United States immediately after which of the following events?

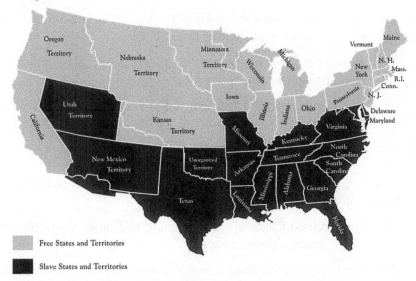

(A)   Passage of the Compromise of 1850

(B)   Negotiation of the Webster-Ashburton Treaty

(C)   Passage of the Northwest Ordinance

(D)   Settlement of the Mexican War

6.   The principle of "popular sovereignty" was

(A)   first conceived by Senator Stephen A. Douglas.

(B)   applied as part of the Missouri Compromise.

(C)   a central feature of the Kansas-Nebraska Act.

(D)   a policy favored by the Whig party during the late 1840s and early 1850s.

7.   In issuing the Emancipation Proclamation, one of Lincoln's goals was to

(A)   gain the active aid of Britain and France in restoring the Union.

(B)   stir up enthusiasm for the war in such border states as Maryland and Kentucky.

(C)   please the Radicals in the North by abolishing slavery in areas of the South already under the control of Union armies.

(D)   keep Britain and France from intervening on the side of the Confederacy.

8. Which of the following was not one of Hoover's responses to the Great Depression?

(A) He at first stressed the desirability of localism and private initiative rather than government intervention.

(B) He saw the Depression as akin to an act of nature, about which nothing could be done except to ride it out.

(C) He urged the nation's business leaders to maintain wages and full employment.

(D) His strategy for ending the Depression was a failure.

9. Which of the following statements is correct about the case of Whitaker Chambers and Alger Hiss?

(A) Hiss accused Chambers, an important mid-ranking government official, of being a Communist spy.

(B) The case gained national attention through the involvement of Senator Joseph R. McCarthy.

(C) Hiss was convicted of perjury for denying under oath that he had been a Communist agent.

(D) The case marked the beginning of American concern about Communist subversion.

10. Which of the following best characterizes the methods of Martin Luther King, Jr.?

(A) Nonviolent defiance of segregation

(B) Armed violence against police and troops

(C) Patience while developing the skills that would make blacks economically successful and gain them the respect of whites

(D) A series of petitions to Congress calling for correction of racial abuses

11. Which of the following best describes the agreement that ended the 1962 Cuban Missile Crisis?

(A) The Soviet Union agreed not to station troops in Cuba, and the United States agreed not to invade Cuba.

(B) The Soviet Union agreed to withdraw its missiles from Cuba, and the United States agreed not to invade Cuba.

(C) The Soviet Union agreed not to invade Turkey, and the United States agreed not to invade Cuba.

(D) The Soviet Union agreed to withdraw its missiles from Cuba, and the United States agreed not to invade Turkey.

12. The most common form of resistance on the part of black American slaves prior to the Civil War was

(A) violent uprisings in which many persons were killed.

(B) attempts to escape and reach Canada by means of the "Underground Railroad."

(C) passive resistance, including breaking tools and slightly slowing the pace of work.

(D) arson of plantation buildings and cotton gins.

13. Which of the following best describes the attitudes of Southern whites toward slavery during the mid-nineteenth century (ca. 1835–1865)?

(A) Slavery was a necessary evil.

(B) Slavery should be immediately abolished.

(C) Slavery was a benefit to both whites and blacks.

(D) Slavery should gradually be phased out and the freed slaves colonized to some place outside the United States.

14. For farmers and planters in the South, the 1850s was a period of

(A) low prices for agricultural products.

(B) rapid and violent fluctuations in crop prices.

(C) high crop prices due to repeated crop failures.

(D) high crop prices and sustained prosperity.

15. Immigrants coming to America from Eastern and Southern Europe during the late nineteenth century were most likely to

(A) settle in large cities in the Northeast or Midwest.

(B) settle on farms in the upper Midwest.

(C) seek to file on homesteads on the Great Plains.

(D) migrate to the South and Southwest.

16. Which of the following had the greatest effect in moving the United States toward participation in the First World War?

    (A) The German disregard of treaty obligations in violating Belgian neutrality

    (B) Germany's declaration of its intent to wage unrestricted submarine warfare

    (C) A German offer to reward Mexico with U.S. territory should it join Germany in a war against the United States

    (D) The beginning of the Russian Revolution

17. The Berlin Airlift was America's response to

    (A) the Soviet blockade of West Berlin from land communication with the rest of the western zone.

    (B) the acute war-time destruction of roads and railroads, making land transport almost impossible.

    (C) the unusually severe winter of 1947.

    (D) a widespread work stoppage by German transportation workers in protest of the allied occupation of Germany.

18. The economic theory of mercantilism would be consistent with which of the following statements?

    (A) Economics will prosper most when trade is restricted as little as possible.

    (B) A government should seek to direct the economy so as to maximize exports.

    (C) Colonies are of little economic importance to the mother country.

    (D) It is vital that a country imports more than it exports.

19. The primary American objection to the Stamp Act was that

    (A) it was an internal tax, whereas Americans were prepared to accept only external taxes.

    (B) it was the first tax of any kind ever imposed by Britain on the colonies.

    (C) its proposed tax rates were so high that they would have crippled the colonial economy.

    (D) it was a measure for raising revenue from the colonies but it had not been approved by the colonists through their representatives.

20. In seeking diplomatic recognition from foreign powers during the War for Independence, the American government found it necessary to

    (A) make large financial payments to the governments of France, Spain, and Holland.

    (B) promise to cede large tracts of American territory to France upon a victorious conclusion of the war.

    (C) demonstrate its financial stability and self-sufficiency.

    (D) demonstrate a determination and potential to win independence.

21. William Lloyd Garrison, in his publication *The Liberator,* was outspoken in calling for

    (A) the gradual and compensated emancipation of slaves.

    (B) colonization of slaves to some place outside the boundaries of the United States.

    (C) repeal of the congressional "gag rule."

    (D) immediate and uncompensated emancipation of slaves.

22. The Congressional "gag rule" stipulated that

    (A) no law could be passed prohibiting slavery in the territories.

    (B) no member of Congress could make statements or speeches outside of Congress pertaining to slavery.

    (C) no antislavery materials could be sent through the mail to addresses in Southern states.

    (D) no antislavery petitions would be formally received by Congress.

23. The main idea of Theodore Roosevelt's proposed "New Nationalism" was to

    (A) make the federal government an instrument of domestic reform.

    (B) undertake an aggressive new foreign policy.

    (C) increase economic competition by breaking up all trusts and large business combinations.

    (D) seek to establish a large overseas empire.

24. Franklin D. Roosevelt's New Deal program attempted or achieved all of the following EXCEPT

    (A) Raised farm prices by paying farmers not to plant.

    (B) Encouraged cooperation within industries so as to raise prices generally.

(C) Supported creation of the Reconstruction Finance Corporation.

(D) Invigorated the economy by lowering tariff barriers.

25. The Haymarket Incident involved

(A) a riot between striking workers and police.

(B) a scandal involving corruption within the Grant administration.

(C) allegations of corruption on the part of Republican presidential candidate James G. Blaine.

(D) a disastrous fire that called attention to the hazardous working conditions in some factories.

26. The "New Immigration" was made up primarily of

(A) Europeans who came for economic rather than religious reasons.

(B) Europeans who were better off financially than those of the "Old Immigration."

(C) persons from Northern and Western Europe.

(D) persons from Southern and Eastern Europe.

27. As a result of the Spanish-American War, the United States gained possession of Puerto Rico, Guam, and

(A) the Philippines.   (C) Bermuda.

(B) Cuba.   (D) the Panama Canal Zone.

28. The term "Long Hot Summers" refers to

(A) major outdoor rock concerts during the late 1960s and early 1970s.

(B) major Communist offensives against U.S. troops in Vietnam.

(C) protests held in large American cities against the Vietnam War.

(D) race riots in large American cities during the 1960s.

29. The immediate issue in dispute in Bacon's Rebellion was

(A) the jailing of individuals or seizure of their property for failure to pay taxes during a time of economic hardship.

(B) the under-representation of the backcountry in Virginia's legislature.

    (C)   the refusal of large planters to honor the terms of their contracts with former indentured servants.

    (D)   the perceived failure of Virginia's governor to protect the colony's frontier area from the depredations of raiding Indians.

30.   The Newburgh Conspiracy was concerned with

    (A)   betrayal of the plans for the vital fort at West Point, New York.

    (B)   the use of the Continental Army to create a more centralized Union of the states.

    (C)   resistance to the collection of federal excise taxes in western Pennsylvania.

    (D)   New England's threat to secede should the War of 1812 continue.

31.   The Wilmot Proviso stipulated that

    (A)   slavery should be prohibited in the lands acquired as a result of the Mexican War.

    (B)   no lands should be annexed to the United States as a result of the Mexican War.

    (C)   California should be a free state while the rest of the Mexican Cession should be reserved for the formation of slave states.

    (D)   the status of slavery in the Mexican Cession should be decided on the basis of "Popular Sovereignty."

32.   Which of the following was a goal of the Populist movement?

    (A)   Free coinage of silver

    (B)   Reform of child labor laws

    (C)   Using modern science to solve social problems

    (D)   Eliminating the electoral college as a method of choosing the nation's president

33.   The settlement-house movement drew its workers primarily from which of the following groups?

    (A)   Young, affluent, college-educated women

    (B)   Poor Eastern European immigrants

    (C)   Disabled veterans of the Spanish-American War

    (D)   Idealistic young men who came to the city largely from rural areas

34. In its decision in the case of *Dred Scott v. Sandford,* the Supreme Court held that

    (A) separate facilities for different races were inherently unequal and therefore unconstitutional.

    (B) no black slave could be a citizen of the United States.

    (C) separate but equal facilities for different races were constitutional.

    (D) Affirmative Action programs were acceptable only when it could be proven that specific previous cases of discrimination had occurred within the institution or business in question.

35. The Whig party turned against President John Tyler because

    (A) he was felt to be ineffective in pushing the Whig agenda through Congress.

    (B) he spoke out in favor of the annexation of Texas.

    (C) he opposed the entire Whig legislative program.

    (D) he criticized Henry Clay's handling of the Nullification Crisis.

36. In coining the phrase "Manifest Destiny," journalist John L. O'Sullivan meant that

    (A) the struggle for racial equality was the ultimate goal of America's existence.

    (B) America was certain to become an independent country sooner or later.

    (C) it was the destiny of America to overspread the continent.

    (D) America must eventually become either all slave or all free.

37. All of the following were causes of the Mexican War EXCEPT

    (A) American desire for California.

    (B) Mexican failure to pay debts and damages owed to the U.S.

    (C) U.S. annexation of the formerly Mexican-held Republic of Texas.

    (D) Mexican desire to annex Louisiana.

38. The primary motive of those who founded the British colony in Virginia during the seventeenth century was the

    (A) desire for economic gain.

    (B) desire for religious freedom.

(C)   desire to create a perfect religious commonwealth as an example to the rest of the world.

(D)   desire to recreate in the New World the story of feudalistic society that was fading in the Old.

39.   Which of the following is true of the Gulf of Tonkin incident?

(A)   It involved a clash of U.S. and Soviet warships.

(B)   In it, two North Vietnamese fighter-bombers were shot down as they neared U.S. Navy ships.

(C)   It involved the seizure, by North Vietnam, of a U.S. Navy intelligence ship in international waters.

(D)   It led to major U.S. involvement in the Vietnam War.

40.   Which of the following statements is true of the SALT I treaty?

(A)   It brought sharp reductions in the number of ballistic missiles in both the U.S. and Soviet arsenals.

(B)   It was intended to encourage the deployment of defensive rather than offensive strategic weapons.

(C)   It indicated U.S. acceptance of the concept of Mutual Assured Destruction.

(D)   It was never ratified by the U.S. Senate.

Answer Key

1.	(C)	11.	(B)	21.	(D)	31.	(A)
2.	(D)	12.	(C)	22.	(D)	32.	(A)
3.	(D)	13.	(C)	23.	(A)	33.	(A)
4.	(D)	14.	(D)	24.	(C)	34.	(B)
5.	(A)	15.	(A)	25.	(A)	35.	(C)
6.	(C)	16.	(B)	26.	(D)	36.	(C)
7.	(D)	17.	(A)	27.	(A)	37.	(D)
8.	(B)	18.	(B)	28.	(D)	38.	(A)
9.	(C)	19.	(D)	29.	(D)	39.	(D)
10.	(A)	20.	(D)	30.	(B)	40.	(C)

▌Detailed Explanations

1.   **(C)**   The Republican party came into being primarily out of the controversy stirred up by the Kansas-Nebraska Act. While this same controversy did cause a sizable splinter faction to leave the Democratic party and join the newly formed Republican party, it did not cause the disintegration of the Democratic party (A), which continued as a political force up to and beyond the Civil War. It is also true that the Kansas-Nebraska Act applied popular sovereignty to territory north of the Missouri Compromise line for the first time, but far from preserving the nation's fragile sectional harmony (D), it had quite the opposite effect. Although the South generally supported the Act, most Southerners had given the area little thought before Douglas introduced the issue (B).

2.   **(D)**   U.S. Marines were stationed in Iceland, not Scotland, to guard against possible German attack. Choice (C) may seem impossible, but the United States first instituted the Cash-and-Carry System and later began the Lend-Lease Act when British financial assets began to dwindle. The sale of destroyers to Britain (A) and the growing role of the U.S. Navy in the struggle to keep the Atlantic sea lanes open (B) were both steps taken by President Franklin D. Roosevelt prior to official U.S. entry into the war.

3.   **(D)**   Thomas Nast was a famous American political cartoonist of the late nineteenth century. He is remembered most of all for his criticism of the political machine of William M. "Boss" Tweed in New York City.

4.   **(D)**   One of the most important aspects of the Stamp Act Congress was the opportunity it provided for colonial leaders to meet and establish acquaintances with one another. Nine colonies—not merely Georgia, Virginia, and the Carolinas (C)—were represented at it, but far from being a unified government for all the American colonies (A), it simply passed mild resolutions protesting the Stamp Act. It was not, therefore, a vehicle for enforcing the act (B).

5.   **(A)**   The map depicts the United States after the Compromise of 1850. The states of Texas and California as well as the Utah and New Mexico Territories were not part of the United States at the time of the 1842 Webster-Ashburton Treaty (B), dealing with the Maine-New Brunswick boundary; and the 1787 Northwest Ordinance (C), organizing what was to become the states of Ohio, Indiana, Illinois, Michigan, and Wisconsin. California and the two territories were gained as a result of the Mexican War (D), but California statehood, as well as territorial status for Utah and New Mexico, had to await the Compromise of 1850.

6.   **(C)**   The principle of popular sovereignty was a central feature of the Kansas-Nebraska Act. Though championed by Senator Stephen A. Douglas (A), it had previously been put forward by 1848 Democratic presidential candidate Lewis Cass. A favorite policy of Democrats—not Whigs (D)—during the late 1840s and early 1850s, it proved a failure in solving the impasse over the status of slavery in

the territories. It differed from the system of congressionally specified free and slave areas used in the Missouri Compromise (B).

7. **(D)** One of Lincoln's reasons for issuing the Emancipation Proclamation was to keep Britain and France from intervening on the side of the Confederacy. Lincoln neither needed, wanted, nor could have obtained the active aid of these countries in restoring the Union (A). The Radicals in the North would indeed have been pleased had Lincoln freed the slaves in areas of the South already under the control of Union armies (C), but it was precisely that which the Emancipation Proclamation did not do, largely out of concern for the more-or-less loyal slave-holding border states such as Maryland and Kentucky, who were not at all enthused about Lincoln's action even as it was (B).

8. **(B)** Hoover did *not* see the Depression as akin to an act of nature, about which nothing could be done. He did stress the desirability of localism and private initiative (A) and urged the nation's business leaders to maintain wages and full employment (C), but his efforts ended in failure (D).

9. **(C)** Hiss, a mid-ranking government official, was convicted of perjury for denying under oath that he had been a Communist agent, after being accused as such by admitted former Communist Whitaker Chambers, not the other way around (A). The case gained national attention through the involvement of young Congressman Richard Nixon, not Senator Joseph R. McCarthy (B), and while it did increase American concern about Communist subversion, it was by no means the beginning of such concern (D).

10. **(A)** Martin Luther King's methods were characterized by nonviolent defiance of segregation. While King and/or his supporters might make speeches or send petitions (D), civil disobedience gave his movement its urgency. Patience while developing the skills that would make blacks economically successful and gain them the respect of whites was the advice of late nineteenth century black leader Booker T. Washington (C), while armed violence was called for by King's more radical contemporaries of the 1960s (B).

11. **(B)** The agreement ending the Cuban Missile Crisis called for the Soviet Union to withdraw its missiles from Cuba while the United States agreed not to overthrow Castro's regime there. Turkey pertained to the matter involving Soviet's objections to U.S. missiles there, but it was not included in the agreement (C) and (D). The agreement also said nothing with regard to Soviet troops in Cuba (A).

12. **(C)** Blacks most commonly resisted slavery passively, if at all. The Underground Railroad (B), though celebrated in popular history, involved a relatively minute number of slaves. Arson (D) and violent uprising (A), though they did sometimes occur and were the subject of much fear on the part of white Southerners, were also relatively rare.

13. **(C)** During the period from 1835-1865 Southerners generally defended slavery as a positive benefit to society and even to the slaves themselves. That slavery was a necessary evil (A) and should be gradually phased out as the slaves were colonized outside the United States (D) was the attitude of an earlier generation of white Southerners, including Thomas Jefferson. That slavery should be immediately abolished (B) was the view of the Abolitionists, a minority even in the North during this period.

14. **(D)** Farmers and planters in the South enjoyed high crop prices and sustained prosperity during the 1850s. Crops were large (C) and prices were high and steady (A) and (B).

15. **(A)** For whatever reasons, immigrants of the "New Immigration" tended to settle in the large cities of the Northeast and Midwest. Very few of them settled on farms (B), filed on homesteads (C), or migrated to the South and Southwest (D).

16. **(B)** Germany's 1917 declaration of its intent to wage unrestricted submarine warfare was the most important factor in bringing the United States into World War I. German violation of Belgian neutrality in 1914 (A) did nothing to aid Germany's cause in America, and the revelation of Germany's suggestions to Mexico (C) was even more damaging, but neither of these had the impact of the U-boats. The fall of the czar and beginning of the Russian Revolution (D) may or may not have had an influence on President Woodrow Wilson.

17. **(A)** The Berlin Airlift was Truman's response to the Soviet blockade of Berlin. Neither wartime destruction (B) nor a severe winter (C) would have necessitated such a measure and no such work stoppage (D) occurred.

18. **(B)** Mercantilists believed the government should seek to direct the economy so as to maximize exports. Mercantilists *did*, however, believe in government interference in the economy (A) and the possession of colonies (C). Exports, they asserted, must exceed imports, not the other way around (D).

19. **(D)** Americans' primary objection to the Stamp Act was its purpose of raising revenue from the Americans without the consent of their representatives. A few Americans and a future British prime minister mistook this for opposition to internal taxes only (A). The proposed tax rate was not ruinously high (C), and the British had previously imposed taxes on America (B).

20. **(D)** In order to gain foreign recognition during the War for Independence, it was necessary for the United States to demonstrate a determination and potential to win independence. The U.S. could not have demonstrated financial stability (C) at this time, nor could it have made financial payments (A). It did not prove necessary to make territorial concessions to France (B).

21. **(D)** Garrison called for the immediate and uncompensated emancipation of all slaves. He definitely opposed either gradualism or compensation (A). He also

opposed colonization (B). Though he opposed the congressional gag rule (C), its repeal was not his main issue of concern.

22. **(D)** The congressional "gag rule" held that no antislavery petitions would be formally received by Congress. It did not directly govern the laws that could be considered (A) nor did it limit what a member could say outside of Congress (B). Anti-slavery materials sent through the mail would not be delivered to Southern addresses (C), but this was a separate matter.

23. **(A)** Roosevelt's New Nationalism pertained to domestic reform. Unrelated was the fact that Roosevelt always favored an aggressive foreign policy (B), including the establishment of an overseas empire (D). Though he gained a reputation as a trust-buster, Roosevelt was by no means in favor of breaking up all trusts and large business combinations (C).

24. **(C)** FDR's predecessor, Herbert Hoover, established the Reconstruction Finance Corporation in 1932. In doing so, he broke with many Republican leaders, including Secretary of the Treasury Andrew Mellon, who believed government had no choice but to let the business cycle run its course. Roosevelt's New Deal contained every other element listed.

25. **(A)** The Haymarket Incident involved the throwing of a bomb at Chicago police and a subsequent riot involving police and striking workers. There were plenty of scandals within the Grant administration (B), but this was not one of them. Allegations of corruption on the part of Republican presidential candidate James G. Blaine (C) were contained in the Mulligan Letters. The disastrous fire that pointed out the hazardous working conditions in some factories (D) was New York's Triangle Shirtwaist Company fire on March 25, 1911.

26. **(D)** The "New Immigration" was made up primarily of persons from Southern and Eastern Europe. Some, such as persecuted Russian Jews, came for religious reasons (A). The great majority were financially less well off (B) than those of the "Old Immigration," who came from Northern and Western Europe (C). Persons from Asia, Africa, and the Americas would not generally be considered part of the "New Immigration."

27. **(A)** The U.S. gained possession of the Philippines through the Spanish-American War. Cuba (B), though originally the primary issue of contention between Spain and the United States, was not annexed but rather granted its independence under the terms of the Platte Amendment. The Panama Canal Zone (D) was acquired within a few years of the Spanish-American War but in unrelated incidents and not from Spain. Bermuda (C) has never been acquired by the United States.

28. **(D)** The "Long Hot Summers" were filled with race rioting in America's large cities during the 1960s. Major outdoor rock concerts (A), such as the 1969 Woodstock concert, did occur during these years. The large Communist offensives

against U.S. troops in Vietnam (B) went by the name Tet. The protests (C), which were numerous, were called anti-war protests.

29. **(D)** Bacon's followers were disgruntled at what they saw as the governor's refusal to protect their frontier area from Indian raids. The jailing of individuals or seizure of their property for failure to pay taxes during a time of economic hardship (A) was the source of Shays' Rebellion in 1786. The under-representation of the backcountry areas in colonial legislatures (B) was an ongoing source of irritation in the colonial South. The mistreatment of former indentured servants by large planters (C) and the favoritism of Virginia's Governor Berkeley to his clique of friends may have been underlying causes but were not the immediate issue in dispute in Bacon's Rebellion.

30. **(B)** The Newburgh Conspiracy was composed of army officers disgusted with a central government too weak to collect taxes to pay them and their troops. Betrayal of the plans for the fort at West Point (A) was Benedict Arnold's treason. Resistance to the collection of federal excise taxes in western Pennsylvania (C) took the form of the Whiskey Rebellion of 1791. New England's threat to secede should the War of 1812 continue (D) was made at the 1814 Hartford Convention.

31. **(A)** The Wilmot Proviso was intended to prohibit slavery in the area acquired through the Mexican War. Congress generally agreed that the United States would acquire some territory from the war (B). That California should be a free state while the rest of the Mexican Cession was reserved for slavery (C), and that the status of slavery in the Mexican Cession should be decided on the basis of "Popular Sovereignty" (D), were suggestions for a compromise that might calm the furor aroused by the Wilmot Proviso.

32. **(A)** The Populists desired free coinage of silver. They also desired direct election of U.S. Senators, not necessarily an end to the electoral college (D). The Progressive movement, which followed Populism, favored the reform of child labor laws (B) and the use of modern science to solve social problems (C).

33. **(A)** The settlement-house workers were often young, affluent, college-educated women such as Jane Addams. Poor immigrants (B) and disabled veterans (C) would have had less opportunity for such things. Idealistic young men (D) were apparently drawn to such enterprises in smaller numbers.

34. **(B)** In the 1857 case *Dred Scott v. Sandford* the Supreme Court held that no black slave could be a citizen of the United States. It was in the 1954 case *Brown v. Topeka Board of Education* that the court held separate facilities for the races to be unconstitutional (A). The reverse (C) was the court's holding in the 1896 case *Plessy v. Ferguson*. Affirmative Action was limited (D) in the 1970s and 1980s.

35. **(C)** The Whigs turned on Tyler because he opposed their entire legislative program. He did speak out in favor of Texas annexation (B), but this offense would have been relatively minor in Whig eyes by comparison.

36. **(C)** O'Sullivan spoke of America's "manifest destiny to overspread the continent." The idea that America must eventually become either all slave or all free (D) was expressed by Lincoln in his "House Divided" speech and was called by William H. Seward the "Irrepressible Conflict." Racial equality (A) was still not a popular idea when O'Sullivan wrote in the first half of the nineteenth century. By that time, of course, America was already an independent country (B).

37. **(D)** Mexico did expect to win the war, invade the U.S., and dictate a peace in Washington, but whatever desire, if any, the Mexicans may have had for the state of Louisiana was not a factor in the coming of the war. The U.S. did, however, desire to annex California (A) and did annex Texas (C); Mexico did refuse to pay its debts (B) and did claim Texas (C). All of these contributed to the coming of the war.

38. **(A)** The colony at Jamestown was founded primarily for economic gain. Desire for religious freedom in some form (B) was the motivation of the settlers of Plymouth and some of those who settled Maryland and Pennsylvania. Desire to create a perfect religious commonwealth as an example to the rest of the world (C) was the motive for the Massachusetts Bay colony; and desire to recreate in the New World the sort of feudalistic society that was fading in the Old World (D) was probably a motive of some of the colonial proprietors such as those of the Carolinas.

39. **(D)** The Gulf of Tonkin Incident led to major U.S. involvement in the Vietnam War. In the Gulf of Sidra during the 1980s, two clashes occurred involving the shooting down of Libyan, not Vietnamese, jets approaching U.S. ships (B). Off the coast of North Korea in 1968, North Korean, not Vietnamese, forces seized the U.S. Navy intelligence ship *USS Pueblo* (C).

40. **(C)** The SALT I Treaty indicated U.S. acceptance of the concept of Mutual Assured Destruction. It was ratified by the U.S. Senate (D)—unlike the SALT II Treaty—but did not bring substantial reductions in the number of missiles on either side (A). It discouraged the deployment of defensive weapons (B).

PRACTICE TEST 1

CLEP Social Sciences and History

This practice test is also offered online at the REA Study Center *(www.rea.com/studycenter)*. Since all CLEP exams are administered on computer, we recommend that you take the online version of the test to receive these added benefits:

- **Timed testing conditions** – Gauge how much time you can spend on each question
- **Automatic scoring** – Find out how you did on the test, instantly
- **On-screen detailed explanations of answers** – Learn not just the correct answer, but also why the other answer choices are wrong
- **Diagnostic score reports** – Pinpoint where you're strongest and where you need to focus your study

PRACTICE TEST 1

CLEP Social Sciences and History

(Answer sheets appear in the back of the book.)

TIME: 90 Minutes
120 Questions

Directions: Each of the questions or incomplete statements below is followed by five possible answers or completions. Select the best choice in each case and fill in the corresponding oval on the answer sheet.

1. In 1804, Aaron Burr killed Alexander Hamilton in a duel that was fought because

    (A) Hamilton had formally accused Burr of treason and Burr felt he had to defend his honor

    (B) Burr blamed his loss of the 1804 election for governor of New York on Hamilton's charges that Burr was dangerous and untrustworthy

    (C) Hamilton had uncovered Burr's plan to form an independent republic comprised of American territories west of the Appalachians

    (D) Burr had caught his wife in a sexual liaison with Hamilton and felt that he had to defend his honor

    (E) Burr believed that Hamilton had financially destroyed him in a real estate deal in which Burr lost nearly all of his wealth

2. The following cartoon refers to the results of which war?

President McKinley (the tailor) measures Uncle Sam for a new suit to fit the fattening results of his imperial appetite.

(A) War of 1812   (D) World War I

(B) Civil War   (E) World War II

(C) Spanish-American War

3. "...there is no place for industry... no arts; no letters; no society; and which is the worst of all, continual fear, and danger of violent death; and the life of man, solitary, poor, nasty, brutish, and short." This quotation from Thomas Hobbes' *Leviathan* (1651) described the concept known as

(A) natural rights   (D) reason of state (raison d'état)

(B) state of nature   (E) nationalism

(C) social contract

4. Which one of the following would most likely oppose *laissez-faire* policies in nineteenth century Europe?

(A) A factory owner   (D) A socialist

(B) A liberal   (E) A middle-class businessman

(C) A free trader

5. The first time the Japanese people heard the voice of Emperor Hirohito on the radio was

(A) during his coronation

(B) when he announced his wedding

(C) when he announced that Japanese troops were moving into Manchuria

(D)   when he announced Japan's surrender to the Allied Powers

(E)   when he declared war on the United States

6.   Which was the first European power to seize control of African territories?

(A)   Portugal   (D)   France

(B)   Belgium   (E)   Germany

(C)   England

7.   The ancient world leader who created the Persian Empire and who also freed the Jews from their Babylonian captivity was

(A)   Julius Caesar   (D)   Cyrus the Great

(B)   Marc Antony   (E)   Pompey

(C)   Augustus Caesar

8.   The five pillars of faith require that Muslims do each of the following EXCEPT

(A)   acknowledge that there is only one God and that Mohammed is his prophet

(B)   pray five times per day

(C)   make a pilgrimage to Medina

(D)   fast during Ramadan

(E)   give alms to the poor

9.   The ancient Athenians contributed all of the following to the subsequent development of Western Civilization EXCEPT

(A)   philosophy   (D)   tragedy

(B)   geometry   (E)   the Olympic Games

(C)   monotheism

10.   During the 6th and 5th centuries BCE, a Chinese scholar by the name of _____ helped establish a better system of government by promoting various virtues among the ruling class. His teachings also led to the development of a civil service exam.

(A)   Wang Mang   (D)   Confucius

(B)   Buddha   (E)   Shihuangdi

(C)   Kublai Kahn

11. In his theory, Karl Marx explained that conflict between industrial workers and the owners of industry was

    (A) likely to decline in future years

    (B) usually harmful to social institutions

    (C) an inevitable consequence of capitalism

    (D) of little importance to social change

    (E) a rare occurrence in modern societies

12. When ratified by the original thirteen states in 1781, the weaknesses of the Articles of Confederation included the federal government's inability to levy taxes or regulate interstate commerce. Both weaknesses stemmed from a fear of

    (A) the Dutch Republic   (D) mobs

    (B) the Spanish   (E) tyranny

    (C) the French

13. The primary influence on the U.S. Constitution's separation of powers was derived from

    (A) Plato's *Apology*

    (B) Baron de Montesquieu's *The Spirit of the Laws*

    (C) Machiavelli's *The Prince*

    (D) Thomas Hobbes' *Leviathan*

    (E) Aristotle's *Politics*

14. Which of the following is used to effect the release of a person from improper imprisonment?

    (A) A writ of mandamus

    (B) A writ of habeas corpus

    (C) The Fourth Amendment requirement that police have probable cause in order to obtain a search warrant

    (D) The Supreme Court's decision in *Roe v. Wade*

    (E) The constitutional prohibition against *ex post facto* laws

15. When a member of the House of Representatives helps a citizen from his or her district receive some federal aid to which that citizen is entitled, the representative's action is referred to as

(A) casework

(B) pork barrel legislation

(C) lobbying

(D) logrolling

(E) filibustering

16. One advantage incumbent members of Congress have over challengers in election campaigns is the use of

(A) unlimited campaign funds

(B) national party employees as campaign workers

(C) the franking privilege

(D) unlimited contributions from "fat cat" supporters

(E) government-financed air time for commercials

QUESTIONS 17 to 18 refer to the table below.

GRAIN PRODUCERS				GRAIN IMPORTERS			
Grain	1st	2nd	3rd	Grain	1st	2nd	3rd
Corn	USA	China	Brazil	Corn	CIS	Japan	Spain
Wheat	CIS	USA	China	Wheat	China	CIS	Japan
Rice	China	India	Indonesia	Rice	Indonesia	Iran	CIS

17. Which nation—or group of nations—seems to have the LEAST efficient agricultural system?

(A) Brazil

(B) Indonesia

(C) CIS

(D) India

(E) China

18. Which nation seems to have the MOST self-sufficient agricultural system?

(A) USA

(B) China

(C) Brazil

(D) Indonesia

(E) India

19. Which is NOT a characteristic of American agriculture?

    (A) The rich ecosystem of North America

    (B) The use of mechanization

    (C) The diversity of climate and soil

    (D) Total free market capitalism

    (E) The trend toward agribusiness

20. All of the following are true of the Confederate war effort during the Civil War EXCEPT:

    (A) Confederate industry was never able to adequately supply Confederate soldiers with the armaments they needed to successfully fight the war.

    (B) Confederate agriculture was never able to adequately supply the people of the South with the food they needed.

    (C) Inflation became a major problem in the South as the Confederate government was forced to print more paper currency than it could support with gold or other tangible assets.

    (D) The inadequate railroad system of the South hindered movement of soldiers, supplies, and food from the places where they were stationed (or produced) to the places where they were most needed.

    (E) Tremendous resentment at the military draft developed among poor and middle-class Southerners because wealthy Southern males could pay to have a substitute take their place in the army.

21. What was the OVERALL U.S. unemployment rate during the worst periods of the Great Depression?

    (A) 10%   (D) 60%

    (B) 25%   (E) 90%

    (C) 40%

QUESTION 22 refers to the following.

22. The painting above by François Dubois, an eyewitness, describes the massacre on St. Bartholomew's Day of 1572 of

    (A) Dutch nobility   (D) Spanish Catholics

    (B) German peasants   (E) English merchants

    (C) French Calvinists

23. Which one of the following was a characteristic of the peace settlements at the end of World War I?

    (A) Division of Germany into two parts

    (B) Expansion of the territory of the Ottoman Empire

    (C) The emergence of the Soviet Union as a significant part of the European diplomatic system

    (D) The long-term stationing of American troops in Europe

    (E) Germany was not required to pay reparations.

24. Which of the following has NOT been a leader of an African country?

    (A) Kwame Nkrumah   (D) Julius Nyerere

    (B) Jomo Kenyatta   (E) Patrice Lumumba

    (C) Aimé Césaire

25. When Chinese students held a protest in Beijing's Tiananmen Square on May 4, 1989, they were commemorating the May 4 movement of what year?

    (A) 1919   (D) 1895

    (B) 1911   (E) 1969

    (C) 1901

26. A major difference between the early river valley civilization in Egypt and that of Mesopotamia is that the Egyptians

    (A) tended to believe in an afterlife, in part because of their relatively favorable geographical conditions and natural resources

    (B) were constantly under the threat of being attacked by various regional enemies

    (C) had a pessimistic view toward life, as reflected in the *Epic of Gilgamesh*

    (D) built many large structures called ziggurats

    (E) mostly did not believe in an afterlife

27. In a remarkable chain of events that linked together four famous figures from the ancient world, Socrates taught Plato, who in turn taught Aristotle, who then taught a Macedonian named _____, who later spread Greek learning throughout much of the then-known world.

    (A) Peter the Great   (D) Charles the Great

    (B) Alexander the Great   (E) Frederick the Great

    (C) Alfred the Great

28. Japan's Meiji Restoration led to the end of the Tokugawa Shogunate and a period of

    (A) increased power for the samurai class

    (B) rapid industrialization

    (C) greater reliance on farming as a driving force of the economy

    (D) increased acceptance of feudal practices

    (E) increased fear of foreigners

29. Today, most people in Sub-Saharan Africa make their living based on

    (A) long-distance trade   (D) subsistence farming

    (B) light manufacturing   (E) tourism

    (C) heavy manufacturing

30. The Second Amendment to the U.S. Constitution was drafted to protect the right to

(A) freedom of religion

(B) freedom of speech

(C) peaceably assemble

(D) bear arms

(E) a speedy trial

31. In *Federalist #10*, James Madison wrote: "The latent causes of faction are thus sown into the nature of man." In asserting this claim, he also argued that

(A) "Men are born free, but everywhere they are in chains."

(B) all levels of government must work together to restrict the rise of factions at all costs.

(C) attempts by the government to restrict the organization of factions would be futile given the human tendency toward self-interest

(D) the United States government should encourage factions by embracing the philosophy of "live and let live."

(E) the United States government should ensure that each citizen has the right to bear arms, for, according to Madison, life in the state of nature is a "war of all against all."

32. In its 1920 census, the United States government showed the culmination of a long-term trend, where, for the first time, more people were living in

(A) Texas than New York

(B) Colorado than Pennsylvania

(C) Nevada than Massachusetts

(D) urban areas than rural areas

(E) rural areas than urban areas

33. Major differences between procedures in the House of Representatives and the Senate would include:

I. In the House, time for debate is limited, while in the Senate it is usually unlimited.

II. In the House, the rules committee is very powerful, while in the Senate it is relatively weak.

III. In the House, debate must be germane, while in the Senate it need not be.

(A) I only

(B) II only

(C) III only

(D) I and II only

(E) I, II, and III

34. In the case *McCulloch v. Maryland* (1819), the Supreme Court

    (A) gave a broad interpretation to the First Amendment right of freedom of speech

    (B) claimed the power of judicial review

    (C) struck down a law of Congress for the first time

    (D) gave a broad interpretation to the "necessary and proper clause"

    (E) denied that the president has the right of executive privilege

35. Which of the following statements about the U.S. president's cabinet is FALSE?

    (A) It includes heads of the 15 executive departments.

    (B) It includes members of the House of Representatives.

    (C) Although not mentioned in the Constitution, the cabinet has been part of American government since the presidency of George Washington.

    (D) Presidents may appoint special advisors to the cabinet.

    (E) Senators may not serve in the cabinet.

QUESTIONS 36 and 37 refer to the following graph.

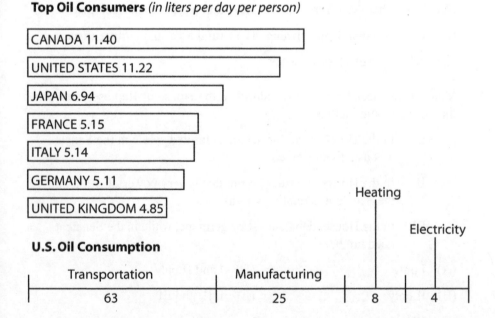

Top Oil Consumers (in liters per day per person)

CANADA 11.40

UNITED STATES 11.22

JAPAN 6.94

FRANCE 5.15

ITALY 5.14

GERMANY 5.11

UNITED KINGDOM 4.85

U.S. Oil Consumption

Transportation	Manufacturing	Heating	Electricity
63	25	8	4

36. Which is NOT a conclusion that can be drawn from the graphs?

    (A) Transportation takes up too high a proportion of U.S. oil usage

    (B) U.S. per capita consumption is over twice that of most European nations

    (C) North American oil demands are the highest

    (D) Manufacturing is a major consumer of oil

    (E) Heating needs take less than 10 percent of oil use

37. Which would be LEAST likely to explain the statistics in the graph?

    (A) The area size of a nation has a relationship to oil usage.

    (B) The European nations consume large quantities of oil.

    (C) The larger the population, the greater the usage.

    (D) Japan is the largest industrial power in Asia.

    (E) Industrial nations' people have lifestyles that use more oil.

38. Which is NOT true about the petroleum industry?

    (A) It is dealing with a nonrenewable resource.

    (B) It is essential to the plastics industry.

    (C) It reacts quickly to the law of supply and demand.

    (D) It is an example of a monopoly.

    (E) It is truly a multinational industry.

39. All of the following were main principles of the Navigation Acts EXCEPT:

    (A) Trade in the colonies was limited to only British or colonial merchants.

    (B) The laws prohibited the colonies from issuing their own paper currencies, greatly limiting their trading capabilities.

    (C) All foreign goods bound for the colonies had to be shipped through England where they were taxed with British import duties.

    (D) The colonists could not build or export products that directly competed with British export products.

    (E) Colonial enumerated goods could be sold only in England.

40. The reason slavery flourished in the Southern English colonies and not in New England is

    (A) most New England farms were too small for slaves to be economically necessary or viable, whereas in the South the cultivation of staple crops such as rice and tobacco on large plantations necessitated the use of large numbers of indentured servants or slaves

    (B) blacks from the tropical climate of Africa could not adapt to the harsh New England winters. Their high death rates made their use as slave laborers unprofitable

    (C) a shortage of females in the Southern English colonies led to many female black Africans being imported as slaves and as potential wives for white planters in the region

    (D) whereas New England religious groups such as the Puritans forbade slavery on moral grounds, the Anglican church, which dominated the Southern English colonies, encouraged the belief that blacks were inferior, and thus not deserving of equal status

    (E) the Stono uprising in 1739 convinced New Englanders that the cost of controlling slaves was not worth their marginal economic benefits

41. All of the following are characteristics of Renaissance humanism EXCEPT:

    (A) sanctity of the Latin texts of Scriptures

    (B) belief that ancient Latin and Greek writers were inferior to later authors

    (C) rejection of Christian principles

    (D) it functioned as a primary cause of the Reformation.

    (E) it accomplished scholarship in ancient languages

42. The October Manifesto of Czar Nicholas II promised all of the following EXCEPT:

    (A) a Duma   (D) a fair, democratic voting system

    (B) political reforms   (E) full civil liberties

    (C) a Russian parliament

43. Which independent Asian nation did NOT exist before 1947?

    (A) Thailand   (D) Korea

    (B) Pakistan   (E) Vietnam

    (C) India

44. All of the following were aspects of Britain's policy of indirect rule in colonial Africa EXCEPT

   (A) subsidizing primary education for Africans

   (B) the expectation of eventual self-government

   (C) decentralized administration

   (D) uniform government policy throughout the colonized territories

   (E) incorporating traditional rulers into the government structure

45. The Glorious Revolution of 1688–89 resulted in all of the following EXCEPT

   (A) the flight and abdication of James II

   (B) an agreement that in the event of no heirs, the Hanover house would succeed the Stuarts

   (C) the elevation of William III and Mary as the monarchs

   (D) specification that all future monarchs must be members of the Church of England

   (E) the passage of the Bill of Rights

46. Churchill gave his "Iron Curtain" speech in Missouri in 1946, and the Berlin Wall later became a manifestation of his dire warning. Construction of that wall began in

   (A) 1948   (D) 1957

   (B) 1951   (E) 1961

   (C) 1955

47. After Asoka rose to power as Emperor of the Mauryan Empire in India in 268 BCE, he emphasized the practice of _____, which helped him promote a sense of unity among his diverse peoples.

   (A) Buddhism   (D) Zoroastrianism

   (B) Confucianism   (E) Taoism

   (C) Catholicism

48. Although China had a much more impressive navy than any European nation by the early 1400s, during the Europe's Age of Exploration, the first country to take the lead in exploration was _____.

    (A) England   (D) Spain

    (B) Portugal   (E) the Dutch Republic

    (C) France

49. The so-called Pax Romana was initiated during the reign of Augustus Caesar (27 BCE to 14 CE) and ended after the reign of _____, a man many historians believe to be the embodiment of Plato's concept of a philosopher-king.

    (A) Tiberius   (D) Justinian I

    (B) Nero   (E) Marcus Aurelius

    (C) Constantine

50. John Marshall served as the U.S. Supreme Court Chief Justice from 1801-1835. With regard to what he considered to be the proper role of the federal government, he opposed each of the following presidents EXCEPT

    (A) Thomas Jefferson   (D) John Quincy Adams

    (B) James Madison   (E) Andrew Jackson

    (C) James Monroe

51. In the study of economics, the Production Possibilities Curve is used to show a trade-off between

    (A) two goods   (C) eight goods

    (B) four goods   (D) ten goods

    (E) as many goods as it takes to analyze a given problem

52. The major responsibility of the Federal Reserve Board is to

    (A) implement monetary policy

    (B) control government spending

    (C) regulate commodity prices

    (D) help the president run the executive branch

    (E) keep records of troop strength in army reserve units across the country

53. Which of the following statements most accurately compares political parties in the United States with those in other Western democracies?

   (A) Parties in the United States exert a greater influence over which candidates run for office.

   (B) Parties are much more centralized in the United States.

   (C) There are usually more political parties in other Western democracies.

   (D) Party members in the national legislature are much freer to vote against the party line in other Western democracies.

   (E) Party label is the principal criterion for voting for a candidate in the United States, whereas it is relatively unimportant in other Western democracies.

54. Which of the following is among the differences between a parliamentary and a presidential system?

   I. In a parliamentary system, there is little or no separation of powers as in a presidential system.

   II. In a parliamentary system, the chief executive officer is not chosen by a nationwide vote as in a presidential system.

   III. In a presidential system, the chief executive officer may call elections for all members of the legislature at any time, unlike in a parliamentary system.

   (A) I only   (D) I and II only

   (B) II only   (E) I, II, and III

   (C) III only

QUESTIONS 55 to 57 refer to the following.

   • We must develop the vision to see that, in regard to the natural world, private and corporate ownership should be so limited as to preserve the interest of society and the integrity of the environment.

   • We need greater awareness of our enormous powers, the fragility of the earth, and the consequent responsibility of men and governments for its preservation.

   • We must redefine "progress" toward an emphasis on long-term quality rather than immediate quantity.

   • We, therefore, resolve to act. We propose a revolution in conduct toward an environment which is rising in revolt against us. Granted that ideas and institutions long established are not easily changed; yet today is the first day of the rest of our life on this planet. We will begin anew.

55. Which group is NOT called upon to act in the statement?

    (A) Private and corporate ownership

    (B) Government

    (C) Individuals

    (D) Society

    (E) Communities

56. What makes this quote relevant to economics?

    (A) Ethical use of the environment

    (B) Man as a member of the "community of all living things"

    (C) Need for individual responsibility

    (D) References to man's machines and past abuses

    (E) Progress, in terms of quality of life

57. Which is NOT an example of how environmental concerns can become eco-nomic priorities?

    (A) Recycling

    (B) Reforestation

    (C) Strip-mining restoration

    (D) Greenhouse effect

    (E) Coal-generated electricity to replace imported oil

58. Which battle was the turning point in the Pacific war between Japan and the United States?

    (A) Leyte Gulf   (D) Midway

    (B) Pearl Harbor   (E) Guadalcanal

    (C) Coral Sea

59. The United States Supreme Court case of *Brown v. Board of Education of Topeka* was significant because it

    (A) prohibited prayer in public schools on the grounds of separation of church and state

    (B) legally upheld the doctrine of "separate but equal" educational facilities for blacks and whites

(C) clarified the constitutional rights of minors and restricted the rights of school administrators to set dress codes or otherwise infringe on students' rights

(D) upheld school districts' rights to use aptitude and psychological tests to "track" students and segregate them into "college prep" and "vocational" programs

(E) ordered the desegregation of public schools, prohibiting the practice of segregation via "separate but equal" schools for blacks and whites

60. Ferdinand and Isabella's policies of Spanish nationalism led to the expulsion, from Spain, of large numbers of Spanish

(A) Protestants   (D) Calvinists

(B) Catholics   (E) Monks

(C) Jews

61. During the Thirty Years' War, the Lutheran movement was saved from extinction by the military intervention of which foreign monarch?

(A) The French king, Philip the Fair

(B) The English king, Henry VIII

(C) The Swedish king, Gustavus Adolphus

(D) The Austrian emperor, Charles V

(E) The Spanish king, Philip II

62. In 1898, the United States took control of the Philippines from which country?

(A) China   (D) Spain

(B) Japan   (E) Portugal

(C) England

63. The following pairs of names are the names of African countries before and after achieving independence EXCEPT

(A) Bechuanaland – Botswana

(B) Dahomey – Benin

(C) Gold Coast – Ghana

(D) Swaziland – Malawi

(E) Angola – Angola

64. Between 1929 and 1933, the Federal Reserve Bank made the economic ca-lamities associated with the Great Depression significantly worse by

(A) increasing the money supply

(B) decreasing the money supply

(C) leaving the money supply unchanged

(D) decreasing government spending

(E) increasing taxes

65. After the start of the Great Recession in 2007, the Federal Reserve Bank used a tactic known as _____ to significantly increase the money supply.

(A) going-for-broke   (D) qualitative easing

(B) beggar-thy-neighbor   (E) qualitative tightening

(C) quantitative easing

66. To protect the borders of their sprawling empire, the Romans built two defen-sive barricades in Britain during the 2nd century CE; one was called Antonine's Wall, while the other (more famous) wall became known as

(A) Caesar's Wall   (D) Nero's Wall

(B) Augustus Caesar's Wall   (E) the Great Wall of Britain

(C) Hadrian's Wall

67. The Ural Mountains run through which of the following countries?

(A) Switzerland   (D) Hungary

(B) Finland   (E) Russia

(C) Germany

68. With regard to fiscal policy, the federal government has two basic tools at its disposal: it can raise or lower

(A) taxes and the money supply

(B) government spending and interest rates

(C) interest rates and the money supply

(D) government spending and taxes

(E) taxes and interest rates

69. In 1954, the Supreme Court ruled in *Brown v. Board of Education of Topeka* that, "We conclude that in the field of public education the doctrine of 'separate but equal' has no place. Separate educational facilities are inherently unequal." In doing so, this decision overturned the decision of the Supreme Court in the case of

   (A) *Dred Scott v. Sandford*

   (B) *Gibbons. v. Ogden*

   (C) *Griswold v. Connecticut*

   (D) *Plessy v. Ferguson*

   (E) *Gideon v. Wainwright*

70. Prior to Central and South America being conquered by the Spanish during the first half of the 16th century, the region contained two major empires. One was founded by the Aztecs, the other by the

   (A) Powhatan Confederacy   (D) Hopi

   (B) Incas   (E) Huron

   (C) Iroquois Confederacy

71. The statement "America has a pluralistic political system" means

   (A) there are many subcultures within American society

   (B) political power is divided between national and state governments

   (C) many interest groups compete in the political arena to influence public policy

   (D) rural interests are overrepresented in the national legislature

   (E) candidates for national office are usually elected by plurality vote

72. Which of the following best describes the relationship between educational background and participation in politics?

   (A) The more schooling one has, the more likely one is to vote.

   (B) The less schooling one has, the more likely one is to run for public office.

   (C) There is no relationship between educational background and participation in politics.

   (D) People with a high school education are more likely to vote than either those who did not finish high school or those with a college degree.

   (E) Those with no formal schooling have a greater personal interest in policy and tend to vote more often than those with high school diplomas.

73. All of the following are recognized functions of the major political parties EXCEPT

    (A) recruiting candidates for public office

    (B) aggregating interests into electoral alliances

    (C) establishing channels of communication between public and government

    (D) providing personnel to staff elections and run the government

    (E) articulating interests

QUESTIONS 74 and 75 refer to the diagram below.

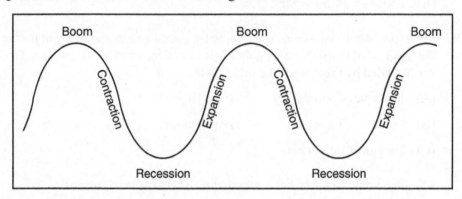

74. Which is the best title for the diagram above?

    (A) Boom and Bust

    (B) Causes of Economic Change

    (C) The Business Cycle

    (D) Causes of Recession

    (E) The History of Business Activity

75. In referring to the stages of the cycle, depicted above, which would not be a factor considered by economists?

    (A) Unemployment figures

    (B) Manufacturing production

    (C) Income levels

    (D) War or peace

    (E) Retail sales

76. Which is not a method used to encourage expansion during a recession?

    (A) Political crisis, such as war

    (B) Increased government spending

    (C) Increased taxation

    (D) Deregulation of industry

    (E) Restriction of imports

77. The Great Awakening of the mid-eighteenth century refers to

    (A) a series of religious revivals that swept through the English colonies spreading evangelistic fervor and challenging the control of traditional clerics over their congregations

    (B) the intellectual revolution which served as a precursor to the Enlightenment and challenged orthodox religion's claims to knowledge of humankind and the universe

    (C) the beginnings of the Industrial Revolution in England and its New World colonies

    (D) the growing realization among English colonists that independence from England was only a matter of time and was the key to their future success

    (E) the sudden awareness among North American Indians that their only chance for survival against the rapidly growing number of European colonists was to fight them before the Europeans grew any stronger

78. One of the major effects of the Industrial Revolution of the late nineteenth century in the United States was

    (A) an increased emphasis on worker health and safety issues

    (B) an increased emphasis on speed rather than quality of work

    (C) an increased emphasis on high-quality, error-free work

    (D) an increase in the number of small industrial facilities, which could operate more efficiently than larger, more costly industrial plants

    (E) a decrease in worker productivity as a result of continuous clashes between unions and management

79. All of the following were significant economic trends in Germany during the 1920s EXCEPT

    (A) large amounts of money leaving the country to pay reparations

    (B) periods of high inflation

    (C) a very stable currency (the mark)

    (D) periods of high unemployment

    (E) the German government placed large amounts of paper money in circulation

QUESTION 80 refers to the following.

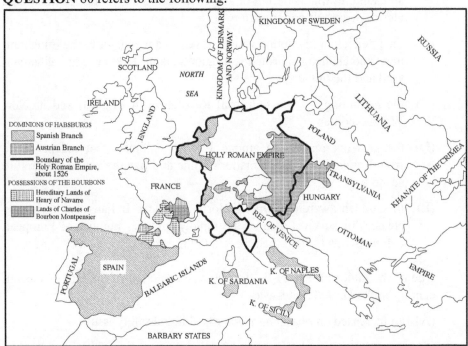

80. The map depicts Europe around

    (A) 1800   (D) 1950

    (B) 1500   (E) 1900

    (C) 1700

81. By 1914 which of the following countries was still an independent state not under colonial control?

(A) Algeria   (D) Egypt

(B) Congo   (E) Ethiopia

(C) Angola

82. Thailand is bordered by which of the following countries?

    I.   Myanmar

    II.   Laos

    III. Vietnam

    IV. Cambodia

(A) I, II, and III   (D) II and III only

(B) I, II, and IV   (E) IV only

(C) I and II only

83. During the Yalta Conference in February 1945, Joseph Stalin demanded a buffer zone to the west of Moscow, noting that this area was especially vulnerable to attack. Since 1800, the two most notable invasions that came from the west of Russia were: (1) the attack by the Nazis in 1941, known as Operation Barbarossa; and (2) the attack by the troops of _____, which took place in 1812.

(A) the Duke of Wellington   (D) Rochambeau

(B) Napoleon   (E) Lafayette

(C) Lord Nelson

84. During the 1930s and 1940s, the main challenge to John Maynard Keynes' school of economic thought came from

(A) Friedrich Hayek

(B) Milton Friedman

(C) Adam Smith

(D) Arthur Laffer

(E) John Kenneth Galbraith

85. In 1776, Adam Smith famously stated: "It is not from the benevolence of the butcher, the brewer, or the baker that we expect our dinner, but from their regard to their own _____."

    (A) hunger and appetites

    (B) tendency toward altruism

    (C) tendency toward greed

    (D) interest

    (E) foolish entrepreneurial spirit

86. When Thomas Jefferson completed the Louisiana Purchase in 1803, the western border of the United States shifted from the Mississippi River to the

    (A) Great Plains

    (B) Rocky Mountains

    (C) the Pacific Ocean

    (D) the western boundary of the Dakotas

    (E) the western boundary of Kansas

87. Which of the following accurately describes the European Union today?

    (A) An economic union that includes countries of roughly equal economic power.

    (B) A political union that includes countries of roughly equal political power.

    (C) An economic and political union that includes countries of roughly equal economic and political power.

    (D) An economic and political union that includes countries of unequal economic and political power.

    (E) An economic union that includes countries with varying degrees of economic power.

88. After the Berlin Conference of 1884-1885 and the subsequent "Scramble for Africa," the existing boundaries and tribal affiliations in Sub-Saharan Africa were

    (A) not modified

    (B) modified, but only to a limited extent

    (C) mostly ignored

    (D) ignored, but only by the British and French

    (E) ignored, but only by the Germans and Italians

89. Which of the following early river valley civilizations is matched incorrectly with the river(s) listed alongside of it?

(A) Egypt / Nile River

(B) Mesopotamia / Tigris and Volga Rivers

(C) Chinese / Yellow and Yangtze Rivers

(D) Indus / Indus River

(E) Mesopotamia / Tigris and Euphrates Rivers

QUESTION 90 refers to the following.

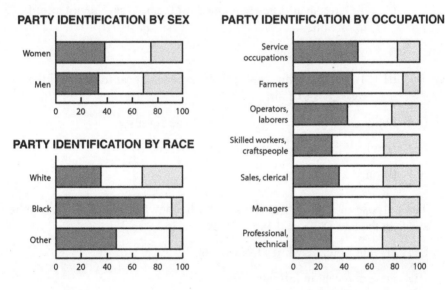

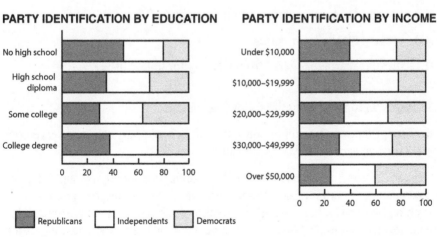

From Janda, Berry, Goldman, *The Challenge of Democracy*, 4th ed., 2001, p. 286. Copyright © 2001 Houghton mifflin.

90. Based on the graphs above, which of the following were least likely to have voted for Franklin Roosevelt in 1940?

    (A) Southerners

    (B) White northern business leaders

    (C) Blue-collar workers

    (D) Racial minorities

    (E) Union members

91. The federal Constitution guarantees which of the following rights to persons arrested and charged with a serious crime?

    I.   To have an attorney appointed for them if they cannot afford to hire one

    II.   To remain silent

    III. To compel witnesses in their favor to appear to testify if the case goes to court

    (A) I only   (D) I and II only

    (B) II only   (E) I, II, and III

    (C) III only

92. The purpose of grandfather clauses and literacy tests, used in the southern states in the late 1800s and early 1900s, was to

    (A) prevent illiterate whites from voting

    (B) prevent recent immigrants from voting

    (C) prevent Hispanics from running for public office

    (D) prevent blacks from voting

    (E) prevent "carpetbaggers" from running for public office

QUESTIONS 93 to 95 refer to the following passage.

Business functions by public consent, and its basic purpose is to serve constructively the needs of society – to the satisfaction of society.

"Historically, business has discharged this obligation mainly by supplying the needs and wants of people for goods and services, by providing jobs and purchasing power, and by producing most of the wealth of the nation. This has been what American society required of business, and business on the whole has done its job remarkably well...

"In generating… economic growth, American business has provided increasing employment, rising wages and salaries, employee benefit plans, and expanding career opportunities for a labor force….

"Most important, the rising standard of living of the average American family has enabled more and more citizens to develop their lives as they wish with less and less constraint imposed on them by economic need. Thus, most Americans have been able to afford better health, food, clothing, shelter, and education than the citizens of any other nation have ever achieved on such a large scale….

Source: U.S. Government report

93. Which statement best summarizes the attitude of the excerpt?

    (A) Business has successfully met all the needs of society.

    (B) Business has done a good job supplying the economic needs of society.

    (C) Americans are best off with the least government.

    (D) All Americans have benefited from the rising living standard.

    (E) Government and business, in partnership, have created prosperity.

94. Which of the following organizations would be most likely to endorse this quote?

    (A) Chamber of Commerce   (D) Socialist Labor party

    (B) Department of Labor   (E) AFL/CIO

    (C) General Accounting Office

95. Which of the following economic goals is not addressed by the quote?

    (A) Economic growth   (D) Economic justice

    (B) Economic stability   (E) Economic freedom

    (C) Economic security

96. Which is NOT one of the four basic economic activities of capitalism?

    (A) Production   (D) Service

    (B) Distribution   (E) Labor

    (C) Manufacturing

97. The key event that guaranteed Lincoln's reelection in 1864 was

    (A) the fall of Vicksburg to General Grant

    (B) the capture of New Orleans by Admiral Farragut

(C) the defeat of Lee's army by General Meade at Gettysburg

(D) the fall of Atlanta to General Sherman

(E) the successful defense of Nashville by General Thomas against repeated Confederate counterattacks

98. The American Hostage Crisis in Iran was precipitated by which of the following?

(A) The American government allowing the deposed Shah of Iran to come to the United States for cancer treatment.

(B) President Jimmy Carter's involvement in arranging the Camp David accords between the Egyptians and the Israelis.

(C) American air strikes against Iran's ally, Libya.

(D) American support for Israel's 1980 invasion of southern Lebanon.

(E) American attempts to overthrow the newly emplaced government of Ayatollah Khomeini.

99. During the era of European imperialism in Africa, 1870-1914, a "Cape to Cairo railway" was a project envisioned by

(A) Italy   (D) Germany

(B) Britain   (E) Spain

(C) France

100. Which European nation failed to establish an African colony when its expeditionary force was overwhelmingly defeated by a native force at Adowa, Ethiopia, in 1896?

(A) Italy   (D) Britain

(B) Belgium   (E) Austria

(C) Portugal

101. The Himalayan mountain range runs through which of the following Asian countries?

  I. China

  II. Nepal

  III. India

  IV. Bangladesh

(A) I and II only

(D) I, III, and IV only

(B) II and III only

(E) All of the above

(C) I, II, and III only

102. Which of the following was the first European country to make the slave trade illegal?

(A) Holland

(D) Spain

(B) Britain

(E) Portugal

(C) France

103. The Federal Deposit Insurance Corporation (FDIC) was created by

(A) John F. Kennedy as part of his New Frontier

(B) Franklin Delano Roosevelt as part of his New Deal

(C) Theodore Roosevelt as part of his Square Deal

(D) Harry Truman as part of his Fair Deal

(E) Lyndon Johnson as part of his Great Society

104. Located in modern-day Israel, the city of Jerusalem is considered sacred to all of the following EXCEPT

(A) Muslims

(D) Shintoists

(B) Catholics

(E) Presbyterians

(C) Jews

105. The Andes Mountain range (excluding its foothills) intersects with all of the following countries EXCEPT

(A) Argentina

(D) Colombia

(B) Chile

(E) Peru

(C) Uruguay

106. To geographers, "CBD" stands for

(A) Central Basin (of) Denmark

(B) Central Business District

(C) Central Baltic District

(D) Central Basin District

(E) Central Basin (of) Delhi

107. When considering the proper role of government, _____ believed that the average citizen would be easily swayed by demagogues and thus be prone to join mobs. As a consequence, he asserted that a strong central government was needed to control its citizenry.

    (A) Thomas Jefferson   (D) James Monroe

    (B) James Madison   (E) Andrew Jackson

    (C) Alexander Hamilton

108. During the 4th and 5th centuries CE, as the city of Rome continued to decline, the city of _____ continued to grow in terms of political and economic importance.

    (A) London   (D) Constantinople

    (B) Moscow   (E) Berlin

    (C) Paris

109. Which of the following rivers is associated with the incorrect city?

    (A) Rome / Arno River   (D) Paris / Seine River

    (B) London / Thames River   (E) Budapest / Danube River

    (C) Prague / Vltava River

110. Believing that he had landed in India in October, 1492, Columbus and his crew had actually landed in modern-day

    (A) Puerto Rico   (D) Haiti

    (B) Jamaica   (E) Honduras

    (C) Cuba

QUESTION 111 refers to the following excerpt from a Supreme Court decision.

It is emphatically the province and duty of the courts to say what the law is… If two laws conflict with each other, the courts must decide on the operation of each… If, then, the courts are to regard the Constitution, and the Constitution is superior to any ordinary act of the legislature, the Constitution and not such ordinary act, must govern the case to which they both apply.

111. This decision of the Supreme Court upheld the principle that

   (A) a law contrary to the Constitution cannot be enforced by the courts

   (B) Congress has the power to pass laws to carry out its constitutional duties

   (C) interpretation of laws is a legislative function

   (D) a law passed by Congress overrides a constitutional provision with which it conflicts

   (E) courts are not equipped to decide questions of constitutional law

112. "Mark-up sessions," where revisions and additions are made to proposed legislation in Congress, usually occur in which setting?

   (A) The majority leader's office

   (B) On the floor of the legislative chamber

   (C) In party caucuses

   (D) In joint conference committees

   (E) In committees or subcommittees

113. Which of the following has chief responsibility for assembling and analyzing the figures in the presidential budget submitted to Congress each year?

   (A) Department of Commerce

   (B) Department of Treasury

   (C) Federal Reserve Board

   (D) Office of Management and Budget

   (E) Cabinet

QUESTIONS 114 to 118 refer to the charts below.

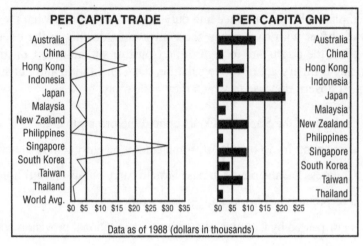

Data as of 1988 (dollars in thousands)

114. Comparing the two charts, the best conclusion is that

    (A) there is a direct relationship between GNP and trade

    (B) the nations all have increased their GNP

    (C) they all exceeded the world average in trade

    (D) Japan is the leader in both GNP and trade

    (E) China ranks lowest in both categories

115. Which is NOT true about both charts?

    (A) Both are figured per person

    (B) Both are in thousands of dollars

    (C) Both compare the same nations

    (D) Both are the same type of graph

    (E) Both use the same year's data

116. Which economic region of the world is reflected in the graphs?

    (A) East Asia   (D) All Pacific

    (B) All Asia   (E) All ex-British colonies

    (C) Northwest Asia

117. According to the charts above, the nation that is increasing its prosperity the most is probably

    (A) Australia   (D) Singapore

    (B) Hong Kong   (E) Taiwan

    (C) Japan

118. Which is the best way to describe the GNP?

    (A) Total goods and services

    (B) Total national production

    (C) Greater national production

    (D) Government natural production

    (E) Gross national resources

119. The Compromise of 1877 resulted in

    (A) the ascension of Republican Rutherford B. Hayes to the presidency in return for assurances that what was left of Reconstruction in the South would be ended.

    (B) the division of the Dakota Territory into North Dakota and South Dakota.

    (C) government financing for a Southern transcontinental railroad route in return for financial grants allowing the completion of the Great Northern Railroad from Minnesota to the Pacific Northwest.

    (D) the ascension of Republican Rutherford B. Hayes to the presidency in return for the passage of an Amnesty Act which would pardon former Confederate soldiers, allowing them to regain their voting rights.

    (E) the formal separation of Virginia and West Virginia and the official acceptance of statehood for West Virginia.

120. The Albany Congress of 1754 was convened for the major purpose of

    (A) adding New York to the Dominion of New England

    (B) getting the colonies to form a "grand council" to coordinate their western expansion and their common defense against Indians

    (C) uniting the colonies under a "grand council" to resist British economic sanctions and coordinate activities against British tax officials

    (D) cooperating with the French in their efforts to rid western New York and southern Canada of raiding Indian tribes

    (E) writing a proclamation to be sent to King George in protest of the Stamp Act

PRACTICE TEST 1

Answer Key

1.	(B)	25.	(A)	49.	(E)	73.	(E)	97.	(D)
2.	(C)	26.	(A)	50.	(D)	74.	(C)	98.	(A)
3.	(B)	27.	(B)	51.	(A)	75.	(D)	99.	(B)
4.	(D)	28.	(B)	52.	(A)	76.	(C)	100.	(A)
5.	(D)	29.	(D)	53.	(C)	77.	(A)	101.	(C)
6.	(A)	30.	(D)	54.	(D)	78.	(B)	102.	(B)
7.	(D)	31.	(C)	55.	(A)	79.	(C)	103.	(B)
8.	(C)	32.	(D)	56.	(D)	80.	(B)	104.	(D)
9.	(C)	33.	(E)	57.	(E)	81.	(E)	105.	(C)
10.	(D)	34.	(D)	58.	(D)	82.	(B)	106.	(B)
11.	(C)	35.	(B)	59.	(E)	83.	(B)	107.	(C)
12.	(E)	36.	(A)	60.	(C)	84.	(A)	108.	(D)
13.	(B)	37.	(C)	61.	(C)	85.	(D)	109.	(A)
14.	(B)	38.	(D)	62.	(D)	86.	(B)	110.	(D)
15.	(A)	39.	(B)	63.	(D)	87.	(E)	111.	(A)
16.	(C)	40.	(A)	64.	(B)	88.	(C)	112.	(E)
17.	(C)	41.	(E)	65.	(C)	89.	(B)	113.	(D)
18.	(A)	42.	(D)	66.	(C)	90.	(B)	114.	(E)
19.	(D)	43.	(B)	67.	(E)	91.	(E)	115.	(D)
20.	(A)	44.	(D)	68.	(D)	92.	(D)	116.	(A)
21.	(B)	45.	(B)	69.	(D)	93.	(B)	117.	(D)
22.	(C)	46.	(E)	70.	(B)	94.	(A)	118.	(A)
23.	(A)	47.	(A)	71.	(C)	95.	(D)	119.	(A)
24.	(C)	48.	(B)	72.	(A)	96.	(E)	120.	(B)

PRACTICE TEST 1

Detailed Explanations of Answers

1.   **(B)**   Burr and Hamilton had never been close friends, and Hamilton made no secret of the fact that he did not trust Burr. During the congressional voting to resolve the outcome of the presidential election of 1800, when Burr might have become the third president of the United States, Hamilton had made attacks against Burr's personal character. In 1804, as Burr ran for governor of New York, Hamilton repeated and expanded those charges. When Burr lost the election, he blamed Hamilton, although there is no clear evidence that Hamilton's charges led to Burr's defeat. Burr demanded "satisfaction" through a duel and Hamilton accepted. Hamilton's death not only deprived the young nation of one of its premier thinkers and statesmen, but it ruined Burr's political career. He was charged with murder and forced to flee to avoid arrest. It was after this disaster that he began formulating his plan for an independent Western empire. Thus, choice (C) is incorrect.

2.   **(C)**   The question deals with the growth of the United States during President McKinley's tenure. President Madison was in office during the War of 1812. President Lincoln headed the government during the Civil War. President Wilson led the country during World War I. President F. D. Roosevelt was the leader during World War II. Thus, the correct answer is (C).

3.   **(B)**   Although "quotation" questions may ask the name of the author or the book title, this question requests more than factual recall. It requires an ability to recognize the main idea of the passage—to read the quotation and understand its philosophic implications. Knowledge of the terminology of seventeenth-century writers is also helpful. Hobbes' *Leviathan* described early human society (the "state of nature") as an anarchic "war of all against all." For self-protection, citizens agreed among themselves to form the first government, an agreement termed by Hobbes as the "social contract." It is especially important to read the quotation carefully, since two of the answers, (B) and (C), are from the *Leviathan*; you may be misled into choosing (C) because you have studied the *Leviathan* in a class and the "social contract" sounds familiar. If the correct answer is not apparent after a second reading of the quotation, it may at least be possible to eliminate the other two answers. The concept of natural rights, incorporated into the French Declaration of the Rights of Man and the Bill of Rights to the United States Constitution, was summarized by John Locke as the idea that human beings are born "free, equal, and independent." "Reason of state" was the justification used by French statesmen such as Cardinal Richelieu to defend measures to create a centralized absolute monarchy in France. Choice (E), nationalism, is not only incorrect but also irrelevant to this question.

4. **(D)** *Laissez-faire* (from the French *laissez-nous faire,* leave us alone) described the economic outlook of nineteenth-century liberals, many of whom were businessmen or industrialists who sought an end to government regulation of business. Proponents of *laissez-faire* envisioned an era of free economic activity in Europe without tariff barriers ("free trade"). Thus factory owners, liberals, and free traders were all supporters of *laissez-faire.* Not so with nineteenth-century socialists, who saw *laissez-faire* as an obstacle to even minimal measures to help the working class, such as government safety inspections of factories.

5. **(D)** On August 15, 1945, traffic came to a halt in Japan, as the nation listened to a prerecorded message in which Emperor Hirohito declared his acceptance of the Potsdam Declaration and Japan's defeat in the Second World War. This was the first time that the country had heard the emperor's voice. In the past, the emperor was considered to hold god-like status, and to allow his subjects to hear his voice, even for events and announcements like his coronation (A), his wedding (B), and declarations of war (C) and (E), would bring him down to the level of a human being. The fact that the emperor himself read the notice of surrender reinforced the completeness of Japan's defeat. They were no longer an imperial power, and their emperor was no longer a deity.

6. **(A)** In 1415 the Portuguese captured Ceuta, one of the first of a series of bases they were to take along the African coast. This marked the first incident of European colonial aggression on the African continent. Portugal's interests in Africa were to find a sea route to India, to explore trade possibilities in the continent (which later developed into transatlantic trade in slaves), to convert the people of Africa to Catholicism, and to assess the strength of the Muslim enemy. By 1640, when Ceuta passed to the Spanish, other European powers had already entered Africa for the same reasons as Portugal. While Belgium (B), England (C), France (D), and Germany (E) all eventually had colonial holdings in Africa, the door was opened up by Portugal (A).

7. **(D)** Prior to creating the Persian Empire, Cyrus the Great had been a shepherd, but he eventually became known as a fierce warrior and sagely leader. In addition to unifying various regional tribes to create the Persian Empire, he also had the reputation for treating his conquered foes fairly. The other answers—Julius Caesar, Marc Antony, Augustus Caesar, and Pompey—were all connected to the Roman Empire and therefore incorrect.

8. **(C)** Muslims are expected to make a pilgrimage to Mecca, not Medina. Although Medina is also considered a holy city (it is where Mohammed is buried), it ranks below Mecca in terms of importance. In addition to being the birthplace of Mohammed, Mecca serves as the center of the Islamic faith, as it contains the faith's most sacred shrine.

9.   **(C)**   Most historians attribute the concept of monotheism to the Israelites, and the figure of Abraham continues to be revered by the worshippers of three main monotheistic religions: Judaism, Christianity, and Islam. The other four answers all refer to legacies of the Greeks. The development of philosophy (A) is generally credited to Socrates (c. 469–399 BCE); geometry (B) to Euclid (c. 300–366 BCE); and tragedy (D) to Aeschylus (c. 525–466 BCE). The Greeks initiated the original Olympic games in 776 BCE.

10.   **(D)**   Confucius (551 to 479 BCE) was an extremely influential scholar and philosopher in China. Among other things, his teachings emphasized the importance of learning, humility, self-discipline, and concern for others. Wang Mang (A) ruled during the short-lived Xin Dynasty (9–23 CE) and was killed after his ambitious attempts at land reform failed badly. Buddha, or Siddhartha Gautama (563 – 479 BCE) was also a scholar, but he was from India. Like Confucius, his teachings had a profound influence on his followers who sought to find the best way to live, which he considered to be the "Middle Way." Kublai Kahn (C) was the grandson of Genghis Kahn and founded the Yuan Dynasty in China in 1271. Shihuangdi (E) founded the Qin Dynasty in 221 BCE. Known for his ruthless leadership tactics (including burning the books of Confucian scholars), he was the first person to unify China.

11.   **(C)**   Marx concluded that conflict between workers and owners was an intrinsic feature of capitalist societies. Since Marx saw this conflict as the principal reason for social change, (D) is incorrect. He also believed this conflict would intensify over time and result in a socialist revolution, so (A) is also incorrect. (B) is incorrect because Marx felt this conflict would ultimately benefit society instead of harming it.

12.   **(E)**   By the mid-1760s, after Britain's passage of the Proclamation of 1763, the Sugar Act, and the Stamp Act, America's colonial leaders increasingly became weary of the tyrannical nature of Britain's King George III and the British Parliament. These tensions rose to a crescendo after the passage of the Coercive Acts in 1774 (which, to be fair to the British, came after the willful destruction of British property in the Boston Tea Party in 1773). Given the foregoing, when the Articles of Confederation were finally ratified by all of the colonies in 1781, there existed an excessive fear of tyranny, which explains why the Articles provided the federal government with such a limited degree of power. Choices (A), (B), and (C) are incorrect because all three countries had become allies to the newly-born United States of America by the signing of the Treaty of Paris in 1783. Choice (D) is incorrect because fear of mobs (the viewpoint held by Alexander Hamilton) is the opposite of the fear of tyranny (the viewpoint held by Thomas Jefferson).

13. **(B)**   Baron de Montesquieu's *The Spirit of the Laws*, published in 1748, provided a thoughtful defense for a country's constitution to include a clear separation of powers. James Madison was intimately familiar with Montesquieu's work when he helped draft the U.S. Constitution. The other four choices are all important works in terms of their contributions to the field of political philosophy, but it was Montesquieu who had the most influence on America's founders when they constructed their new constitution.

14. **(B)**   A writ of habeas corpus is a court order which directs an official who is detaining someone to produce the person before the court so that the legality of the detention may be determined. The primary function of the writ is to effect the release of someone who has been imprisoned without due process of law. For example, if the police detained a suspect for an unreasonable time without officially charging the person with a crime, the person could seek relief from a court in the form of a writ of habeas corpus. (A) is incorrect because a writ of mandamus is a court order commanding an official to perform a legal duty of his or her office. It is not used to prevent persons from being improperly imprisoned. The Fourth Amendment requirement that police have probable cause in order to obtain a search warrant regulates police procedure. It is not itself a mechanism for effecting release of a person for improper imprisonment, so (C) is incorrect. Choice (D) is incorrect since the decision in *Roe v. Wade* dealt with a woman's right to have an abortion. It had nothing to do with improper imprisonment. Choice (E) is incorrect since the prohibition against ex post facto laws is not a mechanism for effecting the release of someone who is improperly imprisoned. Rather, it declares that changing the legal implications of an act, after the act has been committed, is improper.

15. **(A)**   is the best answer since the term "casework" is used by political scientists to describe the activities of members of Congress on behalf of individual constituents. These activities might include helping an elderly person secure Social Security benefits, or helping a veteran obtain medical services. Most casework is actually done by congressional staff and may take as much as a third of the staff's time. Congresspersons supply this type of assistance for the good public relations it provides. Choice (B) fails because pork barrel legislation is rarely, if ever, intended to help individual citizens. Pork barrel legislation authorizes federal spending for special projects, such as airports, roads, or dams, in the home state or district of a congressperson. It is meant to help the entire district or state. Also, there is no legal entitlement on the part of a citizen to a pork barrel project, such as there is with Social Security benefits. (C) is not the answer because lobbying is an activity directed toward congresspersons, not one done by congresspersons. A lobbyist attempts to get members of Congress to support legislation that will benefit the group which the lobbyist represents. Logrolling (D) is incorrect because it does not refer to congressional service for constituents. It refers instead to the congressional practice of trad-

ing votes on different bills. Congressperson A will vote for Congressperson B's pork barrel project and in return B will vote for A's pork barrel project. Filibustering (E) is incorrect. It is a technique used in the Senate to postpone a vote on a piece of legislation. The Senate has a tradition of unlimited debate and nongermane debate. This means that a senator may hold the floor for as long as (s)he likes and need not confine his/her remarks to the bill under consideration. Senators opposing a bill might get control of the floor and talk until the supporters agree to withdraw the bill from consideration.

16. **(C)** The franking privilege is the right of members of Congress to send mail to constituents at public expense. Challengers do not enjoy this privilege. Observers have noticed that the amount of free congressional mail increases during election years, as members try to keep their names before their constituents. Choice (A) is incorrect since incumbent congresspersons certainly do not have access to unlimited campaign funds. Congresspersons may spend as much of their own money as they wish, and they are free to raise money from contributors. But no candidate has unlimited personal funds, nor can incumbents raise unlimited funds from contributions. Choice (B) is incorrect because incumbents and challengers may both have access to national party employees as campaign workers. Both political parties have campaign committees for the House and Senate. All of the committees supply campaign managers, communications directors, and fundraising experts to challengers and incumbents during election campaigns. (D) is incorrect because the Federal Election Campaign Act of 1974 placed a limit of $1,000 per election on individual contributions to political candidates. This put an end to so-called "fat cat" contributors who used to contribute vast sums to candidates. (E) is incorrect because the federal government does not finance any aspect of congressional campaigns.

17. **(C)** is correct. Despite the fact that it comprises leading wheat-producing regions, the former Soviet Union, or CIS, is the only entity that is in the top three in having to *import* extra grain in all three categories, including wheat.

18. **(A)** The United States is the only nation listed that does not import any of the grains but is listed in two categories as a top producer.

19. **(D)** is least correct. The American farmer has traditionally had government assistance available in the form of loan programs, subsidies, price supports, and tariff protection. (A) and (C) are natural assets that American farmers have enjoyed. (B) and (E) have made American farms more efficient and cost effective.

20. **(A)** Contrary to myth, Confederate industry did a masterful job in producing weapons and ammunition for the Confederate military during the war. While it is true that the Confederates never had the abundance of weapons possessed by Union forces, particularly in artillery, it was only near the end of the

war, when Union forces had overrun many production centers and totally destroyed the South's transportation network, that severe shortages of ammunition and weapons developed. It is also true that at the start of the war, Confederate industry could not arm everyone who volunteered for military service; the Union had that same problem. Most Southerners had their own weapons so that despite the lack of government-produced weapons, there was no shortage of available weapons for soldiers. The biggest problem faced by the Confederate armies in regard to weapons and ammunition was a lack of uniformity for the vast array of "homegrown" weapons and ammunition used by their soldiers, not a shortage of weapons themselves.

21. **(B)** The national unemployment rate soared to approximately 25 percent of the workforce in early 1933. This meant that approximately 13 million workers were unemployed. While 25 percent was the national unemployment rate, in some cities the number of unemployed approached 90 percent. This was at a time when there were no welfare benefits or unemployment funds in most areas of the country. What made things worse was the sheer amount of time workers remained unemployed. By early 1937, unemployment had fallen to 14.3 percent, still representing 8 million unemployed workers. Then the recession of 1937 put an additional 2 million workers out of work again. The suffering of being unemployed as long as many of these workers is beyond description. Hobo camps and "Hoovervilles" popped up in virtually every American city. Worse, even for those who kept their jobs, poverty became widespread. Crop prices for farmers dropped by 60 percent. Wages, for workers who still had jobs, dropped 40 percent. Banks continued to collapse, taking the personal savings of depositors down with them, leaving depositors with no savings to help them through this period. So, while 25 percent may not sound catastrophic at first, combined with the collapse of wages and crop prices, as well as the collapse of banks and the sheer amount of time many people were out of work, the nation's economy was close to total collapse.

22. **(C)** The St. Bartholomew's Day Massacre in Paris of French Calvinists, often termed "Huguenots," led to a civil war in France (the War of the Three Henries) and the first Bourbon monarch (Henry IV). When dealing with questions based on illustrations (paintings or drawings), it is important to look for explicit details or other information in the question and in the illustration itself, since it is usually not possible to arrive at a correct answer by eliminating answers. The clues in this case are in the question rather than in the painting. If the primary clue is not sufficient ("St. Bartholomew's Day"), there is a secondary clue in the obviously French name of the painter. Do not be misled by the use of the term "French Calvinists" instead of the name "Huguenots," which is the term usually used by textbook writers; the use of the term "French Calvinists" is another detail testing your knowledge and understanding of European history.

23. **(A)** At first glance this question appears to test only the memorization of facts, but another look will show that it also requires understanding of the diplomatic situation in Europe around 1920. The correct answer may require some thought, since there was no political division of Germany into two governments, as happened at the end of World War II. The "division of Germany into two parts" refers to the "Polish Corridor," created by the peacemakers in order to give Poland an "outlet to the sea." The "Polish Corridor," a strip of formerly German land ceded to Poland in order to provide access to the port city of Danzig, isolated eastern Prussia from the remainder of Germany. It may be possible to arrive at the correct answer by analyzing the other four answers and eliminating them; each is untrue. The end of World War I brought the final collapse of the Ottoman Empire and its reduction to the borders of modern Turkey. The new Communist government of Russia, which came to power in 1917, was ostracized by the other great powers when the war ended. Choice (D) may be tempting because the United States left large numbers of troops in Europe after World War II. This question refers to World War I, however. The United States withdrew from Europe both militarily and diplomatically after that war, preferring to return to "normalcy." Under the terms of the Treaty of Versailles, Germany was required to pay reparations.

24. **(C)** Aimé Césaire was a poet from Martinique (in the West Indies). Although poetry and political writing have been widely influential for writers and thinkers like Franz Fanon, Césaire has never been the leader of an African country. (A) Kwame Nkrumah was the prime minister of Ghana, (B) Jomo Kenyatta was president of Kenya, (D) Julius Nyerere was president of Tanzania, and (E) Patrice Lumumba was prime minister of the Congo.

25. **(A)** When Beijing students chose to hold a protest for the democracy movement in Tiananmen Square, they were making reference to the May 4 Movement of 1919. On this day, students in Beijing demonstrated in Tiananmen Square in protest of the Treaty of Versailles, ending World War I, which denied China all of its demands for return of territory held by foreigners. The demonstrations led to strikes by students and workers, and as a result, the Chinese delegation at Versailles refused to sign the treaty.

26. **(A)** Relative to the Mesopotamians, the Egyptians were blessed in terms of natural resources and geographical conditions. First, the Nile River overflowed on a regular basis, which made for predictable growing seasons. Second, Egypt had excellent natural boundaries that made it difficult to attack; these boundaries included the Sahara Desert, the Red Sea, and the Mediterranean Sea. Third, Egypt had excellent natural building materials, which allowed them to build impressive structures, including the pyramids. Choices (B), (C), and (E) are incorrect, because they all referred to conditions relevant to the Mesopotamians. Ziggurats (D) were buildings found in Mesopotamia, not in Egypt.

27. **(B)** During the 4th century BCE, Aristotle served as a private tutor for the future Alexander the Great. Choice (A), Peter the Great (1672–1725), was a czar of Russia. Choice (C), Alfred the Great (c. 849–899), was a king of Wessex in the south of England. Choice (D), Charles the Great—also known as Charlemagne (1742–1814), was a legendary king of the Franks before being crowned as the Holy Roman Emperor in 1800. Answer (E), Frederick the Great (1712–1786), was a king of Prussia.

28. **(B)** While the Tokugawa Shoganate relied on an agricultural-based feudal structure and developed an insular nature, the Meiji Restoration, which began in 1868, embraced an outward-looking focus, and included the goal of modernizing Japan through rapid industrialization. As a result, the samurai class (A) lost power. In addition, there was a decreased emphasis on subsistence farming (C) and the previous feudal structure (D). Moreover, the xenophobia (E) that had been an integral component of the Tokugawa era slowly began to shift during the Meiji Restoration.

29. **(D)** In spite of a great deal of money being lent to and invested in various countries throughout Sub-Saharan Africa over the past six decades—most notably by the Chinese during the past ten years—this sub-continent mostly remains mired in corruption, poverty, and high infant mortality rates. As such, most people living in Sub-Saharan Africa do what they can to scratch out a living through subsistence agriculture.

30. **(D)** The Second Amendment concerns the right to bear arms. Choices (A), (B), and (C) are all protected by the First Amendment, while Choice (E) is protected by the Sixth Amendment.

31. **(C)** In *Federalist #10*, Madison gave a brilliant defense as to why a government could not prevent the creation of factions. His argument essentially came down to this: the "cure" (a police state that seeks to force the same opinions on all of its citizens) is worse than the "ailment" (factions may form and seek to harm others as well as influence political discourse). Choices (A) and (E) include famous quotations from Thomas Hobbes' *Leviathan*, a work that defends the need for a totalitarian state. Choice (B) is the antithesis of what Madison wrote. Choice (D) is incorrect because Madison certainly did not want the government to encourage the development of factions.

32. **(D)** America's industrial revolution began in earnest during the 1820s with the opening of the Lowell and Waltham textile mills outside of Boston. By the 1830s, a railroad boom had commenced as well. Over time, rapid industrialization and westward expansion led to a transportation revolution (roads, canals, and railroads) and a market revolution (selling goods to distant markets). As more fac-

tories opened up, more people left their family farms and moved to cities in search of work. This trend toward urbanization increased during the 1840s and 1850s, as large waves of German and Irish immigrants came to America, seeking jobs and a better life. Between 1890 and 1920, millions of new immigrants arrived in America, providing a steady source of cheap labor. Most of these immigrants came from southern and eastern Europe and were both poor and unskilled. As such, they were forced to accept low-paying factory jobs and live in tenement houses near their factories. Between 1820 and 1920, millions of struggling farmers and poor immigrants moved to American cities, mostly in the Northeast and Midwest. As a result, the 1920 census showed that more Americans were now living in urban areas rather than rural ones.

33. **(E)** The correct response is (E), since major differences between procedures in the House and Senate include all three of the features mentioned. Because the size of the House is fairly large, with 435 members, time for debate must be limited. If each member was allowed to speak as long as (s)he wanted on every bill, the House could not complete all of its business. Also, debate in the House must be germane. That is, when a member rises to speak, his/her comments must be related to the subject under consideration. This is another time-saving mechanism. The Senate has only 100 members and is not as rushed for time as the House. The Senate has traditionally allowed members to speak as long as they wish and does not force them to confine their remarks to the subject at hand. In the House, the rules committee is very powerful. No bill may get to the House floor without a rule from the rules committee. The rule gives the conditions for debate. The rule sets the time limit for debate and states whether and on what conditions the bill can be amended. The rules committee in the Senate has no such powers.

34. **(D)** In *McCulloch v. Maryland* (1819), the Supreme Court struck down a Maryland law which levied a tax on the Baltimore branch of the Bank of the United States. The Court's ruling was based on its interpretation of the "necessary and proper clause" of the Constitution. This clause may be found in Article I, section 8, of the Constitution. The Court ruled that the necessary and proper clause gives to Congress all powers which make it more convenient for Congress to carry out the enumerated powers of Article I, section 8. (Enumerated powers are those which are specifically mentioned.) The clause is also known as the "elastic clause" since the Court ruled that it gives unspecified powers to Congress. The Court's ruling gave the broadest possible interpretation to the clause, making it possible for Congress to do many things which are not specifically mentioned in the Constitution. By contrast, the Court could have ruled that the clause gave Congress only those powers which are absolutely indispensable to carrying out the enumerated powers. Such a narrow interpretation of the clause would have limited Congress to those activities without which it could not possibly carry out the enumerated powers. (A) is incorrect since *McCulloch v. Maryland* did not deal with freedom

of speech. Choice (B) fails because the power of judicial review (the right of the Court to strike down laws of Congress and to review the actions of the executive) was claimed by the Court in *Marbury v. Madison,* 1803. (C) is incorrect since the Court had previously struck down a law of Congress in *Marbury v. Madison.* Finally, (E) is incorrect because *McCulloch v. Maryland* had nothing to do with the question of executive privilege.

35. **(B)** The question asks which statement about the cabinet is false. Choice (B) is false, and, therefore, the correct answer. The Constitution states in Article I, section 6, that no person holding any office "under the United States" may be a member of Congress. Since cabinet positions are offices "under the United States," cabinet officials may not also be members of Congress. Choices (A) and (D) are true. The cabinet includes the heads of each of the 15 executive departments (State, Treasury, Interior, etc.) as stated in (A). In addition, the president may appoint any other high ranking official whom he wishes to the cabinet, as stated in (D). Choice (C) is true. President Washington was the first to hold cabinet meetings. Every president since Washington has used the cabinet as a tool for managing the federal bureaucracy. So choice (C) is not the correct answer. Choice (E) is not the correct choice. As we saw in the explanation for choice (B), the Constitution states that no one holding office "under the United States" may be a member of Congress. This means that senators may not be members of the cabinet.

36. **(A)** is not a proper conclusion because it is an opinion. The facts from the graph may be used to try to prove the need to cut transportation oil consumption, but the graph itself makes no conclusions. (B) This is true if the average of Germany, Italy, France, and Great Britain is used. (C) Since the United States and Canada top the chart, this is true. (D) This is true, with 25 percent. (E) is true, with about 8 percent.

37. **(C)** This cannot be a conclusion from the graphs, which are per person. Also, Canada, ranking second, has the smallest population on the list. (A) This could be a conclusion because the two largest nations are also the top two consumers. (B) Since four of the top seven consumers are European, this is true. (D) Japan is the only Asian nation listed. (E) This is a probable conclusion, especially when the quantity used for manufacturing in the United States is used as an indicator.

38. **(D)** This is no longer true. Today's industry is divided between many private and nationalized companies. (A) The supply of petroleum is limited and exhaustible. (B) Oil is the key ingredient in plastics. (C) Prices and supply are very sensitive to many conditions. (E) Oil supplies and prices are affected by conditions all over the world with many producers.

39. **(B)**   The Navigation Acts were designed to force the colonies to trade exclusively with England and to give the British government extensive regulatory control over all colonial trade. All of the choices except choice (B) were major principles of these acts. The prohibition of the colonies from issuing paper currencies, while also having a major impact on colonial trade, was the focal point of the Currency Act of 1764 (approximately 100 years later than the Navigation Acts).

40. **(A)**   Slavery never effectively established itself in New England, in large part because the economic system of the New England colonies and the large population of New England, which provided a large pool of workers, rendered the need for large numbers of slaves unnecessary. Most New England farms were relatively small, self-sufficient farms, and the members of farming communities depended on each other to keep their communities economically viable. In the Southern English colonies, there was less community cohesion among the colonists, there were fewer people, and there was a constant demand for laborers to cultivate the cash crops necessary to keep the colonies economically afloat. At first this demand was met by the use of indentured servants, but after the 1660s the supply of potential servants dwindled and the only immediate replacement labor pool was imported slave labor.

41. **(E)**   This question is partly knowledge-based, but it also requires an understanding of the principles of Christian Humanism and an ability to analyze what ideas they would disapprove, (A) and (C), and approve, (E). Renaissance Humanism, also known as Christian Humanism, combined studies of ancient languages with a zeal to make the Scriptures available in the local languages. Virtually all Christian Humanists translated portions of the Scriptures into European languages, using the Latin text which was the sole version available during the Middle Ages. Very few Christian Humanists were connected with the Reformation; the most famous of them, Erasmus of Rotterdam, criticized laxness within the Catholic church but refused to join with the Protestant reformers.

42. **(D)**   Although the czar's manifesto succeeded in calming and ending the Revolution of 1905, the document's promises of reforms contained a loophole: no mention was made of election procedures for the promised Duma, or parliament. When Nicholas II called the Duma into session after the revolution of 1905, he instituted voting procedures which gave considerably heavier representation to the wealthy and to districts around Moscow, which were considered the most loyal to the government.

43. **(B)**   Pakistan, which includes parts of the Punjab, was carved from India in 1947. All of the other choices, Thailand (A), India (C), Korea (D), and Vietnam (E), existed as independent countries before 1947, though because of the partition, India's borders and political situation changed significantly after 1947. It is worthwhile to note that Pakistan, as created in 1947, was later split apart by the secession of Bangladesh in 1971.

44.   **(D)**   The British policy of indirect rule in Africa was designed to reduce tensions and minimize financial costs. It included flexibility and a minimum of direct British intervention. For this reason, the British tried to adapt their colonial policies to fit the wide variety of native systems in and between countries, and they did *not* want a tribal uniform policy (D), which would have been more rigid. Instead they modified the role of traditional rulers in local areas (E) and relied on a decentralized administration (C). The goal for these colonies was eventual self-rule (B), and for this reason they supported basic primary education for Africans which would equip them for this eventuality (A).

45.   **(B)**   The Glorious Revolution of 1688–89 did not result in an agreement that in the event of no heirs, the Hanover house would succeed the Stuarts. Such an arrangement was specified in the Act of Succession of 1701, a year before William III's death and the succession of Queen Anne. She outlived all her children. Upon her death in 1714, George I became the first Hanoverian King of England.

46.   **(E)**   In 1961, after John F. Kennedy gave his approval to overthrow Fidel Castro in what later became known as the Bay of Pigs fiasco, the Russian leader Nikita Khrushchev took advantage of Kennedy's vulnerability and went on the attack. He met with Kennedy in Vienna in June 1961 to address various Cold War-related issues, and after their meetings, Kennedy privately acknowledged that Khrushchev had "savaged him." By August 1961, construction of the Berlin Wall had already begun. In 1963, Kennedy gave a famous speech in West Berlin, where he pledged his solidarity with West Berliners by proclaiming, "Ich bin ein Berliner" ("I am a Berliner."). He also provided a poignant backdrop for his defense of democracy: "Freedom has many difficulties, and democracy is not perfect, but we have never had to build a wall up to keep our people in." The Berlin Wall, the darkest and most enduring symbol of the Cold War, was torn down in 1989, two years before the dissolution of the Soviet Union.

47.   **(A)**   After experiencing a religious conversion after a brutal war against the Kalingans, where he adopted a firm belief in the teachings of Buddhism, Asoka sought to support his newfound belief system by building monasteries and sending out missionaries. The other answers were incorrect in that Confucianism (B) and Taoism (E) primarily took root in China, while Zoroastrianism (D) was an important religion in ancient Persia. Portuguese traders and missionaries did help establish a base for Catholicism (C) in the Indian port city of Goa in the early 1500s, but the Catholic faith did not spread extensively throughout the Indian subcontinent in the same manner that it did in other regions, such as South and Central America.

48.   **(B)**   Portugal's Prince Henry established a navigation school c. 1420, which helped propel his country to an early lead in the Age of Exploration. By 1498, for instance, Vasco da Gama had reached the coast of India. By the mid-1500s, how-

ever, Spain (D) had overtaken Portugal's lead in terms of colonization in the New World. England (A), France (C), and the Dutch Republic (E) were all much slower to devote the resources needed for exploration and colonization.

49. **(E)** The end of the *Pax Romana* (or the "Roman Peace") occurred at the end of the reign of Marcus Aurelius, who ruled from 161–180 CE. Among his major accomplishments, he wrote a series of reflections entitled *Meditations*, a book that serves as an excellent example of stoic philosophy. Sadly, his son, Commodus, was a terrible leader, who ushered in a long period of decline for Rome. The remaining answers are incorrect in that Tiberius (A) ruled Rome from 14 to 37 CE; Nero (B) from 37 to 68; and Constantine (C) from 306 to 337. Justinian I (D) served as a legendary ruler of the Byzantine Empire from 527 to 565.

50. **(D)** Although Alexander Hamilton's Federalist Party had ceased to exist by the time John Quincy Adams was elected president in 1824, like John Marshall, Quincy Adams still embraced many of the principles that Hamilton had set forth. This included the need for an active federal government that used its influence and resources to build a strong national economy by supporting merchants and manufacturers. The other four choices—Jefferson, Madison, Monroe, and Jackson—all sought to minimize the rights of the federal government.

51. **(A)** The Production Possibilities Curve (or Frontier) is a basic economic model that shows the trade-off between two goods. The classic example is the trade-off that shows a society which must choose between producing guns (representing military goods) and butter (representing consumer goods). The reason these two items were first chosen remains unclear, but Nazi Herman Göring once stated, "Guns will make us powerful; butter will only make us fat."

52. **(A)** The Federal Reserve Board is a government agency consisting of seven members appointed for 14-year terms by the president, with the consent of the Senate. This board is at the head of the Federal Reserve System, which is comprised of member banks across the country. The primary function of the Federal Reserve Board is to implement monetary policy. The Federal Reserve Board has three methods of implementing monetary policy. First, it can change the reserve requirement, which is the amount of cash that member banks must keep on deposit in a regional Federal Reserve Bank. An increase in the requirement reduces the amount of cash a bank has on hand to loan. Second, the board can change the discount rate, which is the interest rate that member banks must pay to borrow money from a Federal Reserve Bank. A higher rate discourages a member bank from borrowing and lending more money. Third, the board can buy and sell government securities. To increase the money supply, the board sells securities. To decrease the money supply, the board buys securities. Choice (B) is the most plausible alternative to (A), but fails because controlling government spending is a function of

Congress and the president. Choice (C) is incorrect because the Federal Reserve Board has nothing to do with regulating commodity prices. Choice (D) is incorrect because the board does not help the president run the executive branch. Choice (E) is incorrect because the board does not keep records of troop strength in army reserve units.

53. **(C)** The three largest countries of Western Europe—the United Kingdom, France, and the Federal Republic of Germany—have either a multi-party system or a two-plus party system. A multi-party system is one in which three or more major parties compete for seats in the national legislature, while a two-plus party system has two large parties and one or more small parties. The United Kingdom has a two-plus party system. There are two large parties, the Conservatives and Labour. The Liberals are a smaller third party and there are even smaller regional parties in Scotland, Northern Ireland, and Wales. France has a multi-party system. The Socialists, Neo-Gaullists, and Republicans are major parties, while the Communists and the National Front are small parties with few seats in parliament. The Federal Republic of Germany has a two-plus party system. The major parties are the Christian Democratic Union and the Social Democratic party. At the fringes of public life are the Greens and the Neo-Nazis. The United States, by contrast, has only two parties, which successfully compete on a national basis from one election to the next. These are, of course, the Democrats and the Republicans. Choice (A) is incorrect. In Western European countries, party leaders determine which persons will run for office under the party banner. In the United States, on the other hand, candidates for office are selected by the voters in primary elections. Sometimes in the United States a candidate whom the party leadership detests wins the primary, and thus the right to run for office under the party banner. In most Western European countries, political parties are much more centralized than in the United States; therefore, (B) is false. Choice (D) is false. Because the parties are centralized in Western Europe, and because party leaders select candidates for national office, a party member in the national legislature seldom votes against the party. If one did, party leaders would remove his or her name from the ballot in future elections. Choice (E) is incorrect. Since party members vote the party line almost all of the time in Western Europe, voters tend to not focus on the personalities of candidates, but rather on the party label. In the United States, where legislators vote their personal preference as often as the party line, party label is less important to voters. Voters in the United States tend to focus more on the personalities of candidates than European voters.

54. **(D)** In a parliamentary system the chief executive, normally called the prime minister, is a member of parliament, the legislative body. The majority party in the lower house of the parliament selects its leader to be prime minister. The prime minister then selects a cabinet from among the members of the lower house who are in his/her party. The prime minister and cabinet are the highest executive officers of the country and are usually referred to as the government. There is no

strict separation of powers, since the executive branch is made up of members of the legislature. In a presidential system, by contrast, the president is not a member of the legislature and is selected by popular, not by legislative vote. Cabinet members may not sit in the legislature. There is, then, a strict separation of powers, and thus Statement I is true. In a presidential system, the voters choose the president either by direct popular vote or through an electoral college. In a parliamentary system, the majority party in the lower house of parliament chooses one of its members as prime minister. The general public does not participate in choosing the prime minister. So Statement II is also true. In a parliamentary system the prime minister may call special elections for the lower house of the legislature whenever (s)he wants. In a presidential system the president may not call a special election for members of the legislature, so III is false. The answer, then, is (D), I and II only.

55. **(A)** The first bulleted paragraph states that private and corporate ownership should be limited but they are not directly called upon to act. All other groups are called upon to band together to help the environment.

56. **(D)** These are obvious references to the past use of the environment for economic purposes rather than environmental concerns. (A) and (B) are moral statements, not economic ones. (C) This is a call to action. (E) This tries to redefine society's values.

57. **(E)** This is a political cost concern. Coal is more polluting than oil. (A) This is now used to sell products and is becoming profitable. (B) This is an attempt to replace trees as a renewable resource. (C) Repair and replacement of topsoil, erosion control, and replanting are attempts to reuse mined areas for agriculture. (D) Concern over this has changed products' chemical contents and created new laws to reduce airborne pollution.

58. **(D)** In early 1942, the Japanese high command, angered at air raids from American aircraft carriers, decided to force what was left of the American Pacific fleet into a decisive battle in which the American Navy and its carriers would be destroyed. They decided on an invasion of the American-held island of Midway. Midway was a logical choice. It was 1,100 miles northwest of Hawaii. More importantly, it had a seaplane base and an airstrip. In American hands it provided the United States with an observation post to monitor Japanese actions throughout the central Pacific. In Japanese hands, it would provide them with an airbase from which they could launch continuous air attacks on Pearl Harbor, making it unusable as an American base. If Japan invaded Midway, the Americans would have to send their fleet to defend it or face the loss of Pearl Harbor and Hawaii.

On paper, the plan seemed ideal. The Japanese could throw up to 10 aircraft carriers into the operation. They believed the Americans had only two available aircraft carriers (actually, the Americans had three usable carriers because the

USS *Yorktown,* which the Japanese thought they had sunk at the Battle of Coral Sea, had survived and was repaired in time to fight at Midway). The Japanese had dozens of battleships and heavy cruisers. The Americans had only two battleships available, which they chose not to use, and only eight heavy cruisers. On paper, there seemed to be no way the Americans could win.

Unfortunately for the Japanese, the battle was not fought on paper. American cryptographers deciphered enough Japanese messages to uncover the plan. In addition, the overconfident Japanese, expecting to surprise a scattered American fleet, didn't concentrate their forces into an overwhelming single attack force. Instead they divided their fleet into four separate attack forces, each of which was vulnerable to American attack if caught off guard. When the Japanese arrived at Midway, a well-prepared, tightly concentrated American fleet was waiting. Despite a series of nearly catastrophic errors, the Americans caught the Japanese by surprise, sinking four of their largest aircraft carriers and killing 600 of Japan's best pilots. Without adequate air protection, the invasion was cancelled and the Japanese fleet returned to base. Midway was saved. At the time, American analysts thought they had just bought the United States some additional time until the Japanese regrouped and attacked again. In reality, the Japanese were so stunned by the defeat that they readjusted their war plans, switching to defensive operations. They never returned to Midway. With the Japanese now on the defensive, the United States was able to seize the initiative at Guadalcanal, beginning an island-hopping campaign that took America to Japan's outer islands. Midway was undoubtedly the turning point, as it marked the first significant American victory over the Japanese and the end of major Japanese offensive operations in the central Pacific.

59. **(E)** *Brown v. Board of Education of Topeka* was the first legal shot in the war to desegregate America's public schools. Up to this time, many school districts, particularly in the South, had segregated schools for black and white schoolchildren under the doctrine of "separate but equal" education. Sadly, most education facilities for black children were anything but equal. Blacks usually got dilapidated facilities, the worst teachers, and an inferior education. Frustrated black parents challenged the "separate but equal" doctrine in several states, and those challenges were consolidated into one case to be presented before the United States Supreme Court in 1954. Up until this case, previous civil rights cases had been heard before conservative Supreme Courts which had upheld the "separate but equal" doctrine. However, by 1954, the Court was a more liberal court, more sensitive to constitutional protections for all people.

60. **(C)** While this question calls for fact retention, it also requires an ability to analyze the implications of their policies—unless the answer is apparent upon first reading. The first monarchs of a united Spain, Ferdinand and Isabella, achieved that unity by gaining control of the remaining Muslim sections of

southern Spain. In an effort to promote cultural unity and establish a national identity, they defined Spanish nationalism in terms of their understanding of orthodox Catholicism. Those not fitting their definition of orthodoxy were condemned as disloyal or subversive. Two particular groups, Jews and Muslims who had converted to Christianity but retained Muslim customs or dress, were forced into exile by Spanish authorities.

61. **(C)** The diversity of monarchs listed in the choices should indicate that guessing is a possibility. Two were devout Catholics (D) and (E), while a third (A) predates the Reformation by almost 200 years. During the Thirty Years' War, when Catholic forces from southern Germany and Austria were close to pushing Lutheran forces into the Baltic Sea, the Lutheran convert Gustavus Adolphus intervened in Germany, saving the Lutheran cause. Adolphus was himself killed during a key battle.

62. **(D)** As a result of the Spanish-American War in 1898, the United States gained control of the Philippines from Spain. The Philippines remained a U.S. territory until the Tydings-McDuffie Act of 1934 provided for its independence. This independence was not realized until 1945. Today, however, Spanish influence, mostly in the shape of religion, language, and culture, is still felt, as is America's presence in the form of popular culture.

63. **(D)** Swaziland, a former British colony, has been called Swaziland both before and after its independence. Malawi is a separate independent country, and the other choices, (A), (B), (C), and (E), are all the former and present names of countries in Africa.

64. **(B)** The Nobel-prize winning economist Milton Friedman asserted that the primary cause of the Great Depression was not the overconcentration of wealth, the overproduction of goods, or the overspeculation on stocks, but rather the Federal Reserve Bank allowing the money supply (as defined by M2) to fall by approximately one-third between 1929 and 1933. This errant policy decision starved the nation of credit, which in turn led to the closure of thousands of the nation's banks, wiping out the life savings of many Americans. While many economists dispute the singular focus of Friedman's analysis (arguing that a multitude of factors worked together to cause the Great Depression), virtually all economists agree that contracting the monetary policy during this time period was a major policy blunder that exacerbated a deep economic decline.

65. **(C)** Ben Bernanke, Chairman of the Federal Reserve Bank ("the Fed") from 2006 to 2014, is a Depression-era scholar who possesses an in-depth knowledge of the Fed's disastrous decision to contract the money supply during the first

four years of the Great Depression (1929–1933). As a result, during the Great Recession of 2007–2009, Bernanke dramatically increased the money supply in a policy known as "quantitative easing." Many economists praised Bernanke's handling of monetary policy during this severe downturn, arguing that it kept the United States from another depression; others predicted that it would lead to massive inflation. By 2016, those who were worried about the development of another inflationary cycle looked to be in the wrong, as inflation has steadily remained below 2%.

66. **(C)**   In 122 CE, after a visit to Britain, the Roman Emperor Hadrian began construction of a wall that would eventually bear his name. The barricade, which runs for roughly 80 miles near the English-Scottish border, stretches from the North Sea to the Irish Sea.

67. **(E)**   The Ural Mountains, which are mainly located in Russia and sit to the east of Moscow, are generally considered to be the dividing line between Europe and Asia.

68. **(D)**   The federal government has two primary tools to influence the economy: it can raise or lower taxes and it can raise or lower government spending. (The Federal Reserve Bank is the institution that can raise or lower interest rates and the money supply.) In 1936, during the worst economic crisis in modern history, economist John Maynard Keynes published his famous work *The General Theory of Employment, Interest and Money*, in which he argued that a country's federal government was the only institution big enough to "prime the pump" and thereby stimulate consumer and business demand. Keynes asserted that in a severe economic downturn the federal government should lower taxes and increase government spending; conversely, during an economic boom, he said the government should raise taxes and lower government spending. In making his argument, Keynes challenged the orthodox view of Adam Smith, who in 1776 argued that governments should take a *laissez-faire* (hands-off) approach to markets.

69. **(D)**   The infamous decision rendered in the 1896 Supreme Court case *Plessy v. Ferguson* legitimized Jim Crow segregation laws with the phrase "separate but equal." The other four choices were all famous Supreme Court cases, but only the 1857 decision in *Dred Scott v. Sandford* involved the rights of African Americans. In that case, the Supreme Court, under Chief Justice Roger Taney, ruled that the institution of slavery was protected by the U.S. Constitution and that Congress lacked the power to alter that protection. That ruling was overturned in 1865 with the ratification of the Thirteenth Amendment.

70. **(B)**   The Aztec Empire was based in modern-day Mexico in Central America, while the Incan Empire was based in modern-day Peru in South America. The Powhatan Confederacy (A), the Iroquois Confederacy (C), the Hopi (D), and the Huron (E) were all based in North America and none of them would have been considered empires.

71. **(C)**   Political scientists use the term "pluralistic" to describe a political system in which innumerable groups of people share cultural, economic, religious, or ethnic interests. These groups organize and spend great amounts of time and money competing to influence government policy-making. The pluralistic concept of democracy is in contrast to the elitist model, which states that policy-making is dominated by elites such as wealthy industrialists, military leaders, or organizations such as the Trilateral Commission. Therefore, the answer is (C). Choice (A) fails because pluralism stresses not only cultural groups but economic, religious, and other types of groups. Also important to pluralism is the idea that the different groups do not merely exist but compete to influence public policy-making. Choice (B) fails because the term to describe a system in which political power is divided between national and state governments is "federalism." Choice (D) fails because to say that one group is overrepresented is more like an elitist view than a pluralistic view of politics. It is true that candidates for national office are elected by a plurality vote method (E). "Plurality vote" means that the candidate who gets the most votes, even if less than a majority, wins the election. However, the term "pluralism" does not refer to this method of election, so choice (E) is wrong.

72. **(A)**   As the graph on the next page shows, there is a direct correlation between voter turnout and educational level. Those with four years or more of college are more likely to vote than are those with one to three years of college. Those with one to three years of college are more likely to vote than are high school graduates. High school graduates are, in turn, more likely to vote than are those with less than a high school education. The answer is (A), the more schooling one has, the more likely one is to vote. Voting is only one form of political participation. Other forms are running for office, working in political campaigns, and contributing to campaigns. While it is difficult to find statistics which show the correlation between educational status and running for office, we do know that most people who are completely inactive (that is, do not participate in politics in any way) typically have little education and low incomes and are relatively young. Therefore, it is safe to conclude that the less education one has (B), the LESS likely one is to run for office; so (B) is not the answer. Choice (C) is clearly wrong, since many studies have shown a direct correlation between advanced educational status and political participation by voting. Choice (D) is wrong, as is clear from the graph on the next page. Those with a high school education are NOT more likely to vote than are those with a college degree. Choice (E) is wrong because, as the graph shows, the less education one has, the less likely one is to vote. It is logical to infer from this that those with no formal schooling are less likely to vote than are those with a high school education.

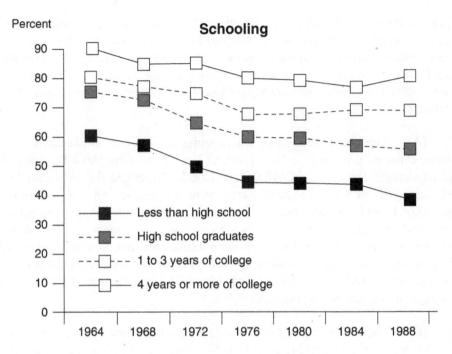

Percent

Schooling

Less than high school

High school graduates

1 to 3 years of college

4 years or more of college

1964 1968 1972 1976 1980 1984 1988

From James Q. Wilson, p. 130, *American Government*

73. **(E)** Articulating interests is generally thought of as the special task of interest groups. Parties, on the other hand, bring together or "aggregate" interests (B) in order to create a working majority to run government. Parties also play a significant role in recruiting candidates (A), serving as channels of communication (C), and staffing elections (D).

74. **(C)** Although the chart can be used for several of the choices, it is a simplified version of the business cycle. (A) The chart does not refer to "bust" or depression. (B) and (D) Changes are shown, but not causes. (E) If you added data, such as dates, it could be used to track historical fluctuations, but doesn't in this form.

75. **(D)** This may influence the other factors, but can have a variety of effects and is not part of the purely economic picture. (A) The number of people employed is used to define whether we are in a recession or not. (B) Obviously directly related to (A), it also shows prosperity, if products are in demand. (C) Personal earnings rise with an economic boom and help sustain it with spending. (E) This is an important indicator of income, production, and consumer confidence in the economy.

76. **(C)** Increased taxation is the most counterproductive to economic growth because it takes money out of spending circulation and reduces sales. (A) is usually not planned, but has been credited with helping the economy as a side effect because of the increased need for services and products. (B) Keynesian economics calls for

"pump-priming" of the economy through government spending to employ people and increase production. (D) Supply-side economics contends that reducing government regulation frees up capital to create products and jobs. (E) This is often used as a short-term solution to help specific industries, such as the auto industry in the early 1980s. Long-term use may trigger international retaliation and create worse problems.

77. **(A)** The Great Awakening was a series of religious awakenings, or rebirths, centered primarily in New England but spread throughout the colonies, which changed the lives of English colonists. It challenged the old hierarchical religious order in which ordained clergy were deferred to and were believed to have knowledge based on extensive formal learning that the average member of a congregation lacked. It brought a much broader sense of community to colonists making them aware of others with similar questions and beliefs who lived outside their village or town. In many ways, it was the first of a series of events that helped to forge distinctively American regional identities, separate from their European heritage, among the North American colonists.

78. **(B)** There were many major changes resulting from the rapid industrial development in the United States from 1860 through 1900. First, there was a shift to building larger and larger industrial facilities to accommodate the new machine technologies coming into existence. Small factories could not absorb the cost of much of the machinery and did not produce enough to make the machinery profitable. So, contrary to choice (D), there was an increase in large industrial plants and a relative decline in small factories.

79. **(C)** Choices (B) and (C) are opposites; high inflation almost always affects the value of a country's currency. If you recognize this conflict, it will become apparent that one of these two answers is the correct answer. If necessary, it is worthwhile guessing, since your odds are 50 percent and only 0.25 point is deducted for an incorrect guess.

80. **(B)** On the map, several areas of Europe are depicted with dark shading. These areas are the lands controlled by the Hapsburgs in the sixteenth century. Choice (C) is incorrect, since Spain was lost by the Hapsburgs in the 1600s. A further clue: the large size of the Ottoman Empire, covering the entire Balkan peninsula, precludes any answer after about 1870.

81. **(E)** In 1914 only Ethiopia, along with Liberia, remained an independent state. Algeria (A) belonged to France; the Congo (B) was Belgian; Angola (C) was occupied by the Portuguese; and Egypt (D) was under British control.

82. **(B)**   Thailand is bordered by Myanmar on the northwest, Laos on the north and east, and Cambodia on the southeast. Vietnam borders Laos and Cambodia on the east with China to its north and the South China Sea to its east. The "Golden Triangle," where Myanmar, Laos, and Thailand meet, is a notorious area for the growing and trafficking of drugs.

83. **(B)**   Hitler, it appears, was not a very good history student, for he basically repeated the same blunders that Napoleon made in 1812, when his troops unsuccessfully invaded Russia. The armies of both men went down in defeat, in part because of the long supply lines and the brutal Russian winters. Stalin successfully negotiated his demand for a buffer zone with Franklin Roosevelt and Winston Churchill, who needed Russia's help to bring about a swift end to the war in Europe. In return, Stalin promised FDR and Churchill that he would hold free elections in Eastern Europe. He later betrayed that promise by holding rigged elections, thereby exacerbating the tensions between Russia and America at the outset of the Cold War.

84. **(A)**   During the 1930s and 1940s, a great debate occurred between British economist John Maynard Keynes and Austrian economist Friedrich Hayek concerning the proper role of government in the economy. Keynes argued that governments should intervene during severe recessions or booming economies. Hayek, on the other hand, asserted that government involvement would eventually lead to a dependent people who, over time, would function much like the serfs did in a feudal society.

85. **(D)**   *In The Wealth of Nations*, Adam Smith argued that human self-interest drives human behavior. The context for his quotation about the butcher, brewer, and baker is that if governments get involved in regulating markets, they will pervert individual incentives and cause market inefficiencies. As a result, Smith asserted that governments should keep their hands-off, noting that in the long-run markets always correct themselves.

86. **(B)**   After Jefferson completed the Louisiana Purchase in 1803, the western boundary of the United States was located along the Rocky Mountains. This boundary did not reach the Pacific Ocean until 1848, after the signing of the Treaty of Guadalupe-Hidalgo at the conclusion of the Mexican-American War.

87. **(E)**   Founded in 1993, the European Union (EU) is an economic union but not a political one, a fact that has caused a great deal of controversy, especially after Greece first began defaulting on its debts in 2010 and needed a bailout from stronger EU countries, such as Germany. In terms of economic power, the EU has a mixture of both strong and weak countries. As a result, many economists question the EU's long-term viability, especially after the 2016 vote in which the British decided to pull out of the EU.

88. **(C)**   Manifesting a mindset that "might makes right," thirteen European powers carved up Sub-Saharan Africa with little regard for existing boundaries or tribal affiliations. An underlying motivation for the Berlin Conference was Otto von Bismarck's desire to enhance Germany's colonial holdings so it could compete on the world stage with the likes of England and France. To justify carving up this vast region, the European powers relied on concepts such as "survival of the fittest," a term first coined by English sociologist Herbert Spencer (not Charles Darwin, as most people assume). Perhaps English industrialist Cecil Rhodes best summed up the prevailing European arrogance and racism of his era when he proclaimed that the Anglo-Saxon race was "the finest race in the world, and that the more of the world we inhabit, the better it is for the human race."

89. **(B)**   The early river valley civilization in Mesopotamia was connected to the Tigris and Euphrates Rivers. The Volga River is the longest river in Europe and located in Russia.

90. **(B)**   In 1932, Franklin Roosevelt was elected president in a landslide vote, ending a 12-year period of Republican domination of the presidency. This election is considered by political scientists a "realigning election." A realigning election is one in which a sharp, lasting change occurs in the coalition of voters which supports each of the parties. In the election of 1936, Roosevelt drew into the Democratic party a coalition of urban workers, blacks, southern whites, and Jews. Most of the urban workers were also union members. The coalition did not include large numbers of business interests, which continued to vote for the Republican party. This coalition continued to support the Democratic party until approximately 1968, when white southerners began to vote for the Republican candidate for president more often than for the Democratic candidate. The answer is (B), northern business leaders, since most of these voters supported the Republicans in each of the years Roosevelt ran for president (1932, 1936, 1940, and 1944). Choice (A) is wrong because most southerners, white and black alike, voted for Roosevelt each time he ran for president. Choice (C) is wrong because blue-collar workers heavily supported Roosevelt in each of his elections. Choice (D) is wrong because blacks and Jews, two prominent racial minorities, voted for Roosevelt. Choice (E) is false because union members, who were mostly blue-collar workers, heavily supported Roosevelt.

91. **(E)**   The Fifth Amendment to the U.S. Constitution states, "No person shall be compelled in any criminal case to be a witness against himself…." The Supreme Court held in *Miranda v. Arizona,* 1966, that "In order to…permit a full opportunity to exercise the privilege against self-incrimination, the accused must be adequately and effectively apprised of his rights and the exercise of those rights must be fully honored." This means that when police apprehend a suspect in a criminal case they must immediately tell the person that (s)he has a

right to remain silent. The Sixth Amendment to the U.S. Constitution states: "In all criminal prosecutions, the accused shall enjoy the right…to have compulsory process for obtaining witnesses in his favor, and to have Assistance of Counsel for his defense. The compulsory process clause means that the accused can sub-poena witnesses in his/her favor to appear in court to testify for the defense. (A subpoena is a court order which commands a person to appear at a certain time and place to give testimony upon a certain matter.) The assistance of counsel clause of the Sixth Amendment was interpreted by the Supreme Court in *Argersinger v. Hamlin,* 1972, to mean that if the accused cannot afford an attorney, (s)he is entitled to have one appointed at government expense, in any felony or misdemeanor criminal case in which, if the accused is found guilty, (s)he may be sentenced to jail. It is clear from the above that the rights mentioned in statements I, II, and III are all guaranteed by the Constitution. Therefore, choice (E) is correct.

92. **(D)** Before the Civil War most blacks in the South were slaves. They were not citizens and had no civil or political rights. After the war, the Fourteenth and Fifteenth Amendments were added to the Constitution. The Fourteenth Amendment extended citizenship to blacks. The Fifteenth Amendment stated that the "right of citizens of the United States to vote shall not be denied or abridged by the United States or by any state on account of race, color, or previous condition of servitude." Contrary to what one might assume, blacks did not immediately gain full voting rights. During the 1870s the Supreme Court held that the Fifteenth Amendment did not automatically confer the right to vote on anybody. States could not pass laws to prevent anyone from voting on the basis of race, but they could restrict persons from voting on other grounds. This interpretation of the Fifteenth Amendment allowed southern states to use several techniques to effectively exclude blacks from voting. Since most former slaves were illiterate, prospective voters were often required to pass literacy tests. Poll taxes were also levied, which kept blacks, who were mostly poor, from voting. Since many whites were also poor and illiterate, grandfather clauses were enacted to allow them to bypass the legal restrictions on voting. Grandfather clauses stated that if you or your ancestors had voted before 1867, you could vote without paying a poll tax or passing a literacy test. Choice (D) is correct because the purpose of grandfather clauses and literacy tests was to keep blacks from voting. Choice (A) is wrong because the purpose of the grandfather clause was to allow poor and illiterate whites to escape voting restrictions. Choice (B) is wrong because the intent of the restrictions was to prevent blacks, not immigrants, from voting. In addition, there was little immigration into the South during the time in question. Choices (C) and (E) are wrong because the measures were restrictions on the right to vote, not on the right to run for office.

93. **(B)** is the most specific statement because, although the first paragraph refers to the "needs of society," those needs are specified as economic in the rest of the quote. (A) Many of society's needs—legal rights, social needs, poverty – are not addressed. (C) This is not discussed. (D) The terms "average," "more" and "more," and "most" are used, not "all." (E) The government role is not discussed.

94. **(A)** The Chamber of Commerce represents U.S. businesspeople and this is definitely a pro-business statement. (B) The federal Department of Labor is not anti-business, but it is not its major concern to advocate pro-business stands. (C) The GAO is the auditing branch of the government and doesn't take a stand on pro- or anti-business statements. (D) The Socialist belief would probably be the opposite of the quote. (E) The union position would probably credit workers more and business less.

95. **(D)** Justice means fair treatment for all, sometimes enforced by government regulation. (A) This is specifically referred to in relation to employment, wages, etc. (B) This is indirectly referred to through rising living standards and growth which also provides security (C). (E) This is implied throughout and referred to as "less constraint."

96. **(E)** Labor is a factor in creating all of the others, which are the basic activities.

97. **(D)** In the autumn of 1864, a war-weary North faced a presidential election that offered them a clear choice. Abraham Lincoln ran on a platform of continuing the Civil War until the South was totally defeated. His opponent, former general George McClellan, ran on a platform calling for an armistice and recognition of the South as a separate nation. Early in the campaign, Lincoln looked to be in trouble. Although the Union had made deep penetrations into the western half of the Confederacy and had complete control of the Mississippi River, the Confederate armies in the East still fought valiantly on. It looked as if the Union armies could never destroy them and many people were questioning if it was worth the cost to try. The war had now been raging for $3\frac{1}{2}$ years. The cost in human lives, time, and money had far surpassed everyone's worst fears. Many Northerners just wanted it to be over. Both Lincoln and Confederate President Jefferson Davis realized this. Accordingly, the Confederate strategy was to just hold on and deny the North any major victories before the election. Lincoln realized he needed a decisive victory before the election, pointing to a rapid defeat of the Confederacy, if he was to win. That victory occurred in September 1864 when Union forces under the command of William T. Sherman occupied Atlanta and followed up on this victory with his infamous "march to the sea." This victory pointed to the imminent destruction of the Confederacy. Finally, people could see a "light at the end of the tunnel" and

desire to completely defeat the Confederates rose again in the North. The capture of Atlanta guaranteed Lincoln's reelection and sealed the fate of the Confederate States of America.

98. **(A)** After he was overthrown by revolutionary forces in 1978 the Shah of Iran fled, travelling to several countries. It was from Mexico, that he asked for permission to enter the United States to receive cancer treatment. President Carter was warned that admitting the Shah to the United States, for any reason, would look to the Iranians like America still supported the Shah's regime and would lead to trouble. However, other advisors told Carter that the United States owed the Shah a large debt of gratitude for the favors he had done for America and also for the lack of decisive support from the United States when his government was overthrown. Carter had previously refused to grant the Shah exile in the United States, but when he was told of the Shah's need for cancer treatment, he decided to allow the Shah to enter the United States on humanitarian grounds. As predicted, the Iranians were infuriated by this. On November 4, 1979, young Iranian males, backed by their government and claiming to be students, seized the American embassy compound and took 76 hostages, 62 of whom were held for more than a year. It was the beginning of one of the worst nightmares in American foreign policy, and it helped ruin Carter's presidency.

99. **(B)** Here is a question that may be answered correctly even if, upon first reading, you are tempted to pass it by. The correct answer must be a country which had some degree of control over land in both Egypt and South Africa. If no answer comes to mind, you still may be able to remember the fact that the British had the largest colonial empire. After wrestling control of the Suez Canal in Egypt from its French builders and the Egyptian Khedive, the British government planned construction of a rail line linking Egypt with its recent acquisition of largely Dutch-settled land in South Africa. Typically, other European nations successfully moved to block the railroad by making claims to central African land along the route.

100. **(A)** The mention of Ethiopia may bring Italy to mind. If not, a possible guess is indicated if you are able to remember Mussolini's invasion of Ethiopia during the 1930s. The sole European nation to have its plans to establish an African colony in the late nineteenth century blocked by a native African force, Italy for some time regarded the incident a national humiliation. The incident was one of several reasons the Italian dictator Mussolini gave for his successful military takeover of Ethiopia in 1935.

101. **(C)** The Himalayan mountain range, the highest in the world, runs 1,500 miles from the northernmost tip of India, through Nepal, and along the southwest border of China. The Himalayas include Mt. Everest (Qomolongma), the tallest mountain in the world, and India's tallest mountain, Nanda Devi, which rises 25,645 feet. Bangladesh is almost completely surrounded by the northeastern bor-

der of India, facing the Bay of Bengal. It does have a small border with Burma on its southeast side.

102. **(B)** When Britain, bowing to internal abolitionist pressure, declared the slave trade illegal for its people in 1807, only Denmark, which made illegal the slave trade in 1805, had already outlawed the practice. The next to follow suit was Holland (A) in 1814, France (C) in 1818, and Spain (D) and Portugal (E) which restricted their slave trade to the seas south of the equator in 1815 and 1817, respectively.

103. **(B)** The Federal Deposit Insurance Corporation (FDIC) was an essential component of FDR's New Deal policies in 1933. Prior to its implementation, depositors risked losing their entire savings if a bank became insolvent. As a result of the FDIC, however, the federal government agreed to guaranty bank deposits for up to $5,000, but only in FDIC-approved banks. (Today that guaranty extends to deposits up to $250,000.)

104. **(D)** The Shinto religion is native to Japan and is a polytheistic faith that involves the worship of both nature and ancestors.

105. **(C)** The country of Uruguay is located on the Atlantic Ocean side of South America, whereas the Andes Mountain range runs along the Pacific Ocean side.

106. **(B)** Geographers use the designation "CBD" when referring to the Central Business District of a city. For example, Manhattan is considered the CBD of New York City.

107. **(C)** Unlike Thomas Jefferson, who defended his viewpoint toward a limited role for the federal government based upon his model citizen, the virtuous yeoman farmer, Alexander Hamilton had a rather jaundiced view of the common man. As a result, Hamilton greatly feared mobs and therefore sought a federal government that would swiftly put down rebellion. For example, he used Shays' Rebellion in western Massachusetts in 1786 to call for a convention of delegates in Philadelphia in 1787. At this gathering, Hamilton and James Madison led an assault against the ineffective Articles of Confederation, a document that was drafted based upon an excessive fear of tyranny.

108. **(D)** The modern-day city of Istanbul, Turkey, was known as Constantinople in 330 CE, after the Roman Emperor Constantine the Great made it the new capital of the Roman Empire. Strategically located on both sides of the Bosporus (a narrow straight that connects Europe to Asia), this city played an important role in three different empires: the Roman, Byzantine, and Ottoman. In what ranks as a key turning point in world history, the Ottoman Turks finally conquered this strate-

gically-important city in 1453, putting an end to the last remnants of the formerly glorious Byzantine Empire.

109. **(A)**   The Arno River runs through the city of Florence, not Rome. The primary river in Rome is the Tiber.

110. **(D)**   On his first trip across the Atlantic Ocean, Columbus mistakenly thought he had reached India, but in fact he had landed in modern-day Haiti. Driven by various motives, including "God, Glory, and Gold," Columbus more or less died a failure, never finding the gold or the glory that he so desperately sought. With respect to God, although he maintained his Christian faith until his death in 1506, the interactions between Columbus and the native peoples that he encountered soon led to the forced coercion to Christianity for many, a tactic that clearly runs contrary to basic teachings in the Gospels.

111. **(A)**   The passage is taken from the landmark case *Marbury v. Madison,* 1803. What the passage means, in everyday language, is:

> 1. Interpreting laws is a judicial function. 2. When two laws conflict, the courts must decide which will be enforced. 3. The Constitution is superior to laws passed by Congress or state legislatures (called statutory law). 4. Therefore, if a statute conflicts with the Constitution, the statute cannot be enforced by the courts.

Choice (B) is incorrect because the passage says nothing about Congress's right to pass laws to carry out its duties. Rather, the passage deals with a conflict between statutory and Constitutional law. Choice (C) is incorrect because it contradicts the main thesis of the passage. The passage clearly says that it is the duty of *courts*, not legislatures, to "say what the law is," which means the same as "interpretation of laws." Choice (D) is incorrect because the passage says when an act of the legislature and the Constitution conflict, the Constitution governs the case. Choice (E) is incorrect because the passage states specifically that if two laws conflict, the courts must decide the operation of each. It then posits a case where the two laws in conflict are an act of the legislature and the Constitution. The clear implication is that, in such a case, the courts must decide on the operation of the Constitution, which means deciding questions of Constitutional law.

112. **(E)**   After a bill is introduced into either house of Congress, it is referred to the appropriate committee. The bill will then usually be referred by the committee to a subcommittee. After holding a hearing on the bill, the subcommittee will then have a mark-up session where revisions and additions are made to the bill. The bill is then referred back to the full committee, which may also hold a hearing and have a mark-up session. Choices (A), (B), and (C) are incorrect

because mark-up sessions do not occur in the majority leader's office, on the floor of the legislative chambers, or in party caucuses. Choice (D) is the most plausible alternative to (E), because a joint conference committee is, after all, a committee. However, proposed legislation goes to a joint conference committee only after it has passed both houses of Congress. The Constitution requires that before a piece of legislation can become law, it must pass both houses in identical form. The purpose of the joint conference committee is to iron out differences in a bill that has passed one house in a different form than in the other. It is true that changes are made to such a bill in a joint conference committee, to satisfy members of both houses. However, the term "mark-up session" refers only to the activity of standing committees and subcommittees in Congress, not to joint conference committees.

113. **(D)** The Office of Management and Budget is the chief presidential staff agency. Its primary responsibility is to put together the budget that the president submits to Congress. Each agency and office of the executive branch must have its budget requests cleared by OMB before it gets into the president's budget. The OMB also studies the organization and operations of the executive branch, to ensure that each office and agency is carrying out its appropriate duty, as assigned by law. Choice (A) is incorrect because the Department of Commerce does not help the president to draw up his annual budget. The Department of Commerce was created in 1903 to protect the interests of businesspeople at home and abroad. Choice (B) is incorrect because the Department of Treasury is not involved in drawing up the president's budget. The functions of the Treasury Department include collecting taxes through the Internal Revenue Service, an administrative unit of the Department, administering the public debt, and coining money. Choice (C) is incorrect because the main responsibility of the Federal Reserve Board is the implementation of monetary policy. It has nothing to do with drawing up the president's annual budget. Choice (E) is incorrect because the cabinet does not help the president draw up his budget. It advises the president on the administration of the executive departments.

114. **(E)** is correct. (A) is not correct, because there are some variances between nations high in GNP while not so high in trade. (B) is incorrect because there is no data comparing previous years. (C) is incorrect. Thailand, the Philippines, and Indonesia did not exceed the world average in trade. (D) is incorrect; Japan was not the leader in trade.

115. **(D)** is not true. The trade graph is a line graph, and the GNP is a bar graph. All the others are true. (A) Per capita means per person.

116. **(A)** is most accurate; all are on the eastern edge of Asia. (B) is incorrect because all of Asia is not represented, for example, India or the Persian Gulf. (C) is wrong; northwest Asia would be either the Persian Gulf area or Asian USSR. (D) is

incorrect; Malaysia and Thailand are as close to the Indian Ocean as to the Pacific. (E) is wrong; only Australia, Hong Kong, Malaysia, New Zealand, and Singapore were ever British colonies. Japan and Thailand were never colonized by foreigners.

117. **(D)**   Singapore shows the greatest growth rate because its per capita trade is not only highest but exceeds its GNP, which means its people are producing exportable products which bring money back into the nation. Hong Kong is second.

118. **(A)**   GNP is the gross national product and is defined as the total goods and services produced by the nation in a given year. (B) is only partially correct because services are not specified. The other choices are not correct.

119. **(A)**   In the presidential election of 1876, Samuel Tilden defeated his Republican opponent, Rutherford B. Hayes, in the popular vote by 250,000 votes. However, there were 20 contested votes in the electoral college. If Hayes received all the contested electoral votes, he would win the election by one vote in the electoral college and he would gain the presidency. The matter was turned over to Congress, where a Republican-dominated commission awarded the disputed electoral votes to Hayes. The Senate ratified the commission's decision, but the Democrats in the House threatened to use political means to gain Tilden's victory through a House vote. Republicans negotiated the issue and the Compromise of 1877 was the result. Hayes won the presidency. Democrats received assurances that federal soldiers would be withdrawn from Southern states (effectively ending Reconstruction) and that blanket federal government support for Republicans in the South would end. This opened the door for Democrats to regain control in all the Southern states (they had already effectively regained control in all but three). None of the other choices listed in the question were in any way involved in the Compromise of 1877.

120. **(B)**   After the defeat of George Washington's Virginian forces at Fort Necessity by the French, it became clear that the colonies were too weak to individually tackle either the French or their various Indian allies. Benjamin Franklin perceived that united action by the colonies was the only hope of providing for their security. He called together the Albany Congress to discuss plans to enlist the aid of the various Iroquois tribes in colonial defense and to coordinate defense plans between the English colonies. It also called for the establishment of a "grand council" with representatives from each of the colonies to enact taxes and coordinate colonial economic activity. The plan is notable because it was the first to call for the individual colonies to act as a single, united entity. While the plan was visionary and ultimately necessary, the colonial legislatures ultimately rejected it.

PRACTICE TEST 2

CLEP Social Sciences and History

This practice test is also offered online at the REA Study Center *(www.rea.com/studycenter)*. Since all CLEP exams are administered on computer, we recommend that you take the online version of the test to receive these added benefits:

- **Timed testing conditions** – Gauge how much time you can spend on each question
- **Automatic scoring** – Find out how you did on the test, instantly
- **On-screen detailed explanations of answers** – Learn not just the correct answer, but also why the other answer choices are wrong
- **Diagnostic score reports** – Pinpoint where you're strongest and where you need to focus your study

PRACTICE TEST 2

CLEP Social Sciences and History

(Answer sheets appear in the back of the book.)

TIME: 90 Minutes
120 Questions

Directions: Each of the questions or incomplete statements below is followed by five possible answers or completions. Select the best choice in each case and fill in the corresponding oval on the answer sheet.

1. The policy promoted by Theodore Roosevelt and most blatantly pursued in Central America was the

    (A) "New Deal" policy

    (B) "Big Stick" policy

    (C) "Good Neighbor" policy

    (D) "Fair Deal" policy

    (E) "Square Deal" policy

2. The Newburgh Conspiracy resulted from

    (A) attempts to bring Kansas into the Union as a slave state

    (B) a plot by the Nationalist faction to overthrow the Articles of Confederation and replace the Continental Congress with a strong central government headed by a European-style monarch

    (C) fears, at the conclusion of the Revolutionary War, that the Continental Congress would disband the army without funding the soldiers' pensions

    (D) plans by Aaron Burr to create a separate republic, with himself as the leader, in the American lands west of the Appalachians

    (E) schemes by France to regain dominance in the Mississippi Valley by enlisting the aid of several prominent Americans, promising them large tracts of land in the region in return for their assistance in the scheme

3. All of the following inventions or processes were significant parts of the Industrial Revolution EXCEPT the

   (A) spinning jenny   (D) flying shuttle

   (B) steam engine   (E) electric motor

   (C) Bessemer process

4. Which one of the following individuals was an example of nineteenth-century liberalism?

   (A) Proudhon   (D) Napoleon III

   (B) Disraeli   (E) Mill

   (C) Fourier

5. In 1956 Britain and France, with Israeli help, attacked Egypt over what issue?

   (A) Egyptian resistance to decolonization

   (B) Intervention in civil war

   (C) Tariff reform

   (D) Control over the Suez Canal

   (E) Egyptian foreign policy in the Middle East

6. Which of the following is NOT one of Japan's islands?

   (A) Honshu   (D) Shikoku

   (B) Kyushu   (E) Yokohama

   (C) Hokkaido

7. When sociologists use the term "ethnic group," they are referring to people who have

   (A) a shared cultural heritage   (D) common political views

   (B) low social status   (E) the same occupation

   (C) similar physical appearance

8. A key difference between the ancient Athenians and the ancient Romans was that the Romans tended to

(A) copy from the Carolingians

(B) use the same names as the Athenians for their most important gods

(C) reject any and all things Athenian in origin

(D) copy and adapt many concepts from the Athenians to suit their own particular needs

(E) be jealous of the Athenians, so they completely destroyed the original Parthenon

9. The Protestant Reformation became a "push" factor from Europe to the New World. A primary cause that led Martin Luther to initiate this Reformation was that the Catholic Church had allowed

(A) Henry VIII to separate England from the Church

(B) the Pilgrims to establish a colony in the New World

(C) John Calvin to publish his heretical work entitled *Institutes of the Christian Religion*

(D) John Winthrop to give his famous "City upon a Hill" speech, indicating that the Puritans would soon show the world how to create a religious utopia

(E) the sale of indulgences, partially as a means of raising funds to build Saint Peter's Basilica in Rome

10. When Karl Marx and Friedrich Engels published the *Communist Manifesto* in 1848, they were primarily responding to the problems associated with the

(A) Scientific Revolution

(B) Glorious Revolution

(C) American Revolution

(D) French Revolution

(E) Industrial Revolution

11. The first people to circumnavigate the globe were

(A) Christopher Columbus and his crew

(B) Vasco da Gama and his crew

(C) Ferdinand Magellan and his crew

(D) Vasco da Gama's crew (because he was lost at sea in the Indian Ocean)

(E) Ferdinand Magellan's crew (because he was killed in the Philippines)

12. Under a confederation-based system of government, such as the one the United States had under the Articles of Confederation, governmental power tends to mostly reside at the _____ level.

    (A) national

    (B) local

    (C) federal

    (D) state or regional

    (E) party

13. When Ho Chi Minh wrote the Vietnamese Declaration of Independence in 1945, he figuratively hurled the U.S. Declaration of Independence back at the West for allowing which of the following countries to regain power in Vietnam after the end of World War II? This same country later suffered an embarrassing defeat in 1954 at Dien Bien Phu.

    (A) Britain

    (B) France

    (C) Germany

    (D) Italy

    (E) The Netherlands

14. The term "executive privilege" refers to

    (A) the right of the president to veto legislation proposed by Congress

    (B) the limited right of the president to withhold certain information from Congress and the public

    (C) the right of the president to appoint and receive ambassadors

    (D) the limited right of the president to pardon persons convicted of federal crimes

    (E) the limited immunity of the president from prosecution for certain misdemeanors

15. A U.S. senator gets an item inserted into the federal budget which allocates $6 million for building a ski lift at a resort in his home state. This is known as

    (A) a filibuster

    (B) pork barrel legislation

    (C) logrolling

    (D) grease for the gears

    (E) senatorial courtesy

16. Which of the following statements reflects an elitist view of American politics?

    (A) American politics are dominated by the military-industrial complex.

    (B) Thousands of competing interest groups influence public policy-making.

(C) Large states dominate public policy because of their overrepresentation in Congress.

(D) American politics are dominated by rural areas at the expense of urban areas.

(E) Since only one registered voter in three votes in off-year congressional races, Congress represents only the politically active.

QUESTIONS 17 to 21 refer to the following graphs.

TOP IMPORTERS FROM U.S. in billions of dollars, 1989		TOP EXPORTERS TO U.S. in billions of dollars, 1989		U.S. TRADE BALANCE with MEXICO in billions of dollars, 1989
$78.6	Canada	$93.6	Japan	27.2
$44.6	Japan	$88.2	Canada	25.0
$25.0	Mexico	$27.2	Mexico	
$20.3	Britain	$24.8	Germany	-2.2
$16.9	Germany	$24.3	Taiwan	Exports Imports Deficit

Source: U.S. Commerce Dept.

17. Which nation is a top importer, but not a top exporter?
   (A) Britain
   (B) Canada
   (C) Germany
   (D) Japan
   (E) Mexico

18. Taken together, which area imports the most from the United States?
   (A) Canada
   (B) Latin America
   (C) Asia
   (D) Africa
   (E) Europe

19. Taken together, which area exports the most to the United States?
   (A) Canada
   (B) Latin America
   (C) Asia
   (D) Africa
   (E) Europe

20. Which of the following has the most favorable trade balance with the United States?

   (A) Britain

   (B) Canada

   (C) Germany

   (D) Japan

   (E) Mexico

21. If exports exceed imports, it is called

   (A) favorable balance of payments

   (B) unfavorable balance of payments

   (C) favorable balance of trade

   (D) unfavorable balance of trade

   (E) deficit spending

22. The thrust of Roosevelt's "Good Neighbor" policy was to

   (A) retreat from the military interventionism and blatant economic domination which had characterized previous American policy toward Latin America

   (B) guarantee the protection of Latin America and South America from European aggression by permanently stationing U.S. forces in the region

   (C) promote "Good Samaritanism" in the United States by encouraging people who still owned their own homes to provide temporary housing for their neighbors who had become homeless because of the Great Depression

   (D) force Latin American countries to cooperate peacefully with each other and end their petty border disputes or face United States military intervention

   (E) supply Britain with the food and nonmilitary essentials they needed to maintain their struggle against Nazi Germany

23. Which of the following was NOT true of the Northwest Ordinance of 1787?

   (A) It recognized the territorial claims of the various Indian tribes within the Northwest Territory.

   (B) It guaranteed freedom of religion to settlers in the Northwest Territory.

   (C) It guaranteed the right to a jury trial to settlers in the Northwest Territory.

   (D) It prohibited slavery within the Northwest Territory.

   (E) It specified procedures through which settlers could organize state governments and eventually apply for full statehood.

24. Which one of the following best characterizes the relationship between the Commercial Revolution and the Italian Renaissance?

   (A) The Commercial Revolution caused Europeans to concentrate on their own continent, to the exclusion of the rest of the world.

   (B) The Commercial Revolution was a result of the Italian Renaissance.

   (C) The new merchant class of the Commercial Revolution was more interested in the secular world and less interested in religion.

   (D) There is no connection.

   (E) The Commercial Revolution enriched Italian farmers.

25. "Imperialism emerged as a development and direct continuation of the fundamental properties of capitalism...imperialism is the monopoly stage of capitalism."

   The writer quoted above would most likely accept which of the following statements as true?

   (A) Imperialism was caused by European advances in science and technology.

   (B) A desire for national prestige drove Europeans into a race to gain colonies.

   (C) Imperialism was a natural and predictable result of the growth of capitalism.

   (D) A country with an advanced capitalistic system might become the "colony" of another country.

   (E) Imperialism fed the egos of the smaller, less powerful nations of Europe.

26. The first All-African People's Conference, organized by Kwame Nkrumah, was held in what year?

   (A) 1949   (D) 1960

   (B) 1956   (E) 1963

   (C) 1958

27. What year did the revolution ending the last Chinese dynasty take place?

   (A) 1864   (D) 1911

   (B) 1900   (E) 1950

   (C) 1644

28. The Republican Party, formed in Ripon, Wisconsin, in 1854, developed a party platform that included support for a movement advocating

    (A) abolition

    (B) popular sovereignty

    (C) free soil

    (D) the Missouri Compromise of 1820

    (E) the late John C. Calhoun's assertion that slavery was a "positive good"

29. After the Kuomintang government fell to the communist forces of Mao Ze-dong in 1949, the Kuomintang leader, Chiang Kai-shek (also known as Jiang Jieshi), fled from mainland China to

    (A) Japan   (C) Taiwan

    (B) Indonesia   (D) Ceylon

    (E) the United States (which had backed him in the war against Mao Zedong)

30. The law of supply states that all other things being equal, _____ tend to produce more when prices rise and less when prices fall.

    (A) consumers   (D) states

    (B) governments   (E) armies

    (C) suppliers

31. Among the various major cities that are part of the North American Free Trade Agreement (NAFTA), the city with the largest population is

    (A) New York   (D) Chicago

    (B) Toronto   (E) Washington, D.C.

    (C) Mexico City

32. After the fall of the western half of the Roman Empire in 476 CE, the most famous leader from the Empire's eastern half during the 6th century was

    (A) Alfred the Great   (D) Xerxes

    (B) William the Conqueror   (E) Justinian I

    (C) Charlemagne

33. In 1776, Adam Smith, the father of modern capitalism, argued that in the long run markets correct themselves. As such, he also argued that governments should

    (A) keep their "hands off" markets

    (B) manipulate government spending to stabilize an economy in the short run

    (C) manipulate government taxes to stabilize an economy in the short run

    (D) manipulate interest rates to stabilize an economy in the short run

    (E) manipulate the money supply to stabilize an economy in the short run

34. Before the early Industrial Revolution began to take hold in the mid- to late 1700s, all of the following had occurred EXCEPT

    (A) the Age of Exploration

    (B) the Columbian Exchange

    (C) the Protestant Reformation

    (D) the unifications of Germany and Italy

    (E) the Renaissance

35. All of the following are formal or informal sources of presidential power EXCEPT

    (A) the fact that the president is elected indirectly by the public, not by Congress

    (B) Supreme Court decisions which have expanded the president's emergency powers

    (C) high public approval ratings

    (D) the veto power

    (E) the ability to introduce legislation in either house of Congress

36. Civil servants in the federal bureaucracy may sometimes successfully resist presidential initiatives because

    (A) they can go directly to Congress with their budget requests

    (B) they have more opportunities to influence public opinion than the president does

    (C) they are directly responsible to Congress, but not to the president

    (D) they may not be removed from office for political reasons

    (E) they have influence over the president through campaign contributions

37. The 1985 Gramm-Rudman Act

    (A) outlawed the use of federal funds for abortions

    (B) established a mechanism for balancing the federal budget

    (C) prohibited the use of any federal funds for aiding the Contras in Nicaragua

    (D) changed the tax code to eliminate loopholes for the wealthy

    (E) provided for the destruction of intermediate-range nuclear missiles in Europe

QUESTIONS 38 to 42 refer to the following passage.

Hoover had been in office less than a year, stocks had been falling for over a month; they had lost, on the average, about one-sixth of their quoted value, and looked "cheap," according to the opinion of important bankers, economists, and government officials. Business was still good—the economic position of the country was "sound" and technically the stock market itself had been improved by a "healthy reaction." Almost everyone thought a rally must be close at hand.

The market opened steady with prices little changed from the previous day, though some rather large blocks, of 20,000 to 25,000 shares, came out at the start. It sagged easily for the first half hour, and then around eleven o'clock the deluge broke.

It came with a speed and ferocity that left men dazed. The bottom simply fell out of the market. From all over the country a torrent of selling orders poured onto the floor of the Stock Exchange and there were no buying orders to meet them. Quotations of representative active issues, like steel, telephone, and anaconda, began to fall two, three, five, and even ten points between sales. Less active stocks became unmarketable. Within a few moments the ticker service was hopelessly swamped and from then on no one knew what was really happening. By 1:30 the ticker tape was nearly two hours late; by 2:30 it was 147 minutes late. The last quotation was not printed on the tape until 7:08:05 p.m., four hours, eight and one-half minutes after the close. In the meantime, Wall Street had lived through an incredible nightmare.

38. What is the event the quote describes?

(A) The Panic of 1837

(B) The Great Depression

(C) The Crash of 1929

(D) Pearl Harbor Day

(E) The assassination of John Kennedy

39. What compounded the problems of the day?

(A) The ticker tape was running slow.

(B) Business leaders were pessimistic.

(C) Government leaders were pessimistic.

(D) Major issues were not affected.

(E) There was a lack of selling orders.

40. The stock prices were driven down by

(A) lack of activity

(B) massive activity at the open of the market

(C) the market's rising trend over several months

(D) the general collapsing of businesses nationwide

(E) sell orders overwhelming buy orders

41. The results of the Crash were partially blamed on the administration of

(A) Woodrow Wilson

(B) Warren Harding

(C) Calvin Coolidge

(D) Herbert Hoover

(E) Franklin Roosevelt

42. Which was not a reform created to try to prevent a repetition of 1929?

    (A) SEC

    (B) Margin restrictions

    (C) FDIC

    (D) Restrictions on corporations issuing stocks

    (E) Restrictions on insider trading

43. Reaganomics is most closely associated with

    (A) the "trickle-down" theory

    (B) the "controlled growth" theory

    (C) the "bubble up" theory

    (D) New Deal reform economics

    (E) Fair Deal progressivist economics

44. The "White Man's Burden" referred to

    (A) the financial cost of running the huge European colonial empires

    (B) the cost in human lives of diseases, such as smallpox, to which only white people were susceptible

    (C) the duty of white laborers to rise up and overthrow the wealthy industrialists who were abusing their power and their workers

    (D) the cost of the wars that resulted from nineteenth-century militarism

    (E) the belief that it was the duty of whites to "civilize" nonwhite people through colonization or economic dominance of nonwhite lands

45. "I think, therefore I am" was written by

    (A) Locke   (D) Diderot

    (B) Descartes   (E) Nietzsche

    (C) Leibniz

46. "Intendants" were

    (A) secret letters of arrest

    (B) courts where secret trials were held

(C) censors employed by Louis XIV

(D) secret emissaries of the pope

(E) regional government agents in France

47. The Swahili word "ujamaa," as used by Tanzanian president Julius Nyerere, stands for what political ideal?

(A) African socialism

(B) Pan-Africanism

(C) Economic modernization

(D) The independent nation-state

(E) Tanzanian national supremacy

48. Which of the following rivers is known as "China's Sorrow"?

(A) Yellow River   (D) Wei River

(B) Yangtze River   (E) Tarim River

(C) Ganges River

49. Some parts of the political system in the United States utilize laws and bureau-cratic rules to define who has what kind of power and authority over whom. These laws and rules exemplify which type of authority?

(A) Traditional   (D) Institutionalized

(B) Charismatic   (E) Corporate

(C) Legal-rational

50. Which of the following statements best characterizes the trends in the econo-my of the United States over the past few decades?

(A) The extent of corporate concentration has declined.

(B) Market forces have become a less powerful determinant of the produc-tion and distribution of goods.

(C) The power elite is now concentrated more in the political sphere than the economic.

(D) Union membership has declined steadily as a percentage of the entire workforce.

(E) The industrial sector has grown as a proportion of the overall economy.

51. Sub-Saharan Africa contains some of the world's longest rivers, but it lacks which of the following?

    (A) large mountain ranges   (D) an abundance of minerals

    (B) excellent natural harbors   (E) good farmland

    (C) large lakes

52. Since the 1970s, employment in which of the following sectors has significantly declined in the United States?

    (A) restaurants   (D) technology companies

    (B) factories   (E) defense-related companies

    (C) retail stores

53. During the early 1790s, Alexander Hamilton did all of the following to prop up the United States economy EXCEPT

    (A) establishing a national bank

    (B) having the federal government assume all state and national debts and issue new bonds to reestablish credit

    (C) seeking a protective tariff, and when Congress approved a much lower tariff, he established what came to be called a "whiskey tax"

    (D) putting the U.S. currency on the gold standard

    (E) establishing the U.S. Patent Office to help protect entrepreneurs

54. Put the following in chronological order:

    I.   The Iranian (Islamic) Revolution

    II.   The Glorious Revolution

    III. The French Revolution

    IV.   The Russian Revolution

    (A) I, II, III, IV   (D) II, III, IV, I

    (B) II, IV, III, I   (E) I, III, IV, II

    (C) IV, II, I, III

55. When Karl Marx postulated a new type of society that would develop after the fall of capitalism, he anticipated a classless society based upon

(A) the principle of "every man for himself"

(B) his maxim "from each according to his ability, to each according to his needs"

(C) his belief that in the state of nature life is "solitary, nasty, poor, brutish, and short"

(D) his assertion that "man is born free, and everywhere he is in chains"

(E) his claim that "power tends to corrupt"

56. In a single-member district, plurality vote system

(A) a runoff election is usually necessary to determine the winner

(B) parties are assigned seats based on the proportion of votes they receive in a district

(C) the candidate with the most votes represents the district

(D) some votes count more than others in determining which candidate wins the election

(E) third parties are more likely to win seats than in proportional representation systems

57. The top official in the Department of Justice is the

(A) Solicitor-General

(B) Secretary of Justice

(C) Secretary of State

(D) Attorney General

(E) Chief Justice

58. Which of the following is a FALSE statement about the Democratic party's national convention?

(A) It selects the state party chairmen.

(B) It determines the national party platform.

(C) It nominates the party's candidate for president.

(D) It has "superdelegates" not chosen by state primaries and caucuses.

(E) It sets the time and place for the next national convention.

QUESTIONS 59 to 62 refer to the following graph.

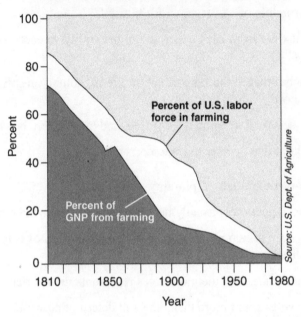

The Growth of Nonfarm Activities, 1810–1980

59. The graph most clearly shows

   (A) the economic impact of farming was always more important than the number of people working in the field

   (B) the GNP and labor force maintained a constant relationship to each other

   (C) farming remained the most important economic activity until about 1900

   (D) the decline in the importance of farming finally reversed itself in the 1970s

   (E) recently, the farming GNP and the farm labor force have more accurately matched each other

60. Which statement is most true about American agriculture and the graph?

   (A) Farming is no longer an important occupation.

   (B) It is not possible to make a good living from farming.

   (C) Farming is becoming more automated.

   (D) American agriculture's production is now possible with fewer workers.

   (E) There was never a time when either GNP or labor force actually increased.

61. Which does not apply to American agriculture?

    (A) Farmers usually have to borrow money to operate.

    (B) The U.S. farmer almost always creates a surplus.

    (C) Farming is one of the last areas to resist big corporations.

    (D) Modern farming still depends on weather conditions.

    (E) Modern farmers have depended heavily on government aid.

62. The best description of American agricultural problems in the near future is

    (A) increasing numbers of Americans will return to agriculture

    (B) world food supplies will increase and the need for U.S. exports will diminish

    (C) efficiency will increase and production will need fewer workers

    (D) water supplies and chemical fertilizers will both increase

    (E) Third World food-growing needs will diminish

63. The paternalistic view of slavery held that

    (A) slavery was a necessary evil that should be phased out as soon as it was economically possible

    (B) slavery was a totally unjustifiable abuse of humanity demanding immediate abolition

    (C) slavery was an artifact of a more primitive past that would eventually fade out on its own

    (D) slavery was necessary to protect blacks from the mistreatment and abuse they would receive if they were freed

    (E) slavery was necessary to keep blacks from developing their superior potential and eventually dominating the white race

64. Mark Twain's classic stories, such as *Tom Sawyer* and *Huckleberry Finn*, were primary examples of the _____ trend in turn-of-the-century American literature.

    (A) romantic   (D) realistic

    (B) gothic   (E) heroic

    (C) fantasy

65. The early twentieth-century pacifist and winner of the Nobel Peace Prize for her book *Lay Down Your Arms* (1889) was

(A) Tirpitz   (D) von Bethmann-Hollweg

(B) Luxemburg   (E) Cosima Wagner

(C) von Suttner

66. When the heir to the Austrian throne was assassinated in August 1914, and the Russian government responded to the ensuing crisis by mobilizing its troops, Germany followed its obligations under the Triple Alliance and declared war on Russia. Which of the following countries did Germany invade first?

(A) Russia   (D) Britain

(B) Austria-Hungary   (E) Italy

(C) France

67. All of the following African countries were colonized by Britain EXCEPT

(A) Nigeria   (D) Northern Rhodesia

(B) Mozambique   (E) Southern Rhodesia

(C) Kenya

68. Which of the following countries would NOT appear on a 1965 map of Asia?

(A) Bangladesh   (D) Laos

(B) Vietnam   (E) North Korea

(C) Cambodia

69. During the election of 1896, the Democrats chose as their candidate a 36-year-old Nebraskan named William Jennings Bryan, who addressed the Democratic Party in what came to be known as the "_____" speech.

(A) Give 'em Hell   (D) Cross of Gold

(B) Buck Stops Here   (E) Low Tariff

(C) Free Silver

70. When the Soviet Union closed off both road and train access from the West into Berlin in 1948, President Truman responded by creating what became known as the

    (A) Berlin Blockade   (D) Berlin Standoff

    (B) North Atlantic   (E) Warsaw Pact
        Treaty Organization

    (C) Berlin Airlift

71. During the Great Depression, the unemployment rate in the United States rose to approximately 25%. Years later, it was finally brought below 5% by

    (A) FDR's many New Deal job creation programs

    (B) FDR's Fair Standard Labor Act, which guaranteed a minimum wage

    (C) World War I factory orders

    (D) World War II factory orders

    (E) Cold War factory orders

72. After Marco Polo set out for Asia during the late 13th century with his uncle and father, he ended up serving in the court of

    (A) Genghis Khan   (D) Hulagu Khan

    (B) Jochi Khan   (E) Kublai Khan

    (C) Bantu Khan

73. In the study of population, the three elements that most directly determine the size, composition, and distribution of a population are

    (A) fertility, mortality, and migration

    (B) fertility, mortality, and community

    (C) fertility, migration, and fecundity

    (D) mortality, migration, and segregation

    (E) fertility, mortality, and ecology

74. In a famous battle, Charles Martel, also known as "the Hammer," stopped the Moors at the Pyrenees in 732; in 800, his grandson, _____, was crowned Holy Roman Emperor by Pope Leo III.

    (A) Louis XIV

    (B) Charlemagne

    (C) Alfred the Great

    (D) Clovis

    (E) Pepin

75. All of the following statements represent positions the U. S. Supreme Court has taken on the First Amendment right to freedom of religion EXCEPT that

    (A) public school officials may write a nondenominational prayer for school children to recite at the beginning of each school day

    (B) public school teachers may not conduct devotional readings of the Bible in class

    (C) a copy of the Ten Commandments may not be posted on the walls of public school classrooms

    (D) creation science may not be taught in public schools

    (E) states may not outlaw the teaching of evolution in the public schools

76. The Constitution, as ratified in 1788, provided for popular vote for the

    (A) election of the president

    (B) election of senators

    (C) ratification of treaties

    (D) ratification of constitutional amendments

    (E) members of the House of Representatives

77. The Great Compromise of 1787

    (A) resolved the controversy over the status of slaves under the Constitution

    (B) provided for an electoral college for selection of the president

    (C) provided for the direct election of senators

    (D) provided for equal representation of states in the Senate and representation based on population in the House

    (E) added a Bill of Rights to the Constitution

QUESTIONS 78 and 79 refer to the following table.

New York Stock Exchange Companies
With the Largest Number of Stockholders, 1985

Company	Stockholders
American Tel & Tel	2,927,000
General Motors	1,990,000
Bell South Corp.	1,685,000
Bell Atlantic	1,413,000
American Information Tech.	1,382,000
NYNEX Corp.	1,348,000
Southwestern Bell	1,320,000
Pacific Telesis Group	1,242,000
US WEST	1,156,000
International Business Machines	798,000
Exxon Corp.	785,000
General Electric	490,000
GTE Corp.	442,000
Bell Canada Enterprises	332,000
Sears Roebuck	326,000

From *1986 Fact Book,* copyright © New York Stock
Exchange, Inc., 1986.

78. Which is most true about the table?

    (A) Telephone companies have the largest number of stockholders.

    (B) Manufacturing companies have more stockholders than service companies.

    (C) Retail merchandise companies have the largest number of stockholders.

    (D) Only domestic companies are represented.

    (E) Oil companies do not have large numbers of stockholders.

79. Which company would you buy if you wanted the greatest voice in its management?

    (A) AT&T   (D) GTE Corp.

    (B) Southwestern Bell   (E) Sears Roebuck

    (C) Exxon Corp.

80. Stockholders control a company through

    (A) the chief executive officer

    (B) the chairperson of the board

    (C) the president of the company

    (D) the elected board of directors

    (E) stock options

81. What proposal did President Woodrow Wilson make in 1918 that convinced the Germans they would be treated fairly if they surrendered?

    (A) The Twenty-One Demands

    (B) The Fourteen Points

    (C) The Versailles Proposals

    (D) The Balfour Declaration

    (E) The "New Freedom" Policy

82. This engraving of the Nat Turner revolt takes what point of view?

HORRID MASSACRE IN VIRGINIA·

    (A) The revolt of the slaves was justified.

    (B) Northern abolitionists were responsible for the revolt.

    (C) The revolt was an attack upon innocent victims.

    (D) The slaves were ineffective revolutionists.

    (E) The slave revolt was successful.

QUESTION 83 refers to the following graph.

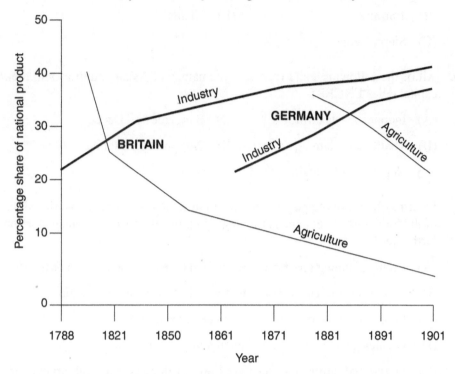

The Triumph of Industry over Agriculture: Germany and Britain

83. According to the graph, which one of the following statements is true?

   (A) Industrial production had a greater impact than agricultural production in Britain in 1800.

   (B) Agricultural production had a greater impact than industrial production in Germany in 1900.

   (C) Agriculture became less significant in Britain and Germany by 1900.

   (D) Britain produced fewer industrial products than Germany.

   (E) During the period shown, industrial production was an insignificant part of the British economy.

84. The Fashoda Crisis involved Britain and France in a dispute over land in

   (A) China   (D) the Balkans

   (B) southern Europe   (E) the Ottoman Empire

   (C) Africa

85. Which of the following countries was an independent state before 1950?

    (A) Liberia   (D) Gambia

    (B) Tanzania   (E) Ghana

    (C) Sierra Leone

86. All of the following pairs represent the names of Asian countries and their capital cities EXCEPT

    (A) Indonesia – Jakarta   (D) Bangladesh – Dacca

    (B) Thailand – Siam   (E) Philippines – Manila

    (C) Nepal – Kathmandu

87. In terms of controlling population growth in societies around the world, which of the following statements is true regarding the effects of various factors on birth rates?

    (A) Family planning programs actually lead to overall increases in birth rates.

    (B) Rising birth rates are associated with increases in urbanization.

    (C) Economic development results in declines in birth rates.

    (D) Greater gender equality results in a higher birth rate.

    (E) Patriarchal family systems have lower birth rates than egalitarian ones.

88. The Berlin Conference of 1884–85 led to

    (A) the Second Industrial Revolution in the United States

    (B) the conquest of the Middle East

    (C) an "Era of Good Feelings"

    (D) the conquest of Sub-Saharan Africa

    (E) a serious financial panic in the United States

89. Before the emergence of Joseph Stalin, who led the Soviet Union from 1929 until his death in 1953, leadership of the U.S.S.R. included Vladimir Lenin and

    (A) Nietzsche   (D Kerensky

    (B) Khrushchev   (E) Trotsky

    (C) Brezhnev

90. The Rocky Mountains run through all of the following states EXCEPT

(A) New Mexico

(D) California

(B) Colorado

(E) Wyoming

(C) Utah

91. The country of Cambodia includes the Mekong Delta and the extensive coast-line along the Gulf of Thailand. In addition, in the northwest of Cambodia sits the ruins of what was originally a _____temple that today is known as Angkor Wat.

(A) Buddhist

(D) Muslim

(B) Hindu

(E) Shinto

(C) Confucian

92. The Crusades were initiated in 1096 by Pope Urban II in an attempt to liberate the Holy Land from the Muslims. The term "Holy Land" includes the city of

(A) Ur

(D) Constantinople

(B) Mecca

(E) Jerusalem

(C) Rome

93. When World War I broke out in 1914, it had been approximately how long since the end of the Napoleonic Wars that devastated Europe during the 19th century?

(A) 100 years

(D) 25 years

(B) 75 years

(E) 10 years

(C) 50 years

94. The structure of the global political system during the Cold War was essentially

(A) monopolar

(D) sophomoric

(B) bipolar

(E) disingenuous

(C) dysfunctional

95. Which of the following best defines the term "judicial restraint"?

(A) A decision by judges to limit the number of cases they decide per year.

(B) Refusal by judges to lobby Congress for funds.

(C) A practice by which judges remove themselves from cases in which they have a personal interest.

(D) The tendency of judges to interpret the Constitution in light of the original intent of its framers.

(E) Willingness of judges to decline participation in partisan political campaigns.

96. A bill introduced in the House or Senate will most likely

(A) be passed by the first house but not the second

(B) be passed by both houses and become law

(C) be sent to the rules committee, then the full House

(D) die before it is referred to committee

(E) be referred to the appropriate committee, but never reach the floor of the house

97. Which of the following is true of the president's veto power?

I. A president may veto certain items in a bill but approve the rest.

II. A president may pocket-veto a bill by refusing to sign it for 10 days while Congress is in session.

III. A presidential veto may be overridden by a two-thirds vote of both houses of Congress.

(A) I only   (D) II and III only

(B) II only   (E) I, II, and III

(C) III only

QUESTIONS 98 to 100 refer to the following graph.

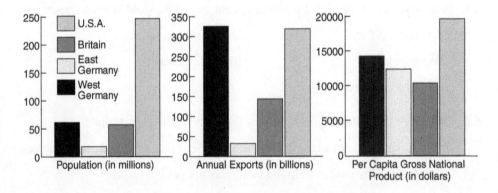

98. Under a unified Germany,

    (A) the United States continues to be the leading exporter

    (B) Britain will export about 60 percent of Germany's total

    (C) the East will increase Germany's exports by nearly 10 percent

    (D) the United States and Germany will almost be tied in exports

    (E) British and German exports together will total nearly $600 billion

99. The best indicator of people's standard of living is the

    (A) per capita gross national product

    (B) population divided into the annual exports

    (C) annual exports

    (D) per capita gross national product divided into the exports

    (E) per capita national product multiplied by the population

100. Which statement would be most true?

    (A) The United States leads in productivity and GNP.

    (B) Germany will go from fourth to second in GNP by unifying.

    (C) For its population, the United States produced the fewest exports.

    (D) For its population, Britain produced the most exports.

    (E) Unified Germany's per capita income will surpass the United States.

101. The main reason that President Grant's administration is considered a failure is

    (A) his failure to retreat from the radical Reconstruction policies of his predecessors

    (B) his failure to effectively quell the Indian uprisings in the Western territories

    (C) his failure to control the corruption permeating his administration

    (D) his attempts to destroy the Democratic party and return the country to a one-party system

    (E) his failure to be reelected after serving his first term in office

102. "If your neighbor's house was on fire, and he didn't have a garden hose, wouldn't it make sense to let him use your hose to fight the fire so the fire could be put out before it spread to your house?" This question was raised by Franklin Roosevelt to justify

    (A) the Neutrality Acts

    (B) the Atlantic Charter

    (C) the Lend-Lease Act

    (D) the Good Neighbor policy

    (E) the Selective Service Act

103. During the Reformation, Anabaptism drew its membership mostly from the ranks of the

    (A) nobility

    (B) middle class

    (C) peasants

    (D) businessmen

    (E) army officers

104. All of the following were part of the Counter-Reformation EXCEPT

    (A) the Index

    (B) the Augsburg Confession

    (C) the Inquisition

    (D) the Council of Trent

    (E) the Society of Jesus

105. The Treaty of Nanjing ended which war in China?

    (A) World War II

    (B) Boxer Rebellion

    (C) First Opium War (1839–42)

    (D) Cultural Revolution

    (E) Taipei Rebellion

106. When the explorer H. M. Stanley's plans for opening the Congo Basin were rejected by the British government in 1877, which European power, headed by King Leopold II, took him into its service?

    (A) Germany

    (B) France

    (C) Belgium

    (D) Italy

    (E) Norway

107. In 1215, King John I signed the *Magna Carta*. In doing so, he agreed to

    (A) increase taxes, but only on foreigners living in England

    (B) increase the power of the king

(C) limit the power of the king

(D) limit the power of the clergy

(E) limit the power of the noble class

108. At the signing of the Treaty of Versailles in 1919, Woodrow Wilson proposed his Fourteen Points, including a League of Nations. After the treaty was signed, the U.S. Senate

(A) rejected the treaty and refused to join the League of Nations

(B) accepted the treaty and played a minor role in the League of Nations

(C) rejected certain parts of the treaty, but still decided to join the League of Nations

(D) rejected the League of Nations and immediately proposed the United Nations instead

(E) joined the League of Nations and did its best to bring down the U.S.S.R. in the 1930s

109. In the ancient world, the first extensive road system was known as the

(A) Persian Royal Road

(B) Roman Road

(C) Silk Road

(D) British Royal Road

(E) Alexander the Great's Royal Road

110. Prior to Columbus sailing under the flag of Spain in 1492, the greatest sailor in the world during the early 1400s was

(A) Vasco da Gama

(B) Bartolomeu Dias

(C) Zheng He

(D) Ferdinand Magellan

(E) Hernando de Soto

111. The Enlightenment thinker John Locke had a great deal of influence on the

(A) Renaissance

(B) Protest Reformation

(C) Age of Exploration

(D) American Revolution

(E) *Magna Carta*

112. After the end of the Napoleonic Wars, the concept of "_____"
dominated important political and economic discussions in Europe during
most of the 19th century.

(A) every country for itself   (D) do unto others

(B) the Scramble for Africa   (E) a balance of power

(C) beggar-thy-neighbor

113. At the Munich Conference in 1938, Britain and France accepted key terms
proposed by Adolf Hitler. This agreement became known as a policy of

(A) lasting peace   (D) fairness

(B) appeasement   (E) good will

(C) mutual admiration

114. Which of the following is true of independent regulatory commissions?

(A) They exercise quasi-legislative, quasi-judicial, and executive functions.

(B) They each form part of one of the 14 cabinet-level executive departments.

(C) They regulate certain parts of the federal bureaucracy.

(D) They are directly responsible to the president.

(E) They were created by the executive branch to help execute federal law.

QUESTION 115 refers to the following.

115. The subject of the cartoon is most likely

    (A) a gerrymandered congressional district

    (B) the influence of environmental issues on congressional behavior

    (C) the role of money in influencing the outcome of an election

    (D) the beastly effect of politics on the character of a congressman

    (E) "dinosaur bills" which congressmen sponsor for the folks back home

116. The War Powers Resolution of 1973 may be invoked by Congress to accomplish which of the following?

    (A) Prevent the president from deploying troops abroad.

    (B) Declare war.

    (C) Force the extradition of foreign ambassadors caught spying in the United States.

    (D) Limit the period for which the president may deploy troops abroad in hostile situations.

    (E) Force reductions in the defense budget in times of peace and stability.

117. Consider a competitive industry composed of firms employing only the labor of their owners as inputs. Let this industry face a downward-sloping demand curve, and let the output price exceed the personal opportunity cost of the labor required to produce the marginal unit of output by the typical firm owner. What should the expected movement of price and market output be in the long run?

    (A) Price up and quantity down

    (B) Price up and quantity up

    (C) Price down and quantity down

    (D) Price down and quantity up

    (E) Price and quantity remain unchanged

118. In general equilibrium and in a situation of perfect competition

    (A) for each consumer, the marginal utility of each good consumed is equal to the price of that good

    (B) for each consumer, marginal utilities of all goods consumed are proportional to the marginal costs of those goods

(C) the marginal physical product of each input is equal to the price of that input

(D) the marginal revenue product of each input is equal to the price of the finished good it produces

(E) the ratio of total expenditure on any good to its price equals marginal utility

119. Consider an outside shock on the value of the dollar that causes it to depreciate. The Fed could defend the dollar by

(A) increasing the money supply, thereby lowering the LM curve and driving the interest rate up

(B) increasing government spending, thereby raising the IS curve and driving the interest rate up

(C) reducing the money supply, thereby raising the LM curve and driving the interest rate up

(D) increasing taxes, thereby lowering the IS curve and driving the interest rate down

(E) simultaneously increasing government spending and the money supply so that the GNP climbs with a fixed interest rate

120. The most significant aspect of the Mexican-American War on the United States during the 20 years following the war was that it

(A) led to the development of the idea of "passive resistance" among those who opposed the war

(B) ended years of hostility between the United States and Mexico

(C) reignited the slavery conflict in regard to all the territories newly acquired from Mexico

(D) gave America undisputed control over Mexican foreign policy for the next 20 years

(E) revealed the shocking ineptitude of American military forces, leading to massive reforms in military training and procedures throughout the 1850s

PRACTICE TEST 2

Answer Key

1.	(B)	25.	(C)	49.	(C)	73.	(A)	97.	(C)
2.	(C)	26.	(C)	50.	(D)	74.	(B)	98.	(C)
3.	(E)	27.	(D)	51.	(B)	75.	(A)	99.	(A)
4.	(E)	28.	(C)	52.	(B)	76.	(E)	100.	(C)
5.	(D)	29.	(C)	53.	(D)	77.	(D)	101.	(C)
6.	(E)	30.	(C)	54.	(D)	78.	(A)	102.	(C)
7.	(A)	31.	(C)	55.	(B)	79.	(E)	103.	(C)
8.	(D)	32.	(E)	56.	(C)	80.	(D)	104.	(B)
9.	(E)	33.	(A)	57.	(D)	81.	(B)	105.	(C)
10.	(E)	34.	(D)	58.	(A)	82.	(C)	106.	(C)
11.	(E)	35.	(E)	59.	(E)	83.	(C)	107.	(C)
12.	(D)	36.	(D)	60.	(D)	84.	(C)	108.	(A)
13.	(B)	37.	(B)	61.	(C)	85.	(A)	109.	(A)
14.	(B)	38.	(C)	62.	(C)	86.	(B)	110.	(C)
15.	(B)	39.	(A)	63.	(D)	87.	(C)	111.	(D)
16.	(A)	40.	(E)	64.	(D)	88.	(D)	112.	(E)
17.	(A)	41.	(D)	65.	(C)	89.	(E)	113.	(A)
18.	(A)	42.	(C)	66.	(C)	90.	(D)	114.	(A)
19.	(C)	43.	(A)	67.	(B)	91.	(B)	115.	(A)
20.	(D)	44.	(E)	68.	(A)	92.	(E)	116.	(D)
21.	(C)	45.	(B)	69.	(D)	93.	(A)	117.	(D)
22.	(A)	46.	(E)	70.	(C)	94.	(B)	118.	(B)
23.	(A)	47.	(A)	71.	(D)	95.	(D)	119.	(C)
24.	(C)	48.	(A)	72.	(E)	96.	(E)	120.	(C)

PRACTICE TEST 2

Detailed Explanations of Answers

1.   **(B)**   Roosevelt's most memorable line was also the underpinning of his foreign policy strategy in Central America: "Speak softly but carry a big stick." The
thrust of this policy was that the United States wouldn't waste a lot of energy on
words in settling issues in Central America. Instead, there would be a focus on action. This served to warn Central American countries to watch their behavior or they
would face U.S. political and military intervention to insure that things were returned
to "proper order." Basically, Roosevelt's policy was an expansion of the Monroe
Doctrine and served notice that the United States intended to be the policeman of
the Caribbean. Roosevelt, true to form, backed up his words with action. The United
States sent troops into six different Latin American nations between 1900 and 1930.
U.S. economic intervention was even more prevalent. Regrettably, while this policy
allowed America to flex its muscles and solved many short-term problems, it ignored
the sensitivities of Latin Americans, building deep resentments that linger today.

2.   **(C)**   The Continental army had been poorly paid, when they were paid at
all, throughout the war. As the war wound down after Yorktown, the army was
camped at Newburgh, New York, waiting for results of peace negotiations. Fears
spread among the soldiers that the army might be disbanded without pay or pen-
sion. Nationalists fueled these fears, encouraging the belief that a military uprising
might take place if the states refused to provide Congress with taxation powers to
raise money to pay the soldiers' pensions, among other things. Only a personal appeal by Washington to his soldiers prevented the situation from exploding into a
military crisis and perhaps an attempted military coup.

3.   **(E)**   Steam and waterpower drove the early machines and the mechanized
looms of the Industrial Revolution, and so choice (B) is an important part of that
event. Choice (E) is unhistorical, since the electric motor was developed after the
First Industrial Revolution; the electricity was often produced by a steam engine.
The spinning jenny and flying shuttle were involved in the production of thread and
cloth, while the Bessemer process was involved in the production of steel.

4.   **(E)**   Although he was not typical of nineteenth-century liberalism in every
respect—he favored the unions as a means of helping the working class, for example—John Stuart Mill wrote extensively on politics and is generally considered
the most notable nineteenth-century liberal writer. His *On Liberty* (1859) is one of
the most famous defenses of individual rights. The other choices may be quickly
eliminated if the identity of the individuals involved is known. As the leader of the

British Conservative party in the second half of the nineteenth century, Disraeli opposed many liberal programs. Napoleon III, emperor of France during the 1850s and 1860s, worked to limit one of the major liberal goals, the achievement of true parliamentary government in France. The other choices list lesser-known individuals but are also incorrect. Proudhon was the most famous anarchist of the first half of the nineteenth century, while Fourier was one of the best-known Utopian Socialists of the same period.

5. **(D)** Of all the choices listed, the only conflict that applies to Egypt in the 1950s was control of the Suez Canal. The conflict began with a plan by Egypt's socialist president Nasser to build a huge dam across the Nile River at Aswan. When the United States withdrew its aid for the project, Nasser nationalized the Suez Canal, seizing control from the Anglo-French company that had been operating it since Britain withdrew its troops from the Canal Zone. His plan was to use the profits to finance the "high dam." The British and French invaded in an attempt to regain financial control of the canal, but UN pressure eventually forced them to withdraw, and the dam was finished with Russian aid.

6. **(E)** Of all the choices, only Yokohama is not an island in Japan. It is actually a port city south of Tokyo on the island of Honshu (A). The largest of Japan's islands, Honshu is the home of about 80 percent of Japan's population and its capital city, Tokyo. Kyushu (B) is the southernmost island and the next most heavily populated. Hokkaido (C) is at the northern tip of Japan and is the second-largest island, and Shikoku (D), between Honshu and Kyushu, is the country's smallest island.

7. **(A)** An ethnic group consists of people who share a common culture and sense of identity. While some ethnic groups are also minorities, others are not. An ethnic group often includes people of *different* social classes (B), occupations (E), and political views (D). Some, like Puerto Ricans and Cubans, include people with a variety of skin colors (C).

8. **(D)** Although the Romans had many innovations of their own (including the clever system of aqueducts and the use of domes and arches), they were adept at copying and adapting from others, especially the Greeks. For example, the Romans' use of epic poetry, philosophy, and various column structures—Doric, Ionic, and Corinthian—were largely borrowed from the Greeks. So, too, were their gods, but the Romans generally used different names. As such, answer (B) is incorrect, and so, therefore, is (C). The Romans never destroyed the Parthenon, so answer (E) is also incorrect, as is answer (A), for the simple reason that the Carolingians arose in modern-day France after the fall of Rome.

9. **(E)** Martin Luther did not originally intend to initiate the Protestant Reformation when he nailed his 95 Theses to the door at the church in Wittenberg in 1517, but a series of events soon caused him to do so. A primary reason for his

CLEP SOCIAL SCIENCES AND HISTORY

dispute with the Catholic Church was its sale of indulgences, which, in essence, allowed an individual—after he or she had confessed to their sinfulness—to purchase entry into heaven. The other answers are incorrect because each of the events involving Henry VIII (A), the Pilgrims (B), John Calvin (C), and John Winthrop (D) took place after the Protestant Reformation had begun, so none of them could have been considered causes.

10. **(E)**   While historians may disagree over the specific trigger event that caused the Industrial Revolution, most would agree that improvements to the steam engine by Scottish inventor James Watt during the late 1700s was a key contributing factor. In addition, most historians would agree that one of the unintended consequences of the Industrial Revolution was the massive creation of wealth that remained in the hands of a small percentage of factory owners. As such, Marx and Engels argued that the proletariat (or the masses) needed to orchestrate a violent overthrow of the factory owners, which would be an important step in the transition from capitalism to communism, where the state would ultimately "wither away."

11. **(E)**   In search of gold and glory, Magellan and his crew set sail from Portugal on five ships in 1519. Although Magellan was killed in the Philippines in 1521, some of his original crew returned home to Portugal in 1522, being the first sailors to successfully circumnavigate the globe.

12. **(D)**   Under the Articles of Confederation, there was no executive or judicial branch, but rather only a unicameral legislative branch. As a result, power mostly resided at the state level, which is exactly where Thomas Jefferson thought it should be. Alexander Hamilton, conversely, thought the power should mostly reside at federal level. The 26 cantons of modern-day Switzerland are a good example of a confederation-based government.

13. **(B)**   French colonization in Vietnam dates back to 1859, and, according to Ho Chi Minh's Declaration of Independence, the tactics used by the French included untold atrocities against both the Vietnamese people and their land. After France fell to Germany in World War II, Germany's ally, Japan, took control of Vietnam until Japan itself suffered defeat in August 1945. In a sad footnote to history, Ho Chi Minh sought an audience with the main leaders at Versailles in 1919, seeking the same principle of self-determination that Woodrow Wilson had articulated as one of his Fourteen Points. Alas, Ho never granted a meeting with Wilson (or David Lloyd George of Great Britain or Georges Clemenceau of France). As a result, Ho eventually turned to communist China and Russia for support, which in turn led to the Vietnam War with the United States.

14. **(B)**   In 1974, in the case *United States v. Nixon,* the Supreme Court declared that the president has an executive privilege to protect military, diplomatic, and sensitive national security secrets from disclosure. However, the material may be

successfully subpoenaed if needed by either the defense or the state in a criminal prosecution. (A) is incorrect since the right of the president to veto proposed legislation is called the veto power. It has nothing to do with the president's right to protect information from disclosure. (C) is incorrect because the right of the president to appoint and receive ambassadors is unrelated to the executive privilege of withholding certain information. (D) is incorrect because the president's power to pardon is unrelated to executive privilege. Also, the president has an unlimited, not a limited, right to pardon persons convicted of federal crimes. (E) is incorrect because the president enjoys no immunity from prosecution for misdemeanors or felonies.

15. **(B)**   Special spending projects sponsored by members of Congress for their home states or districts are known as pork barrel legislation. (A) is incorrect because a filibuster is an attempt in the Senate to talk a bill to death by preventing it from coming up for a vote. (C) is incorrect because logrolling is the term used to designate vote-swapping by members of Congress for special projects. (D) is incorrect because "grease for the gears" is a fictitious term made up as a distractor for this question. (E) is incorrect because "senatorial courtesy" refers to an informal practice whereby the president seeks to have a judicial nominee approved by the senior senator from the state in which the nominee will sit.

16. **(A)**   An elitist view of American politics stresses that the policy-making process is dominated by a small, unrepresentative minority. In *The Power Elite,* published in 1956, the American sociologist C. Wright Mills argued that corporate leaders, top military officers, and key political leaders dominated American politics. (B) is incorrect because the view that thousands of competing interest groups influence policy-making is called a "pluralistic" view of politics. (C) is incorrect because the view that large states dominate public policy, if such a view is held by anyone, has no name. Such a view would be difficult to defend, since all states get two senators regardless of population. (D) is incorrect because such a view has no specific name. Again, such a view would be difficult to defend, since rural areas have such a small population relative to urban areas, and state legislators and U.S. representatives are chosen on the basis of population. (E) is plausible but incorrect. It is true that only about one-third of eligible voters turn out in off-year congressional races (the figure was 33 percent in 1986). However, this fact does not provide the basis for an elitist theory, since it is not clear that election outcomes would have been different if twice as many voters had voted. Also, low voter turnout does not necessarily mean that policy-making is insulated from public opinion and wishes, which is central to elitist theories.

17. **(A)**   is correct. Britain is the only top importing nation that does not appear among the top five exporters.

18. **(A)** is correct. Canada is the largest importer. Even the two European nations, Britain and Germany, combined import less.

19. **(C)** is correct. Japan was the largest single exporter, and combining with Taiwan made it even larger. No other region had two exporters listed.

20. **(D)** is correct, with the difference between exports and imports being the greatest in Japan's favor. The others are relatively close, with no comparisons available for Britain.

21. **(C)** is correct. If your nation sells more exports than it buys imports, it creates a surplus of capital coming in or a profit. (A) and (B) refer to the payments made for many things, including trade. So they may reflect on trade balances, but are not the same. (D) is the opposite. In the graph, the United States imports from Japan reflect a balance of trade unfavorable for the United States and favorable for Japan. (E) This can result from unfavorable trade balances, but reflects many other spending and revenue factors.

22. **(A)** The "Good Neighbor" policy sought to smooth over relations between the United States and Latin America by retreating from the blatant interventionism which dominated U.S. policy into the 1930s. The effects of interventionism had become increasingly costly to the point that the benefits derived were not worth the expense. In 1933, Franklin Roosevelt officially consolidated many changes already under way in U.S. policy toward Latin America under the heading of the "Good Neighbor" policy. Under this plan, the United States would pull back from the nearly constant use of military intervention to control Latin American nations. The U.S. government would cease acting unilaterally in Latin American affairs and would attempt to consult with and seek the approval of Latin American governments before intervening in the region. In addition, the United States would support Latin American governments headed by strong, independent leaders and would help train Latin American military forces so they could defend themselves. U.S. banks would also provide loans and other economic assistance to help stabilize fragile Latin American economies.

While the United States still dominated many aspects of Latin American life, with the enactment of the "Good Neighbor" policy that domination was handled more diplomatically, with somewhat more respect for local authorities. Many of the leaders who emerged at this time were military dictators who were trained by American military personnel as part of the effort to train Latin American military forces. These dictators owed their power to the United States and often stayed in power only as a result of U.S. backing. So, while the days of the "Big Stick" effectively ended with the "Good Neighbor" policy, U.S. domination of the region continued, albeit at a somewhat reduced level of visibility.

23. **(A)** The Northwest Ordinance of 1787, like the previous ordinances of 1784 and 1785, ignored the Indian tribes' claims to the land contained within the Northwest Territory. The Shawnee, Delaware, and Miami, armed with weapons supplied by the British, attacked whites who settled north and west of the Ohio River and prevented settlement of the region for nearly 10 years. While the Northwest Ordinance was a progressive document for its time, it was meaningless until the Indian problem was resolved and settlement of the area was achieved. Contained within the Northwest Ordinance were the provisions listed in choices (B) through (E). The antislavery prohibition is particularly notable because it reflected a growing concern, particularly in the North, about the institution of slavery. It marked the first regional limitation of slavery in the United States beyond individual state boundaries.

24. **(C)** Here two different developments (the Commercial Revolution and Italian Renaissance) are tied, and you are asked to explain the connection. The correct answer requires memory retention, understanding of terminology, and an ability to analyze the social and economic connections between the two developments. The Commercial Revolution describes the expansion of trade and the establishment of a broad system of joint-stock companies and banks in pre-Renaissance Italy. The new merchants of the Commercial Revolution held few ties to the earlier Middle Ages. They established new towns in Italy, such as Florence; they preferred "worldly" reading material on topics such as etiquette and politics; and for some time their new towns held no cathedrals or even smaller churches. In effect, the Commercial Revolution created a new, secular middle class which financed much of the artistic and literary work of the Italian Renaissance.

25. **(C)** Although knowledge of terminology is a great help, in this question careful reading and analyzing of the implication of statements is essential. This quotation, from Vladimir Lenin, father of the Soviet Revolution of 1917, is part of his argument that capitalism held internal contradictions which would lead to its self-destruction; a major contradiction was the uncontrolled race for colonies. (Source: Lenin, *Imperialism: The Highest Stage of Capitalism*, New York: International Publishers, 1934)

26. **(C)** In December 1958, Kwame Nkrumah invited representatives from nationalist movements in 28 territories still under colonial rule to meet in Accra for the first All-African People's Conference. Nkrumah had often stated that once Ghana attained independence, it would be his goal to lead the rest of the African continent to freedom and unity. Ghana achieved independence on March 6, 1957, and he attempted to fulfill the second part of his objective the next year in 1958.

27. **(D)**   On October 10, 1911, the revolutionary army near Hankow rebelled against the government. In January 1912, leaders of the revolt met in Nanjing and declared Sun Yat-sen the new president of the republic, officially ending the rule of the last emperor and the Qing Dynasty.

28. **(C)**   In 1846, a Pennsylvania congressman named David Wilmot proposed a bill that prohibited slavery in any territory acquired from Mexico, and this concept soon became known as "free soil." In 1854, as the Whig Party was collapsing over its inability to come to terms with the Kansas-Nebraska Act, the Republican Party was formed with former Whigs, northern Democrats, and members of the short-lived Free Soil Party.

29. **(C)**   After Chiang Kai-shek fled to Taiwan in 1949, he established a government in exile that was recognized by most countries in the West. In 1972, U.S. President Richard Nixon surprised the world by visiting Chairman Mao in China, ushering in a period of improved relations with the most populous nation on earth. Then, in 1978, after Deng Xiaoping took control of China, he began a rapid period of modernization. To attract foreign capital, he created Special Economic Zones in certain regions of China that effectively functioned as semi-independent capitalist states. Largely as a result of Deng Xiaoping's efforts, the United States formally recognized the communist government of the People's Republic of China in 1979 under the presidency of Jimmy Carter.

30. **(C)**   The law of supply is from the perspective of suppliers (or producers), whereas the law of demand is from the perspective of consumers.

31. **(C)**   Mexico City has a population today of over 20 million, making it by far the most populous city that is part of NAFTA.

32. **(E)**   Justinian I, also known as the Law Giver, ruled the Byzantine Empire from 527 to 565. His famous code of laws borrowed heavily from Roman legal codes, many of which were modified and adapted to meet the needs of his sprawling empire. The remaining answers are wrong for the following reasons: Alfred the Great (A) served as a king of Saxons in the south of England, where he repelled the Danes in 980; William the Conqueror (B) hailed from Normandy, before defeating Harold of Wessex in 1066 in the famous Battle of Hastings; Charlemagne (C) was a king of the Franks before being crowned as the Holy Roman Emperor in 800. Xerxes (D) was the Persian king who lost to the Greeks in the famous the Battle of Salamis in 480 BCE.

33. **(A)**   In the *Wealth of Nations,* Smith argued that since markets always correct themselves in the long run via an "invisible hand" that brings markets back to a state of equilibrium, governments should not interfere. In the 1930s, John Maynard Keynes argued that "in the long run we are all dead." As such, during

severe economic downturns, he asserted that governments should not stand by and do nothing while so much human misery takes place. He thus argued for governments to "prime the pump" by manipulating government spending (A), taxes (B), interest rates (C), and the money supply (D).

34. **(D)** The unifications of Germany and Italy did not occur until the 1870s, long after the early stages of the Industrial Revolution had taken root in England during the mid to late 1700s. All of the other answers list major events or trends that had been initiated long before the beginning of industrialization.

35. **(E)** The president does not have the ability to personally introduce legislation in either house of Congress. To introduce legislation in either house, one must be a member of that house. (A) is incorrect because the fact that he is elected indirectly by the people, not by the legislature as in parliamentary systems, is a source of power and independence for the president. (B) is incorrect because the Supreme Court has expanded the president's emergency powers. See, for example, the Prize Cases, 1863; and *Korematsu v. U.S.,* 1944. (C) is incorrect because when the president has high public approval ratings, as measured in opinion polls, he is in a much better position to push his legislative proposals through Congress. (D) is incorrect because the veto power can be wielded very effectively by presidents to prevent the passage of legislation they don't like. President George H.W. Bush had vetoed more than 20 bills by January 1992, and none of the vetoes had been overridden by Congress.

36. **(D)** Nearly all civil servants have jobs that are, practically speaking, beyond reach of the president. The only reasons for which a federal civil servant can be fired are misconduct or poor performance, and then only if the person's supervisor is willing to invest a great deal of time and effort. Civil servants cannot be fired for political reasons. This gives civil servants the opportunity to thwart or delay presidential initiatives by half-hearted compliance or passive noncompliance with presidential directives. (A) is incorrect because all agency budget requests must be submitted to and approved by the Office of Management and Budget before they can be sent to Congress. (B) is incorrect because the president has many more opportunities to influence public opinion than do civil servants. The presidency is a much more high-profile office than any civil service position, and the president has access to television and newspaper coverage that civil servants generally do not. (C) is incorrect because, technically, the federal bureaucracy is part of the executive branch, and is directly responsible to the president. (E) is incorrect because the Hatch Act, passed in 1939, made it illegal for civil servants to solicit campaign contributions.

37. **(B)** In 1985, Congress passed the Gramm-Rudman Act with the intent to balance the federal budget by 1992. The law created a plan whereby the budget deficit for each year from 1986 through 1991 could not exceed a specified,

declining amount. Therefore, the correct response is (B). (A) is incorrect because the Hyde Amendment of 1976 outlawed the use of federal funds for abortions, except where the life of the mother is at stake. (C) is incorrect because the Boland Amendments outlawed the use of federal funds to aid the Nicaraguan Contras. (D) is incorrect because the Gramm-Rudman Act did not change the tax code. (E) is incorrect because the INF Treaty of 1987 provided for the destruction of intermediate range missiles in Europe.

38. **(C)** is correct because the event was obviously a stock market crash, with no outside event cited as a cause. Historical references, such as ticker tape and anaconda, help pinpoint the era. (A) is incorrect, because modern references, such as telephone, eliminate this era. (B) is incorrect. This will be a partial result of the crash, but no references to it are made. Pearl Harbor Day (D) is also incorrect. No reference to this is made, plus historically the attack occurred on a weekend when the market is closed. (E) is incorrect because there is no reference to point to this event, which occurred in the afternoon while the crash began in the morning.

39. **(A)** The quote says that once the tape lost track, no one knew what was happening. This lack of information would increase the panic. (B) and (C) are cited as being the opposite, with a sound economy waiting for a stock market rally. (D) is incorrect, because three major issues, steel, telephone, and anaconda (copper) were listed. (E) is incorrect. This is the opposite of what happened; there were "no buying orders…."

40. **(E)** is most correct as cited, with sell orders coming in from all over the country, with no buy orders to meet them. (A) is wrong. The passage states that there was so much activity that the ticker tape was overwhelmed. (B) is incorrect. The quote says that the market opened "steady." (C) is incorrect. The opening sentence discusses the general falling market recently. (D) is incorrect. There is no evidence of this in the quote.

41. **(D)** Even though Hoover had been in office for less than a year, the economic conditions were already in place. (A), (B), and (C) were the three presidents before Hoover, and (E) was elected after Hoover to try to solve the depression that followed.

42. **(C)** The FDIC or federal bank account insurance was part of the New Deal to restore confidence in banks, not stocks. (A) is incorrect; the Securities and Exchange Commission was created to regulate the stock market after the crash. Among its reforms were (B), which reduced the percentage of stock that could be bought on credit (margin), tighter checks on the economic soundness of businesses issuing stocks (D), and checks on how people inside a company can buy and sell their own stocks (E).

43. **(A)** "Reaganomics" was the term coined for President Ronald Reagan's supply-side economic policies. Reagan believed that the way to repair the shattered economy he inherited from the Carter administration was to cut federal spending on domestic programs while at the same time cutting taxes for the wealthy and for corporations. The "supply-side" theory advocated by Reagan asserted that by cutting taxes to businesses and to the rich, money would be freed up for future investments and the creation of new jobs. This investment income would offset the initial loss of tax revenue caused by the tax cuts. Eventually, through the creation of new jobs and investments, the money freed up by tax cuts to the rich would "trickle down" to the middle classes and the poor. While this sounded good on paper, it never worked out quite as well in real life. Yes, the tax cuts did spur investment, but the investments often didn't translate into jobs that paid well. The "trickle-down" was uneven and often quite limited. Many wealthy people pocketed the money rather than investing it. Still, new jobs were created and the nation began an economic expansion that lasted well into the 1990s.

44. **(E)** Nineteenth-century Europeans and Americans fully believed in the superiority of their cultures, of the white race, and of Christianity. In their minds, it was perfectly acceptable to go into undeveloped nonwhite lands and do what they pleased with the lands and the natives. Since the natives of these lands were overwhelmingly nonwhite, non-Christian, and technologically undeveloped, Americans and Europeans rationalized their domination of these lands and the subjugation of the natives. They viewed their actions as a noble mission to "civilize" the "savages" and give them the benefits of Western culture. This "mission" was called the "white man's burden" because it was characterized as a burden that only the shoulders of the Western white male were big enough to handle.

45. **(B)** Here the emphasis is entirely upon memory retention; if the quotation is not known, and little is known about the other thinkers, a successful guess is unlikely and is not recommended. This much-quoted passage by the French mathematician and philosopher René Descartes searches for absolute certainty by using a method of "systematic doubt." Rejecting the certainty of all knowledge but the knowledge that a thinking process was occurring, he believed that he had established one certain fact—his own existence.

46. **(E)** In their work to strengthen the French absolute monarchs, royal ministers Cardinals Mazarin and Richelieu placed government agents, or intendants, in areas throughout France, where they acted as both the "king's ears" and as collectors of revenue. The move established a "royal presence" in major areas of the country. Choices (A) (*lettres de cachet*) and (B) were other steps taken to strengthen absolutism in France.

47. **(A)** In Swahili "ujamaa" translates roughly into "brotherhood" or "friendship." Nyerere, the socialist president of Tanzania, developed this concept to represent his search for an ideal socialist society. The concept of "ujamaa" takes its model from traditional African societies in a pre-colonial past. In the words of Nyerere, it looks back to a society in which "nobody starved, whether of food or human dignity, because he lacked personal wealth; he could depend on the wealth possessed by the community of which he was a member. That was socialism. That *is* socialism." The equality inherent in ujamaa could be applied to all of Africa, not only Tanzania (E) or the nation-states created by colonialism (D). While Nyerere did support the pan-African movement (B), ujamaa stood for a specific kind of African socialism. Critics of ujamaa, such as Kwame Nkrumah, charged that it was too idealistic, depending on a mythical African past, as well as unrealistic. Nkrumah supported economic modernization (C) through the action of state-controlled corporations instead of the models of an outdated rural past.

48. **(A)** The Yellow River, about 2,700 miles long, runs west to east across China, bringing in the summer heavy deposits of yellow silt which give the river its name. The river enters the Pacific Ocean near the Shandong Peninsula. The nickname "China's Sorrow" came from the river's tendency to build up its own bed and flood hundreds of square miles of farmland. Since it may take years to recultivate flooded lands, many of the floods in China's history have led to periods of famine. While the Yangtze River (B) is longer than the Yellow River at about 3,200 miles, it has not had the same influence over the land. The Wei River (D) and the Tarim River (E) are both smaller rivers in the eastern and northwestern regions of China, respectively. The Ganges River (C) is in India.

49. **(C)** Legal-rational authority is the type of authority based on rules and laws. (A) and (B) are incorrect because they refer to other bases of authority, namely, authority based on customary and established ways of doing things and authority based on special and extraordinary powers or qualities, respectively. (D) is incorrect because all three types of authority can become institutionalized. (E) is incorrect because the question refers to political, not economic or corporate, authority.

50. **(D)** Union membership peaked in the 1950s at 35 percent of the workforce and has declined steadily to about 13.5 percent today. (A) is wrong because corporate concentration has become even greater than a few decades ago. (B) is wrong because market forces are at least as powerful as a few decades ago. (C) is incorrect because the economic sphere is probably more important to the power elite than in the past. (E) is wrong because the industrial sector has been declining as a proportion of the economy.

51. **(B)** Despite its extensive coastline, Sub-Saharan Africa has no excellent natural harbors, which can be defined as a natural body of water that has: (1) a sufficient depth to allow large ships to anchor there; and (2) strong protection in the form of a land mass. Examples of excellent natural harbors around the world include: Victoria Bay in Hong Kong; Subic Bay in the Philippines; and Pearl Harbor in Hawaii.

52. **(B)** The decline in factory work in America since the 1970s has two broad causes: globalization and technological innovation. Increased industrialization in *developing* nations has benefitted a great deal from the offshoring of jobs from *developed* countries, where wage rates are relatively high compared to those in less-developed countries. Moreover, the decline in U.S. factory jobs has been exacerbated by numerous technological innovations over the last 50 years, mostly because U.S. manufacturers continue to shift their production techniques to include a greater degree of automation and, more recently, robotics. Together, the combined factors of globalization and technological innovation have created a rising gap between the rich and poor in America as well as a growing sense of despair in small "factory" towns that have seen their factories shuttered.

53. **(D)** Hamilton's genius included a profound understanding of economic theory and political philosophy. In terms of setting the United States on the path to economic stability (after a very unstable 1780s, where the U.S. Government could not levy taxes or regulate interstate trade under the ineffective Articles of Confederation), Hamilton took a number of important steps, including establishing a national bank, assuming state and national debt, creating a tariff and a whiskey tax, and establishing a patent office. He did not, however, put the U.S. currency on any type of gold standard.

54. **(D)** The Glorious Revolution was initiated in 1688–89, the French Revolution in 1789, the Russian Revolution in 1917, and the Iranian (Islamic) Revolution in 1978–79, making (D) the only correct answer.

55. **(B)** When he envisioned a communist society, Karl Marx believed that the state would "whither away," and that people would forever live in a state of harmony. This vision seems rather utopian to most people today, for in countries such as Russia and China, which both claimed to implement Marxist doctrine, the state did not wither away, but rather became totalitarian in nature. The other answers are incorrect for the following reasons: "Every man for himself" (A) is a phrase often associated with extreme capitalism; the statement that life in the state of nature is "solitary, nasty, poor, brutish, and short." (C) comes from Thomas Hobbes, who advocated something akin to a totalitarian state; the statement that "power tends to corrupt." (E) comes from a longer quotation from Lord Acton, and the claim that "man is born free, and everywhere he is in chains." (D) is a famous assertion by Jean-Jacques Rousseau.

56. **(C)**   The "single-member district" part of the term means that each district gets a single representative. The "plurality vote system" part means that the candidate with the most votes, even if less than a majority, wins the election. Therefore, (C) is the correct answer. (A) is incorrect because a runoff election is not necessary in a plurality voting system. If the candidate with the most votes wins, whether or not (s)he gets a majority, there is no need for a runoff. (B) is incorrect because each district gets only one representative in a single member district system. (D) is incorrect because there is no requirement that some votes count more than others in a single member district, plurality vote system. Members of the U.S. House of Representatives are chosen by the single member, plurality vote system. In elections for U.S. representatives, each person's vote counts the same as any other person's vote. (E) is incorrect because third parties are more likely to win seats in a multi-member district, proportional representation system. In such systems, each district gets several representatives, and each party gets a number of seats proportionate to its total vote in the district election. Third parties are more likely to gain seats, since it is possible for them to get 10 percent or 20 percent of the vote, and thus 10 percent or 20 percent of the seats for the district. In single member district, plurality vote systems, by contrast, the party with the plurality gets the one seat, and all others get nothing.

57. **(D)**   The Attorney General is the cabinet official in charge of the Justice Department. (A) is incorrect because the Solicitor-General is the third-ranking official at the Justice Department. (B) is incorrect because there is no federal official designated Secretary of Justice. (C) is incorrect because the Secretary of State is in charge of the State Department. (E) is incorrect because the Chief Justice sits on the Supreme Court.

58. **(A)**   The question asks which statement is false. (A) is a correct response because the state party conventions choose their respective state party chairmen. (B) is a true statement. The party platform is written at the national party convention. (C) is a true statement, since the convention does nominate the party's candidate for president. (D) is a true statement since the Democratic party, unlike the Republican party, has several hundred "superdelegates" who are free to vote for the nominee of their choice at the convention. The superdelegates are Democratic governors, congressmen, and other distinguished party members. (E) is a true statement because one of the functions of the convention is to set the time and place of the next convention.

59. **(E)**   is most correct as the two line graphs have met in the 1970s. (A) The opposite has been true as the GNP line was almost always below that of the labor force. (B) is incorrect as the difference between the two lines widened and nar-

rowed in different areas. (C) Farming had declined to below 50 percent well before 1900. (D) Even though the graphs' curves became more level in the 1970s, they still reflected a declining influence.

60. **(D)** The closing of the gap between GNP and labor force reflect the increasing efficiency of each farmer. (A) is not an accurate conclusion because, with fewer farmers growing the food supply, their importance is great. (B) is not addressed by the graph. The range of farm incomes is wide. (C) Automation might be an explanation for the increased efficiency, but the graphs do not supply that information. (E) There was at least one period on each graph when the line went upward.

61. **(C)** Farming has become increasingly agribusiness and the family farm has decreased in influence and number. (A) is a traditional problem as farmers have to borrow until crops are harvested and hope income is good. (B) The United States is usually a food exporter, using its surpluses to sell crops abroad. (D) Several years of severe weather, such as drought, in the 1980s illustrated how dependent agriculture still is on nature. (E) Government farm programs have been very important for 70 years, helping by price supports, quotas, crop limits, and direct payments.

62. **(C)** Efficiency is not necessarily a problem, but the reduction of workers reduces both the earning power of agricultural workers and the political clout of agriculture as an occupation. (A) is the exact opposite of the trend which has continued for most of the twentieth century. (B) World food demands, not supplies, are increasing with population growth and all food exporters will be pressured to increase production. (D) Water supplies are decreasing in relation to the population worldwide. (E) Again, the world population growth will increase food needs.

63. **(D)** The paternalistic view of slavery, held by most Southern plantation owners, held that blacks were inferior, mentally weak and ignorant, requiring "protection" from the evils that could befall them if they were left on their own. In this view, slaveowners were benevolent protectors who took care of their black slaves almost as parents take care of children. This was a comforting myth that most slaveholders really appear to have believed. It was comforting in that if they were really protectors of their poor black "children," then holding slaves wasn't sinful at all. It was, rather, a social service providing a good for everybody involved. Unfortunately, this twisted rationalization denied the fact that slaves were horribly mistreated and often abused or killed for little or no provocation. If they were ignorant or childlike, it is only because they were denied educational opportunities and many slaves learned that acting with childlike deference to their "master" often got them better treatment. In other words, they feigned childishness as part of an act based on a powerful instinct to survive rather than any limitations of mental capacity.

64. **(D)** Mark Twain's writings pioneered a trend toward realism in American literature at the turn of the century. This trend portrayed the lives of real, flawed, and often quite colorful human beings. There was no effort to make the characters in these stories "larger than life" or pillars of virtue to be admired for their flawless character. These people struggled with the everyday issues of life as well as the bigger social and moral questions of the day, sometimes reaching successful resolutions to their quests, more often than not finding only partial answers to their problems. The focus of these stories was often on the temptations of sin, sexuality, and others of life's evils. The hero or heroine often faced difficult tests or questions regarding what was right or wrong in a particular situation. The realistic school of writing was in many ways a coming of age for American literature and bore its own unique stamp as a uniquely American contribution to the world of written fiction.

65. **(C)** The first woman to be awarded the Nobel Peace Prize, Bertha von Suttner, an Austrian, gained wide attention for her book, which contributed to the founding of Peace Societies in Austria and Germany. Admiral Tirpitz represented the opposite pole; he masterminded Germany's plans, beginning in the 1890s, to create a German navy to rival the British navy. Rosa Luxemburg, a German Marxist, was killed during a failed revolutionary attempt in Germany in 1919. Theobald von Bethmann-Hollweg was the chancellor of Germany during the early stages of World War I. Cosima Wagner was the influential wife of composer Richard Wagner.

66. **(C)** This question deals with a complex situation at the start of the war. It requires analytical thinking, an understanding of a complex chain of events, and some knowledge of terminology (although the key term—"Schlieffen Plan"—does not appear in the question). Choice (A) may be eliminated, since such an obvious answer is unlikely to be the correct one on an advanced test. During frequent renewals of the Triple Alliance during the late nineteenth century, Germany was consistently pushed by Austria to make increasingly specific and secret promises of aid to Austria in the event of war. According to one German promise, a Russian mobilization was to lead to a German declaration of war. German military planners, however, were worried about a two-front war, to both the east (Russia) and west (France). A commission working under the German Count Alfred von Schlieffen produced the famous Schlieffen Plan, which required that Germany immediately invade the weaker country of the two in overwhelming numbers, with the goal of quickly defeating the weaker country. The writers of the Schlieffen Plan assumed the weaker nation was France.

67. **(B)** Mozambique, on the Southeast tip of the African continent above South Africa, was colonized by Portugal. All of the other countries—(A), (C), (D), and (E)—were occupied by the British.

68. **(A)** In 1971 India, led by Indira Gandhi, daughter of former Prime Minister Jawaharlal Nehru, joined East Pakistan in a war against West Pakistan. West Pakistan was eventually defeated and East Pakistan became the independent nation of Bangladesh. The countries of Vietnam (B), Cambodia (C), and Laos (D) were all independent countries in 1965 as was North Korea (E), which officially came into existence on September 9, 1948, when North Korean communists established the Democratic People's Republic of Korea.

69. **(D)** In 1896, William Jennings Bryan, a staunch defender of farmers' rights, delivered his "Cross of Gold" speech to a somewhat desperate Democratic Party, which had been searching for an identity after being blamed for the Panic of 1893. A key political issue of the day was whether the U.S. currency should be backed by silver or gold. Whereas most Republicans favored gold, Democrats were somewhat divided between backing gold or silver. By their 1896 national convention, however, the Democrats had attracted Bryan from the Populist Party and adopted a pro-silver, anti-gold stance. In brief, Bryan argued that indebted farmers would benefit from the inflation caused by a silver-backed money supply, which would grow more quickly than it would if it were backed by gold. The logic was as follows: since the supply of silver was more plentiful than the supply of gold, inflation would develop throughout the United States and allow farmers to pay back their outstanding debts in lesser-valued dollars.

70. **(C)** First articulated in 1946 by George Kennan in his "long telegram," the focal point of the Truman Doctrine was containment of Russia's "expansive tendencies." Early examples of containment included the $400 million in American aid to ward off communist insurgents in Greece and Turkey and the Berlin Airlift, which was Truman's response to Stalin's attempt to block the West's access to West Berlin. Choice (A) essentially describes Stalin's actions. Choice (B), NATO, was not established until 1949. Choice (D) describes the situation at hand, not Truman's response, while Choice (E) is the name for the Soviet Union's response to NATO.

71. **(D)** A common misconception is that FDR's New Deal policies, including many job creation programs, such as the Civilian Conservation Corps (CCC) and the Works Progress Administration (WPA), were enough to end the Great Depression and bring down the unemployment rate to pre-depression levels. The primary reason that drove unemployment to below 5% were the massive factory orders associated with World War II.

72. **(E)** The Venetian merchant and explorer Marco Polo arrived at the court of Kublai Khan in 1275. The grandson of Genghis Khan, Kublai Khan established the Yuan Dynasty in China in 1271 and ruled until his death in 1294. After Marco Polo returned from China to Venice, he was imprisoned for a short period by the Genoese (who were at war with the Venetians). While in prison, he told the tales

of his travels to another prisoner, who wrote down these elaborate stories. In time, these stories were published in a book, *The Tales of Marco Polo*. This book excited the imaginations of many Europeans, especially the explorers who set off in search of fame and riches during the so-called Age of Exploration.

73. **(A)** The three core population processes identified by demographers are fertility (births), mortality (deaths), and migration (movement into or out of an area). The other choices are wrong because they include only two of these and a third which is not one of the basic demographic processes. Community (B) refers to a place where people live rather than a demographic process; fecundity (C) refers to the potential number of children that can be born, but actual fertility is the key demographic process; segregation (D) refers to the isolating of people or activities in particular parts of a city; and ecology (E) refers to the field that studies population distributions rather than an element that determines population size and distribution.

74. **(B)** Charlemagne was the grandson of Charles Martel. The remaining answers are incorrect for the following reasons: Louis XIV (A) served as the king of France from 1643 to 1715; Alfred the Great (C) served as a King of the Saxons in the south of England during the latter part of the 10th century; Clovis (D) served as the first king of the Franks from 481 to 511; and Pepin (E) was Charlemagne's father.

75. **(A)** The question requires you to identify the false statement. The correct response is (A), since the Court declared in *Engel v. Vitale,* 1962, that a nondenominational prayer written by New York officials for recitation in public schools at the beginning of each school day was unconstitutional. (B) is a true statement because the Court declared in *Abington School District v. Schempp,* 1963, that a Pennsylvania law which required daily Bible reading in public schools was unconstitutional. (C) is a true statement because in *Stone v. Graham,* 1980, the Court held unconstitutional a Kentucky statute which required the posting of a copy of the Ten Commandments, purchased with private funds, on the wall of every classroom in the state. (D) is a true statement because in *McLean v. Arkansas Board of Education,* 1982, the Court held unconstitutional a law requiring that creation science be taught in public schools. (E) is a true statement because in *Epperson v. Arkansas,* 1968, a law prohibiting the teaching of the theory of evolution in public schools was declared unconstitutional by the Court.

76. **(E)** The Constitution, as it came from the Constitutional Convention in 1788, provided for a direct popular vote for members of the House of Representatives. Direct popular vote means that the general public votes on the item and that vote immediately determines the outcome of the election or issue. (A) is incorrect because the president is elected not by direct popular vote but by the electoral college. Originally, state legislatures chose the electors who made up the electoral college.

(B) is incorrect because senators were originally chosen by the state legislatures. The Seventeenth Amendment, adopted in 1913, provides for popular election of senators. (C) is incorrect because treaties are ratified by a two-thirds vote of the Senate. (D) is incorrect because constitutional amendments are ratified in one of two ways. The first is by three-fourths of the state legislatures. The second is by three-fourths of state ratifying conventions. Congress determines which method will be used.

77. **(D)** The Great Compromise, also known as the Connecticut Compromise, occurred at the Constitutional Convention of 1787. It was a compromise between two plans known as the Virginia, or Large State Plan, and the New Jersey, or Small State Plan. It provided for a Senate in which each state would receive two senators, and a House of Representatives in which representation would be based on population. (A) is incorrect because the Great Compromise had nothing to do with the slavery question. (B) is incorrect because the Great Compromise had nothing to do with the electoral college. (C) is incorrect because senators were selected by state legislatures until the passage of the Seventeenth Amendment. (E) is incorrect because the Great Compromise occurred during the Constitutional Convention, while the Bill of Rights was added to the Constitution after the Convention was over.

78. **(A)** Besides AT&T, the various Bell companies are all on the list. (B) Obvious manufacturing companies, such as General Motors and General Electric, are outnumbered by service companies, such as utilities. (C) Retailers, such as Sears, appear toward the bottom of the list. (D) Bell Canada obviously does foreign business, as do most of the others with their international branches, such as IBM. (E) Exxon appears on the list, with over three-quarters of a million stockholders.

79. **(E)** is correct because it has the least number of stockholders on the list, so, therefore, the fewest number of votes is required to make decisions. All of the others have more stockholders, so each share of stock is less important in a total vote. The reality is that the number of shares in any large company is so great that influence at the annual stockholders meeting is minimal for any one share of stock.

80. **(D)** The stockholders elect a board of directors and give them direction at the annual meeting. The board then directs the company for the rest of the year, appointing a chairperson and setting policy. (A) The chief executive officer (CEO) is appointed or elected by the board of directors. (B) The board elects a chair, but controls its power. (C) The president (often the CEO) directs the day-to-day operations under board direction. (E) Stock options are opportunities for top employees to invest in the company, but do not give control unless the employees buy a large portion of the outstanding stock, thus gaining control.

81. **(B)** In January 1918, Woodrow Wilson proposed the Fourteen Points, which enunciated his goals for the peace that would follow World War I. These were idealistic goals based on notions of open diplomacy, the elimination of secret treaties, self-determination, arms reduction, open trade, and a League of Nations to serve as an international forum to prevent future wars. The thrust of the Fourteen Points emphasized fairness and openness in international relationships. By November 1918, the Germans faced military and political collapse, but they approached an armistice with the Allies convinced that the postwar treaty would be a fair one based upon Wilson's Fourteen Points. They reasoned that since the United States had turned the tide and saved France and Britain from almost certain defeat, the United States would dominate the peace negotiations. Unfortunately, they reasoned incorrectly and the Treaty of Versailles reflected British and French desires for vengeance more than it reflected the Wilsonian principles elucidated in his Fourteen Points.

82. **(C)** This engraving emphasizes the innocence and helplessness of the victims.

83. **(C)** Of the first three choices, the only one that is a correct interpretation of the graph is (C). Choice (D) may or may not be true, but the graph (which indicates percentage shares of national product) does not provide the kind of information required to decide.

84. **(C)** Attempting to guess the location on the basis of the name of the crisis will not be helpful, since "Fashoda" does not sound African. Another approach is recommended: try to remember the geographical areas where Britain and France clashed over colonial claims. This reasoning would eliminate choices (B), (D), and (E). Generally, the two nations acted in concert regarding the Balkans and Ottoman Empire, and they had no colonial claims in southern Europe. Only two answers remain; guessing is strongly recommended. The Fashoda crisis, which stands as an example of the danger that imperialist adventures might lead to a major European war, began when French and British army units contested ownership rights to the village of Fashoda in the African Sudan during the 1890s. The potential for war became increasingly obvious when French and British cabinet debates over the crisis lasted three days; eventually both army units were ordered to withdraw peacefully.

85. **(A)** Liberia has been an independent state since its founding in 1847. Tanzania (B) achieved independence in 1964, Sierra Leone (C) in 1961, Gambia (D) in 1965, and Ghana (E) in 1957.

86. **(B)** The capital city of Thailand is Bangkok. Siam refers to the former name for Thailand. All of the other choices (A), (C), (D), and (E) match the countries with their capitals correctly.

87. **(C)** Research shows that, as economic development (industrialization, urbanization, higher levels of education) expands, birth rates tend to decline. (A) and (D) are wrong because, when women have a choice about how many children to have, they tend to have fewer children; family planning and gender equality give women that choice. (B) is incorrect because urbanization is a part of economic development which tends to reduce birth rates. (E) is wrong because patriarchy involves the subordination of women, which is associated with less choice for women and higher birth rates.

88. **(D)** A main purpose for the Berlin Conference of 1884–85 was to determine an orderly means for the key European powers to carve up Sub-Saharan Africa for themselves. Hence, the Conference led to what became known as the "Scramble for Africa." The historical context for the Berlin Conference was complex, but it clearly included the rapidly expanding Industrial Revolution and the need for additional raw materials. The Second Industrial Revolution in the United States (A) began soon after the end of the Civil War in 1865 and thus preceded the Conference. The European conquest targeted Sub-Saharan Africa, not the Middle East (B). The "Era of Good Feelings" (C) refers to the presidency of James Monroe (1817–25). Within a decade after the Berlin Conference, the United States did experience the Panic/Depression of 1893, but this was mostly caused by over speculation in railroads, not because of decisions made in Berlin.

89. **(E)** Leon Trotsky, a Marxist theorist, was a major figure in the early stages of the Russian Revolution, which began in October 1917. Among other things, Trotsky led the Red Army and he sat on the first Politburo. He was later ousted and exiled by Stalin, who eventually had Trotsky murdered in Mexico in 1940. Nietzsche (A) was a highly controversial German philosopher who claimed "God is dead." He is also known for promoting his concept of the *ubermensch* (or superman). Nikita Khrushchev (B) led the Soviet Union from 1954 to 1964, while Leonard Brezhnev (C) did so from 1964 to 1982. Alexander Kerensky (D) was Prime Minister of the Russian Provisional Government that failed to stop the Russian Revolution.

90. **(D)** The Rocky Mountain range runs well east of California.

91. **(B)** Originally built as a Hindu temple in the early 12th century, Angkor Wat has primarily been used as a place for Buddhist worship since the late 12th century. It also ranks as the largest religious monument in the world.

92. **(E)** Jerusalem lies at the heart of the Holy Land, which, generally speaking, comprises modern-day Israel. The city of Jerusalem is a sacred city for not only Christians, but also for Jews and Muslims. The remaining answers are incorrect for the following reasons: Ur (A) lies in modern-day Iraq; Mecca (B) in modern-day Saudi Arabia; Rome (C) in modern-day Italy; and Constantinople (D) in modern-day Turkey.

93. **(A)** When World War I broke out during the summer of 1914, it had been approximately 100 years since the end of the Napoleonic Wars.

94. **(B)** The global political system was essentially bipolar because there existed two poles of power: one in Washington, D.C., and one in Moscow. As such, the First World (the U.S.-led Western bloc) battled the Second World (the Russian-based Soviet bloc) for dominance in the Third World, or those countries that were not part of either of the two major blocs.

95. **(D)** There are two schools of thought on the proper method of constitutional interpretation by the judiciary. One is called "judicial activism." Advocates of this school believe that the intentions of those who wrote the Constitution should not be authoritative for the decision of controversial matters in the present. They say that judges should be free to adapt the Constitution to changing political and social circumstances. The other school is called "judicial restraint." Advocates of this school stress that the Constitution was a great contract by which the American people created a government. This contract laid the ground rules for the operation of the government, and it provided a formal process of amendment for changing those ground rules. In order to understand the ground rules, say advocates of restraint, one must determine the original intentions of those who wrote and ratified the Constitution. For unelected judges to assume to themselves the power to change the Constitution, according to this school, is for the judges to usurp a power that was not given them by the Constitution or the people. Therefore, the correct answer is (D). Choice (A) is incorrect because there is no general process by which judges limit the number of cases they hear in a year. Justices on the Supreme Court do have a lot of control over which cases they hear, through a process called "certiorari." When litigants appeal to the Court to have their cases heard, the justices vote on the merits of the cases. If four justices vote to hear a particular case, they issue a "writ of certiorari" to the lower court, ordering all documents relevant to the case to be sent up to the Supreme Court. Choice (B) is incorrect because judges do not lobby funds from Congress. Choice (C) is incorrect because when judges remove themselves from a case they are said to recuse themselves. Choice (E) is incorrect because judicial restraint refers to a method of interpreting the Constitution and has nothing to do with political campaigns.

96. **(E)** The vast majority of bills never make it out of committee to the floor of the chamber. Many are introduced by a member only to get publicity, or so the member can tell constituents that (s)he did something about the matter. (A) is incorrect since most bills die in committee. If a bill dies in committee, it cannot be considered, much less passed, by the whole house. There is a seldom-used procedure by which a bill can be forced out of committee in the house. First, 218 members must sign a discharge petition, then the petition must be approved by a majority vote of the full house. However, attempts to force a bill out of committee by discharge petition have

succeeded only about 3 percent of the time in the twentieth century. (B) is incorrect because only a fraction of all bills introduced in either house ever become law. (C) is incorrect because bills are sent to the rules committee only after being reported out of a standing committee. Since most die in standing committee, they never make it to the rules committee. (D) is incorrect because every bill introduced in either house is referred by the presiding officer to the appropriate committee.

97. **(C)**   The correct response is (C) because I and II are false. A president may not veto particular items in a bill (I). Such a power is called a line-item veto, and is held by 43 governors in the United States. A president may not pocket-veto a bill by holding it 10 days while Congress is in session (II). In such a case the bill becomes law without the president's signature. If Congress adjourns during the 10-day period, the bill is pocket-vetoed. The only true statement is III, the president's veto can be overridden if two-thirds of both houses vote to pass the bill despite the veto.

98. **(C)**   is the correct answer because East Germany's $31 billion is 10 percent of West Germany's $323 billion. (A) is incorrect because the United States was not the leading exporter ($322 billion vs. $323 billion for West Germany). (B) is wrong because Britain's $145 billion is less than half of Germany's total of $354 billion. (D) is not correct because with East Germany's $31 billion added to West Germany's $323 billion, the total gap will widen to $32 billion more than the United States. (E) is wrong because the total will be almost $500 billion, not $600 billion.

99. **(A)**   Per capita gross national product is one of the accepted economic figures to compare relative standards of living because it includes all (gross) goods and services produced by a nation. (B) relates to a nation's exporting production per capita only, not standard of living. (C) The annual exports alone do not show a relationship to the number of people who share those sales. (D) is incorrect because it compares an individual figure (per capita) with a total national figure. (E) creates the gross national product of a country, not individuals.

100. **(C)**   The United States, with a population of 248 million, produced $322 billion in exports. Not worrying about the zeroes, the 248 is less than double 322. West Germany produced over five times its population, East Germany nearly double, and the British nearly three times. (A) is incorrect because the graphs do not show total productivity, only the products exported. (B) is wrong. Britain was fourth. It will go to third and the unified Germany will be second behind the United States. (D) is incorrect. As noted in explaining (C), the West Germans produced the most exports per capita. (E) is wrong. In a unified Germany, the East German lower GNP will temporarily create a figure for the total for the whole country somewhere between the two figures $12,480 and $14,260.

101. **(C)**   Grant was an intensely loyal man who was, sadly, not the best judge of character in choosing his administrative appointees. During his first term in office, his administration was beset with financial scandals involving the vice president, Grant's brother-in-law, and a well-known financial entrepreneur named Jay Gould. In his second term, the "whiskey ring" scandal implicated Grant's private secretary. His secretary of war was implicated in a bribery scandal. While few believed Grant to be corrupt, Grant's loyalty to his corrupt associates tarnished his image in virtually everyone's eyes. It also crippled the effectiveness of his administration.

102. **(C)**   While the United States was technically neutral in World War II until the Japanese attack on Pearl Harbor, Franklin Roosevelt made no secret of his distaste for Nazi Germany, Fascist Italy, and militaristic Japan. He openly sought repeal of the neutrality laws so the United States could sell weapons and supplies to Britain and France to help them stop Hitler in Europe. Congress finally agreed, in November 1939, to allow cash sales of goods to European belligerents, meaning France and Britain. When France fell to the Nazi *blitzkrieg*, England stood alone and quickly used up its cash reserves trying to replace its war losses and brace for the expected German invasion. Churchill told Roosevelt of the desperate British situation and predicted that without some means of obtaining American weapons Britain would quickly fall. Realizing that the British needed the help but could not pay for the weapons, Roosevelt proposed Lend-Lease, a policy through which Britain would be allowed to borrow the weapons it needed and would be expected to return the weapons when the war was over. Realizing that there was nothing subtle about this circumvention of the cash-and-carry law, Roosevelt used the analogy of the neighbor's burning house to justify Lend-Lease. Although critics attacked the proposal, it was passed by Congress and was critical in the eventual success of the Allied war effort.

103. **(C)**   This question is a thorough test of your knowledge of the Reformation, since it asks about the social basis of a Protestant group. Some choices may be eliminated, if you already know the social bases of Calvinism and Lutheranism. Each of the three major Protestant groups—Lutheran, Calvinist, and Anabaptist—relied in major ways on particular social elements. Although Lutheranism drew support from a broad social spectrum, Luther himself was forced to rely on sympathetic members of the nobility of the Holy Roman Empire in order to defend Lutheranism against the Holy Roman Emperor. Calvinism held special appeal for the new middle class, particularly business elements. Anabaptism drew most of its membership from the peasantry in western Germany and the Low Countries.

104. **(B)**   If the "Augsburg Confession" is not recognized at first glance, attempt to eliminate the other choices. All of the other terms are part of the Counter-Reformation. Once again, terminology is important. Pope Paul III called the Council of Trent into session in 1545 as a means of revitalizing and reforming parts

of the church. The Council approved restrictions on the reading material of ordinary Catholics (the Index), commissions to investigate the spread of Protestantism (which is what the Inquisition was originally designed to do), and a new group to combat the spread of Protestant ideas (the Society of Jesus, or Jesuits). The Augsburg Confession was a compromise confession of faith written by Luther's friend Philip Melanchthon in a vain attempt to reconcile Protestant and Catholic princes in the Holy Roman Empire.

105. **(C)**   The first Opium War, which ran from 1839 to 1842, began when the Chinese government, in an attempt to stop the trade of opium with the British, seized millions of dollars worth of opium from traders in Canton. In 1839 the British declared war to regain the opium market and other lucrative trading rights. The Opium War ended in 1842 with the Treaty of Nanjing, the first of what China dubbed her "unequal treaties," which gave the British the colony of Hong Kong as well as trading rights at many ports. In addition, China had to pay Britain the cost of fighting the war and the value of the opium seized. The second Opium War raged from 1857–60.

106. **(C)**   After his journey down the Congo River, Stanley approached the government in England with his plans for the geography and resources of the Congo Basin. When the British showed no interest, King Leopold II of Belgium employed Stanley in 1879 to open routes into what would become the Belgian Congo, initiating a brutal and exploitative colonization.

107. **(C)**   Serving as a shining example that self-interest drives much of human behavior, the English noble class forced King John I to sign the *Magna Carta*, mostly to serve their own self-interest. This document therefore limited the power of the king by prohibiting him from acting capriciously toward the barons (or noble class). That said, it did contain a provision that gave "all free men the right to justice and a fair trial," but a great many of those in the peasant class were not considered "free men."

108. **(A)**   Although Wilson's Fourteen Points included many excellent ideas that were later implemented after World War II, his intransigent personality and feud with Henry Cabot Lodge and other leading Republicans in the U.S. Senate, ended with the Senate rejecting the Treaty of Versailles and refusing to join the League of Nations. As a result, the League of Nations lacked sufficient clout to handle international conflicts and it became something of a laughing stock by the 1930s when it lacked the power to stop the fascist states of Italy, Germany, and Japan from annexing and conquering other countries, which in turn led to the start of World War II in September 1939.

109. **(A)**   The origins of the Persian Royal Road date back to the Achaemenid Period (c. 558-330 BCE). These roads were used extensively for trade, troop movements, missionaries, travelers, and postal couriers. Regarding these postal couriers,

the Greek historian Herodotus noted, "Neither snow nor rain nor heat nor gloom of night stays these couriers from the swift completion of their appointed rounds." The Persian Royal Road preceded the Roman Road (B) and the Silk Road (C). Choices (D) and (E) are not actual names for roads.

110. **(C)**   The Chinese explorer Zheng He commanded a navy far greater than any assembled by the Spanish or Portuguese during the 1400s. Zheng He commanded a navy of over 300 ships, some with nine masts and measuring roughly 400 feet in length (more than four times the length of the largest ship that Columbus commanded in 1492). After 1433, however, officials in the Ming Dynasty stopped all further exploration, redeploying their resources to thwart land-based attacks and various internal rebellions.

111. **(D)**   The Enlightenment thinker John Locke had a profound influence on the American Revolution and its central document, the Declaration of Independence. For instance, in his *Two Treatises of Government,* Locke asserts that governments are instituted to protect "life," "liberty," and "possessions." Jefferson slightly altered Locke's emphasis by asserting that governments are established to protect "life, liberty, and the pursuit of happiness." All of the other answers refer to events (or, in the case of the *Magna Carta*, the signing of a document) that occurred long before Locke published his famous book just after England's Glorious Revolution in 1688–1689.

112. **(E)**   At the Congress of Vienna in 1814–1815, Klemens von Metternich led a movement that resulted in a general balance of power between the various European powers. A general goal of this Congress was to create a structure that would prevent any one European country from becoming so powerful that it could threaten the other European powers, as Napoleon's France had just done, with disastrous consequences for the rest of the continent.

113. **(A)**   Neville Chamberlain, the Prime Minister of Great Britain from 1937 to 1940, will forever be remembered—and ridiculed—for what became known as his appeasement policy, whereby he (and the French prime minister) agreed with Hitler's demand at the Munich Conference in 1938 that Germany should be allowed to annex the mostly German-speaking portion of Czechoslovakia. After the conference, Chamberlain famously proclaimed that we had achieved "peace for our time," which was clearly not the case, as World War II began one year later.

114. **(A)**   When it created the independent regulatory commissions, Congress gave them the power to pass regulations (legislative), enforce the regulations (executive), and conduct hearings to determine the punishment for violators of the regulations (judicial). Choice (B) is incorrect because independent regulatory commissions, while nominally in the executive branch, are not included in any of

the 14 executive departments. Choice (C) is incorrect because the regulatory commissions do not regulate the federal bureaucracy. Rather, some guard against unfair business practices, others police the side effects of business, such as pollution, and others protect consumers from unsafe products. Choice (D) is incorrect because the commissions were set up by Congress to be independent of the president. They are headed by commissioners who are appointed for fixed terms and are not removable by the president. The commissions must also be bipartisan in membership. Choice (E) is incorrect because the commissions were created by Congress.

115. **(A)**   This is a famous political cartoon from 1812, when the Massachusetts state legislature created a misshapen district which would be a "safe district" for Congressman Elbridge Gerry. A safe district is one in which a particular political party, or in this case a particular person, is almost certain to win. When cartoonist John Gilbert saw the district he added a head, wings, and claws and called it a salamander. Newspaper editor Benjamin Russell replied that it should be called a "gerrymander." The term has been used ever since to describe any congressional district of contorted boundaries which is created as a safe seat for a political party or candidate. Choice (B) is incorrect because the cartoon has nothing to do with environmental issues or congressional behavior. Choice (C) is incorrect because the cartoon has nothing to do with the influence of money on elections. Choice (D) is incorrect because the cartoon has nothing to do with the character of congressmen. Choice (E) is incorrect because the term "dinosaur bill" is a fictitious term concocted as a distractor for this question.

116. **(D)**   The War Powers Resolution stipulates that the president can deploy troops abroad in situations where hostilities are imminent for only 60 days, unless Congress approves a longer deployment, declares war, or cannot meet because the nation is under attack. (A) is wrong because the War Powers Resolution does not authorize Congress to prevent the initial deployment of troops abroad by the president. Choice (B) is wrong because the Constitution gives Congress the power to declare war. The usual procedure begins with a request from the president for a declaration of war, which is then adopted by the Congress by joint resolution and signed by the president. The War Powers Resolution did nothing to change this procedure. Choice (C) is wrong because the War Powers Resolution has nothing to do with extradition of foreign ambassadors. Choice (E) is incorrect because the War Powers Resolution has no direct relation to the defense budget.

117. **(D)**   Since the opportunity cost of providing more labor (and thus producing more output) is less than the price that can be received for that output, you should expect that each owner will increase his or her effort and thereby produce more output. This should cause industry output to climb, so the price must move down along the demand curve. At the same time, the opportunity cost of producing each unit of output should climb because of diminishing marginal productivity of

labor and increasing marginal utility of leisure. Long-run equilibrium can therefore be achieved at a lower price and a higher output.

118. **(B)** The conditions that define general equilibrium include only one of those listed in the question. In particular, every individual sets every marginal rate of substitution equal to every price ratio. For goods i and j, then, every person maximizes utility where

$$MRS = \frac{MU_i}{MU_j} = \frac{P_i}{P_j}$$

where MU_j represents marginal utility generated by consuming good i, P_i represents the price of good i, etc. Recalling that marginal cost equals price in competitive equilibrium, it is now clear that for every person and every good

$$\frac{MU_i}{MC_i} = \frac{MU_j}{MC_j} \ldots = \text{some constant of proportionality.}$$

Choice (B) is thus correct. Choice (A) is incorrect because marginal utilities are not set equal to prices; ratios of marginal utilities are set equal to ratios of price (see above). Choices (C) and (D) are wrong because it is the marginal revenue products of all inputs that are set equal to prices of the inputs to maximize profits in any (including competitive) equilibrium.

119. **(C)** When the value of the dollar falls, protecting the currency requires that the Fed consider doing something that will increase its demand overseas; i.e., it must somehow make some U.S. assets (whose purchase requires foreign nationals to obtain dollars) more attractive abroad. Restricting the money supply so that domestic interest rates climb is just the ticket. The real return to holding bonds denominated in dollars would then climb, making them more valuable to hold and increasing their demand. Since dollars would be required to purchase these bonds, the price of dollars (i.e., the exchange rate) would also climb according to nothing more mysterious than the simple fundamentals of supply and demand analysis.

120. **(C)** While the slavery issue had never died out, a series of compromises had smoothed over many of the underlying issues left unresolved throughout the 1830s and 1840s. With the acquisition of California, Texas, and the New Mexico Territory from Mexico, combined with the treaty giving the United States complete control of southern Oregon Territory, the whole slavery issue resurfaced like an open wound. Fierce debates would dominate the political scene over which states should be "slave states" or "free states." Some people desired popular sovereignty in which residents of a territory could decide for themselves if they wanted to allow slavery. Others, primarily Southerners, argued that such popular sovereignty was unconstitutional. The debates often turned violent, as was notably true in Kansas in the 1850s. Eventually, the slavery debate, reopened by the Mexican-American War, would lead to the separationism and secessionism in the South that sparked the Civil War.

PRACTICE TEST 1

Answer Sheet

1. Ⓐ Ⓑ Ⓒ Ⓓ Ⓔ	23. Ⓐ Ⓑ Ⓒ Ⓓ Ⓔ	45. Ⓐ Ⓑ Ⓒ Ⓓ Ⓔ
2. Ⓐ Ⓑ Ⓒ Ⓓ Ⓔ	24. Ⓐ Ⓑ Ⓒ Ⓓ Ⓔ	46. Ⓐ Ⓑ Ⓒ Ⓓ Ⓔ
3. Ⓐ Ⓑ Ⓒ Ⓓ Ⓔ	25. Ⓐ Ⓑ Ⓒ Ⓓ Ⓔ	47. Ⓐ Ⓑ Ⓒ Ⓓ Ⓔ
4. Ⓐ Ⓑ Ⓒ Ⓓ Ⓔ	26. Ⓐ Ⓑ Ⓒ Ⓓ Ⓔ	48. Ⓐ Ⓑ Ⓒ Ⓓ Ⓔ
5. Ⓐ Ⓑ Ⓒ Ⓓ Ⓔ	27. Ⓐ Ⓑ Ⓒ Ⓓ Ⓔ	49. Ⓐ Ⓑ Ⓒ Ⓓ Ⓔ
6. Ⓐ Ⓑ Ⓒ Ⓓ Ⓔ	28. Ⓐ Ⓑ Ⓒ Ⓓ Ⓔ	50. Ⓐ Ⓑ Ⓒ Ⓓ Ⓔ
7. Ⓐ Ⓑ Ⓒ Ⓓ Ⓔ	29. Ⓐ Ⓑ Ⓒ Ⓓ Ⓔ	51. Ⓐ Ⓑ Ⓒ Ⓓ Ⓔ
8. Ⓐ Ⓑ Ⓒ Ⓓ Ⓔ	30. Ⓐ Ⓑ Ⓒ Ⓓ Ⓔ	52. Ⓐ Ⓑ Ⓒ Ⓓ Ⓔ
9. Ⓐ Ⓑ Ⓒ Ⓓ Ⓔ	31. Ⓐ Ⓑ Ⓒ Ⓓ Ⓔ	53. Ⓐ Ⓑ Ⓒ Ⓓ Ⓔ
10. Ⓐ Ⓑ Ⓒ Ⓓ Ⓔ	32. Ⓐ Ⓑ Ⓒ Ⓓ Ⓔ	54. Ⓐ Ⓑ Ⓒ Ⓓ Ⓔ
11. Ⓐ Ⓑ Ⓒ Ⓓ Ⓔ	33. Ⓐ Ⓑ Ⓒ Ⓓ Ⓔ	55. Ⓐ Ⓑ Ⓒ Ⓓ Ⓔ
12. Ⓐ Ⓑ Ⓒ Ⓓ Ⓔ	34. Ⓐ Ⓑ Ⓒ Ⓓ Ⓔ	56. Ⓐ Ⓑ Ⓒ Ⓓ Ⓔ
13. Ⓐ Ⓑ Ⓒ Ⓓ Ⓔ	35. Ⓐ Ⓑ Ⓒ Ⓓ Ⓔ	57. Ⓐ Ⓑ Ⓒ Ⓓ Ⓔ
14. Ⓐ Ⓑ Ⓒ Ⓓ Ⓔ	36. Ⓐ Ⓑ Ⓒ Ⓓ Ⓔ	58. Ⓐ Ⓑ Ⓒ Ⓓ Ⓔ
15. Ⓐ Ⓑ Ⓒ Ⓓ Ⓔ	37. Ⓐ Ⓑ Ⓒ Ⓓ Ⓔ	59. Ⓐ Ⓑ Ⓒ Ⓓ Ⓔ
16. Ⓐ Ⓑ Ⓒ Ⓓ Ⓔ	38. Ⓐ Ⓑ Ⓒ Ⓓ Ⓔ	60. Ⓐ Ⓑ Ⓒ Ⓓ Ⓔ
17. Ⓐ Ⓑ Ⓒ Ⓓ Ⓔ	39. Ⓐ Ⓑ Ⓒ Ⓓ Ⓔ	61. Ⓐ Ⓑ Ⓒ Ⓓ Ⓔ
18. Ⓐ Ⓑ Ⓒ Ⓓ Ⓔ	40. Ⓐ Ⓑ Ⓒ Ⓓ Ⓔ	62. Ⓐ Ⓑ Ⓒ Ⓓ Ⓔ
19. Ⓐ Ⓑ Ⓒ Ⓓ Ⓔ	41. Ⓐ Ⓑ Ⓒ Ⓓ Ⓔ	63. Ⓐ Ⓑ Ⓒ Ⓓ Ⓔ
20. Ⓐ Ⓑ Ⓒ Ⓓ Ⓔ	42. Ⓐ Ⓑ Ⓒ Ⓓ Ⓔ	64. Ⓐ Ⓑ Ⓒ Ⓓ Ⓔ
21. Ⓐ Ⓑ Ⓒ Ⓓ Ⓔ	43. Ⓐ Ⓑ Ⓒ Ⓓ Ⓔ	65. Ⓐ Ⓑ Ⓒ Ⓓ Ⓔ
22. Ⓐ Ⓑ Ⓒ Ⓓ Ⓔ	44. Ⓐ Ⓑ Ⓒ Ⓓ Ⓔ	66. Ⓐ Ⓑ Ⓒ Ⓓ Ⓔ

(Continued)

PRACTICE TEST 1

Answer Sheet

67. Ⓐ Ⓑ Ⓒ Ⓓ Ⓔ
68. Ⓐ Ⓑ Ⓒ Ⓓ Ⓔ
69. Ⓐ Ⓑ Ⓒ Ⓓ Ⓔ
70. Ⓐ Ⓑ Ⓒ Ⓓ Ⓔ
71. Ⓐ Ⓑ Ⓒ Ⓓ Ⓔ
72. Ⓐ Ⓑ Ⓒ Ⓓ Ⓔ
73. Ⓐ Ⓑ Ⓒ Ⓓ Ⓔ
74. Ⓐ Ⓑ Ⓒ Ⓓ Ⓔ
75. Ⓐ Ⓑ Ⓒ Ⓓ Ⓔ
76. Ⓐ Ⓑ Ⓒ Ⓓ Ⓔ
77. Ⓐ Ⓑ Ⓒ Ⓓ Ⓔ
78. Ⓐ Ⓑ Ⓒ Ⓓ Ⓔ
79. Ⓐ Ⓑ Ⓒ Ⓓ Ⓔ
80. Ⓐ Ⓑ Ⓒ Ⓓ Ⓔ
81. Ⓐ Ⓑ Ⓒ Ⓓ Ⓔ
82. Ⓐ Ⓑ Ⓒ Ⓓ Ⓔ
83. Ⓐ Ⓑ Ⓒ Ⓓ Ⓔ
84. Ⓐ Ⓑ Ⓒ Ⓓ Ⓔ

85. Ⓐ Ⓑ Ⓒ Ⓓ Ⓔ
86. Ⓐ Ⓑ Ⓒ Ⓓ Ⓔ
87. Ⓐ Ⓑ Ⓒ Ⓓ Ⓔ
88. Ⓐ Ⓑ Ⓒ Ⓓ Ⓔ
89. Ⓐ Ⓑ Ⓒ Ⓓ Ⓔ
90. Ⓐ Ⓑ Ⓒ Ⓓ Ⓔ
91. Ⓐ Ⓑ Ⓒ Ⓓ Ⓔ
92. Ⓐ Ⓑ Ⓒ Ⓓ Ⓔ
93. Ⓐ Ⓑ Ⓒ Ⓓ Ⓔ
94. Ⓐ Ⓑ Ⓒ Ⓓ Ⓔ
95. Ⓐ Ⓑ Ⓒ Ⓓ Ⓔ
96. Ⓐ Ⓑ Ⓒ Ⓓ Ⓔ
97. Ⓐ Ⓑ Ⓒ Ⓓ Ⓔ
98. Ⓐ Ⓑ Ⓒ Ⓓ Ⓔ
99. Ⓐ Ⓑ Ⓒ Ⓓ Ⓔ
100. Ⓐ Ⓑ Ⓒ Ⓓ Ⓔ
101. Ⓐ Ⓑ Ⓒ Ⓓ Ⓔ
102. Ⓐ Ⓑ Ⓒ Ⓓ Ⓔ

103. Ⓐ Ⓑ Ⓒ Ⓓ Ⓔ
104. Ⓐ Ⓑ Ⓒ Ⓓ Ⓔ
105. Ⓐ Ⓑ Ⓒ Ⓓ Ⓔ
106. Ⓐ Ⓑ Ⓒ Ⓓ Ⓔ
107. Ⓐ Ⓑ Ⓒ Ⓓ Ⓔ
108. Ⓐ Ⓑ Ⓒ Ⓓ Ⓔ
109. Ⓐ Ⓑ Ⓒ Ⓓ Ⓔ
110. Ⓐ Ⓑ Ⓒ Ⓓ Ⓔ
111. Ⓐ Ⓑ Ⓒ Ⓓ Ⓔ
112. Ⓐ Ⓑ Ⓒ Ⓓ Ⓔ
113. Ⓐ Ⓑ Ⓒ Ⓓ Ⓔ
114. Ⓐ Ⓑ Ⓒ Ⓓ Ⓔ
115. Ⓐ Ⓑ Ⓒ Ⓓ Ⓔ
116. Ⓐ Ⓑ Ⓒ Ⓓ Ⓔ
117. Ⓐ Ⓑ Ⓒ Ⓓ Ⓔ
118. Ⓐ Ⓑ Ⓒ Ⓓ Ⓔ
119. Ⓐ Ⓑ Ⓒ Ⓓ Ⓔ
120. Ⓐ Ⓑ Ⓒ Ⓓ Ⓔ

PRACTICE TEST 2

Answer Sheet

1. Ⓐ Ⓑ Ⓒ Ⓓ Ⓔ
2. Ⓐ Ⓑ Ⓒ Ⓓ Ⓔ
3. Ⓐ Ⓑ Ⓒ Ⓓ Ⓔ
4. Ⓐ Ⓑ Ⓒ Ⓓ Ⓔ
5. Ⓐ Ⓑ Ⓒ Ⓓ Ⓔ
6. Ⓐ Ⓑ Ⓒ Ⓓ Ⓔ
7. Ⓐ Ⓑ Ⓒ Ⓓ Ⓔ
8. Ⓐ Ⓑ Ⓒ Ⓓ Ⓔ
9. Ⓐ Ⓑ Ⓒ Ⓓ Ⓔ
10. Ⓐ Ⓑ Ⓒ Ⓓ Ⓔ
11. Ⓐ Ⓑ Ⓒ Ⓓ Ⓔ
12. Ⓐ Ⓑ Ⓒ Ⓓ Ⓔ
13. Ⓐ Ⓑ Ⓒ Ⓓ Ⓔ
14. Ⓐ Ⓑ Ⓒ Ⓓ Ⓔ
15. Ⓐ Ⓑ Ⓒ Ⓓ Ⓔ
16. Ⓐ Ⓑ Ⓒ Ⓓ Ⓔ
17. Ⓐ Ⓑ Ⓒ Ⓓ Ⓕ
18. Ⓐ Ⓑ Ⓒ Ⓓ Ⓔ
19. Ⓐ Ⓑ Ⓒ Ⓓ Ⓔ
20. Ⓐ Ⓑ Ⓒ Ⓓ Ⓔ
21. Ⓐ Ⓑ Ⓒ Ⓓ Ⓔ
22. Ⓐ Ⓑ Ⓒ Ⓓ Ⓔ

23. Ⓐ Ⓑ Ⓒ Ⓓ Ⓔ
24. Ⓐ Ⓑ Ⓒ Ⓓ Ⓔ
25. Ⓐ Ⓑ Ⓒ Ⓓ Ⓔ
26. Ⓐ Ⓑ Ⓒ Ⓓ Ⓔ
27. Ⓐ Ⓑ Ⓒ Ⓓ Ⓔ
28. Ⓐ Ⓑ Ⓒ Ⓓ Ⓔ
29. Ⓐ Ⓑ Ⓒ Ⓓ Ⓔ
30. Ⓐ Ⓑ Ⓒ Ⓓ Ⓔ
31. Ⓐ Ⓑ Ⓒ Ⓓ Ⓔ
32. Ⓐ Ⓑ Ⓒ Ⓓ Ⓔ
33. Ⓐ Ⓑ Ⓒ Ⓓ Ⓔ
34. Ⓐ Ⓑ Ⓒ Ⓓ Ⓔ
35. Ⓐ Ⓑ Ⓒ Ⓓ Ⓔ
36. Ⓐ Ⓑ Ⓒ Ⓓ Ⓔ
37. Ⓐ Ⓑ Ⓒ Ⓓ Ⓔ
38. Ⓐ Ⓑ Ⓒ Ⓓ Ⓔ
39. Ⓐ Ⓑ Ⓒ Ⓓ Ⓔ
40. Ⓐ Ⓑ Ⓒ Ⓓ Ⓔ
41. Ⓐ Ⓑ Ⓒ Ⓓ Ⓔ
42. Ⓐ Ⓑ Ⓒ Ⓓ Ⓔ
43. Ⓐ Ⓑ Ⓒ Ⓓ Ⓔ
44. Ⓐ Ⓑ Ⓒ Ⓓ Ⓔ

45. Ⓐ Ⓑ Ⓒ Ⓓ Ⓔ
46. Ⓐ Ⓑ Ⓒ Ⓓ Ⓔ
47. Ⓐ Ⓑ Ⓒ Ⓓ Ⓔ
48. Ⓐ Ⓑ Ⓒ Ⓓ Ⓔ
49. Ⓐ Ⓑ Ⓒ Ⓓ Ⓔ
50. Ⓐ Ⓑ Ⓒ Ⓓ Ⓔ
51. Ⓐ Ⓑ Ⓒ Ⓓ Ⓔ
52. Ⓐ Ⓑ Ⓒ Ⓓ Ⓔ
53. Ⓐ Ⓑ Ⓒ Ⓓ Ⓔ
54. Ⓐ Ⓑ Ⓒ Ⓓ Ⓔ
55. Ⓐ Ⓑ Ⓒ Ⓓ Ⓔ
56. Ⓐ Ⓑ Ⓒ Ⓓ Ⓔ
57. Ⓐ Ⓑ Ⓒ Ⓓ Ⓔ
58. Ⓐ Ⓑ Ⓒ Ⓓ Ⓔ
59. Ⓐ Ⓑ Ⓒ Ⓓ Ⓔ
60. Ⓐ Ⓑ Ⓒ Ⓓ Ⓔ
61. Ⓐ Ⓑ Ⓒ Ⓓ Ⓔ
62. Ⓐ Ⓑ Ⓒ Ⓓ Ⓔ
63. Ⓐ Ⓑ Ⓒ Ⓓ Ⓔ
64. Ⓐ Ⓑ Ⓒ Ⓓ Ⓔ
65. Ⓐ Ⓑ Ⓒ Ⓓ Ⓔ
66. Ⓐ Ⓑ Ⓒ Ⓓ Ⓔ

(Continued)

PRACTICE TEST 2

Answer Sheet

67. Ⓐ Ⓑ Ⓒ Ⓓ Ⓔ
68. Ⓐ Ⓑ Ⓒ Ⓓ Ⓔ
69. Ⓐ Ⓑ Ⓒ Ⓓ Ⓔ
70. Ⓐ Ⓑ Ⓒ Ⓓ Ⓔ
71. Ⓐ Ⓑ Ⓒ Ⓓ Ⓔ
72. Ⓐ Ⓑ Ⓒ Ⓓ Ⓔ
73. Ⓐ Ⓑ Ⓒ Ⓓ Ⓔ
74. Ⓐ Ⓑ Ⓒ Ⓓ Ⓔ
75. Ⓐ Ⓑ Ⓒ Ⓓ Ⓔ
76. Ⓐ Ⓑ Ⓒ Ⓓ Ⓔ
77. Ⓐ Ⓑ Ⓒ Ⓓ Ⓔ
78. Ⓐ Ⓑ Ⓒ Ⓓ Ⓔ
79. Ⓐ Ⓑ Ⓒ Ⓓ Ⓔ
80. Ⓐ Ⓑ Ⓒ Ⓓ Ⓔ
81. Ⓐ Ⓑ Ⓒ Ⓓ Ⓔ
82. Ⓐ Ⓑ Ⓒ Ⓓ Ⓔ
83. Ⓐ Ⓑ Ⓒ Ⓓ Ⓔ
84. Ⓐ Ⓑ Ⓒ Ⓓ Ⓔ

85. Ⓐ Ⓑ Ⓒ Ⓓ Ⓔ
86. Ⓐ Ⓑ Ⓒ Ⓓ Ⓔ
87. Ⓐ Ⓑ Ⓒ Ⓓ Ⓔ
88. Ⓐ Ⓑ Ⓒ Ⓓ Ⓔ
89. Ⓐ Ⓑ Ⓒ Ⓓ Ⓔ
90. Ⓐ Ⓑ Ⓒ Ⓓ Ⓔ
91. Ⓐ Ⓑ Ⓒ Ⓓ Ⓔ
92. Ⓐ Ⓑ Ⓒ Ⓓ Ⓔ
93. Ⓐ Ⓑ Ⓒ Ⓓ Ⓔ
94. Ⓐ Ⓑ Ⓒ Ⓓ Ⓔ
95. Ⓐ Ⓑ Ⓒ Ⓓ Ⓔ
96. Ⓐ Ⓑ Ⓒ Ⓓ Ⓔ
97. Ⓐ Ⓑ Ⓒ Ⓓ Ⓔ
98. Ⓐ Ⓑ Ⓒ Ⓓ Ⓔ
99. Ⓐ Ⓑ Ⓒ Ⓓ Ⓔ
100. Ⓐ Ⓑ Ⓒ Ⓓ Ⓔ
101. Ⓐ Ⓑ Ⓒ Ⓓ Ⓔ
102. Ⓐ Ⓑ Ⓒ Ⓓ Ⓔ

103. Ⓐ Ⓑ Ⓒ Ⓓ Ⓔ
104. Ⓐ Ⓑ Ⓒ Ⓓ Ⓔ
105. Ⓐ Ⓑ Ⓒ Ⓓ Ⓔ
106. Ⓐ Ⓑ Ⓒ Ⓓ Ⓔ
107. Ⓐ Ⓑ Ⓒ Ⓓ Ⓔ
108. Ⓐ Ⓑ Ⓒ Ⓓ Ⓔ
109. Ⓐ Ⓑ Ⓒ Ⓓ Ⓔ
110. Ⓐ Ⓑ Ⓒ Ⓓ Ⓔ
111. Ⓐ Ⓑ Ⓒ Ⓓ Ⓔ
112. Ⓐ Ⓑ Ⓒ Ⓓ Ⓔ
113. Ⓐ Ⓑ Ⓒ Ⓓ Ⓔ
114. Ⓐ Ⓑ Ⓒ Ⓓ Ⓔ
115. Ⓐ Ⓑ Ⓒ Ⓓ Ⓔ
116. Ⓐ Ⓑ Ⓒ Ⓓ Ⓔ
117. Ⓐ Ⓑ Ⓒ Ⓓ Ⓔ
118. Ⓐ Ⓑ Ⓒ Ⓓ Ⓔ
119. Ⓐ Ⓑ Ⓒ Ⓓ Ⓔ
120. Ⓐ Ⓑ Ⓒ Ⓓ Ⓔ

Index

Notes

Notes

Notes

Notes

Notes

Notes

Notes

Notes

Notes